Jeremias David Reuss

Das gelehrte England

Jetztlebende Schriftsteller in Großbritannien, Irland und Nordamerika. Vom Jahr

1770 - 1790

Jeremias David Reuss

Das gelehrte England
Jetztlebende Schriftsteller in Großbritannien, Irland und Nordamerika. Vom Jahr 1770 - 1790

ISBN/EAN: 9783337226626

Hergestellt in Europa, USA, Kanada, Australien, Japan

Cover: Foto ©Thomas Meinert / pixelio.de

Weitere Bücher finden Sie auf **www.hansebooks.com**

ALPHABETICAL REGISTER
OF
ALL THE AUTHORS
ACTUALLY LIVING

IN

GREAT-BRITAIN, IRELAND, AND IN THE
UNITED PROVINCES OF NORTH-AMERICA,

WITH

A CATALOGUE OF THEIR PUBLICATIONS.

FROM THE YEAR 1770 TO THE YEAR 1790.

BY

JEREM. DAV. REUSS,

PROFESSOR OF PHILOSOPHY AND UNDER-LIBRARIAN AT
THE PUBLIC LIBRARY OF THE UNIVERSITY OF
GOTTINGEN.

BERLIN AND STETTIN,
printed for FREDERIC NICOLAI
1791.

DAS
GELEHRTE ENGLAND

ODER

LEXIKON

DER JEZTLEBENDEN

SCHRIFTSTELLER

IN

GROSBRITANNIEN, IRLAND UND NORD-AMERIKA

NEBST EINEM

VERZEICHNIS IHRER SCHRIFTEN.

VOM JAHR 1770 BIS 1790.

VON

JEREMIAS DAVID REUSS,

ORDENTLICHEN PROFESSOR DER PHILOSOPHIE UND UNTER-BIBLIOTHEKAR BEY DER UNIVERSITÄTS-BIBLIOTHEK ZU GÖTTINGEN.

BERLIN UND STETTIN,
BEY FRIED. NICOLAI
1791.

Vorrede.

Bey der Aufmerkſamkeit, die man in Deutſchland auf alle Gattungen von ausländiſcher Litteratur zu richten gewohnt iſt, ſcheint es ein wahres Bedürfnis zu ſeyn, ein Handbuch von den jeztlebenden Schriftſtellern jeder Nation zu beſitzen, worin die Schriften derſelben ſo zuſammengeſtellt wären, daſs man mit einem Blick überſehen kann, was der Fleis eines Mannes geleiſtet, welche Geiſtes-Werke er geliefert, wie viel er zur Aufklärung ſeines Zeitalters beygetragen habe, und wie groſs oder gering die litterariſche Induſtrie einer Nation in einem gewiſſen Zeitraum geweſen ſey. Der wiſſenſchaftliche Gelehrte würde daraus ſehen, welche Wiſſenſchaften oder welche Theile derſelben bey jeder Nation vorzüglich bearbeitet worden und welche Bücher in dieſem oder jenem Fach gegenwärtig bey ihr vorzüglich im Umlauf ſind; dem Litterator, der die Schriftſteller aller Nationen und ihre Schriften in ſeine Verzeichniſſe einträgt, würde durch ſolche einzelne Sammlungen ſeine Arbeit ſehr erleichtert, und ſelbſt die Verbreitung und gegenſeitige Mittheilung der litterariſchen Produkte jeder Nation würde dadurch nicht wenig befördert werden.

Noch haben wir von keiner Nation ein ſolches nüzliches aber auch, mühſames Werk, als von der deutſchen. Für dieſe hat der unermüdete Fleiſs *Homberger's* und ſeines Nachfolgers *Meuſel's* ſo vortreflich geſorgt, daſs wir es dieſen allein zu danken haben, daſs mehrere Gelehrte die Schriftſteller einzelner Provinzen Deutſchland's herausſtellten und auf dieſe Art ein groſſes Hülfsmittel zur Bearbeitung der Gelehrten-Geſchichte einzelner deutſcher Provinzen darreichten. Zu der *France litteraire* iſt ſeit 1784 keine Fortſezung erſchienen; und wie unvollkommen ſind dieſe fünf Bände? Von Spanien hat uns *Juan Sempere* y Guarinos ein ſchäzbares Verzeichnis von Schriftſtellern, welche unter Carl 3. lebten, gegeben, aber dieſes enthält nach ſeinem Plan nur die vorzüglichſten. Von Italien haben wir noch keines und eben ſo wenig von den Nordiſchen Reichen. Auch die Engländer beſizen von ihrer neueſten Litteratur keine ordentlichen und vollſtändigen Jahrbücher.

Das Verzeichnis von fünfhundert Schriftſtellern, welches vor einigen Jahren in London *) herauskam, iſt

---

*) Catalogue of five hundred celebrated Authors of Great - Britain, now living --. London. 1788. 8.

VORREDE.

ist einem Kirchen- und Kezer-Almanach ähnlicher, als daſs es einen Litterator nur einigermaſſen in seinen Unterſuchungen befriedigen könnte. Es scheint, der Verfaſſer oder die Verfaſſer dieſes Buchs stellten aus der ganzen Maſſe von Groſs-Britanniſchen Schriftſtellern blos diejenigen heraus, über welche sie ein richterliches Lob oder Tadel ausſprechen wollten. — *Ayscough* hat sich zwar durch sein Regiſter über 70 Bände der Monthly Review groſſe Verdienſte in dieſem Theil der Engländiſchen Litteratur erworben, aber es enthält nach seiner Abſicht nur diejenigen Schriften, welche in dieſem Journal recenſirt worden sind. Gleichwohl dürfte von keiner andern Nation ein Handbuch ihrer Neueſten Litteratur ſo ſehr unter uns gewünſcht werden als von der Engländiſchen, da ihre Schriften in Deutſchland ſo begierig aufgenommen, überſezt und geleſen werden.

Ich habe es daher verſucht hier ein ſolches Handbuch, das die Litteratur der Britten von den zwey lezten Jahrzehenden enthält, zu liefern. Die Unternehmung scheint für einen Ausländer kühn zu ſeyn; allein, wenn dieſer im Beſiz der meiſten litteraariſchen Hülfs-Mittel iſt, aus welchen der Britte ſelbſt ſchöpfen könnte, und wenn er dieſe mit Fleiſs und Sorgfalt gebraucht; ſo wird es nicht zu viel gewagt ſeyn, wenn er wenigſtens einen Verſuch macht, das zu erſezen, was die Britten ſelbſt bis jezt nicht geleiſtet haben.

* 4   Der

VORREDE.

Der Plan dieses Handbuchs ist dieser. Nur die Schriften der Verfasser, die in dem Zeitraum von 1770 - 1790 geschrieben haben und noch am Leben sind, sind hier aufgenommen und unter dem Nahmen ihrer Verfasser zusammengeordnet. Die Schriftsteller, die in diesem Zeitraum gestorben sind, werden nur kurz angeführt, mit Bemerkung des Jahres ihrer Geburt, ihres Todes, wenn sie mir bekannt waren, und des Amts, welches sie bekleideten. Bey manchen wird freilich der Wunsch entstehen, dafs auch die Schriften, der in diesem Zeitraum gestorbenen Gelehrten hätten angeführt werden sollen, allein diese gehören, so wie die Lebensbeschreibungen für das *Joecher - Adelungische* Gelehrten-Lexicon, und auch diese aufzunehmen würde der Kürze, die ich mir vorsezen muste, nicht entsprechen.

Schriftsteller, welche blos ein Specimen inaugurale vor ihrem Abgang von der Universität, oder Prediger, welche nur einzelne Predigten in Druk gegeben haben, habe ich eben so wenig hier aufgenommen, als diejenigen, welche in diesem Zeitraum ihre litterarische Existenz nicht durch eine Abhandlung erwiesen haben. Teutsche Uebersezungen habe ich sorgfältig angemerkt, aber keine aufgenommen, welche in ausländischen Sprachen gemacht worden sind.

Gelehrte von andern Nationen, unerachtet sie in Engländischer Sprache Abhandlungen geschrieben haben,

ben, find hier, wenn es mir bekannt war, nicht aufgenommen, fondern zu den Schriftftellern ihrer Nation gerechnet worden.

Die Preife der Bücher beyzufügen, fchien mir in gedoppelter Hinficht nüzlich, einmal, um Liebhabern der Engländifchen Litteratur, welche fich darinn Bücher anfchaffen wollen, den Weg dazu zu erleichtern, zweytens, um unfere teutfchen Buchhändler mehr aufzumuntern, Engländifche Bücher in ihre Buchladen aufzunehmen und dadurch die Lectüre derfelben bey uns mehr auszubreiten.

Den Vorwurf der Unvollftändigkeit fürchte ich um fo weniger, da Vollftändigkeit bey einem *Verfuch* diefer Art beinahe unmöglich ift. Ich bin es auch felbft überzeugt, dafs aller angewandten Aufmerkfamkeit und Sorgfalt unerachtet, mir manche Abhandlung entgangen feyn, mancher Irrthum fich eingefchlichen haben mag, welcher nur durch oftmals wiederholte Durchficht und durch anhaltenden, Jahre lang fortdauernden, Fleifs verbeffert werden, und einen höhern Grad der Vollkommenheit erreichen kann. Dafs ich alles genuzt, was ich vor mir hatte, die Kritiken der Bücher felbft gelefen und die in Gefellfchafts-Schriften zerftreueten Abhandlungen mühfam aufgefucht und zu ihren Verfaffern geftellt habe, wird man beinahe auf jeder Seite fehen. Anonymifche Schriften find, wenn fie mir bekannt wurden, zu ihrem Verfaffer gefezt und zum Unterfchied mit

einem

einem Sternchen bezeichnet. Am mühſamſten war mir, gewiſs zu erfahren, ob ein Schriftſteller noch lebt und aufzufinden, in welchem Jahr er geſtorben iſt, denn die Britten ſind in dieſem Theil der Litterargeſchichte ſehr ſorglos. Daher kann auch öfters der Fall eintreten, daſs ich hier einen Schriftſteller noch unter den lebenden aufzähle, welcher ſchon längſt in eine andere Welt übergegangen iſt. Ich wage daher an alle, welche Engländiſche Litteratur lieben, die Bitte, mich mit Beyträgen und Berichtigungen zu unterſtüzen, um in Supplement-Bänden nicht allein die neueſte Litteratur fortzuſezen, ſondern auch die Fehler, welche ſich hier eingeſchlichen haben möchten, zu verbeſſern. Mit dem innigſtem Dank werde ich jedes, was zur Verbeſſerung dieſes Verſuchs der Engländiſchen Gelehrten-Geſchichte in dieſem Zeitraum dienen kann, aufnehmen, ſo wie ich die thätige Unterſtüzung drey, mir ſehr verehrungswürdigen, Freunde, des H. D. *Girtanner*, in Göttingen, H. Hof-Med. D. *Hufeland* in Weimar und H. D. *Kapp* in Leipzig lebhaft und dankbarlichſt erkenne.

Erklärung der Abkürzungen.

A. B: Artium Baccalaureus.

A. M: oder M. A: Artium Magister.

Arch. Archaeologia; or Miscellaneous Tracts relating to Antiquity; published, by the Society of Antiquaries of London. Vol. 1-9. 4to.

Asiat. Res: Asiatick Researches: or Transactions of the Society instituted in Bengal, for inquiring into the history and antiquities, the arts, sciences and litterature of Asia. Vol. I. Calcutta. 1788. 4.

B. D: Bachelor of Divinity.

D. D: Doctor of Divinity.

D. Mus: Doctor Musices.

Duncan's

ERKLäRUNG

Duncan's M. C: Duncan's Medical Commentaries for the Year 1780-1790. Dec. 2. Vol. 5.

Esq: Esquire.

Eſſ. and Obſerv. Edinb: Eſſays and obſervations phyſical and litterary, read before a ſociety in Edinburgh. Vol. 1-3. Edinb. 1754-1771. 8.

F. A. A: Fellow of the American Academy.

F. A. S: Fellow of the Antiquarian Society at London.

F. A. S. Scot: Fellow of the Antiquarian Society of Scotland.

F. I. A: Fellow of the Irish Academy.

F. M. S: Fellow of the Medical Society.

F. R. S: Fellow of the Royal Society at London.

F. R. S. Ed: Fellow of the Royal Society at Edinburgh.

F. T. C D: Fellow of Trinity College, Dublin.

Gren J. d. P: *Gren* Journal der Phyſik. Th. 1. Heft 1-4. Th. 2. Heft 1. 2.

Hunter's G. E: *Hunter's* Georgical Eſſays. Vol. 1-5. 1770-1777. 8.

LL. B: Legum Baccalaureus.

LL. D: Legum Doĉtor.

London M. J: London Medical Journal. Vol. I XI. 1781-1790. 8.

M. B: Medicinae Baccalaureus.

Mem. of B. A: Memoirs of the American Academy of Arts and Sciences. Vol. 1. Boſton. 1785. 4.

M. C: Medical Communications. Vol. 1. 1784. 8.

Med.

Med. Com. of Ed: Medical and philofophical commentaries by a Society of Phyficians in Edinburgh. Vol. 1 - 6. 1774 - 1779. 8. überf. von *Diel.* Th. 1 - 10. 1789. 8.

M. D: Medicinae Doctor.

Med. Obf: Medical Obfervations and inquiries by a Society of Phyficians in London. Vol. 1 - 6. 1762 - 1784. 8. überf. Th. 1 - 7. Altenburg. 8.

Med. Transact: Medical Transactions, published by the College of Phyficians in London. Vol. 1 - 3. 1768 - 1785. 8.

Mem. of M: Memoirs of the Litterary and Philofophical Society of Manchefter. Vol. 1. Warrington. 1785. Vol. 2. 1785. 8. überf. Th. 1. 2. Leipzig. 1788. 8.

Mem. of M. S. of L: Memoirs of the medical Society of London. Vol. 1. 1787. Vol. 2. 1789. 8. überf. Th. 1. Altenb. 1789. 8.

M. R. I. A: Member of the Royal Irish Academy.

Mrs: Miftreff.

N. A: Nautical Almanac for the Year 1771 - 1789.

Phil. Transact: Philofophical Transactions —. Vol. 60 - 80. 1770 - 1790. 4.

Samml. f. A: Sammlung auserlefener Abhandlungen zum Gebrauch practifcher Aerzte. Th. 1 - 13. 8.

Samml. f. W. A: Samml. der auserlefenften und neueften Abhandlungen für Wund - Aerzte. St. 1-9. 8.

Samml. z. P. u. N. G: Sammlung zur Phyfik und Naturgefchichte. Th. 1 - 4. Leipz. 8.

Tr.

Tr. of A. S: Transactions of the American philosophical Society held at Philadelphia for promoting useful knowledge. Vol. 1. 1771. Vol. 2. 1786. 4.

Tr. of E. S: Transactions of the Royal Society of Edinburgh. Vol. 1. 2. Edinb. 1788. 1790. 4. Philosoph. und histor. Abhandlungen übers. von *J. G. Buhle*. Th. 1. Göttingen. 1789. 8.

Tr. of I. A: Transactions of the Royal Irish Academy. Dublin. Vol. 1. 1787. Vol. 2. 1788. 4.

DAS
JEZTLEBENDE
GELEHRTE ENGLAND

ERSTE HÄLFTE
A — L.

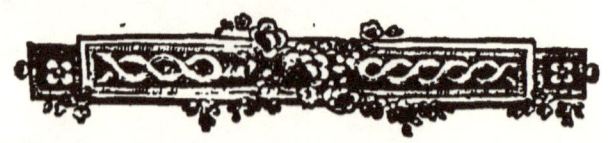

ABERCROMBIE [John] *Gardener at Tottenham-Court.*
J. *Abercrombie* and *Th. Mawe's* univerſal gardener and botaniſt: or, a general dictionary of gardening and botany. 1778. 4. (1 L. 7. Sh.) The garden muſhroom; its nature and cultivation 1779. 8. (1 Sh. 6. d.) The britiſh fruit Gardener; and art of pruning 1779. 8. (4 Sh.) überſ von *G. H. H. Lüder.* Lübek 1781. 8. Every man his own gardener by *Mawe* and *Abercrombie.* 1767. 8. (4 Sh.) Ed. VIII. 1779. 8. überſ. Leipzig. 1776. 8. The complete forcing gardener; or the practice of forcing fruits, flowers and vegetables to early maturity and perfection by the aid of artificial heat. 1781. 8. (2 Sh. 6. d.) The complete wall -- tree pruner. 1783. 8. (3. Sh.) The propagation and botanical arrangements of plants and trees. 1783. 8. Vol. 1. 2. (6Sh.) The Gardener's pocket dictionary. 1786. 8. (10 Sh. 6. d.) The Gardener's daily aſſiſtant. 1787. 8. (3 Sh.) The univerſal gardener's kalender, and ſyſtem of practical gardening. 1789. 8. (5 Sh.) The complete kitchen gardener and hot bed forcer. 1789. 8. (5 Sh) The garden vade mecum or compendium of general gardening. 1789. 8. (4 Sh.) The Hot - houſe gardener. 1789. 8. (8 Sh. 6 d.)

ABINGDON, Earl of, ſee *Willoughby Bertie.*

ACHERLEY, [Roger] *Esq. of the Inner Temple.* Reaſons for uniformity in the ſtate. 1780. 8. (1 Sh.)

ACLAND, [John] *Rector of Broad - cliſt and one of his Majeſty's juſtices of peace for the county of Devon.* Plan for rendering the poor independent on public contribution. 1786. 8. (1 Sh.)

ADAIR, [James] *M. D. Phyſician in Winchester.* Some remarks on certain articles of the materia medica. (*Duncan's* M. C. Vol. 10. p. 233.)

ADAIR, [James] Esq. *Trader with the Indians and Refident in their country 40 Years.* The hiftory of the american indians. 1775. 4. (15 Sh.) überf. (von S. H. Ewald.) Breslau 1782. 8.

ADAIR, [James Makittrick] *M. D. one of the judges of the courts of King's Bench and Common Pleas in the Island of Antigua; Phyfician to the Commander in Chief and the colonial troops of Antigua.* Obfervations on regimen and preparation under inoculation and on the treatment of the natural fmall pox in the Weft-Indies. (*Duncan's* M. C. Vol. 8. p. 211.) A few hints on particular articles of the Materia Medica. (*Duncan's* M. C. Vol. 9. p. 206. überf. Saml. f. A. Th. XI. S. 275. Medical cautions for the confideration of invalids, thofe efpecially who refort tho Bath —. 1786. 8. (3 fh. 6 d.) Ed. 2. 1787. 8. (6 fh.) Sketch of the natural hiftory of the human body and mind —. 1787. 8. (4 fh.) überf. von C. F. *Michaelis.* Zittau u. Leipz. 1788. 8. Cafe of inflammatory conftipation of the bowels fucceffully treated. (Mem. of M. S. of L. Vol. 2.) Unanswerable objections againft the abolition of the Slave trade. 1789. 8. (5 fh.)

—— [Robert] *Surgeon general to the Army.* born... died d. Mart. 1790.

ADAM, [Alexander] LL. D. *Rector of the high fchool at Edinburgh.* The principles of latin and englifh grammar 1772. 8. (3 fh. 6 d.) A fummary of geography and hiftory. 17.. 8.

—— [James] *Esq.* Practical effays on agriculture. 1789. 8. Vol. 1. 2. (12 fh.)

—— [James] and his brother.

—— [Robert] *F. R. S: F. A. S: Architect to the King and to the Queen.* Ruins of the palace of the emperor Diocletian at Spalatro in Dalmatia. 1764. fol. (3 L. 10 fh.) Works in Architecture. *Numb.* 1. Defigns of Sion Houfe, feat of the Duke of Northumberland in the county of Middlefex. 1773. *Numb.* 2. Defigns of Lord Mansfield's Villa at Kenwood. 1774. *Numb.* 3. Defigns of Luton Parkhoufe in Bedfordfhire. 1775. *Numb.* 4. Defigns of public buildings. 1776. fol. (4 L. 7 fh.)

ADAM,

ADAM, [Thomas] *Rector of Winsringham*, *Lincolnshire.* born .... died 17..
ADAMS, [George] *Mathematical Instrumentmaker to his Majesty.* born .... died 1772.
—— [George] *Mathematical Instrumentmaker to his Majesty.* On electricity — with an essay on Magnetism. 1784. 8. (5 sh.) Essay on the Microscope. 1787. 4. (1 L. 6 sh.) History on vision, explaining the fabric of the eye and nature of vision. 1789. 8. (3 sh.) Astronomical and geographical essays. 1789. 8. (10 sh. 6 d.)
—— [John] LL. D. *Member of the Academy of arts and sciences at Boston. Ambassador for the congress of the united states of America to the court of London.* Collection of State papers, relative to the first acknowledgment of the sovereignity of the united states of America. 1782. 8. (2 sh.) History of the disputes with America, from their origin —. 1784. (2 sh. 6 d.) Defence of the constitution of government of the united states of America. Vol. 1. 2. 3. 1787. 1788. 8. (17 sh.)
—— [John] A. M. Lectiones selectae: or select latin lessons in morality, history and biography. 1784. 8. (8 d.) Ed. 2. 1789. 8. (1 sh.) The flowers of ancient history, comprehending the most remarkable and interesting events, as well as characters of antiquity. 1787. 8. (3 sh.) The flowers of modern history — 1788. 8. (3 sh.) The flowers of modern travels. 1788. 8. Vol. 1. 2. (6 sh.) Exercises in latin composition. 1788. 8. (1 sh. 6 d.) Anecdotes, bons mots, and characteristic tracts of the greatest princes, politicians, philosophers, orators and wits of modern times. 1789. 8. (3 sh.)
—— [John] A. B. The english Parnassus — extracted from the works of the latest and most celebrated poets. 1789. 8. (3 sh.)
—— [John] The young Sea-Officers assistant. 1773. 4. (3 sh.)
—— [Samuel] *Member of the General Congress of America.* Oration at the Statehouse in Philadelphia. 1776. 8. (1 sh.)
—— [Thomas Maxwell] *Esq.* On the slave trade. 1788. 8. (1 sh. 6 d.)

ADAMS, [William] *D. D. Prebendary of the cathedral at Gloucester and Master of Pembroke College*, Oxford. born .... died d. 14. Jan. 1789.
—— [William] *Surgeon.* Disquisition on the stone and gravel and other diseases of the bladder. 1773. 8. (2 sh.)

ADDINGTON, [Anthony] *M. D.*
born..... died d. 21. March. 1790.
—— [Stephen] *D. D:* On religious knowledge of the antient jews and patriarchs — 1757. 4. (1 sh. 6 d.) The rudiments of greek tongue. 1761. 8. (2 sh.) Eusebes to Philetus: or a letter to a son on a devout temper and life. 1767. 8. (2 sh.) The Youth's geographical grammar. 1770. 8. (4 sh.) The christian Minister's reasons for baptizing infants. 1771. 8. (2 sh.) Summary of the christian ministers reasons for baptizing infants. 1777. 8. (6 d.) On afflictions, with a discourse on visiting the Sick. 1778. 8. (2 sh.) Sermon on the death of *W. Ford.* 1783. 8. (6 d.) The life of Paul the Apostle with remarks on his discourses and writings 1784. 8. (5 sh.) Sermon on the death of *John Olding*, Pastor at Butt-Lane Deptford. 1785. 8. (6 d.)
—— [William] *Esq. One of the Magistrates presiding at the public office at London.* Abridgment of penal statutes. 1775. (8 sh.) Ed. 3. 1786. 4. (1 L. 6 sh.)

ADEE, [Swithin] *M. D: F. R. S: F. A. S.*
born... died d. 12 Aug. 1786.

AERY, [Lancelot] *M. D: Physician at Whitehaven.* Diss. De Gonorrhoea virulenta. Lugd. Bat. 1772. 4. The symptoms, nature, causes and cure of the essera or nettle rash; with observations on the causes and cure of cutaneous diseases. 1774. 8.
—— [Thomas] *M. D. Physician at Whitehaven.* On the cure of a wound in the cornea of the eye and of a laceration of the uvea. (Phil. Transact. 1755. p. 411.) History of a case of hydrocephalus successfully treated by Mercury. (*Duncan's* M. C. Vol. VIII. p. 332.) A case of hydrocephalus internus cured by Mercury. (London M. J. 1781. p. 424. übers. Samml. f. A. Th. 7. S. 195.) Aphtha, method of curing

curing in infants. (Medical Museum. Vol. 2.) Letter concerning Mrs. *Folke's* cafe. 1773. 8.

AIKIN (. . . .) England delineated; or, a geographical defcription of every county in England and Wales with an account of its moſt important products, natural and artificial. 1788. 8. (4 ſh. 6 d.)

—— [John] *D. D*: born .... died 1781.

—— [John] *M. D*: *Phyſician at Great-Yarmouth in the county of Norfolk.* Eſſay on the ligature of arteries. (vid. *White's* cafes in furgery. P. I. überf. Samml. f. W. A. St. 7. S. 81.) Miſcellaneous pieces in profe. 1773. 8. (3 ſh) nachgedr. Altenburgh 1775. 8. (Dieſe Samml. gab er gemeinſchaftlich mit feiner Schweſter Miſtreſſ *Barbauld* heraus.) Eſſays on fong writing, with a collection of engliſh fongs. Ed. 2. 1774. 8. (4 ſh.) (Einige Stücke überſezt in *Urſinus* Balladen und Lieder altengl. Dichter. 1777. 8.) On the application of natural hiſtory to poetry. 1777. 8. (2 ſh. 6 d.) überf. von *C. H. Schmid.* Leipz. 1779. 8. On the fituation, manners and inhabitants of Germany and the life of Agricola by *C. C. Tacitus*; translated with notes. 1778. 8. (4 ſh.) *Thomſon's* feafons, with an eſſay on the plan and the character of the poem 1778. 8. (4 ſh.) nachgedr. Leipzig 1781. 8. The Calendar of nature — for the inſtruction of young perfons. 1784. 8. überf. Leipzig 1787. 8. *Lewis's* Materia medica. Ed. 3. 1784. 4. Manual of materia medica. 1785. 8. (2 ſh. 6 d.)

—— [Aitken] John, *M. D. fellow of the royal College of Surgeons and lecturer on the practice of phyſik, Anatomy, Surgery and Chemiſtry in Edinburgh.* born .... died d. 22 Sept. 1790.

AINSLIE, [J ....] *M. D.* On the nature and properties of Marle. (*Hunter's* G. E. Vol. 3. p. 25.)

AITON, [William] *Gardener to his Majeſty at Kew.* Hortus Kewenſis, or a catalogue of the plants cultivated in the royal botanic garden at Kew. Vol. 1. 2. 3. 1789. 8. (1 L. 1 ſh.)

AKENSIDE, [Mark] *M. D: F. R. S. and Phyſician to her Majeſty.* born at Newcaſtle-upon-Tyne. d. 9 Nov. 1721. died d. 23 June 1770.

ALANSON (Edward) *Surgeon at Liverpool*, Account of a simple fracture of the tibia in a pregnant woman, in which cafe the callus was not formed till after delivery. (Med. Obf. Vol. 4. p. 410.) Practical obfervations upon amputation and the after treatment. 1779. 8. (1 fh. 6 d.) Ed. 2. 1783. 8. überf. Samml. f. W. A. St. 7. S. 131. überf. Gotha 1785. 8. Th. 1. 2.

ALCHORNE, [Stanesby] *Of his Majefty's Mint and Member of the fociety of Apothecaries.* Catalogue of 50 plants from Chelfea. 1770. (Phil. Transact. 1771. p. 390.) Catalogue of 50 plants from Chelfea. 1771. (Ibid. 1773. p. 30.) Examination of the ores in the mufeum of Dr. *Hunter*. (Ibid. 1779. p. 529.) Experiments on mixing gold with tin. (Ibid. 1784. p. 463.)

ALCOCK, [Nathan] *M. D: F. R. S.* born at Runcorn in Chefhire. 1707. died d. 6 Dec. 1779.

ALDBOROUGH, Earl of; fee *Stratford*.

ALDERSON, [J. ...) *M. D.* On the nature and origin of the contagion of fevers. 1788. 8. (2 fh.) überf. von *W. F. S. Bucholtz*. Jena 1790. 8.

ALEXANDER, [Caleb] Account of eruptions and the prefent appearances in Weftriver-mountain. (Mem. of B. A. Vol. 1. p. 316.)

— [John] *Phyfician in Halifax, Yorkfhire.* The hiftory of an exceffive discharge of water from the uterus during pregnancy. (Med. Comm. of Ed. Vol. 3. p. 187.)

— [John] *Surgeon in the fervice of the Eaft-India Company.* Account of the goods effects derived from the eau de Luce, taken internally, againft the bite of the viper. (*Duncan's* M. C. Dec. 2. Vol. 4. p. 207.)

— [*William*] *M. D. at Edinburgh.* Experimental effays — on the external application of antifeptics in putrid difeafes; on the dofes and effects of Medicines; on diuretics and fudorifics. 1768. 8. (3 fh. 6 d.) On the caufes of putrid difeafes. 1773. 8. (4 fh. 6 d.) (Diefes und das vorhergehende Buch überfezt unter dem Titel: Medizinifche Verfuche und Erfahrungen. Leipzig 1773. 8.) The cafe of a perfon who was feemingly killed by a blow on the breaft, recovered by bleeding and the warm bath.

bath. (Eff. and Obferv. Edinb. Vol. 3. p. 512.)
The hiftory of women, from the earlieft antiquity
to the prefent time. 1779. 4. Vol. 1. 2. (1 L. 10 fh.)
überf. Leipzig. Th. 1. 2. 1781. 8.

ALISON, [Archibald] *LL.B: F.R.S.* On the nature and principles of tafte. 1789. 4. (16 fh.)

ALLEYNE, [John] *Esq. Barrifter at Law.* The legal degrees of marriage ftated and confidered in a feries of letters. 1774. 8. (1 fh.)

ALVES, [Robert] *A.M.* Odes on feveral fubjects. 1778. 8. (1 fh.) Ode to Britannia. 1780. 4. (6 d.) Poems. 1784. 8. (4 fh.) Edinburgh, a poem. 1790. 8. (2 fh.)

AMBROSS [. . . . .] *Mifs.* The life and memoirs of the late Miff *Ann Catley* the celebrated actrefs: with biographical fketches of Sir *Franc. Blake* Delaval and *Ifab. Pawlet*, daughter of the Earl of Thanet. 1789. 8. (1 fh. 6 d.)

AMNER, [Richard] On the inftitution of chriftianity. 1774. 8. (2 fh.) On an interpretation of the prophecies of Daniel. 1776. 8. (3 fh.)

AMORY, [Thomas] *D.D.* born d. 28 Jan. 1700. died d. 24 Jun. 1774.

—— *[Thomas] Esq.* born 1691. died d. 25 Nov. 1788.

AMSTER, [. . . . .] Speculation; or a defence of mankind: a poem. 1780. 4.

ANBUREY, [Thomas] *Officer.* °Travels through the interior parts of America, in a feries of letters, by an Officer. Vol. 1. 2. 1789. 8. (14 fh.)

ANCEL, *[Samuel] Clerk tho the 58 Regiment.* Journal of the late and important blockade and fiege of Gibraltar from 1779 to 1783. 1786. 8. (5 fh.)

ANDERSON, [. . . . .] Account of a large. Honenear Cape Town. (Phil. Transact. 1778. p. 102.)

—— *[Adam]* born . . . . died 17 . .

—— *[Alexander]* Account of a bituminous lake or plain in the island of Trinidad. (Phil. Transact. 1789. p. 65. überf. *Sprengel* u. *Forfter's* N. Beytr. zur Völker u. Länderk. Th. 3. S. 259. und in *Gren* Journ. der Phyf. T. 2. S. 81.

—— *[G . . . .]* * The Arenarius of *Archimedes* translated —. 1784. 8. (2 fh. 6 d.)

—— [James] *LL.D: F.R.S: F.A.S: Farmer at Monkshill, Aberdeenfhire.* born in Scotland. ° Effays rela-

relating to Agriculture and rural affairs. 1775. 8. (6 fh.) Ed. 2. 1777. 8. Vol. 1. 2. (12 fh.) Ed. 3. mit des Verf. Nahmen, 1784. 8. Vol. 1. 2. Obſervations on the means of exciting a ſpirit of national induſtry — and manufactures of Scotland. 1777. 4. (18 ſh.) On the corn laws with a view to the new corn bill propoſed for Scotland. 1777. 8. (1 ſh 6 d.) Inquiry into the cauſes that have hitherto retarded the advancement of agriculture in Europe. 1779. 4 (3 ſh.) Account of ancient monuments and fortifications in the highlands of Scotland. (Arch. Vol. 5. p. 241. Vol. 6. p. 87.) Intereſt of Great Britain, with regard to her American colonies. 1782. 8. (2 ſh 6 d.) On the preſent ſtate of the hebrides and weſtern coaſts of Scotland. 1785. 8. (7 ſh. 6 d.) überſ. Berlin. 1789. 8. --. and Sir *John Sinclair's* Report of the committee of the Highland ſociety of Scotland, to whom the ſubject of Shetland wool was referred — 1790. 8.

ANDERSON, [James] *M. D. Phyſician General at adras in the Eaſt-Indies.* Letters on the ſubject of cochineal inſects diſcovered at Madras. Madras, 1788. 8.

—— [James] *Surgeon.* Account of Morne Garou, a mountain in the Island of St. Vincent, with a deſcription of the Volcano on its ſummit. (Phil. Transact. 1785. p. 16.) Account of a monſter of the human ſpecies. (Ibid. 1789. p. 157.)

—— [John] *M. D.* Medical remarks on natural, ſpontaneous and artificial evacuation. 1787. 8. (2 ſh. 6 d) Ed. 2. 1788. 8. (3 ſh.) überſ. von C. F. *Michaelis.* Breslau, 1789. 8.

—— [John] The tariff or book of rates and duties on goods paſſing through the Sound at Elſinoor — 1771. 8. (1 ſh. 6 d.)

—— [Thomas] *Surgeon in Leith. F. R. S. Edinb.* Account of a very extraordinary enlargement of the Stomach, diſcovered upon diſſection. (Med. Com. of Ed. Vol. 2. p. 294.) Hiſtory of a caſe, in which pus into ſcrotum gave the appearance of a hernia. (Ibid. Vol. 2. p. 423.) Two caſes of dislocation of the femur, with an account of the method of reduction. (Ibid. Vol. 3. p. 424.) Pathological obſervations on the brain. (London M. J. *Vol. XI.* P. 2.)

ANDER-

ANDERSON, [Walter] *D. D.* born in Scotland. Hiſtory of France. 1769-1782. 4. Vol. 1-5. (4 L. 4 ſh.)

—— [William] *Surgeon in Edinburgh.* Obſervations on the uſe of the cabbage-tree-bark, as an anthelmintic. (Med. Com. of Ed. Vol. 4. p 84.) Account of ſome poiſonous fiſh in the ſouth ſeas. (Phil. Transact. 1776. p. 544.) Account of a large ſtone near Cape-Town with a letter from ſir *Will. Hamilton* on having ſeen ſome pieces of the ſaid ſtone. (Ibid. 1778. p. 102.)

ANDRE', [William] *Surgeon.* A microſcopic deſcription of the eyes of the Monoculus Polyphemus Linnaei. (Phil. Transact. 1782. p. 440.) Deſcription of the teeth of the Anarrhichas Lupus *Linnaei* and of thoſe of the chaetodon nigricans of the ſame author; with an attempt to prove that the teeth of cartilagineous fiſhes are perpetually renewed. (Ibid. 1784. p. 274.)

ANDRE'E [John] *Surgeon to the Magdalen-Hospital and Teacher of Anatomy.* Obſervations upon Dr. *Störk's* treatiſe on the virtues of hemlock in the cure of cancers. 1761. 8. (1 ſh.) Inoculation impartially conſidered. 1765. 8. (1 ſh.) A ſuppreſſion of urine, from a ſlough in the urethra. (Med. Obſ. & Inq. Vol. 5. p. 342.) On the Theory and cure of the venereal gonorrhoea. 1777. 8. (1 ſh.) Ed. 2. 1781. 8. überſ. Leipz. 1779. 8. u. 1781. 8. On the theory and cure of the venereal diſeaſe. 1779. 8. (3 ſh.) überſ. Leipz. 1781. 8. Account on an elaſtic trochar. 1781. 8. (1 ſh.)

—— [John] *M. D: at Hertford.* Conſiderations on bilious diſeaſes; and ſome particular affections of the liver and the gall bladder. 1788. 8. (1 ſh. 6 d.)

ANDREWS [. . . . .] *Advice humbly offered to the prince of Wales, by a well meaning Briton. 1789. 8. (6 d.)

—— [John] *LL. D.* The ſcripture doctrine of grace. 1769. 8. (3 ſh.) Hiſtory of the revolutions of Denmark &c. 8. Vol. 1. 2. 1774. (12 ſh.) überſ. Kopenh. u. Flensb. Th. 1. 1786. 8. Letters to the Count de Welderen on the preſent ſituation of affairs between great Britain and the united provinces. 1781. 8. (1 ſh. 6 d.) Two additional letters.

1781. 8. (2 fh.) ' On the manners tafte and amufements of the two laft centuries in England. 1782. 8. (2 fh. 6 d.) On republican principles and on the inconveniences of a commonwealth in a large country and nation. 1783. 8. (1 fh. 6 d.) On the principal duties of focial life. 1783. 8. (3 fh.) Remarks on the french and englifh ladies. 1783. 8. (5 fh.) Letters to a young gentleman on his fetting out for france, containing a furvey of Paris and review of french litterature. 1784. 8. (6 fh.) Hiftory of the war with America, France, Spain and Holland. 1775-1783. Vol. 1-4. 1786. 8. (1 L. 10 fh.) Defence of the ftadholderfhip, wherein the neceffity of that office in the united provinces is demonftrated. 1787. 8. (2 fh.)

ANDREWS [James Petit] F. A. S. Appeal to the humane, on behalf of the moft deplorable claff of fociety, the climbing boys employed by the chimneyfweepers. 1788. 12. (1 fh.) Anecdotes - ancient and modern. 1789. 8. (6 fh.)

—— [Miles Peter] *Esq. Dealer in Gunpowder* The Election. 1774. 8. Summer amufements or an adventure at Margate ; a Comic Opera. 1779. Fire and water, a comic Opera. 1780. I. (1 fh.) Diffipation, a Comedy. 1781. 8. (1 fh. 6 d.) The Baron Kinkvervankotsdorftrakingatchdern, a new mufical comedy. 1781. 8. (1 fh. 6 d.) The beft biddler, a farce. 1782. The reparation, a Comedy. 1784. 8. (1 fh. 6 d.) The enchanted caftle. 1786.

—— [William] *Attorney at Law.* Addreff on the behaviour of the mayor and corporation of Southampton. 1774. 4. (6 d.)

ANSTY. [Charles] ⁰The new bath guide, or, memoirs of the B- R- D- family in a feries of poetical epiftles. 1766. 4. (5 fh.) Ed. 3. 1766. (3 fh. 6 d.) ⁰An Election Ball --. 17.. 4. (2 fh. 6 d.) * The prieft diffected ; a poem. 1774. 4. (2 fh. 6 d.) Ad C. W. Bampfylde epiftola poetica familiaris --. 1776. 4. (5 fh.) Familiar epiftle to C. W. Bampfylde -- translated. 4. 1777. (1 fh.) ⁰Speculation : or, a defence of mankind; a poem. 1780. 4. (2 fh. 6 d.)

ANSTICE,

ANSTICE, [Robert] Remarks on the comparative advantages of wheel, carriages of different ſtructure and draught. 1790. 8. (2 ſh. 6 d.)

ANSTIE, [John] General view of the bill preſented to parliament — for preventing the illicit exportation of wool and live ſheep —. 1787. 8. (2 ſh.)
*Letter to Edw. Philips — on the advantages of manufacturing the combing wool of England — by the chairman of the wool meeting. 1788. 4. (1 ſh. 6 d.)

ANTILL, [Edward] *Eſq. One of his Majeſty's Council for the province of New-Jerſey.* born 17... died. 1770.

APPLEGARTH, [Robert] Theological ſurvey of the human underſtandig. 1779. 8. (5 ſh.) Apology for the two ordinances of Jeſus Chriſt, the holy communion and baptiſm. 1789. 8. A plea for the poor; or, remarks on the price of proviſions, and the peaſant's labour — 1789. 8. (6 d.)

APTHORP, [Eaſt] *DD. Rector of St. Mary-le-Bow, Cheapſide.* Review of Dr. *Mayhew's* remarks on the anſwer to his obſervations on the charter and conduct of the Society for the propagation of the goſpel in foreign parts. 1765. 8. (1 ſh.) Letters on the prevalence of Chriſtianity, before its civil eſtabliſhment; with obſervations on *(Gibbon's)* Hiſtory of the decline of the roman empire. 1778. 8. (5 ſh.) Two ſermons. 1780. 4. (1 ſh.) *Select devotions for families, particular perſons and for the celebration of the holy euchariſt. 1785. 12. (1 ſh.) Diſcourſes on prophecy. 1786. 8. Vol. 1. 2. (10 ſh.)

ARCHDALE, [Mervyn] *A. M. Member of the R. Iriſh Acad. Rector of Slane.* Monaſticum hibernicum, or hiſtory of the abbies, priories and other religious houſes in Ireland. 1786. 4. (1 L. 5 ſh.) *John Lodge's* peerage of Ireland; or, a general hiſtory of the preſent nobility of that kingdom — reviſed, enlarged and continued to the preſent time. *Vol.* 1-7. 1789.

ARCHER, [Anne] *Mrs.* (her maiden name *Sheldon*) Authentic and intereſting memoirs. 1787. 8. Vol. 1-4. (10 ſh.)

ARCHER, [Edward] *M. D. Phyſician of the united hoſpitals for the ſmall pox and Inoculation.*
born 1717. died. d. 28. Apr. 1789.

ARMSTRONG, [Charles] *Surgeon and Man-midwife.* On the ſymptoms and cure of the virulent gonorrhoea in females. 1783. 8. (1 ſh.)

—— [Francis] *M. D. at Uppingham, Rutland.* On the uſe of Matlock waters. (*Duncan's* M. C. Vol. 7. p. 242.) Account of a new invented green paint ——. 1783. 4. (1 ſh.) Account of a ſingular convulſive fits in 3 children of one family. (*Duncan's* M. C. Vol. 9. p. 317.)

—— [George] *M. D: Phyſician to the Diſpenſary.* *Eſſay on the diſeaſes moſt fatal to infants. 1768. 8. (2 ſh. 6 d.) Ed. 2. 1771. 8. überſ. Zelle. 1769. 8. Account of the diſeaſes moſt incident to children. 1777. 8. (3 ſh.) Ed. 2. 1783. 8. überſ. von *J. C. B. Schaeffer*. Regensb. 1786. 8. und in Samml. f. A. Th. 4. S. 52 - 144.

—— [John] *M. D. Phyſician to his Majeſty's Army.* born at Caſtleton, Roxburgſhire. 17.. died d. 7. Sept. 1779.

—— [John] Juvenile poems, with remarks on poetry and a diſſertation on the beſt method of puniſhing and preventing crimes. 1789. 8. (2 ſh. 6 d.)

—— [Mostyn John] *Geographer and County Surveyor.* Actual Survey of the great-poſt-roads between London and Edinburgh. 1776. 8. (7 ſh. 6 d.) Actual ſurvey of the great-poſt-roads between London and Dover. 1777. 8. (3 ſh.)

ARNE [Thomas Auguſtine] *Doctor of Muſic.*
born d. 28 May. 1710. died d. 5 March. 1778.

ARNOLD, [Charles Henry] Hiſtory of South and North America. 1782. 8. (3 ſh.)

—— [John] Account of his pocket chronometer ——. 1780. 4. (1 ſh.) On the longitude ——. 1781. 4. (2 ſh. 6 d.) Anſwer to an anonymous letter on the longitude. 1782. 4. (1 ſh.)

—— [Thomas] *M. D. Phyſician at Leiceſter.* Diſſ. De Pleuritide. Edinb. 1766. 8. Obſervations on the nature, kinds, cauſes and prevention on inſanity, lunacy and madneſs. Vol. 1. 1782. Vol. 2. 1786. 8. (7 ſh.) überſ. von *J. C. B.* Ackermann. Th. 1. 2. Leipz. 1788. 8.

ARNOT,

ARNOT, [Hugo] *Advocate.* History of Edinburgh. 1779. 4. (1 L. 5 sh.) Collection and abridgment of celebrated criminal trials in Scotland from 1536 to 1784. 4. 1786. (18 sh.)
—— [W. . . . .] *Minister of Kennoway.* Harmony of law and gospel, in the method of grace, demonstrated. 1786. 8.
ARTHUR, [Edward] *Minister at Baremore, Etal.* Sermons on various subjects. 1783. 8. (4 sh.)
—— [J. . . .] *Manager of the playhouse at Bath.* born.... died d. 8 Apr. 1772.
—— [Michael] Exposition — of the Assembly's shorter catechism delivered in a series of Sabbath evening lectures. Vol. 1. 1789. 8. (4 sh.)
ASCOUGH, [Charles Edward] born.... died d. 14. Oct. 1779.
ASH [Edward] M. D. "The Speculator, published in weekly Numbers. 1790. 8.
—— [John] LL. D. *Dissenting Minister of Pershore, Worcestershire.* born 1724. died d. 10 Apr. 1779.
—— [John] *M. D: F. R. S: F. A. S.* Experiments and observations to investigate the medicinal properties of the mineral waters of Spa and Aix la Chapelle in Germany and of the Waters — in french Flanders. 1788. 12. (5 sh.)
ASHBY [. . . . .] *B. D. President of St. John's College, Cambridge.* On a singular coin of Nerva. (Arch. Vol. 3. p. 165.)
ASHDOWNE, [William] Essay explaining Jesus true meaning in his parables. 1780. 8. (1 sh. 6 d.) The unitarian, Arian and Trinitarian opinion respecting Christ, examined and tried by scripture evidence alone. 1789. 8. (1 sh.)
ASHE, [Robert] *Curate of Crewkerne and Master of the free grammar school.* published John Browne of Crewkerne, Somerset; (a boy of 11 Years old) poetical translations from various authors. 1787. 4. (2 sh. 6 d.)
ASHMORE, [T. . . . .] Analysis of the several bank annuities. 1774. 4. (1 Sh.)
ASHTON, [James] The christian expositor. 1774. 8. (5 Sh.) The new expositor; containing tables of words from two to seven syllables, accented, explaind

plaind and divided according to the moſt approued
method of pronunciation. 1788. 8. (1 Sh.)
ASHTON, [Thomas] DD. Rector of St. Botolph, Bi-
ſhopsgate. born 1716. died d. 19. March. 1775.
ASHWORTH, [Caleb] Tutor of the diſſenting Academy
at Daventry in Northamptonſhire.
born .... died 1775.
ASKEW, [Anthony] M. D.
. born .... died d. 27 Febr. 1773.
ASTELL, [....] Mrs. *The unfaſhionable wife:
a Novel. Vol. 1. 2. 1771. 8. (5 Sh.)
ASTLE, [Thomas] F. R. S: F. A. S: Keeper of the records
in the tower of London. On the events produced
in England by the grant of Sicily to prince Edmund. (Arch. Vol. 4. p. 195.) Origin and progreſſ
of writing, as, well hieroglyphic as elementary.
1784. 4. (1 L. 11 Sh. 6 d) On the radical letters
of the pelasgians and their derivation. (Arch. Vol.
7. p. 348.) *The will of King Alfred. 1788. 4.
(3 Sh.) *The will of King Henry the VII. 1789.
4. (3 Sh. 6 d.)
ATCHISON, [Robert] Surgeon. Obſervations on the
dyſentery, as it appears among the negroes on the
coaſt of Guinea. (Duncan's M. C. Vol. 9. p. 268.)
ATKINS, [James] M. A. The aſcenſion, a poem.
1780. 4. (6 d.)
—— [John] A meteorological journal for the Year 1782.
(Phil. Transact. 1784. p. 58.)
ATKINSON, [Chriſtopher] Rector of Yelden, Bed-
fordſhire. Poetical ſermon on the benefit of affliction. 1766. 4. (1 Sh. 6 d.) Sermons on the moſt
intereſting and important ſubjects. 1775. 8. (6 Sh.)
—— [William] M. A. fellow of Jeſus College, Cambridge.
Poetical eſſays. 1786. 4. (1 Sh.)
ATWOOD, [George] M. A: F. R. S. A general theory for the menſuration of the angle ſubtended by
two objects, of which one is obſerved by rays after
two reflections from plane ſurfaces and the other
by rays coming directly to the ſpectator's eye.
(Phil. Transact. 1781. p. 395.) On the rectilinear
motion and rotation of bodies. 1784. 8. (10 Sh. 6 d.)
On the principles of natural philoſophy. 1784. 8.
(5 Sh.).

ATWOOD,

ATWOOD, [Thomas] Obfervations on the true methods of treatment and ufage of the Negroflaves
in the britifh Weft-India Islands. 1789. 8. (1 fh.)
AUFRERE, [Anthony] *Efq.* Tribute to the memory
of *Ulric* of *Hutten* — tranflated from the german
of *Goethe.* 1789. 8. (3 fh.)
AUSTIN, [....] *Mrs.* The noble family; in a feries of letters. Vol. 1. 2. 3. 1771. 8. (9 fh.)
—— [William] *M. D.* Examination of the firft fix books
of *Euclids* elements. 1781. 8. (2 fh. 6 d.) Experiments on the formation of volatile alkali and on
the affinities of the phlogifticated and light inflammable airs. (Phil. Tranfact. 1788. p. 379. überf.
Gren J. d. Ph. T. I. S. 418.) Experiments on the
analyfis of the heavy inflammable air. (Phil. Transact. 1790 p. 51.)
AYLOFFE, [Jofeph] *Baronet*, *Viceprefident of the
Antiq. Soc. and F. R. S.*
born 1709. died. d. 19. Apr. 1781.
AYRES, [William Thomas] *Efq.* Comparative view of
the differences between the englifh and irifh fta-
tute and common law -- *Vol.* 1. 2. 1781. 8.
(12 fh.)
AYSCOUGH, [Georg Edward Lyttelton] *Captain.*
(Schwager *George* Lord *Lyttelton's*)
born.... died d. 19 Oct. 1779.
—— [Samuel] *Clerk*, *Affiftant Librarian of the britifh
Mufeum in the department of natural hiftory.* Ca-
talogue of the Manufcrits preferved in the britifh
Mufeum hitherto undefcribed. 1782. 4. Vol. 1. 2.
(2 L. 2 fh.) °Remarks on the letters from an
American farmer: or a detection of the errors of
Mr. J. *Hector St. John.* 1783. 8. (6 d.) General
Index to the Monthly Review from its commence-
ment to the 70 Volume. 1786. 8. Vol. 1. 2. (15 fh.)
General Index to the 56 Volumes of the Gentle-
man's Magazine -- Vol. 1. 2. 1789. 8.

BABINGTON, [William] *Apothecary to Guy's Hof-
pital.* A cafe of hydrophobia. (M. C. Vol. 1. p. 215.)
BACHMAIR, [John James] *M. A.* The revelation of
St. John hiftorically explained -- 1778. 8. (5 fh.)
BACKHOUSE, [William] *D. D. Rector of Deal and
Archdeacon of Canterbury.*
born.... died d. 29 Aug. 1788.

BACON,

BACON, [John] *Apothecary in York.* History of a carcinomatous ulcer in the mouth cured by the application of leeches. (Med. Com. of Ed. Vol. 2. p. 296.)
—— [Manuel] DD. *Rector at Balden and Vicar of Bramber, Suffex.* born.... died d. 2 Jan. 1783.
BADCOCK, [Samuel] *Dissenting minister of South-Moulton, Devonshire.* born 1750. died d. 19 May 1788.
BADENACH [James] *M. D.* Observations on the bilious fever usual in voyages to the East-Indies. (Med Obs. Vol. 4. p. 156.) Observations on the use of wort in the cure of the scurvy at sea. (Ibid. Vol. 5. p. 61.) Technical description of an uncommon bird from Malacca. (Phil. Transact. 1772. p. 1.)
BAGGS [S.....] *M. A. Pinto*, on circulation and credit, translated. 1774. 4. (10 sh. 6 d.)
BAGOT, [Lewis] *D. D. Bishop of Norwich.* (brother of Lord *William Bagot.*) Twelve discourses on the prophecies concerning christianity. 1780. 8. (5 sh.) (Several single sermons.)
BAILEY, [Alexander Mabyn] born.... died 17..
—— [William] *Register to the society for the encouragement of arts, manufactures and commerce.* born.... died 17..
BAILLIE [....] *Captain, late Lieut. Governor of the Royal Hospital for seamen at Greenwich.* Solemn appeal to the public --. 1779. fol. (2 L. 2 sh.)
—— [Hugh] *LL. D. late Judge of the court of Admiralty in Ireland.* Letter to Dr. *Shebbeare*, containing a confutation of his arguments concerning the Boston and Quebec acts of parliament. 1775. 8. (2 sh.)
—— [Matthew] *M. D. Trustee of the Museum of the late Dr. Hunter.* Account of a remarkable transposition of the viscera. (Phil. Transact. 1788. p. 350. London M. J. Vol. X. P. 2.) Account of a particular change of Structure in the human ovarium. (Ibid. 1789. p. 71. London M. J. Vol. X. P. 3. überf. Samml: f. A. Th. 13. S. 354.)
BAKER, [....] *Remarks on the english language --. 1771. 8. (2 sh.)
—— [David Erskine] *Esq.* The Muse of Ossian, a dramatic poem. 1763. 12. Biographia Dramatica, or a companion to the playhouse. 1782. 8. Vol. 1. 2.

BAKER,

BAKER, [George] *M. D: F. R. S. Baronet, Prefident of the College of Phyficians and Phyfician to her Majefty's Houshold.*
Opufcula medica. Innhalt: De Catarrho et De Dyfenteria Londinenfi epidemica. De affectibus animi et morbis inde oriundis. Oratio Harvejana. De *Joh. Cajo* Anatomiae conditore apud nostrates. Ed. 2. 1771. 8. (5 fh.) On the merits of inoculating the fmallpox. 1766. 8. (1 fh. 6 d.) überf. von C. F. T. Leipz. 1767. 8. Inquiry concerning the caufe of the endemial colic of Devonfhire. (Med. Transact. Vol. 1. p. 175. p. 460.) Examination of feveral means by which the poifon of lead may be fuppofed frequently to gain admittance into the human body unobferved and unfufpected. (Ibid. Vol. 1. p. 257. Vol. 2. p. 419.) Attempt towards an hiftorical account of the colic of Poitou. (Ibid. Vol. 1. p. 319.) Examination of the feveral caufes, to which the colic of Poitou has been attributed. (Ibid. Vol. 1. p. 364. Vol. 3. p. 407.) Flos Cardamines recommended to the tryal of phyficians as an antifpafinodic remedy. (Ibid. Vol. 1. p. 442.) Account of a fingular difeafe, which prevailed among fome poor children, maintained by the parifh of St. James in Weftminfter. (Ibid. Vol. 3. p. 113.) Obfervations on the late intermittent fevers; with a hiftory of the Peruvian bark. (Ibid. Vol. 3. p. 141.) Obfervations on *Erafm. Darwin's* account of the ufe of foxglove in fome dropfies and in the pulmonary confumption. (Ibid. Vol. 3. p. 287.) A Sequel to the cafe of *Thom. Wood* of Billericay in the county of Effex. (Ibid. Vol. 3. p. 309.) Several extraordinaries instances of the cure of the dropfy. (Ibid. Vol. 2. p. 235.) Obfervations on the modern method of inoculating the fmall-pox. (Ibid. Vol. 2. p. 275.)

—— [Henry] *F. R. S: F. A. S.*
born.... died at London d. 25 Nov. 1774.

—— [Richard] *A. M. Rector of Cawfton in Norfolk.*
Sermon on falvation. 1782. 4. (1 fh.) Harmony of IV Evangelifts. P. 1-4. 1787. 8. (10 fh. 3 d.)

—— [Robert] *B. D.*
Account of a ftag's head and horns, found at Alport,

port, in the parish of *Youlgreave* in the county of *Derby*. (Phil. Transact. 1785. p. 353.)

BALDWIN, [Loammi] *Esq. F. A. Acad.*
Account of a very curious appearance of the electrical fluid, produced by raising an electrical kite in the time of a thunder shower. (Mem. of B. A. T. I. p. 257.)

—— [Samuel] *of the Customhouse.*
Survey of the british customs, containing the rates of merchandizes — and other statutes. 1775. 4. (18 sh.)

—— [Thomas] *Esq. A. M.*
Airopaedia: or narrative of a balloon excursion from Chester 1785. —. 1786. 8. (7 sh. 6 d.)

BALDWYN, [Edward]
°Critique on the poetical essays of *Will. Atkinson.* — 1787. 8. (2 sh. 6 d.)

BALFOUR, [Francis] *M. D. Physician at Calcutta.*
Dissertatio de Gonorrhoea virulenta. Edinb. 1767. 4.
On the influence of the moon in fevres. Calcutta. 1784. London 1785. 8. (1 sh. 6 d.) übers. von A. T. W. Strafsb. 1786. 8. The forms of Herkern; — translated into english with an index of arabic words. 1787. 4. (1 L. 1 sh.)

—— [James] *Esq.*
Philosophical dissertations. 1782. 8. (2 sh. 6 d.)

BALGUY, [Thomas] *D. D. Arch-Deacon and Prebendary of Winchester.*
W. S. Powell's Discourses on various subjects published. 1776. 8. (5 sh.) Discourses on various subjects. 1785. 8. (5 sh.) (several single sermons.)

BALL, [John] *M. D.*
born.... died d. 15 Oct. 1779.

BALLIN, [....] *Miss.*
The statue room, an historical tale. 1790. 8. Vol. 1. 2. (5 sh.)

BALTIMORE, [Frederic] *Lord.*
born 1731. died at Neapel d. 8 Sept. 1771.

BANCROFT, [Edward] *M. D.*
*Natural History of Guiana in South-America. 1769. 8. (6 sh.) übers. Frankf. u. Leipz. 1769. 8.
°History of Charles Wentworth, Esq. Vol. 1. 2. 3. 1769. 8. (7 sh. 6 d.)

BAN-

BANCROFT, [T. ...]
Prolufiones poeticae; or, a felection of poetical exercifes in greek, latin and englifh. 1788. 8. (3 fh.)
BANDINELL, [James] D. D.
Eight fermons. 1780. 8. (4 fh.)
BANNISTER, [James]
*Select Tragedies of *Euripides*, translated from the greek. 1780. 8. (7 fh.) View of the arts and fciences, from the earlieft times to the age of Alexander the great. 1785. 8. (3 fh.)
BARBAULD, [Anna Laetitia] (Sifter of Dr. *John Aikin*, at *Hampftead near London*.)
Poems. 1773. 4. (6 fh.) Mifcellaneous pieces in profe. 1773. 8. (3 fh.) Devotional pieces, compiled from the Pfalms and the book of Job — thoughts on the devotional tafte, on fects and on eftablifhments. 1775. 8. (2 fh. 6d.) Leffons for children from two to three Years old. 1778. 4. (6 d.) *Hymns in profe for children. 1781. 8. (1 fh.) *An Addrefs to the oppofers of the repeal of the corporation and Teft-Acts. 1790. 8. (1 fh.)
BARBUT, [James]
The genera infectorum of Linnaeus, exemplified by various fpecimens of englifh infects drawn from nature. 1781. 4. (2 L. 12 fh. 6 d.) The genera vermium —. P. 1. 2. 1788. 4. (3 L. 9 fh.)
BARCLAY, [James] *Curate of Edmonton in Middlefex*.
*The greek rudiments. 1754. 8. (4 fh.) The rudiments of the latin tongue. 1758. 8. (2 fh.) Complete and univerfal englifh dictionary on a new plan —. 1774. 8. (6 fh.)
(feveral fingle fermons.)
BARD, [Samuel] *M. D. Profeffor of the practice of Phyfic, Kings-College, New-York.*
Enquiry into the nature caufe and cure of the Angina fuffocativa, or fore throat diftemper. (Tr. of A. S. Vol. 1. p. 322.)
BARFOOT, [P....] *Esq.*
Two letters — for obtaining an equal fyftem of taxation and for reducing the national debt. 1786. 8. (1 fh.)
BARING, [Francis] *Memb. of Parl. Director of the Eaft-India Company.*
The

The principle of the commutation Act eſtabliſhed by facts. 1786. 8. (1 ſh.)

BARKER, [John]
On Cheltenham water, and its great uſe in the preſent peſtilential conſtitution. 1786. 8. (1 ſh. 6 d.) Obſervations on the publication on Cheltenham water. 1787. 8.

—— [Robert] *Sir, Knight. Commander in chief of the Eaſt-India Company's forces in Bengal.* born.... died d. 14 Sept. 1789.

—— [Thomas] *Esq. of Lyndon in Rutlandſhire.* Account of a meteor ſeen in the county of Rutland which reſembled a water ſpout. (Phil. Transact. 1756. p. 248.) On the return of the comet expected in 1757 or 1758. (Ibid. 1759. p. 347.) On the mutations of the ſtars. (Ibid. 1761. p. 498.) Account of a remarkable Halo, May 20. 1737. (Ibid. 1762. p. 3.) Obſervations on the quantities of rain fallen at Lyndon, in Rutland, for ſeveral Years. (Ibid. 1771. p. 221.) On the ſame ſubject, with obſervations for determining the latitude of Stamford in Lincolnſhire. (Ibid. 1771. p. 227.) The duty, circumſtances and benefits of baptiſm. 1771. 8. (3 ſh. 6 d.) Regiſter of the Barometer, Thermometer and rain at Lyndon in Y. 1771. (Phil. Transact. 1772. p. 42.)
—— 1772. (ibid. 1773. p. 221.)
—— 1773. (ibid. 1774. p. 202.)
—— 1774. (ibid. 1775. p. 199.)
—— 1775. (ibid. 1776. p. 370.)
—— 1776. (ibid. 1777. p. 350.)
—— 1777. (ibid. 1778. p. 554.)
—— 1778. (ibid. 1779. p. 547.)
—— 1779. (ibid. 1780. p. 474.)
—— 1780. (ibid. 1781. p. 351.)
—— 1781. (ibid. 1782. p. 281.)
—— 1782. (ibid. 1783. p. 242.)
—— 1783. (ibid. 1784. p. 283.)
—— 1784. (ibid. 1785. p. 481.)
—— 1785. (ibid. 1786. p. 236.)
—— 1786. (ibid. 1787. p. 368.)
—— 1787. (ibib. 1788. p. 408.)
—— 1788. (ibid. 1789. p. 162.) Meſſiah. 1780. 8. (2 ſh. 6 d.) The nature and circumſtances of the demo-

demoniacs in the Gofpel ſtated, methodized and
confidered in the feveral particulars. 1783. 8. (1 ſh.
6 d.)
BARKER, [William] *Hair - Dreſſer.*
On the principles of hair dreſſing —. 1784. 8.
(1 ſh. 6 d.)
—— [W.... H....] *A. B. Maſter of the grammar ſchool,
Carmarthen.*
Grammar- of the hebrew language. — 1774. 8.
(1 ſh. 6 d.)
BARLOW, [Frederic] *M. A.*
Complete engliſh Dictionary. 17.. The complete
engliſh peerage; or, a genealogical and hiſtorical
account of the peers and peereſſes of this realm.
Vol. 1. 2. 1773. 8. (12 ſh. 6 d.) Ed. 2. Vol. 1. 2.
1775. 8. (12 ſh.)
—— [Joel]
The viſion of Columbus, a poem. 1787. 8. (2 ſh.
6 d.)
BARNARD, [....] *D. D. Biſhop of Killaloe. M. R. Iriſh
Acad. and F. R. S.*
Enquiry concerning the original of the Scots in
Britain. (Tr. of J. A. 1787. p. 25.)
—— [James]
The divinity of our Lord Jeſus Chriſt demonſtrated
from the holy ſcriptures and from the doctrine of
the primitive church; —. 1789. 8. (3 ſh.)
—— [William] *Ship - Builder.*
Of an exploſion in a coal - pit. (Phil. Transact.
1773. p. 217.) Method for the removal of Ships
that have been driven on ſhore and damaged in
their bottoms. (Ibid. 1780. p. 100)
BARNES, [Thomas] *D. D. Member of the litterary and
philoſophical ſociety of Mancheſter.*
On the nature and eſſential character of poetry as
diſtinguiſhed from proſe. (Mem. of M. Vol. 1. p.
54.) On the affinity, ſubſiſting between the arts,
with a plan for promoting and extending manufactures by encouraging thoſe arts, on which manufactures principally depend. (Ibid. Vol. 1. p. 72.)
On the pleaſure which the mind in many caſes
receives from contemplating ſcenes of diſtreſſ. (Ibid.
Vol. 1. p. 144.) On the influence of the imagina-
tion and the paſſions upon the underſtanding.
B 3 (Mem.

(Mem. of M. Vol. 1. p. 375.) On public and private education. (Ibid. Vol. 2. p. 1.) Plan for the improvement and extenfion of liberal education in Manchefter. (Ibid. Vol. 2. p. 16.) Propofals for eftablifhing a plan of liberal education in Manchefter. (Ibid. Vol. 2. p. 30.) On the voluntary power which the mind is able to exercife over bodily fenfation. (Ibid. Vol. 2. p. 451.)
(feveral fingle fermons.)

BARR, [.....]
Journal of the weather at Montreal from Dec. 1776 to March 1777. (Phil. Transact. 1778. p. 557.)
—— from Dec. 1778 to April 1779. (Ibid. 1780. p. 272.)

BARRET, [John] B. D. *fellow of Trinity College, Dublin.* Account of a greek Manufcript of St. Matthew's gofpel in the library of Trinity College, Dublin. (Tr. of J. A. 1787. p. 121. überf. *Eichhorn's* Biblioth. der bibl. Litterat. Th. 2. S. 584.)
—— [Onflow] M. D.
On the gout. 1785. 8. (1 fh. 6 d.)
—— [Phineas] *Merchant at Lisbon.*
Tables of the feveral european exchanges —. 1771. 4. (2 L. 2 fh.)
—— [William] F. A. S. *Surgeon at Briftol.*
born.... died d. 15 Sept. 1789.

BARRINGTON, [Daines] F. R. *and* A. S. *Vice-Prefident of the Royal fociety at London.*
Letter on fome particular fifh, found in Wales. (Phil. Transact. 1767. p. 204.) Invefigation of the difference between the prefent temperature of the air in Italy and fome other countries, to what it was 17 centuries ago. (Ibid. 1768. p. 58.) On the trees, which are fuppofed to be indigenous in Great-Britain. (Ibid. 1769. p. 23.) Account of a very remarkable young mufician. (Ibid. 1770. p. 54.) Letter concerning Chesnut trees. (Ibid. 1771. p. 167.) Account of a mole from North-America. (Ibid. 1771. p. 292.) Account of fome experiments made in North-Wales, to afcertain the different quantities of rain, which fell in the fame time at different heights. (Ibid. 1771. p. 294.) Invefigation of the fpecific characters, which diftinguifh the rabbit from the hare. (Ibid. 1772. p. 4.)
On

On the periodical appearing and disappearing of certain birds at different times of the Year. (Phil. Transact. 1772. p. 265.) Account of a foſſil lately found near Chriſt-church in Hampſhire. (Ibid. 1773. p. 171.) Obſervations on the lagopus or ptarmigan. (Ibid. 1773. p. 224.) Experiments and obſervations on the ſinging of birds. (Ibid. p. 249.) Of the Gillaroo trout. (Ibid. 1774. p. 116.) Obſervations on the welſh caſtles. (Arch. Vol. 1. p. 278.) Account of two muſical inſtruments uſed in Wales. (Ibid. Vol. 3. p. 30.) Anſwer to Mr. *Pegge*, on the growth of the vine in England. (Ibid. Vol. 3. p. 67.) On the expiration of the corniſh language. (Ibid. Vol. 3. p. 278.) Obſervations on the Corbridge Altars. (Ibid. Vol. 3. p. 324.) On the term Levant. (Ibid. Vol. 4. p. 27.) On the Apamean medal. (Ibid. Vol. 4. p. 315.) Obſervations on *Caeſar's* invaſion of Britain and — his paſſage acroſſ the thames. (Ibid. Vol. 2. p. 134.) On the corniſh language. (Ibid. Vol. 5. p. 81.) Obſervations on patriarchal cuſtoms and manners. (Ibid. Vol. 5. p. 119.) The probability of reaching the Northpole diſcuſſed. 1775. 4. (2 ſh 6 d.) überſ. von *S. Engel*, Bern 1777. 4. Miſcellanies. 1781. 4. (18 ſh.) Obſervations on St. *Juſtin's* tomb. (Arch. Vol. 5. p. 143.) Obſervations on the earlieſt introduction of cloks. (Ibid. Vol. 5. p. 416. überſ, von *Joh. Beckmann*, Beytr. zur Geſch. der Erfind. Th. 1. S 301.) Obſervations on the vitrified walls in Scotland. (Ibid. Vol. 6. p. 100.) Obſervations on the practice of Archery in England. (Ibid. Vol. 7. p. 46.) On the progreſſ of gardening. (Ibid. Vol. 7. p. 113.) Account of pits or caverns in the earth in the county of Berks. (Ibid. Vol. 7. p. 236.) Obſervations on a picture by Zuccaro — ſuppoſed to repreſent the game of Primero. (Ibid. Vol. 8. p. 133.) Obſervations on the antiquity of card-playing in England. (Ibid. Vol. 8. p. 134.) Obſervations on the grey weathers in Berkſhire and the crypts in Canterbury cathedral. (Ibid. Vol. 8. p. 442.) Hiſtorical disqniſition on the game of cheſſ. (Ibid. Vol. 9. p. 16.) On the origin of the arms — the Pegaſus and the holy lamb. (Ibid. Vol. 9. p. 187.

BARRY,

BARRY, [Edward] *Sir: Baronet, M. D: F. R. S: Phyfician in general to his Majesty's forces in Ireland.*
born.... died d. 29 March. 1776.
—— [Edward] *A. M. et M. D. Chaplain to the Lord Bishop of Kildare.*
Twelve fermons on particular occasions. 1789. 8.
(5 fh.) Letter on the practice of boxing. 1790. 8.
(1 fh.)
(feveral fingle fermons.)
—— [James]· *Professor of painting to the Royal Academy.*
born at Cork in Ireland.
Enquiry into the real and imaginary obstructions to the acquifition of the arts in England. 1775. 8. (4 fh.) Account of a series of pictures in the great room of the fociety of arts, manufactures and commerce at the Adelphi. 1783. 8. (3 fh. 6 d.)

BARTLET, [Benjamin] *F. A. S. Quacker.* (formerly Apothecary at Bradford.)
born.... died d. 3 March. 1787.

BARTON, [Benjamin Smith] *Member of the Royal Society of Edinburgh.*
Obfervations on fome parts of natural hiftory —.
P. I. 1787. 8. (2 fh.)

BARTRAM. [Ifaac]
Memoir on the deftillation of perfimons. (Tr. of A. S. Vol. I. p. 231.)
—— [Mofes]
Obfervations on the native filk worms of North-America. (Tr. of A. S. Vol. I. p. 224.)

BARUH, [Raphael]
Critica facra examined —. 1775. 8. (5 fh.)

BASTARD, [William] *Esq. of Kitley in Devonshire.*
On the culture of pine-apples. (Phil. Transact. 1777. p. 649.)

BATE, [Henry] fee *Dudley.*
—— [Julius] *M. A. Rector of Sutton, Suffex.*
born.... died 1771.

BATEMAN, [Thomas] *A. M. Chaplain to his Grace the Duke of Gordon, Vicar of Whaplode, Lincolnshire.*
On agiftment tithe — 1778. 8. Appendix 1779.
(5 fh. 6 d.) Two fermons on the refurrection of the body —. 1780. 4. (1 fh.) The royal ecclefiaftical gazetteer, or, Clergyman's pocket kalender —.

dar —. 1781. 8. (3 ſh.) The eccleſiaſtical patronage of the church of England. 1783. 8. (3 ſh. 6 d.)

BATH, [Robert] *Surgeon.*
Addreſſ on the ſubjeƈt of inoculation —. 1778. 8. (6 d.) On the nature and quality of diſeaſes of the liver and biliary duƈts —. 1777. 8. (2 ſh.) On the medical charaƈter, with a view to define it. 1785. 8. (2 ſh. 6 d.) Ed. 3. 1789.

BATLEY, [Jeremiah] *Eſq.*
Two letters on parliamentary repreſentation. 1783. 8. (1 ſh. 6 d.)

BATT, [Charles William] *M. A. Chaplain to Lord Malmesbury.*
* Diſſertation on the meſſage from John the Baptiſt to our Saviour Luk. VII. 9. Ed. 2. 1789. 8. (2 ſh. 6 d.)

BATTIE, [William] *M. D.*
born at Devon 1704. died d. 13 Jun. 1776.

BAVERSTOCK [....] *Brewer at Alton, Hampſhire.*
* Hydrometical obſervations and experiments in the brewery. 1785. 6. (2 ſh.)

BAXTER, [Alexander] *Eſq.*
Deſcription of a ſet of Halo's and parhelia, ſeen in the Year 1771. in North-America. (Phil. Transaƈt. 1787. p. 44.)

BAYFORD, [David] *of Lewes. M. D: F. R. S.*
born 1739. died d. 16 Apr. 1790.

—— [Thomas] *Surgeon at London.*
The effeƈts of injeƈtions into the urethra and the uſe and abuſe — in the cure — of the virulent gonorrhoea. 1773. 8. (1 ſh. 6 d.) überſ. Altenb. 1777. 8.

BAYLEY, [Anſelm] *LL. D. ſub-Dean of his Majeſty's Chapels Royal.*
The antiquity, evidence and certainty of chriſtianity canvaſſed, on *Middleton's* examination of the biſhop of London's diſcourſes on prophecy. 1750. (1 ſh. 6 d.) On ſinging and playing with juſt expreſſing and real elegance —. 1771. 8. (2 ſh.) Grammar of the engliſh language. 1772. 8. (2 ſh.) The old teſtament, engliſh and hebrew with remarks critical and grammatical on the hebrew and correƈtions of the engliſh. Vol. 1-4. 1774. 8. (2 L. 2 ſh.) Grammar of the hebrew language. 1774. 8. (2 ſh.) Two ſermons, the command-

mandments of God, in nature, inftitution and religious ftatutes in the jewifh and chriftian churches. 1778. 8. (1 fh.) ◦ Remarks on *David Levi's* fecond letter to Dr. *Prieftley* — by Anti-focinus. 1787. 8. (1 fh.) The alliance of Mufic, Poetry and Oratory. 1789. 8. (6 fh.)

BAYLEY, [C.....]
Entrance into the facred language containing the neceffary rules of hebrew grammar. 1782. 8. (5 fh.) Sermon on Galatians IV. 6. Ed. 2. 1786. 8. (1 fh.)
—— [E.....]
Addreff to perfons, afflicted with the gout. 1783. 8. (6 d.)
—— [John] *Student of Gray's Inn.*
On the law of bills of exchange, cafh bills and promiffory notes. 1789. 8. (2 fh.)
—— [Richard] *Surgeon.*
Cafes of the angina trachoalis with the mode of cure —. New-York. 1781. 8.
—— [T... B...] *Esq. of Hope near Manchefter: F. R. S.*
On a cheap and expeditious method of draining land. (*Hunter's* G. E. Vol. 4. p. 143.) On the culture of cabbages. (Ibid. Vol. 5. p. 167.) On fecuring apple trees from cattle. (Ibid. Vol. 5. p. 268.)

BAYLIE, [William] *Königl. Preuffifcher Geheimer Rath und Leibarzt.* born 1718. died at Berlin d. 2 Merz. 1787.

BAYLY, [William] *Affiftant at the Royal obfervatory at Greenwich.*
born.....died 17..

BEARDSLEY, [Ebenezer] *Surgeon of the 22d Regiment of the American Army in the campaign of 1776.*
Remarks on the effects of ftagnant air. (Mem. of B. A. Vol. 1. p. 542.)

BEATSON, [Robert] *Esq.*
Political index to the hiftories of great Britain and Ireland, or, a complete regifter of the hereditary honours, public offices and perfons in office from the earlieft periods to the prefent time. 1786. 8. (9 fh) Ed. 2. Vol. 1. 2. 1788. 8. (15 fh.)

BEATTIE, [James] *LL. D: F. R. S. Edin: Profeffor of moral philofophy and Logic in the Univerfity of Aberdeen.*

Origi-

Original poems and translations. 1780. 8. (3 fh.)
The judgment of Paris. 1764. 4. (1 fh. 6 d.) On
the nature and immutability of truth. 1770. 8. (6 fh)
Ed. 2. 1777. 4. (1 L. 1 fh.) überf. von *H. W. Ger-
stenberg.* Kopenh. u. Leipz. 1772. 8. The Min-
strel, or, the procefs of Genius, a poem. Book 1.
2. 1774. 4. (3 fh.) nachgedrukt in *Benzler's* poetical library. Leipzig. Vol. 1. Poems on feveral occafions. 1780. Differtations moral and critical.
1783. 4. überf. von *K. Groffe* Th. 1 - 3. Göttingen 1789. 8. On the evidences of the chriftian
religion. 1787. 8. Vol. 1. 2. The Theory of language. 1788. 8. (5 fh.) Elements of Moral fcience.
Vol. 1. 1790. 8. (6 fh.) überf. von *K. P. Moritz*
Th. 1. Berlin 1790. 8.

BEATY, [M....] *Teacher of the claffics.*
The Monitor, or an addrefs — on the prefent fituation of affairs. 1786. 8. (3 fh.)

BEAUCHAMP, [....] *Lord.*
Account of a fire ball feen in the air and of an
explofion heard Dec. 11. 1741. near London. (Phil.
Transact. 1751. p. 870.) * Letter to the firft bel-
faft company of volunteers by a member of the
britifh parliament. 1782. 8. (1 fh. 6 d.)

BEAUFORD, [William] *A. M.*
Account of antient coins, found at Ballylinam in
the Queen's County, Ireland. (Tr. of J. A. 1787.
p. 139.) Account of an antient fepulchre, difcovered in the county of Kildare at Colverfton, near
Kilcullen. 1788. (Tr. of J. A. 1788.)

BEAUFOY, [Henry] *Member of Parliament, F. R. S.*
Life of Lord *Robert Clive's*. (vid. *Kippis* Biographia
Britannica. Vol. 3. p. 645.) Speech on his motion
for the repeal of the teft and corporation acts —.
1786. 8. (1 fh.) Speech — for extending the fifhe-
ries. 1787. 8. (1 fh. 6 d.)

BECKET, [J... B....] *Bookfeller in Briftol.*
The ufe of the hydroftatic balance made eafy and
applied particularly to the purpofe of detecting
counterfeit gold coin 1775. 8. (1 fh.) On the air
extracted from the water of the hotwell and on the
air of that city and the neighbourhood. (*Prieftley's*
Experiments on Natur. Philof. Vol. 1. p. 466.) On
the fubject of air from feawater. (Ibid. p. 468.)

BECK-

BECKFORD, [Peter] *Esq.*
    Thoughts on hunting. 1782. 4. (7 sh. 6 d.)
—— [W....] *Jun.*
    Remarks upon the situation of Negroes in Jamaica. 1788. 8. (2 sh.) Description of Jamaica. Vol. 1. 2. 1790. 8. (14 sh.)
BECKWITH, [Josiah] *F. A. S.*
    Thom. Blount's fragmenta antiquitatis; or ancient tenures of land and jocular customs of some manors. 1784. 8. (6 sh.)
BEDDOES, [Thomas] *at Edinburgh. M. D.*
    ° The chemical essays of C. *W. Scheele* translated 1785. 8. (6 sh.) Account of some new experiments on the production of artificial cold. (Phil. Transact. 1787. p. 282. überf. Samml. zur P. u. N. G. Th. 4 S. 225.) (*John Mayow's*) chemical experiments and opinions; extracted from a work published in the last century. 1790. 8. (2 sh. 6 d.)
BELCHIER, [William] *Esq. Kent.*
    Essays on various subjects, critical and moral —. 1786. 8. Vol 1. 2. (5 sh.)
BELFOUR, [John]
    New history of Scotland from the earliest accounts to the present time. 1770. 8. (3 sh. 6 d.)
BELKNAP, [Jeremy] *A. M. Member of the American philosophical Society at Philadelphia. F. A. A.*
    History of New-Hampshire. Vol. 1. 1784. 8. (5 sh. 3 d.) Description of the white mountains in New-Hampshire. (Tr. of A. S. Vol. 2. p. 42.) Observations on aurora borealis. (Ibid. Vol. 2. p. 196.) On the preserving of parsnips by drying. (Ibid. Vol. 2. p. 199.) Account of large quantities of a fossil substance containing vitriol and sulphur, found at Lebanon, in the state of New-Hampshire. (Mem. of B. A. Vol. 1. p. 377.)
BELL, [Andrew] *F. A. S.*
    Prospectus of a system of anatomy illustrated with 240 copper plates. 1787. fol.
—— [Archibald]
    The church members directory; or, a gospel church described —. 1776. 8. (2 sh.)
—— [Beaupré] *Esq.*
    On the horologia of the antients. (Arch. Vol. 6. p. 133.)

                                        BELL,

BELL, [Benjamin] *Surgeon at Edinburgh.*
On the theory and management of Ulcers, and Differtation on white fwellings of the joints with an effay on the chirurgical treatment of inflammation and its confequences. 1778. 8. (5 fh.) überf. Leipz. 1779. 8. Syftem of Surgery. Vol. 1-6. 1788. 8. (L. 16 fh.) überf. Leipz. Th. 1-5. 1791. 8. The cafe of a man affected with an obftinate epilepfy confiderably relieved by the ufe of the flowers of zink. (Med. Com. of Ed. Vol. 1. p. 204.) The hiftory of a cafe, in which fome of the vertebrae were found diffolved. (Ibid. Vol. 3. p. 82.)

—— [Benjamin] *Surgeon at Wigton in Cumberland.*
Hiftory of a cafe of obftinate cough, returning at intervals, removed by the vfe of the cuprum ammoniacum. (*Duncan's* M. C. Dec. 2. Vol. 4. p. 307.)

—— [George] *M. D Phyfician at Manchefter.*
born in the county of Dumfries. died d. 2 Febr. 1784.

—— [George] *Surgeon, at Redditch.*
Thoughts on the cancer of the breaft. 1788. 8. (1 fh.)

—— [John] *M. D.* born... died at his country-houfe, at Antermonie d. 28 Aug. 1780.

—— [Robert] *Surgeon in Cork.*
Account of a cafe, in which a very large portion of the lungs was protruded and ftrangulated, occafioned by a wound in the thorax. (*Duncan's* M. C. Dec. 2. Vol. 1. p. 349.)

—— [Thomas] *Sir, Knights. M. D. of the city of Dublin,*
The hiftory of a cafe, in which two faetufes, that had been carried near 21 months, were fuccefffully extracted from the abdomen by incifion. (Med. Com. of Ed. Vol. 1. p. 72.)

—— [Thomas] *Major.*
On military firft principles. 1770. 8. (4 fh.)

—— [William] *D. D. Prebendary of Weftminfter, Treafurer of St. Paul's and Chaplain to the Princefs Amelia.*
Differtation — what caufes principally contribute to render a nation populous? and what effect has the populoufnefs of a nation on its trade? 1756. 4. (1 fh.) überf. Wien 1768. 8. Enquiry into the divine

divine miſſions of John the Baptiſt and Jeſus Chriſt —.
1761. 8. (5 ſh.) überſ. von *H. P. C. Henke*. Braun-
ſchw. 1779. 8.   Attempt to illuſtrate the nature
and effects of the Lord's ſupper. 1780. 8. Supplem.
1790. 8. (4 ſh.)   *P. F. le Courayer* ſentiments on
the different doctrines of religion — with his life.
1787. 8. (2 ſh. 6 d.)
(ſeveral ſingle ſermons.)

BELL, [William] *A. B. private Teacher of the latin and greek languages*
Grammar of the latin tongue. 1772. 8. (1 ſh. 6 d.)
1775. 8. (1 ſh. 6 d.) Grammar of the greek tongue.
1775. 8. (1 ſh. 6 d.)

BELLAMY, [Daniel] *Vicar at Kew and Petersham,*
born.... died d. 15 Febr. 1788.

—— [George Anne] *Actreſſ.*
died d. 16 Febr. 1788.

—— [Thomas]
The benevolent planter; a dramatic piece. 1789. 8.
(1 ſh.)

BELOE, [William] *of Norwich.*
Ode to Miſſ Boscawen. 1783. 4. (1 ſh.) *The rape
of Helen, from the greek of Coluthus, with notes.
1786. 4. (2 ſh. 6 d.) Poems and translations. 1788.
8. (5 ſh.)

BENNET, [....] *Mrs.*
The welch heireſſ and juvenile indiſcretions. 17..
Agnes de Courci, a domeſtic tale. Vol. 1-4. 1789.
8. (12 ſh.)

—— [Abraham] *M. A.*
Deſcription of a new electrometer. (Phil. Transact.
1787. p. 26. überſ. Samml. zur P. u. N. G. Th. 4.
S. 419.) Account of a doubler of electricity, or a
machine by which the leaſt conceivable quantity of
poſitive or negative electricity may be continually
doubled, till it becomes perceptible by common
electrometers, or viſible in ſparks. (Phil. Transact.
1787. p. 288.)

—— [H....] *M. A.*
The treaſury of wit. Vol. 1. 2. 1786. 8. (5 ſh.)

—— [James] *M. D. Phyſician in Cork.*
Hiſtory of a ſingular affection of the action of the
heart, terminating favourably. (*Duncan's* M. C.
Dec. 2. Vol. 2. p. 316.)

BENNET,

BENNET, [John] *Curate of St. Mary's, Manchester.*
 Divine revelation, impartial and univerſal, or, an attempt to defend Chriſtianity —. 1783. 8. (3 ſh.)
 Letters to a young lady. Vol. 1. 2. 1789. 8. (5 ſh. 6 d.)
 (ſeveral ſingle ſermons.)
—— [John] *a journeyman Shoemaker.*
 Poems on ſeveral occaſions. 1774. 8. (2 ſh. 6 d.)
—— [Thomas] *M. A.*
 Lectures on — the Apoſtle's creed. 1776. 8. (5 ſh.)
—— [William] *Surgeon.*
 On the teeth and gums and the ſeveral diſorders to which they are liable. 1779. 8. (1 ſh.)
BENSON, [....] of Steinley.
 A new and profitable method of raiſing a crop of turnips in Drill. (*Hunter's* G. E. Vol. 5. p. 210.)
BENT, [James] *Surgeon at Newcaſtle under Line, Staffordſhire.*
 Account of a woman enjoying the uſe of her right arm after the head of the os humeri was cut away. (Phil. Transact. 1774. p. 553.)
—— [William]
 A meteorological journal of the Year 1787. kept in Paternoſter-Row, London. 17.. 4.
BENTHAM, [Edward] *D.D. Prof. of Divinity at Oxford.* born at Ely d. 23 Jul. 1707. died d. 1 Aug. 1776.
—— [James] *M. A: F. A. S. Rector of Feltwell St. Nicholas, Norfolk.*
 Hiſtory and antiquities of the conventual and cathedral church of Ely from the foundation of the monaſtery A. D. 673. to the Y. 1771. 1771. 4. (1 L. 11 ſh. 6 d.) Account of certain diſcoveries in Ely Minſter. (Arch. Vol. 2. p. 364.)
—— [Jeremy] of Lincoln's-Inn: at preſent at *Cherſon* in the *Crimea.*
 View of the hard labour bill —. 1778. 8. (2 ſh 6 d.) Defence of uſury, ſhewing the impolicy of the preſent legal reſtraints on the term, of pecuniary bargains; with a letter on the diſcouragement oppoſed — to the progreſs of inventive induſtry. 1787. 8. (3 ſh. 6 d.) Introduction to the principles of morals and legiſlation. 1789. 8. (19 ſh)
BENTLEY, [....] *Surgeon at Paterington near Hull.*
 Caſe of ſuppreſſion of urine, ſucceſsfully treated,
 in

in which the bladder was punctured through the rectum. (M. C. Vol. I. p. 256.)

BENTLEY, [Richard] Sohn des Philologen *Rich. Bentley*. born.... died d. 23 Oct. 1782.

―― [Samuel]
The river dove; a lyric pastoral. 1768. 4. (1 sh.) Poems on various occasions. 1776. 8. (6 sh.)

―― [Thomas] *LL. D. Rector at Narlston, Leicestershire.* born 1704. died d. 4 March. 1786.

BERDMORE, [Thomas] *Surgeon - Dentist to the King.* On the disorders and deformities of the teeth and gums. 1770. 8. (3 sh.)

BERDOE, [Marmaduke] *M. D.* Enquiry into the influence of the electric fluid in the structure and formation of animal beings. 1771. 8. (4 sh.) On the pudendagra. 1771. 8. (1 sh.) On the gout. 1772. 8. (1 sh. 6 d.) Doubts concerning the inversion of objects on the retina. 1772. 8. (1 sh. 6 d.) On the nature and circulation of the blood. P. 1. 2. 1772. 8. (1 sh. 6 d.) Theory of the human sensations. 1773. 8. (1 sh.)

BERENGER, [Richard] *Gentleman of the horse to his Majesty.*
Translation of *Bourgelas's* new system of Horsemanship. 1754. 4. (10 sh. 6 d.) The history of the art of Horsemanship. Vol. 1. 2. 1771. 4. (2 L. 2 sh.)

BERINGTON, [Joseph] *a Roman Catholic Clergyman.*
a Letter on materialism and *Hartley's* Theory of the human mind. 1776. 8. (3 Sh.) Immaterialism delineated; or, a view of the first principles of things. 1779. 8. (5 Sh.) Address to the protestant dissenters who have lately petitioned for a repeal of the corporation and test acts. 1786. 8. (1 Sh.) Reflexions — with an exposition of roman catholic principles in reference to god and the country —. 1787. (1 Sh. 6 d.) History of the lives of Abeillard and Heloisa —. 1784. Ed. 2. 1787. 4. (1 L. 1 Sh.) Account of the present state of the Roman Catholics in Great - Britain. 1787. On the depravity of the nation, with a view to the promotion of Sunday schools —. 1788. 8. (1 Sh.) The rights of dissenters from the established church, in relation, principally, to english catholics. 1789. 8. (1 Sh.)

(1 Sh.) The hiftory of the reign of Henry II.
and of Richard and John, his fons —. 1790. 4.
(1 L. 1 fh.)

BERKELEY; [George-Monck] *Esq.* LL. B: *F. A. S.*
and of the Inner temple London.
Literary relics: containing original letters from
King Charles II. King James II. the Queen of Bo-
hemia, Swift —. with an inquiry into the life of
Swift. 1789. 8. (6 fh.)

BERKENHOUT, [John] *M. D.*
Account of the laft attempt on the coaft of france.
17..8. (1 fh.) *Count *Teffin's* letters from an
old man to a young prince with the anfwers, tranf-
lat: from the Swedifh. Vol. 1 - 3. 1759. 8. (9 fh.)
*Clavis Anglica linguae botanicae; or a botanical
lexicon. 1763. 8. (3 fh. 6 d.) Pharmacopoea medica. 1766. 8. (2 fh. 6 d.) Outlines of the natural hiftory of great Britain and Ireland. Vol. 1 - 3.
1771. 8. (11 fh. 6 d.) *Ed.* 2. 1789. 8. Vol. 1. 2.
(10 fh.) Dr. *Cadogan's* differtation on the gout
and all other difeafes examined and refuted. 1772.
8. (1 fh.) *Pomme* on hyfterical and hypochon-
driacal difeafes, translated. 1777. 8. (5 fh.) Bio;
graphia litteraria. Vol. 1. 1777. 4. (18 fh.) Lucu-
brations on ways and means. 1780. 8. (2 fh.) On
the bite of a mad-dog. 1783. 8. (1 fh. 6 d.) Sym-
ptomatology. 1784. 8. (3 fh.) Firft lines of the
theory and practice of philofophical chemiftry. 1788.
8. (6 fh. 6 d.)

BERKLEY, [....]
*Maria, or the generous ruftic. 1784. 8. (2 fh.
6 d.) *Heloife; or, the fiege of Rhodes, a legendary tale. Vol. 1. 2. 1788. 8. (3 fh. 6 d.)

BERNARD, [Francis] *Sir. Baronet.*
born.... died d. 16 June 1779.
—— [....] *Governor at Bofton.*
Letters on the trade and government of America
and the principles of law and polity applied to the
american colonies. 1774. 8. (2 fh.)
—— [Giffard]
Translation of *Bemetzrieder's* mufic made eafy to
every capacity —. 1778. 4. (3 fh. 6 d.)
—— [William] *Ship-Builder, Grove-ftreet, Deptford.*
Account of an explofion of air in a coal-pit at
C Middle-

Middleton, near Leeds in Yorkſhire. (Phil. Transact. 1773. p. 217.) Method for the removal of ſhips that have been driven on ſhore and damaged in their bottoms. (Ibid. 1780. p. 100.)

BERROW, [Capel] *A. M.* Rector of Finningley, Nottinghamſhire.
A pre-exiſtent lapſe of human ſouls demonſtrated from reaſon —. 1762. 8. (2 ſh. 6 d.) A lapſe of human ſouls in a ſtate of pre-exiſtence —. 1766. 8. (3 ſh.) Deiſm not confiſtent with the religion of reaſon and nature. 1780. 4. (4 ſh.)

BERTEZEN, [S. ...]
Thoughts on the different kinds of food given to young ſilk worms and the poſſibility of their being brought to perfection in the climate of England —. 1789. 8. (1 ſh.)

BERTIE, [Willoughby] *Earl of Abingdon.*
Thoughts on the letter of — Edm. Burke — on the affairs of America. 1777. 8. (1 ſh.) Dedication to the collective body of the people of England on the preſent political diſtractions. 1780. 8. (1 ſh. 6 d.)

BEST, [....]
Matilda an original poem. 1789. 4. (2 ſh. 6 d.)
— [Thomas] *Gentl. late of his Majeſty's Drawing room in the tower.*
On the art of angling — with the complete flyfiſher. 1787. 12. (2 ſh.)

BETTESWORTH, [John] *Maſter of the naval Academy at Chelſea.*
The univerſal reckoner; or, every trader's infallible guide —. 1778. 8. (1 ſh.) Arithmetic in the firſt four fundamental rules. 1779. 8. (3 d.) Syſtem of naval mathematics; or, practical rules of the art of navigation. 1787. 12. (5 ſh.)

BEVER, [Thomas] *LL. D.*
On the ſtudy of Jurisprudence and the civil law —. 1766. 8. (1 ſh. 6 d.) Hiſtory of the legal polity of the roman ſtates and of the riſe, progreſſ and extent of the roman laws. 1781. 4. (18 ſh.) überſ. von *C. Völkel.* Leipz. 1787. 8.

BEVERLEY, [John] *M. A.*
The poll for the election of two repreſentations in
parlia-

parliament for the univerſity of Cambridge. 3 Apr. 1784 —. 1784. 8.

BEVIS, [John] *M. D: F. R. S.*
born.... died d. 6 Nov. 1771.

BEW, [George] *M. D. Phyſician at Mancheſter.*
Obſervations on blindneſſ and on the employment and of the other ſenſes to ſupply the loſſ of ſight. (Mem. of M. Vol. I. p. 159.) Of the epidemic catarrh of the Year 1788. (Lond. M. J. Vol. IX. Part. 10.) Caſe of a ſtudent who ſwallowed a golden breaſtpin four inches in length, and voided it by ſtool, without any ill conſequence. (Ibid. Vol. 4. p. 77.)

BEWLEY, [William] *Surgeon and Apothecary at Great-Maſſingham in Norfolk.*
born 1725. died d. 5 Sept. 1783.

BICKERSTAFF, [Iſaac] *Marine - Officer.* born in Ireland.
Leucothoe. 1756. 8. Thomas and Saily; or the ſailor's return. 1760. 8. Judith. 1761. 4. Love in avillage 1762. 8. (1 ſh. 6 d.) The maid of the mill. 1765. 8. (1 ſh. 6 d.) Daphne and Amintor. 1765. 8. (1 ſh.) The plain dealer. 1766. 8. Love in the city. 1767. 8. (1 ſh. 6 d.) The Royal Garland. 1768. 8. Lionel and Clariſſa. 1768. 8. Ed. 2. 1770. 8. The abſent man. 1768. 8. The Padlock. 1768. 8. The Hypocrite. 1768. 8. The epheſian matron. 1769. 8. Dr. *Laſt* in his chariot. 1769. 8. The captive. 1769. 8. 'Tis well it's no worſe. 1770. 8. The recruiting ſerjeant. 1770. 8. He would if he could; or, an old fool worſe than any. 1771. 8. The ſultan; a farce. 1787. 8. (6 d.)

BICKNELL, [Alexander] *Esq.*
Hiſtory of Lady Anne Neville; 17.. Hiſtory of Iſabelle, or the reward of good nature. 17.. *Philoſophical disquiſitions on the chriſtian religion —. 1777. 12. (2 ſh. 6 d.) °The hiſtory of Edward Prince of Wales commonly termed the black prince —. 1777. 8. (5 ſh.) The life of Alfred the great King of the Angloſaxons. 1777. 8. (6 ſh.) The putrid Soul: a poetical epiſtle —. 1780. 4. (1 ſh. 6 d.) The patriot king; or, Alfred and Elvida, a Tragedy. 1788. 8. (2 ſh. 6 d.) Doncaſter races; or the hiſtory of Miſſ Maitland, a tale

tale of truth: — Vol. I. 2. 1789. 8. (5 fh.) Painting perfonified, or, the caricature and fentimental pictures of the principal artifts of the prefent times fancifully explained. Vol. I. 2. 1790. 8. (6 fh.) The grammatical wreath; or, a complete fyftem of englifh grammar —. 1790. 8. (3 fh.)

BIDDLE, [Owen]
Obfervations on the tranfit of venus, June 3. 1769 made at Leweftown in Penfylvania. (Phil. Transact. 1769. p. 414.) Account of the tranfit of venus over the fun's difc, as obferved near Cape-Henlopen on Delaware-Bay June 3. 1769. (Tr. of A. S. Vol. I. p. 89.)

BINGHAM, [George] *B. D. Rector of Pimperne and of Moo-Critchell in the county of Dorfet and Diocefe of Briftol.*
Vindication of the doctrine and liturgy of the church of England —. 1774. 8. (1 fh. 6 d.)

BINGLEY, [W....]
* The riddle by the late unhappy *George Rob. Fitzgerald* with notes. 1787. 4. (1 fh.)

BINNEY, [Barnabas] *Hofpital-Phyfician and Surgeon in the American Army* 1782.
A remarkable cafe of gunfhot wound. (Mem. of B. A. Vol. I. p. 544. London M. J. Vol. VII. P. 3.)

BIRCH, [John] *Army-Surgeon.*
On the efficacy of electricity in removing female obftructions. 1779. 8. (1 fh. 6 d.) Ed. 2. 1780. 8. (1 fh. 6 d.) überf. Samml. f. A. Th. 5. S. 575.

—— [Samuel] *Paftry-Cook.*
Confilia, or thoughts on feveral fubjects. 1785. 8. (2 fh. 6 d.) Ed. 2. (with the author's name) 1786. 8. (2 fh. 6 d.) The Abbey of Ambresbury, a poem. P. I. 2. 1789. 4. (4 fh.)

BIRD, [John] *Mathematical Inftrumentmaker at London.*
born 1709. died d. 31 March. 1776.

—— [Robert] *Efq.*
Propofals for paying great part of the national debt and reducing taxes —. 1780. 8. (1 fh.)

—— [William] *Surgeon and Man-midwife at Chelmsford, Effex.*
Account of a retroverfio uteri. (Med. Obf. Vol. 5. p. 110.)

BISSET

BISSET, [....]
Three difcourfes — on the character and office of a clergyman of the excellency of the britifh conftitution, — of liberty, public fpirit and the power of the britifh legislature. 1775. 8. (1 fh.)
—— [Charles] *M. D. Phyfician at Knayton Yorkfhire.*
On the fcuruy, defigned chiefly for the ufe of the Britifh nauy. 1756. 8. (2 fh. 6 d.) *Effay on the medical conftitution of Great-Britain —. 1762. 8. (5 fh.) überf. von *J. W. Müller*. Warfchau 1779. Medical effays and obfervations — 1766. 8. (5 fh.) überf. von *P. W. Möller*. Breslau 1781. 8. Obfervations on lymphatic encyfted tumours. (*Duncan's* M. C. Vol. 8. p. 244.)
—— [Thomas] *D. D. Minifter of Logierait.*
Sermons. 1789. 8. (6 fh.)

BLACK, [J....]
The vale of innocence; a vifion; verfes and fonnets. 1785. 4. (1 fh.)
—— [James] *of Morden in Surry.*
Obfervation on the tillage of the earth and on the theory of inftruments adapted to his end. 1778. 4. (5 fh.)
—— [Jofeph] *M. D. Profeffor of Medicine and Chemiftry in the Univerfity of Edinburgh.*
Diff. De humore acido a cibis orto et magnefia alba. Edinb. 1754. Experiments upon Magnefia alba, Quic-lime and fome other alkaline fubftances. (Eff. and Obferv. Edinb. Vol. 2. p. 157.) The fuppofed effect of boiling upon water, in difpofing it to freeze more readily, afcertained by experiments. (Phil. Transact. 1775. p. 124.)
—— [William] *M. D. Of the Royal college of Phyficians.*
Obfervations on the fmall-pox and inoculation. 1781. 8. (2 fh. 6 d.) Hiftorical fketch of Medicine and furgery from their origine to the prefent time. 1782. 8. (5 fh.) überf. von *J. C. F. Scherf.* 1789. 8. Comparative view of the mortality of the human fpecies at all ages and of the difeafes and cafualities by which they are deftroyed or annoyed. 1788. 8. (6 fh.) überf. Leipz. 1789. 8.

BLACKBURNE, [Francis] *M. A. Archdeacon of Cleveland.*

Enqui-

Enquiry into the use and importance of external religion. 1752. (and in the Pillars of Priester Vol. 4.) *The confessional; or, enquiry into the right, utility, edification and success of establishing systematical confessions of faith and doctrine in protestant churches. 1766. 8. (5 sh.) Ed. 2. 17.. Ed. 3. 1770. 8. (7 sh.) Considerations on the present state of the controversy between the protestant and papists of Great-Britain and Ireland. 1768. 8. (5 sh.) Four discourses. 1775. 8. (3 sh.) (several single sermons.)

BLACKBURNE, [Thomas] *M. D: Physician at Durham: F. R. S.*
born 1749. died d. 23 June 1782.

—— [William] *M. D: F. R. S.*
Differt. De sale communi. Edinb. 1781. Case in which the substance of the uterus was in a great measure destroyed during pregnancy. (London M. - J. Vol. VIII. P. 1.) On the effects of a large dose of emetic tartar. (Ibid. Vol. IX. p. 61. überf. Samml. f. A. Th. 12. S. 737.)

BLACKETT, [Mary Dawes]
Suicide, a poem. 1789. 4. (1 sh. 6 d.)

BLACKLOCK, [Thomas] *LL. D. at Edinburgh.*
born at Anan in Scotland 1721. (deprived of his eye-sight by the small-pox in the sixth month of his life.)
Joseph *Spence's* account of the life, characters and poems of Mr. *Blacklock.* 1754. 8. (1 sh.) Collection of originals poem. 1761. 8. (2 sh. 6 d.) Paraclaesis; or, consolations deduced from natural and revealed religion: in two dissertations. 1767. (5 sh.) Translation of *Armand's* two discourses on the spirit and evidences of christianity. 1768. 8. (2 sh.) The Graham, an heroic ballad. 1774. 4. (2 sh. 6 d.)

BLACKRIE, [Alexander] *Apothecary at Bromfield.*
born.... died d. 29 May 1772.

BLACKSTONE, [Henry] *Esq. of the Middle-Temple.*
Reports of cases argued and determined in the court of common pleas — in the 28 Year of Georg III. Part. 1-3. fol. 1789. (15 sh.)

—— [William] *Professor of law at Oxford.*

born

born at Cheapfide d. 10 July 1723. died d. 14 Febr. 1780.

BLAGDEN, [Charles] *M. D: F. R. S: F. A. S: Phyfician to the army.*
Diff. De caufa apoplexiae. Edinb. 1768. 8. Experiments and obfervations in an heated room. (Phil. Transact. 1775. p. 111. and p. 484.) On the heat of the water in the gulf-ftream. (Ibid. 1781. p. 334.) Account of fome late fiery meteors; with obfervations. (Ibid. 1784. p. 201.) Obfervations on ancient inks, with the propofal of a new method of recovering the legibility of decayed writings. (Ibid. 1787. p. 451.) Experiments on the cooling of water below its freezing point. (Ibid. 1788. p. 125. überf. *Gren* J. d. P. Th. 1. S, 87.) Experiments on the effect of various fubftances in lowering the point of congelation in water. (Ibid. 1788. p. 277. überf. *Gren* J. d. P. Th. 1. S. 389.) Hiftory of the congelation of Quickfilver. (Ibid. 1783. p. 329. überf. Samml. zur P. u. N. G. Th. 3. S. 347. u. S. 515.)

BLAGRAVE, [J....] *Notary public.*
Laws for regulating bills of Exchange, inland and foreign —. 1783. 12. (1 fh.) *Ed.* 2. 1788. 12. (1 fh.)

BLAIR, [Hugh] *D. D. Emeritus Profeffor of Rhetorik in the Univerfity of Edinburgh.*
*Critical Differtation on the poems of Offian, the Son of Fingal. 1762. 4. (2 fh. 6 d.) überf. von *O. A. H. Oelrichs.* Hannover 1785. 8. Sermons. Vol. 1-3. 1777-1790. 8. (18 fh.) überf. (von *F. S. G. Sack*) Th. 1. 2. Leipz. 1781. 8. Lectures on Rhetoric and belles lettres. Vol. 1. 2. 1783. 4. (1 L. 16 fh.) nachgedr. Bafil. T. 1. 2. 3. 1788. 8. überf. von *K. G. Schreiter.* Th. 1-3. Liegniz. 1788. 8.

BLAIR, [John] *D. D. Rector of St. John, Weftminfter, and Prebendary of Weftminfter-Abbey. F. R. S: F. A. S.*
born .... died d. 24 June 1782.

—— [Robert]
Defcription of an accurate and fimple method of adjufting *Hadley's* Quadrant for the back obfervation. (Nautical Almanac 1788.)

BLAKE,

BLAKE, [Francis] *Sir, Baronet.*
On the beft proportion for fteam engine cylinders of a given content. (Phil. Transact. 1757. p. 379.) Spherical Trigonometry reduced to plain. (Ibid. 1757. p. 441.) On the greateft effects of engines, with uniformley accelerated motions. (Ibid. 1757. p. 1.) The lunar eclipfe Oct. 11. 1772. obferved at Canton. (Ibid. 1774. p. 45.) The efficacy of a finking fund of one million per annum confidered. 1785. 8. (1 fh.) The propriety of an actual payment of the public debt confidered. 1786. 8. (1 fh) The true policy of great Britain confidered. 1787. 8. (1 fh.) Political tracts. 1790. 8, (5 fh.)

—— [John] *Surgeon at Briftol.*
On Inoculation. 1771. 8. (1 fh. 6 d.)

—— [W....]
King Edward the third. Drama. 1783. 8.

BLAND, [Robert] *M. D. Phyfician Man - Midwife to the Weftminfter General difpenfary.*
Some calculations of the number of accidents or deaths which happen in confequence of parturition and of the proportion of male to female children as well as of twins, monftrous productions, and children that are dead — born; taken from the midwifery reports of the Weftminfter General difpenfary —. (Phil. Transact. 1781. p. 355. überf. Journal für Geburtshelfer. St. 1.) On the treatment of convulfions during parturition. (London M. J. Vol. 2. p. 328. überf. Samml. f. A. Th. 7. S. 498.) Account of a woman who had the fmall pox during pregnancy and who communicated the fame difeafe to her foetus. (Ibid. Vol. 2. p. 204.) Account of two cafes of haematuria. (Ibid. Vol. 4. p. 282.)

BLAND, [T....] *M. D. of Blandford in Virginia.*
Account of a extra uterine conception. (*Duncan's* M. C. Dec. 2. Vol. 1. p. 334.)

—— [Thomas] *Surgeon at Newark.*
Account of the effects of the cuprum ammoniacum in the cure of epilepfy. (*Duncan's* M. C. 1780. p. 240. überf. Samml. f. A. Th. XI. S. 176.)

BLANE, [Gilbert] *M. D: F. R. S: Phyfician extraord. to the Prince of Wales, Phyfician to St. Thoma's Hofpital.*

Obfer-

Obfervations on the difeafes incident to feamen. 1785. 8. (6 fh.) überf. Marburg 1788. 8.

BLANE, [William] *Esq.*
Effays on hunting — with an account of the *Vizier's* manner of hunting in the mogul empire. 1788. 8. (4 fh.) Ed. 2. 1788. 8. (6 fh.)
Some particulars relative to the production of borax. (Phil. Transact. 1787. p. 297. überf. Samml. zur P. u. N. G. Th. 4. S. 285.)

BLAYMIRES, [J....]
The chriftian's fpelling-book, for the ufe of fchools and private families. 1790. 8. (1 fh.)

BLAYNEY, [Benjamin] *D. D. Profeffor of Hebrew in the Univerfity of Oxford.*
Differtation on — Daniel's prophecy of 70 weeks — with remarks on J. D. *Michaelis* letters. 1775. 4. (2 fh. 6 d.) überf. (von *J. C. F. Schulz*) Halle 1777. Anhang 1780. 8. Jeremiah and lamentations, a new translation with notes. 1784. 4. (1 L. 1 fh.) (feveral fingle fermons.)

BLICKE, [Charles]
On the bilious or yellow fever of Jamaica. 1772. 8. (1 fh. 6 d.)

BLIGH, [William] *Lieutenant in the navy.*
Narrative of the mutiny on board his Majefty's fhip Bounty and the fubfequent voyage of part of the crew in the fhip's boat from Tofoa, one of the friendly Iflands, to Timor, a dutch fettlement in the eaftindies — with charts. 1790. 4. (7 fh.)

BLIZARD, [William] *F. A. S. Surgeon to the London Hofpital and Lecturer in Anatomy. F. R. S. of Gottingen.*
Experiments and obfervations on the danger of copper and bell-metal in pharmaceutical and chemical preparations. 1786. 8. (1 fh.) Defcription of the fituation of the large blood-veffels of the extremities, the inftrument Tourniquet and the methods of making effectual preffure on the arteries in cafes of dangerous effufions of blood from wounds. 1786. 8. (1 fh. 6 d.) Defultory reflections on police with an effay on the means of preventing crimes and amending criminals. 1786. 8. (2 fh.) A new method of treating the fiftula lachrymalis. (Phil. Transact. 1780. p. 239. London M. J.

M. J. Vol. 1. p. 62.) überf. Leipz. 1784. 8. On the external ufe of emetic tartar. (Ibid. Vol. VIII. P. 1. überf. Samml. f. A. Th. XI. S. 726.) On the ufe of electricity in deafneff. (Ibid. Vol. XI. P. 1.)

BLOWER, [Eliza] *Miſſ.*
*Maria: the genuine memoirs of an admired lady of rank and of fome of her friends. Vol. 1. 2. 1763. 8. (4 Sh.) *George Bateman. Vol. 1-3. 1782. 8. (7 Sh. 6 d.) Features from life; or a fummer vifit. Vol. 1. 2. 1788. 8. (6 Sh.)

BLUNT, [John] *Surgeon at Leominſter, Herefordſhire.*
Practical farriery —. 1773. 8. (3 Sh. 6 d.)

—— [Robert] *Surgeon at Odiham, in Hampſhire.*
Cafe of a painful affection of the face cured by electricity. (London M. J. Vol. VII. P. 2.) überf. Samml. f. A. Th. XII. S. 8.

BODDINGTON, [John] *Esq.*
Account of fome bones found in the rock of Gibraltar with remarks by Dr. *Hunter.* (Phil. Transact. 1770. p. 414.).

BOLTON, [James] *Member of the Natural Hiſt. Society at Edinburgh.*
Hiftory of tunguffes growing about Halifax (Yorkſhire). —. Vol. 1. 2. 1788. 4. (2 L. 2 Sh.) Filices Britannicae; an hiftory of the britifh proper ferns. 1785. 4. (13 Sh.) (coloured 1 L. 1 ſh.)

BOLTS, [William] *Merchant, and Alderman or Judge of the Mayor's Court of Calcutta.*
Confiderations on india affairs; particularly refpecting the prefent ftate of Bengal and its dependencies —. Vol. 1. 2. 1772. 4. (1 L. 10 ſh.) überf. von *J. C. F. Schulz.* Leipz. 1780. 8.

BONHOTE, [Elizabeth] *Mrs.*
The parental monitor. Vol. 1. 2. 1788. 8. (5 Sh.) Darnley vale; or Emilia Fitzroy, a novel. Vol. 1-3. 1789. 8. (9 Sh.) Olivia. 17.. Ellen woodley, a novel. Vol. 1. 2. 1790. 8. (5 Sh.)

BONNYCASTLE, [John] *of the royal military academy, Woolwich.*
The fcholar's guide to arithmetic —. 1780. 12. (2 Sh.) Introduction to menfuration and practical geometry —. 1782. 12. (3 Sh.) Introduction to Algebra. 1782. 12. (3 Sh.) Introduction to aftronomy.

nomy. 1786. 8. (7 Sh.) Ed. 2. 1787. 8.   *Euclid's*
Elements of geometry. 1789. 8. (5 ſh.)

BOOKER, [Luke]
Poems on ſubjects ſacred, moral and entertaining.
Vol. 1. 2. 1785. 8. (5 ſh.)   The Highlanders, a
poem. 1787. 4. (2 ſh. 6 d.)   Miſcellaneous poems.
1790. 8. (6 Sh.)

BOOTE, [Richard] *Attorney at Law, at Abingdon, Berks.*
born.... died d.   Febr. 1782.

BOOTH, [....]   *Mrs.*
The little french lawyer. a Comedy. 1778. 8.
―― [Abraham]   *Methodiſtical Preacher.*
Apology for the baptiſts. 1778. 8. (1 ſh.)   Paedo-
baptiſm examined. 1784. 8. (4 ſh.) Ed. 2. Vol. 1. 2.
1787. 8. (8 ſh.)
(ſeveral ſingle ſermons.)
―― [Joſeph]   *Portrait - Painter.*
Addreſſ to the public on the polygraphic art, or
the copying or multiplying pictures in oil colours,
by a chemical and mechanical proceſſ―. 1786. 8.
(1 ſh.)

BORLASE, [William]   *D. D: F. R. S.*
born at Pendeen. Cornwallis 1695. died d. 24
Aug. 1772.

BORTHWICK, [George]   *Surgeon of the XIV. Regiment of Dragoons.*
A Cataract in the eye, with a preternatural mem-
brance attacted to the iris, extracted. (Med. Com.
of Ed. Vol. 2. p. 84.)   Treatiſe upon the extraction
of the chryſtalline lens. 1775. 8. (1 ſh.)   The hiſtory of a fractured ſternum. (Med. Com. of Ed.
Vol. 5. p. 185.)   The hiſtory of a ſingular caſe of
delirium from a wound of the head. (*Duncan's*
M. C. 1780. p. 439.)   Account of the ſucceſſfull
operation of the trepan on the left temple, with
the extraction of a ſplinter of ſtone, penetrating
the dura mater. (*Duncan's* M. C. Vol. 8. p. 322.)
―― [William]   *Esq.*
Inquiry into the origin and limitations of the feudal
dignities of Scotland. 1775. 8. (1 ſh. 6 d.)   Remarks on britiſh antiquities ―. 1776. 8. (2 ſh. 6 d.)

BOSWELL, [....]
*Treatiſe on watering meadows. 1780. 8. (2 ſh.
6 d.)

BOSWELL,

BOSWELL, [James] *Esq.* (Son to Lord *Auchinleck.*)
"Account of Corfica, the journal of a tour to that island and memoirs of *Pafcal Paoli.* 1768. 8. (6 fh.) überf. von *A. E. K.* (Klaufing) Leipz. 1768. 8. Ausg. 2. Leipz. 1769. 8. überf. im Auszug (von *H. A. Mertens*) Augsb. 1769. 8. Britifh effays in favour of the brave Corficans by feveral hands. 1769. 8. (2 fh.) Letter to the people of Scotland, on the prefent ftate of the nation. 1784. 8. (1 fh.) Letter to the people of Scotland on the alarming attempt to infringe the articles of the union. 1785. 8. (2 fh. 6 d.) Journal of a tour to the hebrides with *Sam Johnfon* —. 1774. Ed. 2. 1785. überf. 1775. überf. (von *A. Wittenberg*) Lübek 1787.

BOTT, [Edmund] *Esq. Barrifter: F. A. S.*
Collection of decifions of the court of King's bench upon the poor's laws, down to the prefent time. 1773. 8. (7 fh.)

BOURN, [Daniel]
On Wheel-Carriages —. P. 1-3. 1769. 8. (3 fh.) Remarks on Mr. *Jacob's* treatife on wheel-carriages. 1773. 8. (1 fh.)

BOURNE, [Vincent] *M. A: Ufher of Weftminfter fchool.*
Mifcellaneous poems. 1772. 4. (11 fh.)

BOUTCHER, [William] *Nurferyman, at Comely Garden.*
On foreft trees —. 1775. 4. (15 fh.)

BOWDLER, [....] *Miff. of Bath.*
born.... died 17..

—— [Thomas] *F. R. S: F. A. S.*
Letters written in Holland in the months of Sept. and Oct. 1787. 1788. 8. (5 fh.)

BOWDOIN, [James] *Esq. L. L. D. Governour of the Commonwealth: Prefident of the American Academy at Bofton.*
Philofophical difcourfe - when he was inducted into office as prefident. (Mem. of B. A. Vol. 1. p. 1.) Obfervations upon an hypothefis for folving the phenomena of light —. (Ibid. Vol. 1. p. 187.) Obfervations on light and the wafte of matter in the fun and fixt ftars, occafioned by the conftant efflux of light from them —. (Ibid. Vol. 1. p. 195.) Obfervations tending to prove — the exiftence of an orb which furrounds the whole vifible material fyftem —. (Ibid. Vol. 1. p. 208.)

BOWEN,

BOWEN, [James] *Surgeon to the 30th Regiment.*
    Account of a fingular tumour in the groin, removed by extirpation. (*Duncan's* M. C. Vol. 9. p. 233.)
—— [....]
    Hiftorical account of the origin progreff and prefent ftate of Bethlehem hofpital —. 1783. 4. (—)
BOWLE, [John] *M. A*: *F. A. S. Vicar of Idmifton, near Salisbury.*
    born.... died d. 26 Oct. 1788.
BOWLES, [W.... Lisle] *A. B. of Trinity College.*
    *Fourteen Sonnets: 1789. 4. (1 fh.) Ed. 2. (with the author's name) 1789. 4. (2 fh.) Verfes on the benevolent inftitution of the philantropic fociety. 1789. 4. (2 fh.) Verfes to *John Howard* on his ftate of prifons and lazarettos. 1789. 4. (1 fh. 6 d.) The grave of *Howard*, a poem. 1790. 4. (2 fh.)
BOWYER, [William] *F. A. S: Printer.*
    born at London d. 17 Dec. 1699. died d. 18 Nov. 1777.
BOX, [George] *of Abingdon ftreet, Weftminfter.*
    Plans for reducing the extraordinary expences of the nation, and gradually paying of the national debt —. 1784. 8. (1 fh.)
BOYCE, [....] *A. M. Rector of Worlingham in Suffolk and Chaplain to the Earl of Suffolk.*
    Harold; a Tragedy. 1786. 4. (3 fh.)
—— [Gilbert]
    Reply to *Dan. Taylor's* differtation on finging. in the Worfhip of God. 1787. 8. (1 fh.)
—— [Samuel]
    born.... died d. 16 March. 1775.
—— [Thomas]
    *Specimen of elegiac poetry. 1773. 4. (1 fh.)
BOYD, [Henry] *A. M.*
    Translation of the inferno of *Dante Alighieri*, in englifh verfe — with a fpecimen of a tranflation of the Orlando furiofo of *Ariofto*. Vol. 1. 2. 1785. 8. (10 fh. 6 d.)
—— [Robert] *LL. D.*
    Office, powers and jurisdiction of his Majefty's juftices of the peace and commiffioners of fupply. Vol. 1. 2. 1787. 4. (1 L. 11 fh. 6 d.)
BOYDELL, [James] *Wine Merchant.*
    The Ullage cafk gauger —. 1784. 8. (12 fh. 6 d.)
                                           BOYDELL,

BOYDELL, [John]
Collection of prints, engraved after the moſt capital paintings in England. Vol. 1. 2. 1772. fol. (12 Guin.)
BOYER, [Iſaac]
Propoſal for determining the longitude at ſea by obſervation, independent of any time-keeper or of the truth of the magnetic compaſſ —. 1774. 8. (6 d.)
BOYS, [....] *Mrs.*
The coalition: or family anecdotes. Vol. 1. 2. 1785. (6 ſh.)
—— [....]
Collection for a hiſtory of Sandwich. P. I. 1788. 4.
—— [William] *F. A. S. Surgeon at Sandwich, Kent.*
Caſe of a child who ſwallowed a pin. (London M. J. Vol. 6. p. 401.)
BRADBERRY, [David]
Letter to *Edw. Jefferies* — for applying to Parliament for a repeal of the corporation and teſt acts, ſo far as they concern proteſtant diſſenters. 1789. 4. (1 ſh.)
BRADLEY, [John]
born.... died 17..
BRAND, [....] *Secretary.*
Explanation of the inſcriptions on a roman Altar and tablet found at Tinmouth Caſtle in Northumberland. 1783. (Arch. Vol. 8. p. 326.)
—— [....] *M. A.*
Obſervations on Mr. *Gilbert's* bill. 1776. 8. (2 ſh.)
—— [Charles]
On aſſurances and annuities on lives —. 1775. 8. (3 ſh. 6 d.) Letter in defence of his treatiſe on aſſurances — with notes. (Critical Review Vol. XLI. p. 160.)
—— [F.... J....] *M. A.*
Select diſſertations from the amoenitates academitae, a ſupplement to *Stillingfleet's* tracts relating to natural hiſtory — translated. Vol. I. 2. 1781. 8. (5 ſh. 3 d.)
—— [John] *M. A: Fellow and Secretary of the Society of Antiquaries at London.*
Conſcience, an ethical eſſay. 1772. 4. (2 ſh.) On illicit love, a poem. 1776. 4. (1 ſh. 6 d.) Obſervations

vations on popular antiquities, including the whole of Mr. *Bourne's* Antiquitates vulgares —. 1777. 8. (5 fh.) Hiftory and Antiquities of Newcaftle upon Tyne. Vol. 1. 2. 1789. 4. (3 L. 3 fh.)

BRAND, [Robert]
The true method of reducing ruptures and retaining them in the abdomen and in the navel. 1771. 8. (1 fh.)

—— [Thomas] *Surgeon.*
Translation of M. *Sage's* treatife on the fluor alcali. 1778. 8. (1 fh.) Chirurgical effays on the caufes and fymptoms of ruptures. 1783. 8. (2 fh.) Strictures in vindication of fome of the doctrines mifreprefented by Mr. *Foot* in his obfervations upon the new opinions of *John Hunter*, in his late treatife —. 1787. 4. (2 fh. 6 d.) The cafe of a boy who had been miftaken for a girl —. 1787. 4. (2 fh.)

BRANDER, [Guftavus] *Esq. F. R. S: F. A. S: Curator of the Britifh Mufeum.*
born 1717. died d. 21 Jan. 1787.

BRANDISH, [Jofeph] *Surgeon at Alcefter in Warwickfhire.*
Account of a cafe in which the head of the os femoris, fhattered by a gun fhot, is fuppofed to have been regenerated. (London M. J. Vol. VII. P. 2) Cafe of mortification of the leg. (Ibid. Vol. VIII. P. 2.) Account of a cafe; in which a confiderable portion of the lower jaw bone was removed —. (Ibid. Vol. VIII. P. 3.)

BRAY, [William] *F. A. S.*
* Sketch of a tour into Derbyfhire and Yorkfhire —. 1778. 8. (2 fh. 6 d.) Ed. II. (with the author's name) 1783. 8. (6 fh.) Obfervations on the indian method of picture-writing. (Arch. Vol. 6. p. 159.) On the Leicefter roman miliary ftone. (Ibid. Vol. 7. p. 84.) Remark on *Mooke's* account of fome druidical remains in Derbyfhire. (Ibid. Vol. 7. p. 178.) Account of the obfolete office of purveyor to the King's houfehold. (Ibid. Vol 8. p. 329.) Account of a roman road leading from Southampton by Chicefter and Arundell through Suffex and Surrey to London —. (Ibid. Vol. 9. p. 96.)

BREAKS,

BREAKS, [Thomas]
Complete fyftem of Land - Surveying, both' in theory and practice. 1771. 8. (7 fh. 6 d.)
BRERETON, (Owen Salisbury) *Esq. F. R. S; F. A. S.*
Obfervations on *Pet. Collinfon's* paper on the round towers in Ireland. (Arch. Vol. 2. p. 80.) Obfervations in a tour through South - Wales Shropfhire. (Ibid. Vol. 3. p. 111.) Extracts from a Mf. dated apud Eltham Jan. 22. Hen. VIII. (Ibid. Vol. 3. p. 154.) Defcription of a third unpublifhed royal feal. (Ibid. Vol. 5. p. 280.) Account of the violent fturm of lightning at Eaftbourn in Suffex. Sept. 17. 1780. (Phil. Transact. 1781. p. 42.)
BRETT, [John] *Captain:*
born.... died 1785.
BREWSTER, [John] *M. A.*
Sermons for prifons with prayers for the ufe of prifoners in folitary confinement. 1790. 8. (2 fh. 6 d.)
BRICE, [Andrew] *Printer.*
born at Exeter. 1690. died d. 14 Nov. 1773.
—— [Thomas] *Printer.*
The ftate coach in the mire, a tale. 1783. 4 (1 fh.)
BRICKNELL, [A.....]
The life of Alfred the great king of the Anglofaxons. 1777. (6 fh.)
BRIDGES, [George] *Sir.* fee Lord *Rodney.*
—— [Thomas] *Wine Merchant at Hull.*
born at Yorkfhire.
·Under the fuppofed name *Cauftic Barebones* he publifhed: New translation of *Homer's* Iliad adapted to the capacity of honeft englifh roaft beef and pudding eaters. Vol. 1. 2. 1764. 12. (5 fh. 6 d.) Dido. a comic opera. 1771. 8. The dutchman; a mufical entertainment. 1775. 8. (1 fh.)
BRIGGS, [Richard] *Cook at the Temple Coffeehoufe.*
The englifh art of cookery —. 1788. 8. (7 fh.)
BRIGHT, [Henry] *M. A. Mafter of New College fchool, Oxford.*
The praxis; or a courfe of englifh and latin exercifes —. 1784. 8. (5 fh.)
BRISBAINE, [John] *M. D. Phyfician to the Middlefex hofpital at London.*

The

The anatomy of painting —. 1769. fol. (1 L. 8 ſh.)
Select caſes in the practice of medicine. 1772. 8.
(1 ſh. 6 d.)

BRISTOW, [W.....] *Esq.*
On the policy, juſtice and expediency of repealing the teſt and corporation acts. 1789. 8. (1 ſh. 6 d.)

BROCKLESBY, [Richard] *M. D: F. R. S: Phyſician to the Army.*
Diſſert. De ſaliva ſana et morboſa. Lugd. Bat. 1745. 4. Eſſay concerning the mortality of horned cattle. 1746. 8. On the Indian poiſon. (Phil. Transact. 1754. p. 408.) On the ſounds and hearing of fiſh. (Ibid. 1755. p. 233.) On a poiſonous root lately found among gentian. (Ibid. 1755. p. 240.) Experiments on the ſenſibility and irritability of the ſeveral parts of animals. (Ibid. 1759. p. 240.) Eulogium medicum, ſ. Oratio anniverſarii *Harvejana.* 1760. 4. (1 ſh.) Oeconomical and medical obſervations — tending to the improvement of military hoſpitals and to the cure of camp diſeaſes —. 1764. 8. (5 ſh.) überſ. von *Chr. Gottl. Selle.* Berlin. 1772. 8. The caſe of a lady labouring under a diabetes, attended with uncommon irregularities of the pulſe and palpitations of the heart. (Med. Obſ. Vol. 3. p. 274.) Experiments relative to the analyſis and virtues of Selzer water. (Ibid. Vol. 4. p. 7.)

BROCKWELL, [Joſeph] *M. A. Rector of Weſt-Merſea, Eſſex.*
Practical expoſition on the Lord's prayer. 1783. 8. (1 ſh.)

LE BROCQ, [Philipp] *M. A: Curate of Eling.*
Project for the payment of the national debt. 17.. Hints relative to the management of the poor. 1784. 8. (1 ſh. 6 d.) Deſcription of certain methods of planting, training and managing all kinds of fruit trees, vines —. 1785. 8. (1 ſh. 6 d.)
(ſeveral ſingle ſermons.)

BROMEHEAD, [Joſeph] *M. A.*
The melancholy ſtudent, an elegiac poem. 1769. 4. (1 ſh.) Ed. 2. 1776. Oration on the utility of public infirmaries. 1772. 4. (1 ſh.)

BROMFIELD, [William] *Surgeon to the Queen's Houshold, and to St. George's and the Lock's - Hoſpitals.*

Cafe of a woman who had a foetus in her abdomen for 9 years. (Phil Transact. 1751. p. 697.) Account of the englifh nightfhades, and their effects —. 1757. 12. (2 fh) Narrative of a phyfical transaction with Mr. *Aylett*, Surgeon and Apothecary at Windfor. 1759. 8. (1 fh.) Thoughts concerning the prefent peculiar method of treating perfons inoculated for the Small-Pox —. 1767. 8. (2 fh. 6 d.) Chirurgical obfervations and cafes. Vol. 1. 2. 1773. 8. (14 fh.) überf. Leipz. 1774. 8.

BROMLEY, [George] *Sir, Baronet*.
Collection of original royal letters, written by King Charles 1. and 2, King James II and the King and Queen ot Bohemia — from 1619 to 1665. 1787. 8. (10 fh. 6 d.)

—— [Robert Anthony] *Rector of St. Mildred's in the Poultry. Lecturer of St. John's Hackney and Minifter of Fitzroy Chapel.*
Inquiry into the neceffity of preparation for the Lord's fupper. 1770. 8. (3 fh.) Difcourfe on the confideration of our letter end. 1772. 8. (5 fh.) (feveral fingle fermons.)

BROMWICH, [Bryan J'Anfon]
* The experienced bee-keeper; containing an effay on the management of bees —. 1783. 8. (2 fh.) überf. von *C. F. Michaelis*. Leipz. 1785. 8.

BROOKE, [....] *Mifs*.
Reliques of irifh poetry — with notes. 1790. 4. (16 fh.)

BROOK, [Abraham]
Mifcellaneous experiments and remarks on electricity, the air pump, and the barometer; with the defcription of an electrometer of a new conftruction. 1789. 4. (1 fh.) Account of a new electrometer. (Phil. Transact. 1782. p. 384.)

BROOKE, [Francis] *Mrs.* (late Miff *Moore*, her husband *Brooke*, *Rector of Colney in Norfolk*.) born.... died d. 23 Jan. 1789.

—— [Edward]
Table or chronological index to the books of reports of the determinations in the feveral courts of judicature in England. 1780. (10 fh. 6 d.) Bibliotheca legum Angliae —. Vol. 1. 2. 1788. 12. (5 fh.)

BROOKE,

BROOKE, [Henry] *Barrak-Mafter of Mellingar in Ireland.*
born.... died 1783.
—— [John Charles] *Esq. of the Herald's College.* F. A. S.
Conjecture on Sir *Rich. Worsley's* Seal. (*Arch.*
Vol. 4. p. 182.) The ceremonial of making the
King's bed. (Ibid. Vol. 4. p. 311.) Illuftration of
a Saxon infcription on the church of Kirkdale in
Rydale in the North - Riding of the county of York.
(Ibid. Vol. 5. p. 188.) Account of an ancient feal
of Robert, Bar. *Fitzwalter.* (Ibid. Vol. 5. p. 211.)
Defcription of the great Seal of Queen *Catherine*
Parr the 6 Wife of Henry VIII. (Ibid. Vol. 5. p.
232.) Defcription of the great Seal of Mary d'Efté,
the fecond wife of King James II. (Ibid. Vol. 5.
p. 367.) Account of a Saxon infcription in Ald-
brough church, in Holderneffe in the eaft riding
of the County of York. (Ibid. Vol. 6. p. 39.)
—— [Thomas Digby]
Short and eafy method of prayer translated from
the french of Mad. *Guion.* 1775. 12. (1 fh.)
—— [W.....] *Major.*
*Plans of the funday-fchools and fchool of indu-
ftry, eftablifhed in the city of Bath —. 1789. 8.
(6 d.)
BROMHEAD; [Jofeph] *M. A.*
Oration on the utility of public infirmaries. 1772.
4. (1 fh.)
BROUGH, [Anthony] *Esq.*
On the neceffity of lowering the exorbitant freight
of fhips employed in the fervice of the eaft india
Company. 1786. 8. (1 fh.) View of the importance of the trade between great Britain and Ruffia.
1789. 8. (1 fh.)
BROUGHTON, [Arthur] *M. D. Phyfician to the
hofpital at Briftol.*
Obfervations on the influenza or epidemic cattarrh —
during the Months of May and June 1782. 1782.
8. (1 fh.) Enchiridion botanicum —. 1782. 8.
(4 fh.) The hiftory of two cafes of dropfy. (*Duncan's* M. C. Vol. 9. p. 368.)
—— [Thomas] *Rector of Alhallows, Lombard - Street and
of Wotton in Surry: Secretary to the fociety
for promoting chriftian knowledge.*
born.... died d. 14 Dec. 1777.

BROUGHTON, [Thomas] *Vicar of Bedminster, near Briftol.*
  born d. 5 Jul. 1704. died d. 21 Dec. 1774.
BROWN, [Hugh]
  The true principles of gunnery inveftigated and explained, comprehending translations of *Euler's* obfervations upon the new principles of gunnery by *Benj. Robins* —. with additions. 1777. 4. (15 fh.)
—— [John] *Painter.*
  born.... died 17..
—— [John] *M. D.*
  born.... died d. 7 Oct. 1788.
—— [Jofeph] *Esq.*
  Obfervation of a folar eclipfe Oct. 27. 1780. at Providence. (Mem. of B. A. Vol. 1. p. 149.)
—— [Jofiah] *Esq. Barrifter at law.*
  Reports of cafes upon appeals and writs of error in the high court of parliament from the Year 1701-1779. Vol. 1-7. fol. 1779-1783. (10½ Guin.)
—— [Peter]
  Illuftrations of zoology —. 1776. 4. (3 L. 3 fh.)
—— [Richard] *Profeffor of Hebrew and Arabic in the Univerfity of Oxford.*
  born.... died d. 20 March 1780.
—— [Thomas]
  The evangelical hiftory of our lord and faviour Jefus Chrift —. Vol. 1. 2. 1777. 8. (6 fh.)
—— [Thomas] *Surgeon, near Glasgow.*
  Defcription of the exocoetus volitans, or flying fifh. (Phil. Transact. 1778. p. 791.)
—— [William] *Phyfician at Kolyvan in Siberia.*
  On the fcurvy, which prevailed in Ruffia. 1785. *(Duncan's* M. C. Dec. 2. Vol. 2. p. 339.)
—— [William] *Esq. Of the Inner-Temple; Barrifter at Law.*
  Reports of cafes argued and determined in the high court of chancery — from 1778-1787. fol. 1788. (2 Guin.)
—— [W....L....] *D. D. Minifter of the englifh church at Utrecht.*
  Effay on the folly of fcepticifm; the abfurdity of dogmatizing on religious fubjects —. 1788. 8. (2 fh. 6 d.)

BROWNE,

BROWNE, [Arthur] *Esq. Repreſentative in Parliament for the Univerſity of Dublin.*
Review of the queſtion, whether the articles of Limerick have been violated? 1788. 8.
—— [Moſes] *Chaplain of Morden College, Vicar of Olney and of Sutton, Lincolnſhire.*
born 1703. died d. 13 Sept. 1787.
—— [Robert] *Gardener at Gunton in Norfolk.*
Method to preſerve peach and nectarine trees from the effects of the mildew. 1786. 12. (5 ſh.)
—— [Thomas] *Esq.*
The times. a ſatire —. 1783. 4. (2 ſh.)
—— [William] *Sir: M D: Phyſician at Lynn, Norfolk.*
born 1692. died at London 1774.
BROWNRIGG, [John]
Account of the fort of Ardnorcher or Horſeleap near Kilbegan, in the county of Weſtmeath. (Tr. of J. A. 1788.)
—— [William] *M. D: F. R. S: Phyſician at Keswick, Cumberland.*
Diſſ. De praxi medica ineunda. Lugd. Bat. 1737. 4. The art of making common ſalt. 1748. 8. überſ. von *F. W. Henn.* Leipz. 1776. 8. Thoughts on Dr. *Hale's* method of deſtillation. (Phil. Transact. 1759. p. 534.) Enquiries on the nature of the mineral elaſtic ſpirit, or air, contained in the Spa water. (Ibid. 1765. p. 218. 1774. p. 357.) Extract of an eſſay, intituled, „on the uſes of a knowledge of mineral exhalations when applied to diſcover the principles and properties of mineral waters, the nature of burning fountains and of thoſe poiſonous lakes, which the ancients called Averni. (Ibid. 1765. p. 236.) Conſiderations on the means of preventing the communication of peſtilential contagion. 1771. 4. (1 ſh 6 d.) Of the ſtilling of waves by means of oil. (Phil. Transact. 1774. p. 445.) On ſome ſpecimens of native ſalts. (Ibid. 1774 p. 480.)
BRUCE, [James] *of Kinnaird, Esq. F. R. S.*
Some obſervations upon Myrrh, made in Abyſſinia in the Year 1771. (Phil. Transact. 1775. p 408.) Travels to diſcover the ſource of the nile in the Year 1768-1773. containing a yourney through Egypt, the three Arabias and Ethiopia —. Vol. I 5. 1790.

1790. 4. (5 L. 5 fh.) überf. von *J. J. Volkmann,* mit Zuf. u. Anmerk. von *J. F. Blumenbach.* Th. I. 2. 1790. 8.

BRUCE, [John] *A. M: F. R. S. of Edinb. Profeſſor of Logic in the Univerſity of Edinburgh.*
Firſt principles of philoſophy. 1780. 8. (2 fh. 6 d.) *Ed.* 2. 1782. 8. (3 fh.) *Ed.* 3. 1785. 8. (3 fh) überf. von *K. G. Schreiter* 1788. 8. Elements of ſcience of Ethics. 1786. 8. (5 Sh.]

BRUCE, [Robert] *M. D.*
Account of the ſenſitive quality of the tree Averrhoa Carambola. (Phil. Transact. 1785. p. 356. überſ. Samml. zur P. u. N. G. Th. 3. S. 659.)

BRUCKSHAW, [....]
One more proof of the iniquities of private madhouſes. 1774. 8. (1 Sh. 6 d.)

BRUEN, [Lewis]
A Book of truly chriſtian pſalms, anthems and a chant —. 1788. 12. (1 Sh.)

BRUMWELL, *Surgeon in the Suſſex militia.*
Dangerous effects from eating a quantity of ripe berries of Belladonna. (Med. Obſ. Vol. 6. p. 222.)

BRYANT, [Charles] *Norwich.*
Account of two ſpecies of Lycoperdon —. 1782. 8. (2 Sh.) Flora Diaetetica: or, hiſtory of eſculent plants, both domeſtic and foreign. 1783. 8. (6 Sh.) überſ. Th. 1. 2. Leipz. 1786. 8.

—— [Henry] *A. M: Rector of Colby and Vicar of Langham, Norfolk.*
Enquiry — of the diſeaſe in wheat called brand —. 1783. 8. (1 fh.)

—— [James] *Esq.*
Obſervations on ancient hiſtory. 1767. 4. (15 Sh.) aus dieſer überſ. von den Menſchenopfern der Alten (von *C. F. Michaelis*). Gött. u. Gotha. 1774. 8. °Vindication of the Apamean medal. 1775. 4. (1 Sh.) New ſyſtem or an Analyſis of ancient mythology. Vol. 1 - 3. 1776. (3 L. 6 Sh.) Vindiciae Flavianae; or a vindication of the teſtimony given by Joſephus concerning our Saviour Jeſus Chriſt. 1780. (1 fh. 6 d.) °Addreſs to *Prieſtley* upon his doctrine of philoſophical neceſſity illuſtrated. 1780. 8. (2 Sh.) Obſervations on the poems of Thomas *Rowley.* Vol. I. 2. 1781. 8. (8 Sh. 6 d.)

Colle-

Collections on the Zingara or Gypfey language.
(Arch. Vol. 7. p. 387.) *Gemmarum antiquarum
delectus ex praeltantioribus defumtus in dactylio-
theca Ducis Marlburienfis. Vol. 1. fol. 1783.
BRYANT, [William] Esq.
Account of an electrical eel, or the torpedo of Su-
rinam. (Tr. of A. S. Vol. 2. p. 166.)
BRYDGES, [S Egerton] Esq.
Sonnets and other poems. 1785. 8. (2 fh. 6 d.)
BRYDONE, [Patrick] Esq. F. R. S: F. A. S.
Inftance of a palfy cured by electricity. (Phil.
Transact. 1760. p. 392.) Effects of electricity in
the cure of fome difeafes. (Ibid. 1760. p. 695.)
Tour through Sicily and Malta. Vol. 1. 2. 1773.
(12 fh.) überf. Th. 1. 2. Leipz. 1774. Aufl. 2. Th.
1. 2. Leipz. 1777. 8. Account of a fiery Meteor,
feen on the 1cth of Febr. 1772. and alfo of fome
new electrical experiments. (Phil. Transact. 1773.
p. 163.) Account of a thunder - ftorm in Scotland;
with fome meteorological obfervations. (Ibid. 1787.
p. 61.)
BRYMMER, [Alexander] *Surgeon at Stirling.*
Account of the happy effects of a feton in the fide
(Med. Com. of Ed. Vol. 3. p. 422.)
BRYSON, [James] *A. M.*
Sermons on feveral important fubjects. 1778.
BUCHAN, [William] *M. D. at London.*
Diff. de infantum vita confervanda. Edinb. 8. 17..
Domeftic medicine; or, on the prevention and cure
of difeafes by regimen and fimple medicines. Ed. 2.
1772. 8. (7 fh.) überf. Altenb. 1774. 8. Ed. 9. 17..
Caution concerning cold bathing, and drinking
the mineral waters. 1786. 8. (6 d.)
—— Earl of, fee *David Erskine.*
BUCHANAN, [George] *M. D. Prefident of the Roy.
Phyf. Soc. of Edinb. and Member of the Amer.
Philof. Soc.*
On the typhus fever. 1789. 8. (1 fh.)
BUKINGTON, [Nathaniel] *Esq. Barrifter at Law.*
Confiderations on the political conduct of Lord
North —. 1783. 8. (2 fh.)
BULKELEY, [Charles] *Methodiftical Preacher.*
Difcourfes —. 1752. 8. (5 fh.) Vindication of Lord
Shaftsbury, on the fubjects of morality and reli-
gion.

gion. 1752. 8. (1 sh. 6 d.) Two discourses on catholic communion. 1755. 8. (1 sh.) Notes on the philosophical writing of Lord Bolingbroke. 1755. 8. (2 sh. 6 d.) Observations upon natural religion and christianity. 1757. 8. (1 sh 6 d.) Sermons on public occasions. 1760. 8. (5 sh.) The oeconomy of the gospel in 4 books. 1765. 4. (10 sh. 6 d.) Discourses on the parables of our blessed saviour and the miracles of his holy gospel. Vol. 1-4. 1771. 8. (1 L.) Catechetical exercises. 1774. 8. (3 sh.) (several single sermons.)

BULLER, [Francis] Esq. *Judge of the Court of King's Bench.*
Introduction to the law relative to trials at nisi prius. 1772. 4. (18 sh.)

BULLIVANT, [Daniel] *Surgeon at Oakham, Rutlandshire.*
Case of violent spasms which succeded the amputation of an arm. (Med. Com. of Ed. Vol. 4. p. 447.)

BURDER, [George]
Evangelical truth defended —. 1788. 8. (6 d.) Pilgrim's progress by *John Bunyan,* a new edition with notes. 1786. 12. (3 sh. 6 d.)

BUREAU, [James] *Surgeon at Aldermanbury.*
On the erysipelas, or that disorder commonly called St. Anthony's fire. 1777. 8. (1 sh.) Case of an ileus, with observations on an hydraulic machine. (Mem. of M. S. of L. Vol. 2.)

BURGES, [James Bland] *Barrister at Law and Member of Parliament.*
(He assist in the House of Commons the cause of Mr. Hastings.)
Considerations on the law of insolvency. 1783. 8. (5 sh.) Letter to the Earl of Effingham on his lately proposed act of insolvency. 1783. 8. (2 sh.) Address to the country Gentlemen of England and Wales. 1780. 8. (1 sh. 6 d.)

BURGESS, [....] *Mrs.*
The oaks, or the beauties of Canterbury. a Comedy. 1780. 8.

—— [Thomas] *of Corpus Christi College, Oxford. Domestic Chaplain to the Lord Bishop of Salisbury.*
John Burton's pentalogia s. tragoediarum graecarum delectus —. Vol. 1.2. 1780. 8. (10 sh. 6 d.)
Mich.

Mich. Dawes Mifcellanea critica, iterum edita —.
1781. 8. (7 fh.) *Effay on the ftudy of antiquities. Ed. II. 1783. 8. (2 fh. 6 d.)   Confpectus cri-
ticarum obfervationum in fcriptores graecos et la-
tinos ac locos antiquae eruditionis edendarum una
cum enarrationibus, collationibusque veterum co-
dicum-Mftorum et fylloge anecdotorum graecorum.
1788. 8.   Initia Homerica f. excerpta ex Iliade *Ho-
meri* cum locorum omnium graeca metaphrafi, ex
codicibus Bodlejanis et Novi Collegii MfT. majo-
rem in partem nunc primum edita. 1788. 8. (2 fh.
6 d.) Remarks on *Jofephus's* account of Herod's
rebuilding of the temple at Jerufalem. 1788. 8.
(2 fh. 6 d.) *Tractatus varii latini a *Crevier, Bro-
tier, Auger* aliisque — confcripti et ad rem, cum
criticam tum antiquariam, pertinentes —. 1788. 8.
*Conliderations on the abolition of flavery and the
flave trade upon grounds of natural, religious and
political duty. 1789. 8. (2 fh. 6 d.)

BURGH, [James] *Mafter of an Academy at Newing-
ton Green.*
born at *Madderty in Pertfhire* 1714. died d. 26.
Aug. 1775.

—— [William]
Inquiry into the belief of the chriftians of the firft
three centuries refpecting the godhead —. 1778. 8.
(6 fh. 6 d.) Scriptural confutation of the arguments
againft the one godhead of the father, fon and holy
ghoft —. 1774. 8. (3 fh.)

BURGOYNE, [Bourgoyne] John; *Member of Parliament: Lieutenant General and privy Counfellor of
Ireland.*
*The maid of the oaks: a dramatic entertainment.
1774. 8. (1 fh. 6 d.)   The fubftance of his fpeeches —. 1778. 8. (1 fh.) Letter to his conftituents
on his late refignation with the correfpondences
between the fecretaries of war and him —. 1779. 8.
(1 fh.) State of the expedition from Canada; with
fupplement, containing orders, refpecting the principal movements and operations of the army, to
the raifing of the fiege of Ticonderoga. 1780. 4.
(14 fh.) Ed. 2. 17..   *The Lord of the Manor, a
comic opera. 1781. 8. (1 fh. 6 d.) The Heirefs a

Comedy. 1785. 8. Richard coeur de Lion; an Opera. translated from the French. 1786. 8.

BURKE, [Edmund] LL. D. *Member of Parliament.* born in Ireland.
°Vindication of natural fociety. 1756. 8. (1 fh. 6 d.) °Account of the European Settlements in America. 1757. 8. Vol. 1. 2. (8 fh.) Ed. 3. 1760. 8. überf. (von *Sam. Wilh. Turucr*) Th. 1 - 4 Danzig 1781. *Enquiry into the origin of our ideas of the fublime and beautiful: 1757 8. (3 fh.) Ed. 5. 17.. überf. von *Ch. Garve*. Riga 1773. 8. Thoughts on the caufe of the prefent difcontents. 1770. 8. (2 fh. 6 d.) Speech on american taxation. 1774. 4. (2 fh. 6 d.) 8. (2 fh.) Speeches at his arrival at Briftol and at the concluſion of the poll 1774. 4. (6 d.) Speech on moving his refolutions for conciliation with the colonies. 1775. 4. (2 fh. 6 d.) De Tumultibus Americanis, deque eorum concitatoribus. 1776. 8. (1 fh.) Letters on the affairs of America. 1777. 8. (1 fh. 6 d.) Two letters relative to the trade of Ireland. 1778. 8. (1 fh.) Speech on the independency of Parliament and the oeconomical reformation of the civil and other eftablifhments. 1780. 8. (2 fh.) Speech in the houfe of commons on his motion for a plan of public oeconomy. 1780. 8. (1 fh. 6 d.) *Letter from a gentleman in the englifh houfe of commons in vindication of his conduct, with regard to the affairs of Ireland. 1780. 8. (1 fh. 6 d.) Speech upon certain points relative to his parliamentary conduct. 1780. 8. (1 fh. 6 d.) Speech — on *Fox's* eaſt India bill. 1783. 8. (2 fh.) überf. (von *J. M. Sprengel*) Hiftor. Portefeuille. 1784. S. 75. A reprefentation to his majefty. 1784. 4. (1 fh. 6 d.) Speech on the Nabob of Arcot's debts to Europeans, on the revenues of the Carnatic. 1785. 8. (3 fh. Charges againſt *Haftings*. P. 1 - 4. 1786. 8. (8 fh.) Letter to *Philip Francis*. 1788. 8. (1 fh.) Subftance of his fpeech, in the Debate on the Army eftimates in the Houfe of Commons the 9 Febr. 1790. comprehending a difcuffion of the prefent fituation of affairs in France. 1790. 8. Reflections on the revolution in France and on the proceedings in certain focieties in London relative to that event,

in

in a letter intended to have been fent to a gentleman in Paris. 1790. 8.

BURKE, [John] M. D.
Translation of *Tiſſot's* letter to *Zimmermann* on the morbus niger. 1776. 8. (1 ſh. 6 d.)

BURMAN, [Charles]
The lives of thoſe eminent antiquaries, *Elias Aſhmole*, and *William Lilly* —. with *Lilly's* life and death of Charles I. 1774. 8. (6 ſh.)

BURN, [....]
° Miſcellany ſermons, extracted chiefly from the works of divines of the laſt century. Vol. 1 - 4. 1773. 8. (1 L.) überſ. Th. 1 - 3. Halle 1778. 8.

—— [A....] *Teacher of the mathematics in Tarporley, Cheſhire.*
Geodoeſia improved. 1771. Ed. 2. P. 1. 2. 1775. 8. (6 ſh.)

—— [Edward] A. B.
Letters to Dr. *Prieſtley* on the infallibility of the apoſtolic teſtimony concerning the perſon of Chriſt. 1790. 8. (1 ſh.)

—— [Richard] LL. D: *Vicar of Orton, in the county of Weſtmoreland.*
born at Winton in Weſtmoreland 17.. died d. 20 Nov. 1785.

BURNABY, [Andrew] D. D. *Vicar of Eaſt Greenwich, Kent and Archdeacon of Leiceſter.*
Travels through the middle ſettlements in North-America in the Years 1759 and 1760. with obſervations upon the ſtate of the Colonies —. 1775. 4. (3 ſh. 6 d.) überſ. (von C. D. *Ebeling*). Hamb. u. Kiel 1776. 8. (ſeveral ſingle ſermons.)

BURNBY, [John]
Hiſtorical deſcription of Canterbury Cathedral. 17.. Addreſſ to the people of England on the increaſe of their poor rates. 1780. 8. (1 ſh.) Summer amuſement; or, miſcellaneous poems. 1783. 8. (2 ſh. 6 d.) Thoughts on the freedom of election. 1784. 8. (6 d.)

BURNE, [James]
The man of nature. translated from the french. Vol. 1. 2. 1773. 12. (5 ſh.)

BURNET, [....] *Judge.* (Son of the Biſhop *Burnet.*)
Verſes

Verſes written on ſeveral occaſions between the Years 1712 and 1721. 1777. 4. (2 ſh. 6 d.)

BURNET, [George]
A ſhort catechiſm — on ſome of the main points of the chriſtian religion. 1773. 12. (6 d.)
—— [James] Lord *Monboddo. One of the Lord of Seſſion for the Kingdom of Scotland.*
* On the origin and progreſſ of language. Vol. 1-4. 1773-1787. (1 L. 4 ſh.) überſ. von *F. A. Schmidt* Th. 1. 2. Riga 1785. 8. * Ancient metaphyſics; or the ſcience of Univerſals. Vol. 1-3. 1779-1784. 4. (1 L. 11 ſh.)

BURNEY, [Charles] *D. Muſ. F. R. S.*
The cunning man, a muſical entertainment. 1766. 8. Preſent ſtate of Muſic in France and Italy; or the journal of a tour through thoſe countries. 1771. 8. (5 ſh.) Ed. 2. 1773. 8. (6 ſh.) * Translation of Sign. *Tartini's* letter to Sign. *Lombardini* publiſhed as an important leſſon to performers on the violin. 1771. 4. (1 ſh.) Preſent ſtate of Muſic in Germany, the Netherlands and united provinces, or the journal of a tour through thoſe countries. Vol. 1. 2. 1773. 8. (10 ſh.) überſ. Tagebuch ſeiner muſikaliſchen Reiſen von *C. D. Ebeling* u. *Bode* Hamb. 1773. 8. Th. 1-3. General Hiſtory of Muſic, from the earlieſt ages to the preſent period with a diſſertation on the muſic of the antients. Vol. 1-4. 1776 1789. 4. (5 L. 5 ſh.) überſ. Ueber die Muſik der Alten, von *J. J. Eſchenburg.* 1781. Leipz. 4. Account of the muſical performances in Weſtminſter Abbey in Commemoration of *Handel.* 1785. 4. (1 L. 1 ſh.) überſ. von *J. J Eſchenburg.* Berlin u. Stettin. 1785. 8. Account of an infant muſician. (Phil. Transact. 1779. p. 183.)
—— [Frances] *Miſſ.* (Daughter of *Charles Burney D. Muſ.*) *Keeper of the Robes to her Majeſty.*
* Evelina; or a young lady's entrance into the world. 1778. 8. Vol. 1-3. (9 ſh.) überſ. Leipz. 1783. 8. neu bearbeitet u. abgekürzt von *Brömel.* Berlin. 1789. 8. * Cecilia, or memoirs of an heireſſ. 1785. 8. Vol. 1-5. (15 ſh.) * Georgina. 17.. überſ. Tübingen. 1790. 8.

BURNS, [Robert] *A Ploughman in the county of Ayr as Scotland.*

Poems,

Poems, chiefly in the fcottifh dialect. 1786. 8.
Ed. 2. 1787. 8. (6 fh.)

BURROW, [James] *Sir. Knight, Mafter of the Crown-Office: F. R. S: F. A. S:*
born.... died d. 5 Nov. 1782.

—— [Reuben] *Esq.*
Reftitution of the geometrical treatife of *Apollonius Pergaeus* on inclinations; alfo the theory of gunnery —. 1779. 4. (2 fh.) Hints relative to friction in Mechanics. (Aliat. Ref. Vol. I. p. 171.) Method of calculating the 'moon's parallaxes, in latitude and longitude. (Ibid. p. 320.) Remarks on the artificial horizons —. (Ibid. p. 327.) Demonftration of a theorem concerning the interfections of curves. (Ibid. p. 330.) Corrections of the lunar method of finding the longitude. (Ibid. p. 433.)

BURROWES, [Robert] *A. M. and M. R. J. A.*
On the ftile of *Sam. Johnfon.* (Tr. of J. A. 1787. p. 27.)

BURT, [Adam] *Surgeon.*
A tract on the biliary complaints of europeans in hot climates, founded on obfervations in Bengal and confequently defigned to be particularly ufeful to thofe in that country. Calcutta. 1785. 8.

BURTENSHAW, [....]
Letter to — the Earl of *Mansfield.* 1781. 4. (10 fh. 6 d.) Specimens of juftice, humility and uniformity —. 1782. 4. (3 fh.)

BURTON, [Edmund] *A. M.*
The fatyrs of *Perfius*, translated into Englifh. 1752. 4. (3 fh.) Antient characters deduced from claffical remains. 1764. 8. (4 fh.) Manilii aftronomicon Lib. V. 1783. 8. (5 fh.)

—— [George] *M. A. Rector of Eldon in Suffolk.*
Analyfis of two chronological tables — the one being a table to affociate fcripturally the different chronologies of all ages and nations, the other, to fettle the pafcha feaft from the beginning to the end of time. 1787. 4. (2 fh. 6 d,)

—— [John] *D. D: of Eton.*
born at Wembworth in Devonfhire 1696. died d. 10 Febr. 1771.

—— [John] *M. D: F. A. S.*
Cafe of the extirpation of an excrefcence from the womb.

womb. (Phil. Transact. 1756. p. 520.) Account of a roman sepulchre, found near York 1768. (Arch. Vol. 2. p. 177.) Extract of two letters concerning the roman antiquities discovered in Yorkshire. (Ibid. p. 181.)

BURTON, [Philip] *Secondary and first Attorney in the court of Exchequer.*
Nature and extent of the business in the exchequer office of pleas —. Vol. I. 1770. 8. (7 sh. 6 d.)

—— [Philippina]
Fashion displayed. a Comedy. 1770.

—— [William]
Superstition, fanaticism and faction; a poem. 1781. 4. (1 sh.)

BUSBY, [Thomas]
The age of genius! a satire on the times. 1786. 4. (3 sh.)

BUTLER, [Charles] *Esq.*
Sir *Edw. Coke's* commentary upon *Littleton* Ed. 13. with additions by *Franc. Hargrave* and *Charles Butler* —. 1788. fol. (3 L. 3 sh.)

—— [James]
Justification of the tenets of the roman catholic religion —. 1787. 8. (2 sh. 6 d.)

—— [Rachael]
The new London and country cook. 1779.

—— [William]
Introduction to Arithmetic —. 1785. 8. (2 sh.)

BUTT, [George] *A. M: Rector of Stanford, Vicar of Clifton upon Teme and Chaplain to the Earl of Finlater.*
Sermon on Bishop of Worcester, *Johnson's* death. 1775. 4. (1 sh.) Isaiah versified. 1785. 8. (5 sh.)

BUTTER, [William] *M. D: Physician at Derby.*
A method of cure for the stone, chiefly by injections. 1754. 8. (1 sh. Diss. De frigore quatenus morborum caussa. Edinb. 1757. 8. Diss. De Arteriotomia. Edinb. 1761. 8. On the kinkcough with an appendix of Hemlot and its preparations. 1773. 8. (3 sh.) übers. von *J. C. F. Scherf.* Stendal. 1782. 8. Account of puerperal fevers in Derbyshire. 1775. 8. (2 sh. 6 d.) On the infantile remittent fever. 1782. 8. (1 sh.) übers. Samml. f. A. Th. 8. S. 347. "On opening the temporal artery

artery and new method for extracting the cataract.
1783. 8. (4 sh.)

BUTTERWORTH, [John] *Minister of the Gospel.*
A new concordance to the holy scriptures of the old and new testament —. 1767. 8. (6 sh.) Ed. II. 1785 8. (8 sh.)

—— [Laur.]
The superexcellency of the christian religion displayed, or, on natural and revealed religion; with an answer to *Lindseys* argument against the divinity of the Lord Jesus Christ. 1784. 8. (2 sh.)

BUTTON, [William]
Remarks on *Andr. Fuller's* treatise „The gospel of christ worthy of all acceptation. 1785. 12. (1 sh.)

BUXTON, [....] *Norfolk.*
On the most profitable method of managing light arable lands (*Hunter's* G. E. Vol. 5. p. 199.) On claying land. (Ibid. Vol. 5. p. 260.)

BYROM, [John] *M. D. F. R. S.*
Remarks on Mr. *Jeake's* plan for short-hand. (Phil. Transact. 1755. p. 388.) Remarks on Mr. *Lodwick's* Alphabet. (Ibid. 1755. p. 401.) Miscellaneous poems. Vol. 1. 2. 1773. 8. (10 sh.)

BYRON, [John] *Admiral.*
born d. 8 Nov. 1732. died 1786.

CADE, [John] *Esq. of Durham.*
On the roman roads and other antiquities in the county of Durham. (Arch. Vol. 7. p. 74.) Conjectures on the name of the roman station Vinovium or Binchester. (Ibid. Vol 7. p. 160.) Observations on the roman station Cataractonium with an account of antiquities in the neighbourhood of Piersbridge and Gainford. (Ibid. Vol. 9. p. 276.)

CADOGAN, [William] *M. D. at London.*
Oratio anniversaria Harvejana. 1764. 4. (1 sh. 6 d.) On the nursing and management of children. 17.. übers. 1782. 8. Dissertation on the gout and all chronic diseases. 1772. 8. (1 sh. 6 d.) Übers. Frankf. u. Leipz. 1772. 1790. 8. °Sermon on temperance and exercise by a physician. 1772. 8. (1 sh.)

CAIRNCROSS, [Andrew] *Surgeon to the 73d regiment.*
A curious case of a — recovery — attended with a fracture of the cranium requiring the trephine, —
a com-

a compound fracture of the lover extremity, requiring amputation, and several other wounds. (*Duncan's* M. C. Vol. 8. p. 296.)

CALDECOTT, [Thomas] *of the Middle temple, Esq.* Reports of cases relative to the duty and office of a justice of. the peace from 1776-1785. Vol. 1. 2. 1789. 4. (19 Sh.)

CALDERWOOD, [Robert] *Surgeon, Dalkeith.* Account of the discharge of animals by the anus, much resembling the common caterpillar, and which were found to be the larva of an insect. (*Duncan's* M. C. Vol. 9. p. 223.)

CALDWELL. [James] *Sir. F. R. S.* Examination of the question whether papishs should take securities for money. 1764. (1 Sh.) Inquiry into the restrictions on the trade of Ireland.—. 1779. 8. (1 Sh. 6 d.)

CALEF, [John] *Agent for the inhabitants of Penobscot.* *The siege of Penobscot by the rebels in the July 1779—. 1781. 8. (2 Sh. 6 d.)

CALEY, [John] *F. A. S.* On the origin of the jews in England. (Arch. Vol. 8. p. 389.) Extract from a Mscpt (*Wardrobe's* account of Henry VIII) in the augmentation office. (Ibid. Vol. 9. p. 243.)

CALL, [John] *Esq.* Sketch of the signs of the Zodiac, found in a pagoda, near Cape *Comorin* in India. (Philos. Transact. 1772. p. 353.)

CALLAM, [James] *Surgeon of his Majesty's ship Supply.* Letter containing an account of a voyage from the cape of good Cape to Botany-Bay with a description of the inhabitants and settlement of the Colony. 1789. 8. (6 d.)

CALLANDER, [James] *Colonel.* Military maxims—. 1782. 12. (2 Sh. 6 d.)

—— [John] *Esq. of Craighforth.* Two ancient scottish poems; the Gaberlunzie-Man and Christ's kirk on the green, with notes — 1785. 8. (2 Sh. 6 d.)

CAMBRIDGE, [Richard Owen] *Esq.* The scribleriad: an heroic poem. 1751. 4. (6 Sh.) Dialogue between a member of parliament and his servant. 1752. 4. (1 Sh.) The intruder, a poem. 1753.

1753. 4. (1 sh.) *The Fakeer, a tale. 1756. 4. (6 sh.) Account of the war in India, between the englifh and french on the coaft of Coromandel from the Year 1750-1760. 1760. 4. (1 L.. 1 sh.) (One of the original contributors to the World, a periodical paper by *Edw. Moore*. Mifcellaneous poems in *Dodsley's* collection of poems.)

CAMERON, [Charles] *Architect.*
The baths of the romans explained and illuftrated. 1772. fol. (4 L. 4 sh.)
—— [Ewen]
The fingal of Offian, an ancient epic poem — now rendered into beroic verfe. 1777. 4. (15 sh)
—— [John]
The Meffiah. 1770. 8. (4 sh.)

CAMMEL, [....] *Surgeon at Bungay in Suffolk.*
Cafe of an extrauterine foetus. (Lond. M. J. Vol. 5. p. 396.)

CAMPBELL, [A....] *M. D. Phyfician, Hereford.*
Account of the fucceffful treatment of a cafe of hydrocephalus, by Mercurials. (*Duncan's* M. C. Vol. 9. p. 240.)
—— [Alexander]
*The Hiftory of Dover Caftle, by *Will. Darell*, Chaplain to Queen Elizabeth —. 1780. fol. (1 sh. 6 d.)
—— [David] *M. D.*
Obfervations on the typhus —. 1785. 8. (2 sh.) überf. von *A. F. A. Diel*. Altenb. 1788. 8.
—— [George] *D. D. Principal of the Marifhall College at Aberdeen. F. R. S.*
Differtation on miracles, containing an examination of the principles advanced by *Dav. Hume*. 1762. 8. (4 sh.) The philofophy of rhetorik. Vol. 1. 2. 1776. 8. (12 sh.) *John Farquhar's* fermons on various fubjects — corrected from the Author's Manufcripts by *G. Campbell* and *Alex. Gerard* D. D. Prof. of Divinity in King's College Aberdeen. Vol. 1. 2. 1772. 8. (7 sh.) Addreff to the people of Scotland upon the alarms that have been raifed in regard to popery. 1779. 8. (1 sh.) The IV Gofpels, translated — with differtations and notes. Vol. 1. 2. 1789. 4. (2 L. 2 sh.) (feveral fingle fermons.)

E   CAMP.

CAMPBELL, [John] *LL. D.*
born at Edinburgh, 1708. died d. 28 Dec. 1775.
—— [Ivie] *near Inverary.*
Account of a fewing needle lodged in the breaſt of a woman being removed by inciſion. (*Duncan's* M C. Vol. 9. p. 275.)
—— [Thomas] *LL. D. Chancellor of St. Macartins Clogher.*
Sermon, for the ſupport of 12 boys and 8 Girls —. 1780. 4. (1 ſh) Strictures on the eccleſiaſtical and literary hiſtory of Ireland —. 1790. 8.
—— [William] *D. D. diſſenting Miniſter of Armagh in Ireland.*
Vindication of the principles and character of the presbyterian of Ireland. Ed. 3. 1787. 8. (1 ſh. 6 d.) Examination of the Biſhop of *Cloyne's* defence of his principles. 1788. 8. (ſeveral ſingle ſermons.)
CANNING, [George] *Esq. of the Middle Temple.*
born in Ireland 17.. died d. 11 Apr. 1771.
CANTON, [John]
born at Strout, Gloucesterſhire 1718. died d. 22 March. 1772.
—— [John] *late private ſecretary to the Marquis of Rockingham.*
The adventures of Telemachus the ſon of Ulyſſes; translated into blank verſe. 1788. 4. (2 ſh.)
CAPEL, [Edward] *Esq. Deputy Inſpector of Plays.*
born.... died d. 24 Febr. 1781.
CAPPER, [James] *Colonel in the ſervice of the Eaſt-India Company.*
Obſervations on the paſſage to India through Egypt and acroſſ the great deſert. 1784. 4. (7 ſh. 6 d.) überſ. *Sprengel's* Beytr. zur Völker und Länderk. Th. 4. S. 183.
CARDALE, [Paul] *Diſſenting Clergyman at Evesham Worceſterſhire.*
born 1705. died d. 1 March. 1775.
CARDONNEL, [Adam de] *Member of the Antiquarian Society of Edinburgh.*
Numismata Scotiae; or a ſeries of the ſcottiſh coinage, from the reign of William the Lion, to the union. 1786. 4. (1 L. 1 ſh.) Picturesque antiquities of Scotland. Vol. 1. 2 1788. 8. (18 ſh.)
CAREY, [George Savile] *Printer.*
The inoculator, a Comedy. 1766. 8. The cottagers,

tagers, an Opera. 1766. 8. Liberty chaſtiſed, or, patriotiſm in chains. 1768. 8. *Shakespeare's* jubilee. 1769. 8. The three old women weather wife. 1770. 8. The magic girdle. 1770. 4. The nut brown maid, a comic opera. 1770. 8. *Poems, written in the time of Oliver Cromwell. 1771. 4. (1 Sh. 6 d.) *Analects, in verſe and proſe. 1771. 8. (2 Sh.) Lecture on mimickry. 1776. 12. (1 Sh.) A rural ramble: with a poetical tagg; or Brighthelmſtone guide. 1777. 8. (2 Sh.) Poetical efforts. 1787. 8. (2 Sh.)

CARLISLE, Earl of, ſee HOWARD.

CARMICHAEL. [James] *Surgeon at Port - Glaſgow.* Hiſtory of a puerperal affection terminating in a diſcharge of pus from the umbilicus. (Med. Com. of Ed. Vol. 4. p. 445.) Hiſtory of a caſe, in which the left arm of a child was torn off by a milt, without any ſucceeding haemorrhage. (Ibid. Vol. 5. p. 79.)

CARPENTER, [B....]
Four ſermons on conformity to the world. 1790. 8. (1 Sh. 6 d.)

CARR, [John] *Maſter of the ſchool at Hertford.*
Epponina, a dramatic entertainment. 1765. 8. Translation of the dialogues of Lucian. Vol. 1-3. 1786. 8. (9 Sh.)

—— [Samuel]
Eugenia, a Tragedy. 1770. 8.

CARROL, [....] *D. D.*
Addreſs to the roman catholics of the united ſtates of North - America —. 1787. 8. (1 Sh. 6 d.)

CARTER, [Francis] *Eſq. F. A. S.*
born.... died at Woodbridge, Suffolk. d. 1 Aug. 1783.

—— [Francis] *M. D.*
Account of the various ſyſtems of medicine, from the days of *Hippocrates*, to the preſent time collected from the beſt latin, french and engliſh authors, particularly from the works of *John Browne*, M. D. Vol. 1. 2. 1788. 8. (10 Sh. 6 d.)

—— [John]
Short ſtrictures on infant baptiſm —. 1780. The reviewer reviewed; or a reply to Mr. *Will. Richard's* review on infant baptiſm —. 1781. 8. (1 Sh.)

(1 Sh.) Remarks on *Will. Richard's* „obfervations on infant fprinkling. 1782. 8. (1 Sh.)
CARTER, [London] *of Sabine-Hall, Virginia.*
Obfervations concerning the fly-weevil, that deftroys the wheat, with fome ufeful difcoveries and conclufions, concerning the propagation and progreff of that-infect and the methods to be ufed to prevent the deftruction of the grain by it. (Tr, of A S. Vol. I. p. 205.)
—— [William] *Lieutenant of the 40th regiment of foot.*
Detail of the feveral engagements, pofitions — of the royal american armies during the Years 1775 and 1776 —. 1784. 4. (2 Sh. 6 d.)
—— [William] *Med. D. at Canterbury.*
Examination of *Cadogan's* differtation on the gout and chronic difeafes. 1771. 8. (1 Sh.) Cafe of a locked jaw. (Med. Transact. Vol. 2. p. 39.)
CARTERET, [Philip] *Captain of the Swallowfloop.*
Letter on the inhabitants of the coaft of Patagonia. (Phil. Transact. 1770. p. 20.) Letter on a Camelopardalis found about the cape of good hope. (Ibid. 1770. p. 27.)
CARTWRIGHT, [....] *Mrs.*
*Armine and Elvira; a legendary tale. 1771. 4. (2 Sh.) Letters on female education —. 1777. 12. (2 Sh.) Memoirs of Lady *Eliza Audley*. Vol. I. 2. 1779. 12. (5 Sh.) The generous fifter. Vol. I. 2. 1779. 12. (5 Sh.) *The Prince of peace and other poems. 1779. 4. (2 Sh. 6 d.) Letters moral and entertaining. 1781. 8. (3 Sh.) The duped guardian: or the amant malade. Vol. I. 2. 1785. 12. (5 Sh.) The platonic marriage, a novel. Vol. 1-3. 1786. 12. (9 Sh.) Retaliation; or the hiftory of Sir Edward Ofwald and Lady Frances Seymour; a novel. Vol. 1-4. 1787. 12. (10 Sh.)
—— [Charles] *Deputy Accomptant to the Eaft-India Company.*
Abftract of the orders and regulations of the court of directors of the Eaft-India Company — to the pains and penalties the commanders and officers of fhips in the Company's fervice are liable to, for breach of Orders, illicit trade — 1788. 8. (5 Sh.)
—— [John] *Major of the Northamptonfhire Militia.*
*American independence the intereft and glory of great

Great Britain. 1774. 8. (1 Sh. 6 d.) Ed. II. 1775. 8. (2 Sh. 6 d.) "Take your choice. 1776. 8. (1 Sh. 6 d.) Ed. 2. (with the author name and with the title) The legislative rights of the commonalty vindicated; or take your choice. 1777. 8. (3 Sh. 6 d.) The legislative rights of the commonalty vindicated. 1778. (3 Sh. 6 d.) Letter to the *Earl* of *Abingdon*, difcuffing a pofition relative to a fundamental right of the conftitution, contained in his lordfhips thoughts on the letter of *Edmund Burke*. 1778. 8. (1 Sh.) The people's barrier againft undue influence and corruption —. 1780. 8. (2 Sh. 6 d.) Give us our rights or a letter to the electors of Middlefex —. 1782. 8. (1 Sh.) Internal evidence;' or an inquiry how far truth and the chriftian religion have been confulted by the author of ,,Thoughts on a parliamentary reform,, 1784. 8. (1 Sh. 6 d.)

CARVER, *[John] Captain of a Company of provincial troops during the late War with France.*
born at Stittwater in New-England 1732. died 1780.

CARWITHIN, *[William] A. B.*
The feafons of life, a poem. 1786. 8. (5 Sh.)

CARY, *[Henry Francis]* (born 1772.)
Ode to General Elliot. 1787. 4. Sonnets and odes. 1788 4. (1 Sh. 6 d.)

CARYSFORT, Lord, fee *Proby.*

CASE, *[Charles] M. A.*
Sermons on primitive chriftianity —. 1774. 12. (3 Sh. 6 d.)

CATLOW, *[Samuel]* . *of Mansfield.*
Addreff to the diffenters on the fubject of their political and civil liberty, as fubjects of Great Britain. 1788. 8. A proteftant catechifm for the ufe of young perfons translated from french. 1789. 8. (6 d.)

CAVENDISH, *[Henry] F. R. S: F. A. S.*
Experiments on factitious air. (Phil. Transact. 1766. p. 141.) Experiments on Rathbone — place water. (Ibid. 1767. p. 92.) Attempt to explain fome of the principal phaenomena of electricity, by means of an elaftic fluid. (Ibid. 1771. p. 584.) On pointed conductors. (Ibid. 1773. p. 66.) Account

count of some attempts to imitate the effects of the torpedo by electricity. (Ibid. 1776. p. 196.) Account of the meteorological instruments used at the royal society's house. (Ibid. 1776. p. 375.) Experiments on air. (Ibid. 1784. p. 119. p. 170. 1785. p. 372.) Experiments on *Hutchins's* experiments for determining the degree of cold at which Quicksilver freezes. (Ibid. 1783. P. 2.) Account of a new eudiometer. (Ibid. 1783. p. 106.) Account of experiments, relating to freezing mixtures. (Ibid. 1786. p. 241.) Account of experiments made by Mr. *John M' Nab* at *Albanyfort*, Hudsonsbay, relative to the freezing of nitrous and vitriolic acids. (Ibid. 1788. p. 166. übers. *Gren* J. d. P. Th. 1. S. 113.) On the conversion of a mixture of dephlogisticated and phlogisticated air into nitrous acid, by the electric spark. (Ibid. 1788. p. 261. übers. *Gren* J. d. P. Th. 1. S. 282.) On the height of the luminous arch which was seen on Febr. 23. 1784. (Ibid. 1790. p. 101.)

CAVERHILL, *[John]* *M. D: F. R. S.*
born.... died at Old-Melrose, Roxburgshire, d. 1 Sept. 1781.

CAUL, *[Goverdhan]*
On the litterature of the Hindus from the sanscrit with a short commentary. (Asiat. Res. Vol. 1. p. 340.)

CAULDWELL, *[Ralph]* *at Goodwickhall near Swaffham in Norfolk.*
On the descent of titles of honour, particularly baronies, through the female line: transcribed from a Mf. of *Saynslowe Kniveton*, (Arch. Vol. 3. p. 285.)

CAULFIELD, *[J. ...]* *Esq. late Cornet, of the Queen's Regiment of Dragoon guards*
The manners of paphos; or triumph of love. 1777. 4. (3 Sh.)

CAUSER, *[John]* *Surgeon at Stourbridge, in Worcestershire.*
Case of a fracture of the scull successfully treated (Lond. M. J. Vol. VII. P. 2.)

CAUTY, *[William]* *Cabinetmaker.*
Natura, philosophia et ars in concordia; or nature, philosophy and art in friendship. 1772. 8. (2 Sh.)

CAWDLE,

CAWDLE, [Amy]
Legal attempt to enforce the practice of infant baptifm being a copy of a petition to parliament — againſt the Anabaptifts. 1780. 12. (6 d.)

CAWLEY, [Thomas] M. D. late chief Surgeon to the forces in Jamaica.
A cafe of inverted uterus fucceſſfully treated; two cafes of the ſpontaneous evolution of 'the foetus; and an inftance of the caefarean operation performed by a woman on herfelf. (London M. J. Vol. 6. p. 366.) Account of the dyfentery, as it appeared amongſt his Majefty's troops in Jamaica during the laft war —. (Ibid. Vol. 7. P. 4. überf. Samml. f. A. Th. 12. S. 113.) A ſingular cafe of Diabetes, confifting entirely in the quality of the urine —. (Ibid. Vol. IX. P. 3. überf. Samml. f. A. Th. 13. S. 112.)

CAWTE, [R....] of Croydon, in Surry.
Academic leſſons; comprizing a fyftem of education particularly adapted to female Seminaries. 1786-8. (2 Sh. 6 d.)

CELESIA, [....] Mrs. (daughter of Dav. Mallet Esq.)
*Almeida: a tragedy. 1771. 8. (1 Sh. 6 d.) *Indolence, a Poem. 1772. 4. (1 Sh.)

CHALMERS, [George]
Political annals of the prefent united colonies from their fettlement to the peace of 1763. Vol. 1. 1779. 4. (1 L. 1 Sh) Eftimate of the comparative ftrength of Britain during the prefent and four preceding reigns — with *Juftice Hale's* eſſay on population. 1782. 4. (5 Sh.) Ed. 2. 1786. 8. (3 Sh. 6 d.) Opinions on interefting fubjects of public law and commercial policy arifing from American independence —. 1784. 8. (3 Sh.) The life of Daniel De Foe. 1790. 8. (3 Sh.)

—— [Lionel] M. D: of Charlestown, South-Carolina.
Obfervations on Opifthotonos and Tetanos. (Med. Obf. Vol. 1. p...) Eſſay on fevers —. 1768. 8. (2 Sh.) überf. Riga. 1773. 8. On the weather and difeafes of South-Carolina. 1776. 8. Vol. 1. 2. (6 Sh.) überf. Th. 1. Stendal. 1788. 8.

CHAL-

CHALMERS. [William] *Surgeon in Edinburgh.*
A cafe of incarcerated hernia cured. (Med. Com. of Ed. Vol. I. p 413.)

CHALONER, [Charles]
The method of making whale-compoſt. (*Hunter's* G. E. Vol. 5. p. 225.) On feeding hogs with potatoes. (Ibid. Vol. 5. p. 243.)

CHAMBERLAINE, [William] *Surgeon.*
On the efficacy of Stizolabium or cowhage in difeafes occafioned by worms with obfervations on other anthelmintic medicines of the Weſtindies. 1784. 8. (1 ſh. 6 d.) überſ. Altenburg. 1786. 8. Remarks on the folvent powers of Camphor. (Mem. of M. S. of L. Vol. 2.)

CHAMBERS, [Amelia] *Mrs.*
The ladies beſt companion, or a golden treafure for the fair fex; containing the whole arts of cookery, paſtry, confectionary, potting, pickling, preſerving — to which are added, every lady her own and family's phyſician. 1772. 8. (2 ſh.)

—— [William] *Sir. Knight. Knight of the Polar ſtar, Surveyor general of the board of Works and Treaſurer of the Royal Academy.*
Plans elevations, feĉtions and perſpective views of the gardens and buildings at Kew. 1762. fol. (2 L. 2 ſh.) On oriental gardening. 1772. 4. (5 ſh.) überſ. (von *S. H. Ewald.*) Gotha. 1775. 8. *W. Chamber's, W. Jones's* and other literary gentleman's afiatic miſcellany, confiſting of translations, imitations, fugitives pieces, original productions and extracts from curious publications. 1785. 8. (3 ſh.) Account of the fculptures and ruins of Mavalipuram, a place, a few miles North of Sadras, and known to feamen by the name of the feven Pagodas. (Afiat. Ref. Vol. I. p. 145.) Account of the Marratta ſtate; written in Perfian by a Munfhy, translated by *W. Chambers* — with M. *Caeſar Frederike's* voyages and travels into the Eaſt-Indies and beyond the Indies, Calcutta, 1787. 8. (2 ſh)

CHAMIER, [John] *Secretary to the military and polical department of the Governmens at Madras.*
* Meteorological account of the weather at Madras from 1 June 1787 to 31 May 1788.

CHAMPION, [Joseph] *Esq.*
The progreß of freedom, a poem. 1776. 4. (1 sh.)
Poems; imitated from the Persian. 1787. 4. (2 sh.
6 d.) The poems of *Ferdosi*, translated from the
Persian. Vol. 1. 1788. 4. (12 sh.)
—— [Richard] *Esq.*
On the present situation of Great-Britain and the
united states of America. 1784. 8. Comparative
reflections on the past and present political, commercial and civil state of Great Britain. 1787. 8.
(5 sh.)

CHANDLER, [Benjamin] *Surgeon.*
Case of a stone in the bladder. (London M. J. Vol.
5. p. 387.)
—— [Bernhard] *M. D. Surgeon at Canterbury.*
On the present succeßfull and most general method
of inoculation. 1767. 8. (1 sh.) On the various
theories and methods of cure in apoplexies and pal-
sies. 1785. 8. (3 sh.) überſ. Leipzig. 1787. 8. Stendal. 1787. 8.
—— [George] *Surgeon at London.*
On cataract, its nature, species, causes and symptoms —. 1775. 8. (2 sh. 6 d.) On the diseases
of the eye and their remedies. 1780. 8. (3 sh.)
überſ. Leipz. 1782. 8.
—— [John] *F. R. S. Apothecary at London.*
born 1700. died d. 12 Dec. 1780.
—— [Richard] *D. D. Fellow of Magdalen College, Oxford.
F. A. S.*
*Marmora Oxoniensia. 1764. fol. Jonian antiqui-
ties. 1769. fol. (1 L. 11 sh. 6 d.) Inscriptiones antiquae — in Asia minori et Graecia praesertim Athe-
nis collectae. 1774. fol. (1 L. 5 sh.) Travels in
Asia minor. 1775. 4. (15 sh.) überſ. (von *H. C.
Boje*) Leipz. 1776. 8. Travels in Greece —. 1776.
4. (16 sh.) überſ. (von *H. C. Boje*) Leipz. 1777. 8.

CHAPMAN, [George] *A. M: Master of the grammar
school of Dumfries.*
On education. 1773. 12. (3 sh.)
—— [John] *D. D. Rector of Mersham and of Aldington.*
born 1704. died 1784.
—— [Samuel] *M. D. of Sudbury in Suffolk.*
Pulmonary and other complaints, apparently sup-

ported by fever, of the intermittent or remittent kind and cured by the bark, (M. C. Vol. 1. p. 260.)

CHAPMAN, [William] *A. M.*
The parriad addreff to the editor of Bellendene upon his preface. 1788. 4. (1 fh. 6 d.)

CHAPONE, [....] *Mrs.*
* Letters on the improvement of the mind. Vol. 1. 2. 1773. 12. (6 fh.) Mifcellanies in profe and verfe. 1775. 12. (3 fh.) Letter to a new married lady. 1777. 12. (6 d.)

CHAPPLE, [William] *of Exeter.*
Review of part of *Risdon's* Survey of Devon, containing the general defcription of that county; with additions —. 1785 4 (6 fh)

CHARFY, [Guiniad] *Esq.*
The fifherman; or, the art of angling made eafy. 1784. 8. (fh. 6 d.)

CHARLEMONT, [....] Earl of, *Prefident of the Roy Irifh Academy.*
Antiquity of the woollen manufacture in Ireland. (Tr of J. A. 1787. p. 17.)

CHARLES, [R....] *Surgeon at Winchefter.*
On the treatment of confumptions. 1787. 8. (1 fh.)

CHARLESWORTH, [J....] *M. A. late Fellow of Trinity College, Cambridge,*
Practical fermons, felected and abridged from various authors. Vol. 1. 2 1789. 8. (5 fh. 6 d.)
(feveral fingle fermons.)

CHARLETON, [Rice] *M. D: F. R. S: Phyfician to the General Hofpital at Bath, Somerfetfhire.*
born .... died d. 23 Oct. 1788.

CHARSLEY, [W....] *M. D.*
On the caufes of the general mortality by fevers —. 1783. 8. (1 fh. 6 d.)

CHARTERS, [Samuel] *Minifter of Wilton.*
Sermons 1786. 8. (5 fh.)

CHATTERTON, [Thomas]
born d. 20 Nov. 1752. died d. 24 Aug. 1770.

CHAVASSE, [Nicholas] *Surgeon at Walfall in Staffordfhire.*
Cafe of chronic dyfentery fucceffully treated by large dofes of the vitrum Antimonii ceratum. (London M. J Vol. 5. p. 297.) Account of a remarkable difeafe of the heart. (Ibid. Vol. 7. p. 407.
überf.

überſ. Samml. f. A. Th. XI. S. 692.) ' Miscellanous obſervations on the medical and ſurgical uſes of cold water. (Ibid. Vol. 7. P. 2. überſ. Samml. f. A. Th. XII. S. 32.)

CHAVASSE, [William] *Surgeon at Burford, Oxfordſhire.*
Hiſtory of a caſe of tetanus ſucceſſfully treated by the uſe of large doſes of Opium. (*Duncan's* M. C. Vol. 9. p. 374.)

CHAUNCY, [Charles] *D. D. Miniſter of the firſt church in Boſton, New-England.*
* The myſtery hid from ages and generations made manifeſt by the goſpel revelation — by one who wiſhes well to the whole human race. 1784. 8. (5 ſh) Five Diſſertations on the ſcripture account of the fall and its conſequences. Boſton 1785. 8. (4 ſh.) The benevolence of the deity - conſidered. 1784. 8. (4 ſh.)

CHELSUM, [James] *D D. Chaplain to the Lord Biſhop of Wincheſter, Rector of Droxford, Hants.*
* Remarks on the two laſt of Mr. *Gibbon's* Hiſtory of the decline and fall of the roman empire. 1776. 8. (1 ſh 6 d.) Ed. 2. (with the author's name) 1778. 8. (2 ſh. 6 d.) Reply to Mr. *Gibbon's* vindication of ſome paſſages in the XV and XVI Chapters of the hiſtory of the decline — of the roman empire —. 1785. 8. (2 ſh.)

CHESSHER, [Robert]
Account of a caſe of luxation of the os humeri, in which the reduction of the bone was facilitated by inducing ſickneſſ and faitneſſ by means of emetic tartar. (Lond. M. J. Vol. VIII. p. 189. überſ. Samml. f. A. Th. 12. S. 561.)

CHESTERFIELD, [Philip Dormer Stanhope, Earl of] born d. 22 Sept. 1694. died d. 24 March 1773.

CHESTON, [Richard Browne] *F. R. S: Surgeon to the Infirmary at Glouceſter.*
Pathological inquiries and obſervations in ſurgery from the diſſection of morbid bodies. 1766. 4. überſ. von *J. C. F. Scherf.* Gotha 1780. 8. Account of an oſſification of the thoracic duct. (Phil. Transact. 1780. p. 323. p. 546.) The caſe of Mr. *Holder* with ſome remarks on the exiſtence of polypoſe

lypofe concretions in the heart. (Lond. M. J. Vol. VI. p 225. überf. Samml. t. A. Th XI. S. 226.)

CHETWYND, [James] *Esq. Barrifter at law.*
Treatife upon fines —. 1773. 4. (5 fh.)

CHILCOT, [Harriet] *Miſſ.* (now Mrs. *Meziere.*)
Elmar and Ethlinda, a tale. Adalba and Ahmora an indian tale; with other pieces. 1783. 8. (3 fh.)
Moreton Abbey or the fatal myftery. Vol. 1. 2. 1786. 8. (3 fh)

CHISHOLM, [C....] *Surgeon at St. George's*, Grenada.
The hiftory of a fingular affection of the liver, which prevailed epidemically in fome parts of the Weft-Indies. *(Duncan's* M. C. *Dec.* 2. Vol. 1. p. 353.)

CHRISTIE, [Thomas] *Member of the Med. und Antiq. Soc. of Edinb.*
Obfervations on pemphigus. (Lond. M. J. Vol. X. P. 4.)

CHRISTIAN, [....] *Lieutenant.*
Relation of the battle of Maxen, with a treatife on profiles —. translated by an Officer. 1785. 4. (12 fh.)

CHRYSEL, [Chriftopher]
Account of a new invention for conftructing and fetting boilers in fire engines, faltworks —. 1775. 8.

CHURCH, [J....] *M. A: F. M. S.*
Remarks on the afcaris lumbricoides. (Mem. of the M. S. of L. Vol. 2.)

CHURCHMAN. [John] *Landfurveyor for the Diſtrict of the Counties of Delaware and Chefter and for part of Lancafter and Berks , Penfylvania.*
Addreſs in fupport of the principles of the magnetic variation and their application in determining the longitude at fea. fol. 1789. Explanation of the magnetic atlas. 1790. 8. Addreſs to the members of the different learned focieties in Europe and America. fol. (1790.)

CHURCHYARD, [Thomas]
The worthines of Wales, a poem —. 1776. 8. (7 fh. 6 d.)

CHURTON, [Ralph] *M. A. one of his Majefty's preachers at Whitehall.*
Eight fermons on the prophecies refpecting the deſtruction of Jerufalem. 1785. 8. (4 fh.) Sermon,

The

The will of God the ground and principle of civil as well as religious obedience. 1790. 8.

CLARE, [....] *Lord.*
  Faith a poem. 1774. 4. (1 sh. 6 d.) Verses addressed to the Queen. 1775. 4. (1 sh.)
—— [Peter] *Surgeon.*
  On the cure of abscesses by caustic and on the treatment of wounds and Ulcers —. 1779. 8. (2 sh. 6 d.) Ed. 2. 1780. Übers. Samml f A. Th. 6. S. 110. S. 626. Samml. f. W. A. St. 1. S. 1. On the Gonorrhoea. 1781. 8. (1 sh.) Ed. 5. 1789. 8. (1 sh.)

CLARK, [Alexander] *Gardener at Drumcrief in Scotland.*
  View of the glory of the Messiah's kingdom —. 1763. 8. (2 sh. 6 d.) Emblematical representation of the paradise of God —. 1779. 8. (3 sh.)

CLARK, [Ewan]
  Miscellaneous poems. 1779. 8.
—— [George]
  Vindication of the honour of god and of the rights of Men in a letter to Mr. de *Coetlogon*, occasioned by the publication of Mr. *Edwards's* sermon on the eternity of hell torments. 1789. 8. (6 d.) Defence of the unity of god in four letters to M. *Harper* —. 1790. 8. (2 sh. 6 d.)
—— [George] *Esq.*
  The penal statutes abridged and alphabetically arranged —. 1777. 8. (3 sh.) Alphabetical epitome of the common law of England —. 1778. 8. (3 sh. 6 d.) The game laws from King Henry III. to the present period —. 1786. 12. (3 sh.) A defence of the unity of God in IV letters —. 1789. 8. (2 sh. 6 d.)
—— [Hugh] *Heraldic Engraver.*
  H. *Clark* and *Thomas Wormull's* Introduction to Heraldry. 1775. 12. (2 sh. History of Knighthood containing the religious and military orders which have been instituted in Europe —. Vol. 1. 2. 1784. 8. (10 sh 6 d.)
—— [James]. *Farrier.*
  Observations upon the shoeing of horses, with an anatomical description of bones in the foot of a horse. P. 1. 2. 1772. 8. (1 sh. 6 d.) Ed. 2. 1776. 8. (3 sh.) Übers. Leipz. 1777. 8. On the prevention

tion of difeafes incidental to horfes from bad management in regard to ftables, food, water, air and exercife with obfervations on fome of the furgical and medical branches of farriéry. 1788. 8. (7 fh. 6 d.) überf. Wien. 1790: 8.

CLARK, [James] *Surgeon in Dominica.*
Hiftory of an anevrifm of the crural artery with fingular circumftances. (*Duncan's* M. C. Dec. 2. Vol. 3. p. 326.) Hiftory of cafes of abfceffes in the liver, with obfervations on the effects of opening them. (Ibid. Dec. 2. Vol. 4. p. 317.) Hiftory of a cafe of fchirrous liver. (Ibid. Dec. 2. Vol. 4. p. 355.)

—— [John] *F. A. S. Scot.* (born in Scotland.)
Anfwer to *Will. Shaw* on the authenticity of the poems of Offian. 1781. 8. (1 fh.) * The works of the Caledonian bards, translated from the Galic. Vol. 1. 1778. 8. (3 fh.) Translation of the adventures of Telemachus. 1773. 4. (1 fh. 6 d.)

—— [John] *M. D. Phyfician at Newcaftle.*
Obfervations on the difeafes in long voyages to hot countries, and particularly — in the Eaft-Indies. 1773. 8. (6 fh.) Obfervations on fevers, efpecially thofe of the continued type —. 1780. 8. (5 fh.) Obfervations on the hepatitis. (Med. Com. of Ed. Vol. 5. p. 423.) Cafe of obftructed fecretion of urine. (Ibid. Vol. 6. p. .) On the influenza as it appeared at Newcaftle upon Tyne. 1783. 8.

CLARKE, [Cuthbert] *Lecturer in experimental philofophy.*
Theory and practice of husbandry — with a compendium of mechanics. 1777. 4. (10 fh. 6 d.) A new complet fyftem of weights and meafures —. 1789. 4. (1 fh. 6 d.)

—— [Edward] *A. M. Rector of Pepperharrow in Surrey.*
born .... died d. Nov. 1786.

—— [Henry]
Practical perfpective —. Vol. 1. 1776. 8. (6 Sh.) The rationale of circulating numbers —. 1777. 8. (3 Sh. 6 d.) *Lorgna* on the fummation of infinite converging feries with algebraic divifors — translated from the latin. 1780. 4. (10 Sh. 6 d.) Supplement. 1782. 4. (2 Sh. 6 d.)

CLAR-

CLARKE, [James] *Land-Surveyor.*
Survey of the lakes of Cumberland, Westmorland and Lancashire —. 1787. fol. (2 L. 5 Sh.) Ed. 2. 1790. fol. (1 L. 1 Sh.)

—— [John] *Licentiate in Midwifery, of the royal college of physicians and Teacher in Midwifery in London.*
Essay on the epidemic disease of lying in women of the Years 1787 and 1788. 1788. 4. (2 Sh. 6 d.) (übers. Samml. f. A. Th. 13. S. 161.) Two successful cases of delivery by the crotchet, in extreme deformity of the pelvis. (Lond. M. J. Vol. VII. P. 1. übers. Journal für Geburtsh. St. 1. On the cause of the death of children when the umbilical cord is compressed during labour. (Ibid. Vol. VIII. P. 2.)

—— [John] *First-Lieutenant of Marines*
Narrative of the battle fought on the 17 June 1775. — on Bunker's hill near Charlestown in New-England —. 1775. 8. (1 Sh.)

—— [Joseph] *M. D. Physician to the lying in Hospital at Dublin. F. J. A.*
Observations on some causes of the excess of the mortality of males above that of females. (Philos. Transact. 1786. p. 349. London M. J. Vol. IX. P. 2.) On the properties commonly attributed by medical writers to human milk on the changes it undergoes in digestion, and the diseases supposed to originate from this source in infancy. (London M. J. Vol XI. P. 1. Tr. of J. A. 1788.)

—— [M... A...] *M. D. and Professor of Midwifry.*
Directions for the management of Children, from the time of their birth to the age of seven Years. 1773. 8. (2 Sh.)

—— [Samuel] *Teacher of the Mathematics.*
The laws of chance —. 1758. 8. (4 Sh.) The british gauger: or trader and officer's instructor in the royal revenue of the excise and customs —. 1761. 12. (5 Sh.) Introduction to the theory and practice of Mechanics —. 1764. 4. (6 Sh.) Sentiments — for the coining of 40,000 pounds worth of silver. 1771. 8. (6 d.) Letter to *Rich. Price* containing a refutation of his treatise on reversionary payments. 1777. 8. (2 Sh.)

CLARKE, [Thomas] *Surgeon at Market Harborough.*
A cafe of epilepfy fuccefTrully treated. (London
M. J. Vol. 1. p. 428. überf. Samml. f. A. Th. 7.
S. 201.)
—— [Thomas] *A. M. at Oxford and Gottingen.*
The Crifis of immediate concernments of the britifh empire. 1786. 8. The fecond edition of Junius Alter's letter to Mr. O'Leary with a fhort examination into the firft caufes of the prefent lawlefT fpirit of the irifh peafantry and a plan of reform. 1787. 8.
—— [William] *M. A: Rector at Chichefter,*
born at Haghman-Abbey, Shroplhire 1696. died d. 21 Oct. 1771.
CLARKSON, [T....] *M. A.*
* Effay on the flavery and commerce of the human fpecies particularly the African. 1786. 8. (4 Sh.) Ed. 2. (with the author's name) 1788. (3 Sh.) On the impolicy of the African flave trade. 1788. 8. (2 Sh. 6 d.) On the comparative efficiency of regulation or abolition, as applied to the flave trade. 1789. (1 Sh. 6 d.) überf. von *M. C. Sprengel.* Leipz. 1789. 8.
CLATER, [Francis] *Farrier at Newark.*
Every man his own farrier. 1783. 8. (5 Sh. 6 d.)
CLAVERING, [Robert] *Architect.*
On the conftruction and building of Chimney's and the caufes of their fmoaking. 1779. 8. (2 Sh. 6 d.)
CLAYTON, [William] *Esq. of his Majefty's Navy.*
An Account of Falkland Islands. (Phil. Transact. 1776. p. 99.)
CLEAVER, [E....] *of Whitwell, near York.*
Comparifon between red and white wheat. *(Hunter's* G. E. Vol. 5. p. 245.) On lime. (Ibid. Vol. 5. p. 246.) On preparing feed-wheat with oil. (Ibid. Vol. 5. p. 255.)
CLEGG, [James] *of Redivales, near Bury.*
Experiments on dying black. (Philof. Transact. 1774. p. 48.)
CLEGHORN, [George] *M. D: Profeffor of Anatomy in Trinity College, Dublin.*
born at Grantar, near Edinburgh 1716. died d. Dec. 1789.

CLEGHORN,

CLEGHORN, [James] *M. B.*
Hiſtory of an Ovarium, wherein were found teeth, hair and bones. (Tr. of I. A. 1787. p. 73.)

CLELAND, [John] *Esq.*
born 1709. died d. 23 Jan. 1789.

CLERKE, [William] *Sir, Baronet: Rector of Bury, Lancaſterſhire.*
Thoughts, on the means of preſerving the health of the poor by prevention and ſuppreſſion of epidemical fevers. 1790. 8. (6 d.)

CLIFFORD, [Charles] *Esq.*
Remarks on the ſpeech of Lord *Thurlow* on a motion for the houſe to reſolve itſelf into a committee on the inſolvent debtors bill —. 1788. 8. (1 ſh.)

CLINTON, [Henry] *Sir, Knight Baron Lieutenant-General in the army, Colonel of the 70 Regim. of Dragoons and of the 84 Regim. of Foot, Governor of Limeric in Ireland.*
Narrative, relative to his conduct during part of his command of the King's troops in North-America particularly that which reſpects the unfortunate iſſue of the campaign in 1781. 1782. 8. (2 ſh.)
Obſervations on ſome parts of the anſwer of Earl Cornwallis to — Narrative —. 1782. 8. (2 ſh 6 d.)
Letter to the Commiſſioners of public accounts, relative to ſome obſervations in their 7 report —. 1784. 8. (1 ſh)

CLIVE, [Catherine] *Actreſſ.*
born.... died d. 5 Dec. 1785.

CLOWES, [Thomas] *Surgeon at Wingham, in Kent.*
A caſe of hernia. (London M J. Vol. X. P. 1.)

CLUBBE, [J...] *Surgeon at Ipswich, Suffolk.*
On the inflammation in the breaſts of lying in women. 1779. 8. (2 ſh. 6 d.) On the nature of the venereal poiſon. 1782. 8. (2 ſh.) On the virulent gonorrhoea. 1787. 8. (1 ſh. 6 d.)

—— [John] *Rector of Wheatfield and Vicar of Debenham, Suffolk.*
The hiſtory and antiquities of the ancient villa of Wheatfield. 1758. 4. (1 ſh. 6 d.) Sermon before the widows and orphans of clergymen. 1752. (6 d.)
°Phyſiognomy. 1764. 4. (1 ſh. 6 d.) Miſcellaneous tracts. Vol. 1. 2. 1771. 8. (6 ſh.)

COBB, [James]
The contract or female captain, a farce. 1779. The wedding night. 1780. Who'd have thought it; a farce. 1781. Kenfington garden, or the walking jockey. 1781. *The ftranger at home, a comic opera. 1785. 8. The humourift, a farce. 1785. The firft floor, a farce. 1787. *Love in the eaft, or the adventures of XI hours, an opera. 1788. 8. (1 fh. 6 d.)

COBB, [John] *D. D. Fellow of St. John's College.*
Eight fermons. 1783. 8. (3 fh. 6 d.)

COCHRANE, [Thomas] *M. D. Phyfician in St. Chriftopher's.*
The ufe of couhage as an anthelmintic. (Med Com. of Ed. Vol. 2. p. 82.) Obfervations on the ufe of cold bathing in the cure of tetanus. (Ibid. Vol. 3. p. 183.) The hiftory of a cafe in which a large wound of the abdomen, with a remarkable protrufion of the inteftines, terminated favourably. (*Duncan's* M C. Vol. 10. p. 276.)

COCKIN, [William]
Account of an extraordinary appearance of a mift. (Phil. Transact. 1780. p. 157.)

COCKELL, [William] *M D of Pontefract.*
On the retroverfion of the uterus —. 1785. 4. (1 fh. 6 d.).

COCKSON, [Thomas] *Surgeon at Campden.*
A peculiar cafe of a fpecies of maggots being difcharged from the uterus during menftruation. (Med. Com. of Ed. Vol 3. p 86.)

COETLOGON, [Charles Edward de] *A. M. Chaplain to the Mayoralty.*
Sermons on the 51 pfalm. 8. Vol. 1. 2. 17,. Caution againft the abominations of the church of Rome. 1779. 8. (6 d.) (feveral fingle fermons.)

COGAN, [E ...]
Addrefs to the diffenters on claffical litterature. 1789. 8. (1 fh.)

COGAN, [Thomas] *M. D. Phyfician in the ftates of the United Provinces.*
Differt. De pathematum animi vi et modo agendi. Lugd. Bat. 1757. 4. Memoirs of the fociety inftituted at Amfterdam in favour of drowned perfons

for

for the Y. 1761-1771. 1775. 8. (2 ſh.) Philoſophical ſurvey of the Creation. 17.. Hiſtory of *John Buncle*, junior. 17..

COKE, [Edward] *Sir.*
The firſt part of the inſtitutes of the laws of England, or a commentary upon *Littleton.* Ed. 13. with notes by *Francis Hargrave* and by *Charles Butler.* — fol. 1788. (4 L.. 4 ſh.)

COLE, [Charles Nalſon] *Esq.*
The works of *Soame Jenyns.* Esq. with his life. Vol. 1-4. 1790.

—— [Mary] *Mrs. Cook to the Earl of Drogheda.*
The lady's complete guide; or cookery and confectionary in all their branches—. 1789. 8. (6 ſh)

—— [William] *F. A. S: Vicar of Burnham in Buckinghamſhire.*
born 1714. died d. 16 Dec. 1782.

—— [W....] *A. M: Fellow of King's College, Cambridge.*
Key to the pſalms —. 1788. 8. (2 ſh.) Exalted affection, or, Sophia Pringle. a poem. 1789. 8. (1 ſh.)

—— [William]
Obſervations — on the nature and properties of light and on the theory of Comets. 1777. 8. (2 ſh.) Oratio de ridiculo habita Cantabrigiae —. 1780. 4. (1 ſh.)

COLEBROOK, [Joſiah]
born.... died d. 16 Aug. 1775.

COLEBROOKE, [Henrietta] *Miſſ.*
Thoughts of *Jean Jacques Rouſſeau.* Vol. 1. 2. 1788. 8. (7 ſh. 6 d.)

COLEMAN, [Charles] *Esq.*
Satirical peerage of England —. 1784. 4. (2 ſh. 6 d.)

COLEMANN, [William] *Surgeon at Sandwich in Kent.*
Two caſes of ſcurvy attended with ſome uncommon circumſtances. (London M. J. Vol. 2. p. 117. überſ. Samml. f. A. Th. 7. S. 205.) Caſe of worms diſcharged through a wound of the groin. (ibid. Vol. 7. P. 3.)

COLERIDGE, [John] *Vicar and Schoolmaſter at Ottery St. Mary, Devon.*
Miſcellaneous diſſertations ariſing from the XVII & XVIII Chapt. of the book of judges. 1768. 8. (5 ſh.

(5 ſh. 6 d.) A critical latin grammar. 1772. 12. (3 ſh.) Faſt-fermon on government not originally proceeding from human agency but divine inſtitution. 1777. 4. (1 ſh)

COLEY, [William] *Surgeon.*
Account of the late epidemic ague, as it appeared in the Neighbourhood of Bridgnorth, in. Shropſhire in 1784. 1784. 8. (1 ſh.)

COLLES,.[Richard] *Esq. Barriſter at Law.*
Reports of cafes, upon appeals and writs of error in the high court of Parliament from the Y. 1697 to the Y. 1709 —. 1790. 8. (9 ſh. 6 d.)

COLLET, [John] *M. D. Phyſician at Newbury, Berkſhire.*
born.... died d. 12 May 1786.

COLLIER, [George] *Sir.*
Selima and Azor, a dramatic romance. 1776. 8.

—— [Joel] *Organiſt.*
Muſical travels through England. 1774. 8. (1 ſh.)

COLLIGNON, [Charles] *M D: Profeſſor of Anatomy at Cambridge: F. R. S.*
born in London d. 30 Jan. 1725. died d. 1 Oct. 1785.

COLLINGWOOD, [Thomas] *Surgeon at Alnwick.*
Account of an uncommon difcharge, from an opening made into a large tumour in the under part of the belly and back. (*Duncan's* M. C. Vol. 9. p. 344.) Obſervations on the peruvian bark. (Ibid. Vol. 10. p. 265.)

COLLINS, [Walſingham] *Merchant at London.*
Addreſs — with propoſals for the regulation of bankers and brokers. 1778. 8. (ſh .6 d)

—— [William] *D. D: F. R. S Edin. Miniſter of Inveresk and Chaplain in Ordinary to his Majeſty.*
born.... died 17..

COLLINSON, [John]
Beauties of britiſh antiquity —. 1779. 8. (6 ſh.)

COLLS, [John]
The poet, a poem. 1785. 4. (1 ſh.)

COLLYER, [Joſeph]
born.... died d. 20 Febr. 1776.

COL.

COLMAN, [George] *Esq. Manager of the Theatres of Coventgarden and the Haymarket.*
born d. 28 Apr. 1733.
The jealous wife; a Comedy. 1761. 8. (1 sh. 6d.) The Mufical lady; a farce. 1762. 8. A Midfummer's night dream, altered. 1763. 8. Philafter, a tragedy; altered from *Beaumont* and *Fletcher.* 1763. 8. The Deuce is in him; a farce 1763. 8. A fairy tale. 1764. 8. The comedies of *Terence*, translated. 1765. 4. (1 L. 1 sh.) Ed. 2. Vol. 1. 2. 1768. (12 sh.) The clandeftine marriage, a Comedy. 1766. 8. (1 sh 6d.) The englifh merchant, a Comedy. 1767. 8. (1 sh. 6d.) The hiftory of King Lear; altered from *Shakespeare.* 1768. 8. T. Harris diffected. 1768. 4. (1 sh. 6d.) The Oxonian in Town, a Comedy. 1769. 8. (1 sh.) Man and wife, or the *Shakespeare* Jubilee; a Comedy. 1769. 8. (1 sh. 6d.) The Portrait. 1770. 8. The fairy Prince. 1771. 8. Comus. 1772. 8. Occafional prelude on opening Covent Garden Theater Sept. 1772. 1776. 8. (6d.) Achilles in petticoats; an Opera. 1774. 8. The man of bufinefs, a Comedy. 1774. 8. (1 sh. 6d.) Epicaene, or the filent woman, altered a Comedy. 1776. 8. (1 sh.) The fpleen or Islington Spa; a comic piece. 1776. 8. (1 sh) New brooms, occafional prelude. 1776. 8. (1 sh.) Dramatic Works. Vol. 1-4. 1777. 8. (1 L. 1 sh) Bonduca, a Tragedy. 1778. The manager in diftrefs. Prelude. 1780. Translation of *Horace's* Art of poetry. 1783. 4. (7 sh. 6d.) Connoiffeur, a periodical paper. Vol. 1-4. 17.. Mifcellaneous Works. Vol 1-3. 1787. Profe on feveral occafions, accompanied with fome pieces in verfe. Vol. 1-3. 1787. 8. (12 sh.)

COLMANN, [George] *Jun.* (Son of the preceding.)
Two to one, a Comedy. 1784. Turk and no Turk, a Comedy. 1785. Inkle and Yarico, an Opera. 1787. 8. (1 sh. 6d.) The manager in diftrefs; a prelude. 1780. 8. (1 sh.) Ways and means; or, a trip to Dover. 1788. 8. (1 sh. 6d.)

COLTMAN, [John]
Every Man's monitor; or the univerfal counfellor, in profe and verfe, being a collection of felect fentences,

F 3

tences, choice maxims and divine precepts. 1781. 8.
(2 fh. 6 d.)

COMBE, [Charles] F. R. S: F. A. S.
Nummorum veterum populorum et urbium in Mu-
feo Guil. Hunteri Defcriptio. 1782. 4. (2 L. 15 fh.)
Obfervations on an inedited coin in the collection
of D. Hunter. (Arch. Vol. 5. p. 280.)

COMBER, [Thomas] LL. D. *Rector of Buckworth and
Morborne, Huntingdonfhire and Chaplain to the
Countefs Dowager of Balcarras.*
Reflections on Dr. *Middleton's* examination of (*Thom.
Sherlok's*) Bifhop's of London difcourfes on prophecy, 1750. 8. (1 fh. 6 d.) Vindication of the great
revolution in England 1688. and of the characters
of King *William* and Queen *Mary* — 1758. 8.
(1 fh. 6 d.) Correfpondance on the (*Young's*) farmer's letters to the people of England. 1770. 8.
(2 fh.) Real improvements in Agriculture. 1772.
8. (1 fh. 6 d.) Translation of *Theodoret's* treatife
of laws. 1776. 8. (2 fh.) °*Chriftopher Wandesforde's* book of inftruction. 1777. 8. (1 fh. 6 d.)
The *part fecond* under the title: Memoirs of the life
and death of the Lord *Wandesforde.* 1778. 8. (2 fh.
6 d.)

CONSETT, [Matthew]
Tour through Sweden, Swedifh-Lapland, Finland
and Denmark in a feries of letters. 1789. 4. (10 fh.
6 d.) überf. Leipzig. 1790. 8.

CONWAY, [Henry Seymour] *Governor of the Island
of Jerfey and privy Counfellor.* (Brother to the
Earl of Hertford.)
The depopulated vale, a poem. 1774. 4. (2 fh.)
Falfe appearances, a Comedy, altered from the
french. 1789. 8. (1 fh. 6 d.) Speech — on moving in the houfe of commons May 5. 1780. 8.
(1 fh. 6 d.) Defcription of a druidical monument
in the Island of Jerfey. (Arch. Vol. 8. p. 386.)

COOK, [.....] *Taylor.*
A fure guide againft wafte in drefs; or the woollen
Draper's Man Mercer's and taylor's affiftant —.
1787. 8. (5 fh.)

COOK, [Adam Mofes Emanuel]
The King cannot err, a Comedy. 1762. 8. The heroic converted, or the maid of bath married. 1771. 8.
—— [James] *Captain, Commander of the ship, the Endeavour.* F. R. S.
born at Whitby in Yorkſhire 1728. died at O·Whyhe d. 14 Febr. 1779.
—— [John] *M. D. Phyſician at Hamilton, Lanerk.*
On difeafes of children. 1769. 8. (1 ſh.) Voyage and travels through the Ruſſian empire, Tartary and part of the kingdom of Perſia. Vol. 1. 2. 1770. 8. (12 ſh.) Treatife of poifons, vegetable, animal and mineral with their cure. 1770. 8. (1 ſh.) Natural hiſtory of Lac, Amber and Myrrh. 1770. 8. (6 d)
—— [R....] *Surgeon at Barking, in Effex.*
Account of a — cure of a dropfy of the belly, after the patient had been tapped fixteen times. London M. J. Vol. VII. P. 1. überſ. Samml. f. A. Th. XI. S. 720.) Account of a fracture of the ſcull, by a piſtol-ball, that entered the cranium at the right temple and was fucceffully extracted. (London M J. Vol. 3. p. 72.)

COOKE, [James] *M. A*
Drill husbandry perfected —. 1784. 12. (1 ſh)
—— [John] *M A. Chaplain of Chriſt church, Oxford, and Rector of Wentnor, Salop.*
The preacher's affiftant — containing a feries of the texts of fermons and difcourfes publifhed either fingles or in volumes, by divines of the church of England and by the diffenting clergy fince the reſtoration to the prefent time. — Vol 1. 2. 1783. 8. (16 ſh.) — and *John Maule's* Account of the royal hofpital for feamen at Greenwich. 1789. 4. (7 ſh. 6 d.)
—— [John] *Surgeon at Gloucefter.*
Account of the difcovery of the corpfe, of one of the abbots of Gloucefter. (Arch. Vol. 9. p. 10.)
—— [William] *Greek Profeffor of King's College, Cambridge, Rector of Hempfted Norfolk.*
Ariſtoteles De poetica, cum verfione et notis. 1785. 8. (3 ſh. 6 d.) Praelectio ad actum publicum habita Cantabrigiae. 1787. 4. (1 ſh.) Poetical effays on

on several occasions. 1775. 4. (5 sh.) The Revelations, translated and explained. 1789. 8. (6 sh.) (several single sermons.)

COOKE, [William] *M. A: Rector of Oldbury and Didmarton, Gloucestershire, Vicar of Enford, Wiltshire and Chaplain to the Earl of Suffolk.*
born.... died d. 25 Febr. 1780.

—— [William] *A. B. Fellow of new College, Oxford and Chaplain to the Marquis of Tweedale.*
The conquest of Quebec, a poem. 1769. 4. (1 Sh. 6 d.) The Way to the temple of true honour and fame by the paths of heroic virtue —. Vol. 1 - 4. 1773. 12. (12 sh.) The capricious lady, a Comedy, altered from *Beaumont* and *Fletcher*. 1783. 8.

—— [William] *Esq. of Lincoln's Inn.*
Compendious system of the bankrupt law. 1786. 8. (8 sh.) Ed. 2. Vol. 1. 2. 1788. 8. (10 sh.)

—— [William] *Esq. of the Middle temple.*
The Elements of dramatic criticism —. 1775. 8. (4 sh.) übers. (von J. Andr. *Engelbrecht* u. Alb. *Wittenberg*) Lübeck. 1777. 8.

COOKSON, [James] *Clerk. A. B. Rector of Colemere and Prior's Deane, Hants.*
Thoughts on polygamy —. 1782. 8. (6 Sh.)

—— [John] *M. B.*
born 1700. died at Wakefield, Yorkshire, d. 4 May 1779.

COOLEY, [William] *Surgeon in Bridgnorth, Shropshire.*
Account of the late epidemic ague in the Y. 1784. with observations on a dysentery that prevailed at the same time. 1785. 8. (1 Sh.)

COOMBE, [Thomas] *D. D.*
The peasant of Auburn, or the emigrant, a poem. 1783. 4. (1 Sh.) (several single sermons.)

—— [Thomas] *Esq.*
Meteorological observations made at Philadelphia. (Tr. of A. S. Vol. 1. p. 70.)

COOPER, [Allen] *Esq. Master of the Atlas East-India Men.*
Account of the effects of lightning on board the Atlas. (Phil. Transact. 1779. p. 160.)

—— [Samuel] *D. D. Minister of Great-Yarmouth.*
Definitions and axioms relative to charity, charitable

table inſtitutions and the poor's laws. 1764. 8.
(2 ſh.) Explanations of ſome difficult textes in the
New Teſtament. 1771. (3 Sh.) Addreſſ to perſons after confirmation. 1783. 8. (1 Sh.) Conſo-
lation to the mourner and inſtruction both to Youth
and old age, from the early death of the righteous.
1786. 8. (2 Sh. 6 d.) The one great argument for
the truth of chriſtianity from a ſingle prophecy,
evinced in a new explanation of the 70 Chapt. of
Iſaiah. 1786. 8. (3 Sh. 6 d.) (ſeveral ſingle ſermons.)

COOPER, [Thomas] *Esq.*
Letters on the ſlave trade. 1787. 8.
—— [William] *D. D: F. R. S: Archdeacon of York,*
born.... died d. 10 Jul. 1786.
—— [William] *M. D: Phyſician at London.*
born.... died d. 4 May 1779.
—— [William]
Poems. 1782. 4.

COOTE, [Charles] *A. M.*
Elements of the grammar of the engliſh language.
1788. 8. (5 Sh.)

COPE, [J... A...] *M. D.*
Eſſay on the virtues and properties of the Ginſeng-
tea. 1786. 8. (1 Sh.)

COPLAND, [Samuel] *D. D. Miniſter of the Goſpel
at Fintray.*
Eſſay on the chriſtian character —. 1785. 8. (3 Sh.)

CORBET, [John]
Conciſe ſyſtem of engliſh grammar. 1784. 12.

CORDINER, [Charles] *Miniſter at Bamff in Scotland.*
Antiquities and Scenery of the North of Scotland.
1780. 4. (12 Sh. 6 d.) Remarkable ruins and romantic proſpects in the North of Scotland. Number 1 - 6. 1786. 4. (1 L. 10 Sh.) überſ. *Ebeling's*
Neue Samml. von Reiſebeſchreib. Th. 5. S. 95.

CORDWELL, [J..]
New ſyſtem of phyſic founded on the principles of
nature and not on the materia medica. 1768. 8.
(1 Sh.) *Second tract. 1770. 8. (1 Sh. 6 d.) °Re-
marks on *Warner's* — account of the gout —.
1769. 8. (1 Sh.)

CORNISH, [James] *Surgeon at Totneſſ, Devonſhire.*
Of the torpidity of ſwallows and martins. (Phil.
Transact. 1775. p. 343.)

CORNISH, [Joseph] *Paſtor to the church of Proteſtant Diſſenters at Colyton, Devon.*
The life of Mr. *Thom. Firmin*, Citizen of London. 1780. 8. (2 Sh.) On importance of claſſical learning with remarks on *Knox's* liberal education. 1783. 8. (1 Sh. 6 d.)

CORNWALLIS, [Charles] *Earl, Lieutenant-General, Knight of the Garter and privy counſellor.*
Anſwer to *Henry Clinton's* narrative —. 1783. 8. (3 Sh. 6 d.)

CORNWELL, [B....] *M. D.*
The domeſtic phyſician or guardian of health. 1784. 8. (7 Sh 6 d.) überſ. Erfurt. 1788. 8.

CORP, [William] *M. D.: Phyſician to the pauper charity of Bath.*
Eſſay on the jaundice in which the property of uſing the Bath waters in that diſeaſe — is conſidered. 1785. 8. (1 Sh. 6 d.)

COSENS, [....] *Miniſter of Teddington, Middleſex; Chaplain to the Earl of Denbigh.*
The oeconomy of beauty; in a ſeries of fables. 1777. 4. (10 Sh. 6 d.)

COSTARD, [George] *M. A. Vicar of Twickenham, Middleſex.*
born 1710. died 1782.

COSTIGAN, [Arthur William] *Eſq. late Captain of the Iriſh brigade in the ſervice of Spain.*
Sketches of ſociety and manners in Portugal. Vol. 1. 2. 1788. 8. (10 Sh. 6 d.) überſ. Th. 1. 2. Leipz. 1789. 8.

COTTER, [Georg Sackville] *A. M. of Trinity College, Cambridge.*
Poems. Vol. 1. 2. 1788. 8. (7 Sh.)

COTTON, [....] *Captain of his Majeſty's ſhip Pallas.*
Extracts relative to the britiſh forts in Africa — with obſervations of *John Roberts* —. 1778. 8. (1 Sh.)

—— [Charles] *M D.* (Proprietor of a private madhouſe near St. Alban's.)
born.... died d. 2 Aug. 1788.

COVEY, [John] *Apothecary at Baſingſtoke in Hampſhire.*
Obſervations and facts on the inoculation of the ſmallpox (London M. J. Vol 7. P. 2.) Further obſervations on the inoculation of the ſmallpox. (Lon-

(London M. J. Vol. 8. P. 1.) überſ. Samml. f. A. Th. 12. S. 57. On the good effects of Mercury in a difeaſe apparently of the lymphatic ſyſtem attended with nervous ſymptoms. (London M. J. Vol. VIII. P. 2. überſ. Samml. f. A. Th. 12. S. 542.)

COURCY, [Richard de] *Vicar of St. Alkmond's, Shrewsbury.*
Two ſermons: National troubles a proper ground for national humiliation. 1776. 8. (1 ſh.) The rejoinder —. P. I. 1777. 8. (3 ſh.) Two ſerm ns: The Lord's controverſy with a guilty nation. 1778. 8. (1 ſh.) Letter of ſolemn counſel from a miniſter of the goſpel to a perſon in a declining ſtate of health. 1778. 8. (6 d.)

COURTENAY, [John] *Member of Parliament.*
Poetical review of the literary and moral character of D. Sam. Johnſon. 1786. 4. (2 ſh.) Philoſophical reflections on the late revolution in France and the conduct of the diſſenters in England. 1790. 8. (2 ſh.) Ed. 3. with additions. 1790. 8. (2 ſh.)

COWLEY, [H....] *Mrs.*
°The Runaway; a Comedy. 1776. 8. (1 ſh. 6 d.) Who's the dupe? a farce. 1779. 8. (1 ſh.) Albina, counteſſ Raimond; a Tragedy. 1779. 8. (1 ſh. 6 d.) The maid of Aragon; a Tale. 1780. 4. (2 ſh. 6 d.) The ſchool for eloquence. 1780. The world as it goes, or a trip to Montpelier, a Comedy. 1781. Second thoughts are beſt; a Comedy. 1781. The Bell's ſtratagem; a Comedy. 1782. 8. (1 ſh. 6 d.) Which is the man? a Comedy. 1783. 8. (1 ſh. 6 d.) A bold ſtroke for a husband, a Comedy. 1784. 8. (1 ſh. 6 d.) More ways than one; a Comedy. 1784. 8. (1 ſh. 6 d.) The ſchool for grey beards, or the mourning bride, a Comedy. 1786. 8. (1 ſh. 6 d.) Scottiſh village or pitcairne green, a poem. 1786. 4. (2 ſh.) The fate of Sparta, or, the rival kings, a Tragedy. 1788. 8. (1 ſh. 6 d.)

COWLING, [Richard] *M. D. Surgeon to the 85 Regiment of footh.*
Diſſ. De rhevmatiſmo. Edinb. 1775. 8. Caſe of hemiplegia, ſucceeded by mania. (London M. J. Vol. 2. p. 198. überſ. Samml. f. A. Th. 7. S. 485.

COWPER, [Henry] *Eſq. Barriſter at law, of the Middle-Temple.*

Reports

Reports of cafes adjudged in the King's bench from 1774-1778. fol. 1788. (1 L. 16 fh.)

COWPER, [Spencer] *D D. Dean of Durham.* born..... died d. 25 March. 1774.

—— [William] *of the Inner - Temple.* Poems Vol. 1. 1782. Vol 2. the tafk a poem with an epiftle to Jof. Hill; Tirocinian or a review of fchools; and the hiftory of John Gilpin. 1785. 8. (8 Sh.)

COX, [A... M...] Jofeph: a poem. 1783. 12. (3 Sh.)

—— [Jofeph Malon] *M. D. at Fifhponds, near Briftol.* Hiltory of a cafe of inianity, cured by the ufe of the Digitalis purpurea. (*Duncan's* M. C. Dec. II. Vol 4. p. 261.)

—— [N. ...] *Efq.* The fowler, containing the methods of taking land and water fowl. 1788. (1 Sh. 6 d.)

COXE, [Samuel Compton] *of Lincoln's Inn.* William Peere William's collection of reports of cafes argued and determined in the high court of chancery —. Ed. IV. 1787. 8. (1 L. 11 Sh. 6 d.)

—— [William] *M A: F R S: F. A. S: Rector of Bemerton and Chaplain to the Duke of Marlborough.* Sketches of the natural civil and political ftate of Swifferland. 1779. 8. (6 Sh.) überf. Zürich. 1781. 8. Travels in Switzerland. Vol. 1-3. 1789. 8. (1 L. 4 Sh.) Account of the Ruffian difcoveries between Afia and America. 1780. 4. (18 Sh.) überf. Frankf. u. Leipz. 1783. 8 Supplement: Comparative view of the ruffian difcoveries, with thofe made by Capt. Cook and Clerke. 1787. 4. (1 Sh. 6 d.) Account of the prifons and hofpitals in Ruffia, Sweden and Denmark. 1781. 8. (1 Sh. 6 d.) Travels into Poland, Ruffia, Sweden and Denmark — with cartes and engravings Vol. 1. 2. 1784. 4. (2 L. 2 Sh.) überf. von *J. Pezzl.* Th. 1. 2. Zürich. 1785. 4. Letter to *Mich. Price* upon his difcourfe on the love of our country. 1790. 8. (1 Sh)

COYTE, [William B...] *M. B. Phyfician at Ipswich, Suffolk.* The confequences of a crown-piece fwallowed by an epileptic man. (Med. Transact. Vol. 3. p. 30.)

COZENS,

COZENS, [Alexander]
Principles of beauty relative to the human mind. 1778. fol. (1 L. 5 Sh.) . A new method of aſſiſting the invention in drawing original compoſitions of Landſcape. 1785.

CRABBE, [George] *Chaplain to the late Duke of Rutland.*
*The library, a poem. 1781. 4. (2 Sh.) The village, a poem. 1783. 4. (2 Sh. 6 d) °The ſkull, a tale. 1783. 4. (2 Sh) The news-paper, a poem. 1785. 4. (2 Sh.) Sermon on the death of the Duke of *Rutland*. 1788. 4 (1 Sh.)

CRADDOCK, [Joſeph] *M. A: F. R. S.*
°Letters from Snowdon deſcriptive of a tour through the northern counties of Wales —. 1770. 8. °Zobeide, a Tragedy. 1771. 8. (1 Sh. 6 d.) °Village memoirs—. 1775. 8. (3 Sh) *Account of ſome of the romantic parts of North-Wales. 1777. 8. (2 Sh. 6 d.)

CRAIG, [William] *D. D. Miniſter of St. Andrew's church, Glasgow.*
born d. Febr. 1709. died 1783.

CRAKELT, [William] *M. A. Rector of Nurſted and Ifield in Kent.*
John Entick's new ſpelling dictionary —. 1785. 12. (2 Sh.) Ed... 1788. 4. (4 Sh.)

CRAMMOND, [Hercules] *M. D.*
Outlines of human life. 1787. 8. (3 Sh.)

CRANE, [John] *Phyſician at Dorcheſter.*
Account of the nature, properties and medicinal uſes of the mineral water at Nottington, near Weymouth, .Dorſet. 1789. 8. (1 Sh.)

—— [Thomas] *Miniſter of St. Olave, Cheſter; Chaplain to Earl Verney.*
The common engliſh translation of the 109 pſalm — corrected —. 1772. 4. (6 d.) The common engliſh translation of the 45 pſalm — corrected 1774. 8. (1 Sh.) The poetic works of *William Smith*, D. D. late Dean of Cheſter, with his life and writings. 1788. 8. (1 Sh. 6 d.)

CRAVEN, [Elizabeth] *Baroneſſ* (Daughter of the Earl Aug. Berkeley. At preſent by the court of Anſpach.)
The ſleep-walker. 1778. 8. The family picture. 17.. Modern anecdote, or the hiſtory of the Baron

Baron Kinkvervankotsdarsprakengotchderns. 17.. The silver tankard. 1781. °The miniature picture; a Comedy. 1781. 8. (1 Sh. 6 d.) Nuriad, Comedie en 3 Actes. Anspac. 1787. Journey through the Crimea to Constantinople. 1789. 4. (18 Sh.) übers. Leipz. 1789. 8.

CRAVEN, [William] *B. D. Professor of Arabic at Cambridge.*
Sermons on the evidence of a future state of rewards and punishments —. 1776. 8. (1 Sh. 6 d.) Ed. 2. 1783. 8. (2 Sh. 6 d.)

CRAUFURD, [C...] *Captain of the Queen's regiment of Dragoon guards.*

—— [R...] *Capt. of the 101 Regt.*
Translation of *J. G. Tielke's* account of events of the war between the Prussians, Austrians and Russians from 1756-1763. Vol. 1. 2. 1788. 8. (1 L. 10 Sh.)

—— [George] *Esq.*.
On the actual resources for establishing the finances of Great-Britain. 1785. 8. (2 Sh 6 d.) Enquiry into the situation of the East-India company. 1789. (3 Sh.)

CRAWFORD, [Adair] *M. D: F. R. S. at Edinburgh and London, Member of the philos. Soc. of Dublin and Philadelphia.*
Experiments and observations on animal heath and the inflammation of combustible bodies. 1779. 8. (2 Sh. 6 d.) Ed. 2. 1788. 8. (7 Sh) übers. mit *W. Morgan's* Erinnerungen wider diese Theory. Leipz. 1785. 8. übers. von *C. Crell.* Leipz. 1789. 8. *Lichtenberg's* u. *Forster's* Göttingisches Magazin. Jahrg. I. St. 5. Experiments on the power that animals, when placed in certain circumstances, possess of producing cold. (Phil. Transact. 1781. p. 479.)

—— [Charles] *Esq. Fellow commoner of Queen's College, Cambridge. M. A.*
Dissertation on the phaedon of Plato; or, dialogue of the immortality of the Soul —. 1773. 8. (4 Sh. 6 d.) Sophronia and Hilario; an Elegy. 1774. 4. (1 Sh. 6 d.) The revolution, a poem. Canto I. 1776. 4. (1 Sh. 6 d.) Richmond-Hill; a poem. 1777. 4. (1 Sh.) The Christian: a poem. 1781.

1781. 8. (2 Sh.) Liberty, a pindaric ode. 1789. 4. (1 Sh.)

CRAWFORD, [James] *Esq.*
born.... died at Edinburgh d. 18 Apr. 1783.

—— [John] *Surgeon.*
On the nature, caufe and cure of a difeafe incident to the liver —. 1772. 8. (2 Sh) The human mufcles claffed as they appear in diffection —. 1785. 4. (2 Sh.)

—— [William] *M. A. one of the Chaplains of the firft Tyrone regiment.*
Remarks on the Earl of *Chefterfield's* letters to his fon. 1776. 12. (2 Sh) Hiftory of Ireland; from the earlieft period to the prefent time. Vol. 1. 2. 1783. 8. (12 Sh.)

CREECH, [....]
* Account of the trial of *William Brodie* and *James Smith* — for breaking into and robbing the general excife office of Scotland. 1788. 4. (3 Sh. 6 d.)

CRESWICK, [....] *Teacher of Elocution.*
The female reader; or mifcellaneous pieces in Profe and verfe; felected from the beft writers — for the improvement of young women with a preface, containing fome hints on female education. 1790. 12. (3 Sh.

CRIBB, [William] *Surgeon in high Holborn.*
On the ufe of injections in the gonorrhoea. 1773. 8. (1 Sh. 6 d) Cafe of a luxation of the thigh bone. (London M. J. Vol. 5. p. 412)

—— [William] *Surgeon at Bifhops Storsford in Hertfordfhire.*
Cafe of a ftrangulated hernia fucceffully treated with remarks on the ufe of cold applications in the reduction of Herniae. (London M. J. Vol. VI. p. 259.)

CRICHTON, [Alexander] *M. D.*
Account of the effects of the Aftragalus Exfcapus *Linn.* in the cure of the venereal difeafe. tranflated from the German. (London M. J. Vol. IX. Part. 4.) On the medicinal effects of the lichen Islandicus and Arnica montana. (London M. J. Vol. X. Part. 3.)

CROCKER,

CROCKER, [Abraham] *Schoolmaster at Ilminster.*
Introduction to english grammar and rhetorik.
1772. 12. Instructions for young people in the
public worship of god. 1776. 12. (3 d.) The catechism of the church of England, with notes.
1780. 12. (2 Sh. 6 d.)

CROFT, [Georg] *D. D. Vicar of Arncliff, Master of
Brewood school and Chaplain to the Earl of Elgin.*
General obfervations concerning education. 1776.
8. (6 d.) A plan for education delineated and vindicated —. 1784. 8. (1 Sh. 6 d.) Eight fermons
preached before the univerfity of Oxford. 1786.
8. (4 Sh.) Sermon; the teft laws defended. 1790.
(1 Sh.)

—— [Herbert]
"Love and madnefs; a ftory. 1780. 8. (3 Sh. 6 d.)
* The will of King Alfred. 1788. 4. (3 Sh, 6 d.)

—— [John] F. A. S.
On the wines of Portugal — on the nature and
ufe of wines in general, or pertaining to luxury
and diet. 1787. 8. (1 Sh.)

—— [Richard] *Surgeon at Tutbury, in Staffordshire.*
Account of a fucceffful method of reducing the
funis in cafes in which it comes down before the
head of the foetus. (London M. J. Vol. VII. P. 1.
überf. Journal für Geburtshelfer. St. 1.)

CROMPTON, [Georg] *Esq. of the Inner Temple.*
Practice common placed; or the rules and cafes of
practice in the courts of King's bench and common
pleas —. Vol. 1. 2. 1780. 8. (16 Sh.) Ed. 2. 1783.
8. (16 Sh.)

CROOKSHANK, [John] *Commander of his Majesty's ship the Lark.*
Conduct and treatment — relating to his attempt
to take the gloriofo, a Spanifh fhip of war 1747 —
1759. 8. Reply to Admiral *Knowles* pamphlet.
1759. 8. (6 d.) Letter to *Rob. Kirke.* 1772. 8.
(6 d.)

CROSS, [John] *Clerk.*
Cafh tables at five pounds and XV per cent, on
the duties of excife and malt —. 1779. 8. (1 Sh.)

CROSSE, [Thomas] *Esq.*
The power of friendfhip, a poetical epiftle. 1785.
4. (1 Sh.)

CROWE,

CROWE, [C....] *Esq. of Kipling.*
Method of making excellent butter from the milk of cows fed upon turnips. (*Hunter's* G. E. Vol. 5. p. 209.)
— — [William] *LL. B. of New-College, Oxford.*
Sermon before the University of Oxford. 1781. 4. (1 sh.), °Lewesdon Hill, a poem. 1788. 4. (2 sh. (6 d.) Oratio. 1788. 4. (1 sh.)

CRUDEN, [Alexander] *M. A.* born at Aberdeen 1701. died d. 1 Nov. 1770.
— — [John] *Esq. President of the assembly of the united loyalists.*
Address to the loyal part of the british empire and the friends of monarchy. 1784. 8.

CRUIKSHANK, [William]
Anatomy of the absorbing vessels of the human body. 1786. 4. (12 sh.) Ed. 2. 1790. 4. überf. von *C. F. Ludwig.* Th. 1. 2. Leipz. 1789. 4.

CRUISE, [William] *Esq. of Lincolns-Inn.*
°Essay on the nature and operation of fines. 1783. 8. (3 sh. 6 d.) On the nature and operation of common recoveries. 1783. 8. (2 sh. 6 d.)

CRUSO, [John] *Apothecary.*
Treasury of easy medicines, translated of latin. 1771. 8. (3 sh.)

CRUTTWELL, [Clement]
The Holy Bible — with notes by *Thom. Wilson* and various renderings —. Vol. 1-3. 1785. 4. (4 L. 14 sh. 6 d.) A concordance of parallels, collected from bibles and commentaries —. 1790. 4.
— — [C....] *Surgeon at Bath.*
Advice to lying in Women, on the custom of drawing the breasts. Ed. II. 1779. 4. (1 sh.)

CRUWYS, [H... S...]
Enquiries into the Archetype of the LXX version, its authenticity and different editions. 1774. 8. (1 sh. 6 d.)

CULLEN, [Charles] (Son to D. *Will. Cullen.*)
Translation of *Luyart's* chemical analysis of Wolfram, with a translation of *Sheele's* analysis of the Tungsten —. 1785. 8. (1 sh. 6 d.) *F. S. Clavigero* History of Mexico — translated. Vol. 1. 2. 1787. 4. (2 L. 2 Sh.)

CULLEN, [Edmund] *M. D. Fellow of the college of Physicians at Dublin.*
T. Bergmann's phyſical and chemical eſſays — tranſlated, with notes. Vol. 1. 2. 1785 8. (13 Sh.)
—— [William] *M. D. Profeſſor of the practice of phyſic in the Univerſity of Edinburg.* born 1709. died d. 5 Febr. 1790.
CULLEY, [George] *Farmer at Fenton, Northumberland.* Obſervations on live ſtock. 1786. 8. (3 Sh.)
CULLUM, [John] *Sir: Baronet: F. R. S: F. A. S.* born 1733. died at London d. 9 Oct. 1785.
—— [Thomas Gery] *Surgeon at St. Edmundsbury.*
An encyſted watery tumour, adhering to the poſterior part of the bladder and to the whole length of the rectum, which brought on a fatal ſuppreſſion of urine. (Med Obſ. Vol. 6. p. 91.) Account of an unuſual exfoliation of the cranium. (Mem. of M. S. of L. Vol. 1. p. 194.)
CUMBERLAND, [Richard] *Solicitor and Clerk of the reports in the trade and plantation Office.*
The baniſhment of *Cicero*, a Tragedy, 1761. 4. (2 Sh. 6 d.) The ſummers tale, a comedy. 1765. 8. (1 Sh. 6 d.). *Amelia, a muſical entertainment. 1768. 8. (1 Sh.) Ed. 2. 1771. 8. (1 Sh.) ° The Brothers, a Comedy. 1769. 8. (1 Sh. 6 d.) Timon of Athens, a Tragedy. 1771. 8. (1 Sh. 6 d.) *The Weſt-Indian, a Comedy. 1771. 8. (1 Sh. 6 d.) überſ. (von *Joh. Joach. Bode*) 1772. 8. °The faſhionable lover, a Comedy. 1772. 8. (1 Sh 6 d.) überſ. durch *K. C. H. Roſt*, unter dem Titel: Miſs *Obre*, oder die gerettete Unſchuld. Leipz. 1774. 8. *The note of Hand, or a trip to new market. 1774. 8. (1 Sh.) The choleric man; a Comedy. 1775. 8. (1 Sh. 6 d.) überſ. Mannheim. 1785 8. Odes. 1775. 4. (1 Sh.) °The princeſs of Parma, a Tragedy. 1778. The battle of Haſtings; a Tragedy. 1778. 8. (1 Sh. 6 d.) Calypſo, a new masque. 1779. 8. (1 Sh. 6 d) Anecdotes of eminent printers in Spain during the XVI and XVII Centuries. Vol. 1. 2. 1782. 8. (5 Sh.) The myſterious huſband, a Tragedy. 1783 8. (1 Sh 6 d.) Letter to Richard Lord Biſhop of Landaff on the ſubject of his Lordſhip's letter to the late Archbiſhop of Canterbury. 1783. 8. (1 Sh. 6 d.) The carmelite, a

Trage-

Tragedy. 1784. 8. (1 Sh. 6 d.) The natural fon, a Comedy. 1785. 8. (1 Sh. 6 d.) überf. Leipzig. 1785. 8. Character of the late Lord *Sackville*. 1785. 8. (6 Sh.) ° The obferver. 1785. 8. (6 Sh. , Ed. 2. Vol. 1 - 5. 1786 - 1790. 8. (17 Sh. 2 d.) Catalogue of the feveral paintings in the kings of fpains palace at Madrid with account of the pictures in the Buen - Retiro. 1787. 12. (2 Sh. 6 d.) ° Arundel. Vol. 1. 2. 1789. 8. (5 Sh.) The impoftors, a Comedy. 1789. 8. (1 Sh. 6 d.)

CUMYNS, [Eliza] *of Brompton*.
Introduction to geography and aftronomy for the ufe of young ladies. 1787. 4. (5 Sh.)

CUNNINGHAM, [John] born at Dublin 1729. died at Newcaftle d. 18 Sept. 1773.

—— [John]
Inquiry into the Copernican fyftem, refpecting the motions of the heavenly bodies. 1789. 8. (1 Sh. 6 d.)

—— [T...] *Esq. Barrifter at law. F. A. S.*
The practice of a juftice of peace: containing the ftatutes which give jurisdiction to that magiftrate. Vol. 1. 2. 1762. 8. (14 Sh.) A new and compleat law dictionary, or, general abridgment of the law —. Vol. 1. 2. fol. 1767. (3 L. 12 Sh.) Hiftory of the cuftoms, aids, fubfidies, national debts and taxes of England from William the conqueror to the Y. 1778. Ed. III. 1778. 8. (6 Sh.) Hiftorical account of the rights of election of the feveral counties, cities and boroughs of Great Britain —. P. 1. 2. 1783. 8. (5 Sh.) The law of Simony —. 1784. 8. (3 Sh. 6 d.) Supplement to *Bacon's* abridgment containing a table of the names of the cafes; a table of the ftatutes, or acts of parliament cited; a table of the reporters and other writers —. fol. 1786. (6 Sh.)

CURREY, [Mary] Mrs. (maiden name *Elliot.*) born 1745. died d. 1 Oct. 1788.

CURRIE, [James] *M. D.*
Memoirs of the late Dr. *George Bell*. (Mem. of M. Vol. 2. p. 381.)

CURRY, [John] *M. D. Phyfician at Dublin.* born... died d. 24 March. 1780.

CURTIN, [Samuel] *Phyſician at Rio Bueno, in Jamaica.*
Obſervations on the Yellow fever of the Weſt-Indies. *(Duncan's* M. C. Vol. 9. p. 256.)

CURTIS, [Anne] (Siſter to Mrs. *Siddons.)*
Poems on miſcellaneous ſubjects. 1783. 12. (5 Sh.)
— [Roger] *Lieutenant of his Majeſty's ſloop the Otter.*
Particulars of the country of Labradore. (Philoſ. Transact. 1774. p. 372.)
— [William] *Demonſtrator of Botany to the Company of Apothecaries.*
Experiments and obſervations on bulbous roots, plants and ſeeds growing in water. (Phil. Transact. 1748. p. 267.) On the ſtructure and formation of the teeth. 1769. 8. (1 ſh 6 d.) Catalogue of the 50 plants from Chelſea garden. (Phil. Transact. 1774. p. 302.) Fundamenta entomologiae. 1772. 4. (2 ſh. 6 d.) Hiſtory of the brown tail moth. 1782. 4. (1 ſh. 6 d.) Flora Londinenſis. Numb. 1-63. 1777-1789. fol. (15 L. 15 ſh.) Catalogue of the britiſh plants in the London botanical garden. 1783. 8. (3 ſh. 6 d.) The botanical magazine; or, flower-garden diſplayed. N. 1-24. 1788. (1 L. 4 ſh)

CUTHBERTSON, [John] *Mathematical Inſtrument-maker at Amſterdam.*
Deſcription on an improved air pump. 1787. 8. überſ. Samml. z. P. u. N. G. Th. 4. S. 83. Allgemeene Eigenſhappen van de Electriciteit. Deel. I. 2. Amſtel. 1782. überſ. Leipz. 1786. 8. Beſchreibung einer Electriſir-Maſchine, überſ. a. d. Holländ. Leipz. 1790. 8.

CUTLER, [Manaſſeh] *F. A. A: F. S. Philad.*
Obſervations of the tranſit of Mercury over the Sun Nov. 12. 1782. (Mem. of B A. Vol. 1. p. 128.) Obſervations of an eclipſe of the Moon March 29, 1782. and of Ecliple of the Sun on the 12 April at Ipſwich. (Ibid. p. 162.) Meteorological obſervations at Ipswich in 1781, 1782, and 1783. (Ibid. p. 336. Account of ſome of the vegetable productions, naturally growing in this part of America botanically arranged. (Ibid. p. 396.)

DADE,

DADE, [William] *F. A. S*; *Rector at Barmston, Yorkshire.* born.... died d. 2 Aug. 1790.

DALE, [....]
*Supplement to calculations of the value of annuities —. 1777. 8. (2 ſh. 6 d.)

DALGLIESH, [William] *Miniſter of the goſpel at Peebles.*
The ſum of chriſtianity —. Vol. 1. 2. 1786. 8. (10 ſh. 6 d.)

DALLAS, [George] *Eſq. Member of the committee — in Bengal.*
Speech-praying redreſs againſt an act of parliament —. 1786. 8. (1 ſh. 6 d.)

DALLAWAY, [James] *M. A. of Trinity-College, Oxford.*
Letters of the late *Thomas Rundle*, L. L. D. Lord-Biſhop of Derry in Ireland to Mrs. *Barbara Sandys*, of Miſerden — with introductory memoirs. Vol. 1. 2. 1789. 8. (6 ſh.)

DALRYMPLE, [Alexander] *Eſq F. R. S.*
Diſcoveries made in South pacific Ocean. 1767. 8. Two letters to the court of Directors for affairs of the united company of merchants of England, trading to the Eaſt-Indies. 1768. 4. (1 ſh. 6 d.) On the formation of Iſlands. (Phil. Tranſact. 1767. p. 394.) Plan for extending the commerce of this kingdom and of the Eaſt-India company. 1769. 8. (1 ſh. 6 d.) Hiſtorical collection of the ſeveral voyages and diſcoveries in the ſouth pacific Ocean — a litterary translation from the ſpaniſh writers. Vol. 1. 2. 1770. 4. (1 L. 11 ſh.) überſ. *Ebelings* N. Samml. v. Reiſebeſchr. Th. 8. S. 175. Letter to D. *Hawkesworth* occaſioned by ſome groundleſs and illiberal imputations in his account of the late voyages to the South. 1773. 4. (1 ſh.) Proof that the Spaniards can have no claim to Balambangan. 1774. 8. (1 ſh.) Collection of voyages, chiefly in the ſouthern Atlantic Ocean, publiſhed from original MSS. 1775. 4. (5 ſh.) Journal of a voyage to the Eaſt-Indies in the ſhip *Grenville*, Capt. *Burnet Abercrombie* in the Y. 1775. (Phil. Tranſact. 1778. p. 389.) Account of the loſs of the Grosvenor Indiaman. 1783. 8. (1 ſh.) *Account of the Gentoo made of collecting the revenues on the coaſt of Co-

romandel. 1783. 8. (1 fh.) *Retrofpective view of the ancient fyftem of the Eaft-India company —. 1784. 8. (1 fh. 6 d.) Account of a curious Pagoda near Bombay, drawn up by Capt. *Pyke*, who was afterwards Governor of St. Helena. (Arch. Vol. 7. p. 323.) The fpanifh pretenfions fairly difcuffed, 1790. 8. (1 fh.) The fpanifh memorial of the 4th of June, confidered: 1790. 8. (1 fh.)

DALRYMPLE, [David] *Sir*, Lord *New-Hales*.
° Memorials and letters relating to the hiftory of Britain in the reign of James I. 1762. 8. (2 fh. 6 d.) * The fecret correfpondence of Sir Rob. Cecil with James VI. King of Scotland. 1765. 8. (3 fh.) ° Memorials and letters relating to the hiftory of Britain in the reign of Charles I. 1766. 8. (3 fh.) Hiftorical memorials. 1769. 4. Remarks on the hiftory of Scotland. 1773. 8..(4 fh. 6 d.) Annals of Scotland, from the acceffion of Malcolm III. — to the acceffion of the houfe of Stewart. Vol. I. 2. 1775. 1779. 4. (1 L. 7 fh. 6 d.) Inquiry into the fecondary caufes which Mr. Gibbon has affigned for the rapid growth of chriftianity. 1786. 4. (7 fh. 6 d.)

—— [George] *Cook by Sir John Whitefoord*.
The practice of modern Cookery —. 1781. 8. (6 fh.)

—— [John] *Sir*, *Earl of Stair*. born... died 1790.

—— [John] *Sir*, *Baronet of the Kingdom of Scotland*.
Memoirs of Great-Britain and Ireland from the diffolution of the laft parliament of Charles II. until the Sea battle of la Hogue. Vol. I. 2. 1773. 4. (2 L. 3 fh.) Three letters to Vifcount *Barrington*, late Secretary at War. 1778. 8. (2 fh.) On the exportation of wool. 1781. (1 fh.) Letter to the landed gentlemen and Graziers of Lincolnfhire. 1782. 8. (1 fh.) Memoirs of Great-Britain and Ireland from the battle of la Hogue till the capture of the french and fpanifh fleets at Vigo. Vol. I. 2. 1771. 1788. 4. (12 fh.) Addrefs — upon the intereft which they have in the ftate of the diftillery laws. 1786. 8. (2 fh.) Queries concerning the conduct which England fhould follow in foreign politics in the prefent ftate of Europe. 1789. 8. (2 fh. 6 d.)

—— [William] *Major*.
Travels through Spain and Portugal in 1774 with an account of the fpanifh expedition againft Algiers

giers in 1775. 1777. 4. (7 Sh. 6 d.) überf. Leipz.
1778. 8. - Tactics. 1781. 8. (5 Sh.)
DALRYMPLE, [William] *D. D. Minifter at Ayr.*
History of Chrift for the ufe of the unlearned —.
1787. 8. (6 Sh.) Family worfhip explained in four
fermons. 1787. 8. (2 Sh.)

DALTON. [Maria Regina]
The vicar of Landsdowne. Vol. 1. 2. 1789. 8. (6 Sh.)
—— [Richard] *Esq Antiquarian to the King.*
Remarks on XII hiftorical defigns of Raphael and
the Mufaeum Graecum et Aegyptiacum or antiquities of Greece and Egypt. 1751. 8. (6 d.) Every
one his own phyfician, or, the prefent practice of
phyfic. 1780. 8. (2 Sh. 6 d.) Remarks on prints
intended to be publifhed, relative to the manners,
cuftoms — of the prefent inhabitants of Egypt —.
1781. 8. (1 Sh.)

DALZEL, [Andrew] *M. A. Profeſſor of greek in the
Univerſity of Edinburgh.*
*Collectanea graeca, minora, cum notis philolo-
gicis atque lexico. 1787. 8. (5 Sh.)

DANCER, [Thomas] *M. D. Phyfician to the troops.*
History of the expedition againft Fort San Inan, fo
far as it relates to the difeafes of the troops —.
1782. 4. (2 Sh. 6 d.)

DANIEL, [Samuel] *M. D. Phyfician at Crewkherne
in Somerfetfhire.*
Diff. De Ictero. Edinb. 1776. 8. A cafe of ptya-
lifm, apparently occafioned by a diminifhed fecretion of urine. (M. C. Vol. 1. p. 155.) A cafe
of painful menftruation, attended with vomiting.
(London M. J. Vol. 5. p. 183.)

DANNET, [Henry] *M. A. Minifter of St. John's,
Liverpool.*
Examination of Mr. Harris's fcriptural refearches
on the Licitneff of the flave trade. 1788. 8. (2 Sh.)

DARBEY, [....] *Apothecary to the Infirmary at Manchefter.*
Account of good effects from the vapour-bath in
an hydropic cafe. *(Duncan's* M. C. Vol. 9. p. 305.)

DARBY, [John] *Jun. Surgeon at Diff, in Norfolk.*
Cafe of emphyfema. (London M. J. Vol. VIII.
p. 4.)

DARWALL, [John] Political lamentations —. 1777.
4. (2 Sh.)

DARWIN, [....] ° The botanic garden — a poem.
1789. 4. (12 Sh.)

—— [Charles] born at Lichtfield d. 3 Sept. 1758. died at Edinburgh, (where he was ſtudying phyſic,) d. 15 May. 1778.

—— [Eraſmus] *M. D: F. R. S.* Remarks on the opinion of *Henry Eeles* concerning the aſcent of vapours. (Phil. Transact. 1760. p. 240.) An uncommon caſe of an haemoptyſis. (Ibid. 1761. p. 526.) Experiments on animal fluids in the exhauſted receiver. (Ibid. 1774. p. 344.) A new caſe in ſquinting. (Ibid. 1778. p. 86. Account of the ſucceſſfull uſe of foxglove in ſome dropſies and in the pulmonary conſumption. (Med. Transact. Vol. 3. p. 255.) Account of an artificial ſpring of water. (Phil. Transact. 1785. p. 1.) Frigorific experiments on the mechanical expanſion of air, explaining the cauſe of the great degree of cold on the ſummits of high mountains. the ſudden condenſation of aerial vapour and of the perpetual mutability of atmoſpheric heat. (Ibid. 1788. p. 43. überſ. *Gren* J. d. Ph. Th. I. S. 73.)

—— [Robert Waring] *M. D.* New experiments on the ocular ſpectra of light and colours. (Phil. Transact. 1786. p. 313.)

DAVIDSON, [David] Thoughts on the ſeaſons — partly in the ſcottiſh dialect. 1789. 8. (3 Sh.)

—— [George] Account of a new ſpecies of the bark-tree found in the island of St. Lucia. (Phil. Transact. 1784. p. 452.)

—— [Thomas] *Surgeon in Carriacou.* Facts relative to the ſmall-pox. (Lond. M. J. Vol. X. P. 4.)

—— [William] *Architect and Landſurveyor.* Arithmetic and meaſurement, improved by examples and plain demonſtrations —. 1779. 8. (2 Sh. 6 d.)

DAVIES, [Arabella] *Mrs.* Letters from a parent to her children. 1788. 12. (2 Sh. 6 d.)

—— [David] *Esq. of the Middle-Temple.* The jury-man's guide; or the engliſhman's right —. 1779. 8. (1 Sh. 6 d.)

—— [Edward] *Lecturer of Sodbury.* Vacunalia: conſi-
ſting

fting of effays in verfe, on various fubjects; with fome translations. 1788. 8. (4 Sh,)

DAVIES, [Thomas] *Captain Lieutenant of Artillery.* Method of preparing birds for prefervation. (Philof. Transact. 1770. p. 184.)

—— [Thomas] *Bookfellor at London.* born.... died d. 5 May. 1785.

—— [William] Plays. 1786. 8. (6 Sh.)

DAVIS. [Henry Edward] *B. A. of Balliol College, Oxford.* born d. 11 July 1756. died d. 19 Febr. 1784.

DAVISON, [J....] A fyftem of Algebra. 1789. 8. (4 Sh.)

DAVY, [C....]

—— [F....] Translation of *Bourris's* journey to the glacieres. 1775. 8. (6 Sh.)

—— [Charles] *M. A. Rector of Onehoufe in Suffolk.* Letters — upon fubjects of litterature; including a translation of *Euclid's* fection of the canon and his treatife on harmony with an explanation of the greek mufical modes, according to the doctrine of Ptolemy. Vol. 1. 2. 1787. 8. (14 fh.)

—— [William] *A. B.* Syftem of divinity in a courfe of fermons —. Vol. 1 - 6. 1786. 12. (1 L. 1 fh.)

DAWES, [Matthew] *Efq.* Two fermons. 1763. 8. (1 fh.) Philofophical confiderations, or a free enquiry into the merits of a controverfy between Dr. *Prieftley* and Dr. *Price* on matter and fpirit and philofophical neceffity —. 1780. 8. (1 fh. 6 d.) On Intellectual liberty and toleration. 1780. 8. (2 fh. 6 d.) Letter to *John Horne Tooke.* 1782. 8. (1 fh.) On crimes and punifhments. 1782. 8. (5 fh.) The nature and extent of fupreme power. 1783. 8. (1 fh.) England's Alarm! on the prevailing doctrine of libels —. 1785. 8. (1 fh. 6 d.) The deformity of the doctrine of libels. 1785. 8. (1 Sh.) Vindication of the proceedings of the Lords and Commons upon the regency —. 1789. 8. (1 Sh.) Commentaries on the laws of arrefts in civil cafes —. 1789. 8. (1 Sh.)

DAWSON, [Abraham] *M. A. Rector of Ringsfield, Suffolk.* Englifh translation of the Chapt. 1. 2. 3. of Genefis with illuftrations and notes. 1763. 4. (2 Sh. 6 d.) Englifh translation of the Chapt. 4. 5. of Genefis —. 1772. 4. (3 Sh.) The VI and XI following

wing Chapters of Genesis translated with illustrations and notes. 1786. 4. (3 Sh. 6 d.)

DAWSON, [Ambrose] *M. D. fellow of the college of Physicians.* On human calculi; shewing them to be of very different kinds. (Med. Transact. Vol. 2. p. 105.) Thoughts on the hydrocephalus internus (Letters and Essays by different practitioners. Artic. IX.) Observations on the hydatides in the heads of cattle. (ibid. Art. X.)

—— [Benjamin] *LL. D. Rector of Burgh in the County of Suffolk.* Sermons VIII. on logos. 1765. 8. (4 Sh.) Address to the writer of a second letter to the author of the confessional. 1767. 8. (1 Sh. 6 d.) Examination of an essay on establishments in religion, with remarks upon it, considered as an answer to the confessional. 1767. A short and safe expedient for terminating the present debates about subscriptions occasioned by — the confessional. 1769. 8. Letter in vindication of the petition for the removal of subscription to human formularies of religious faith and doctrine. 1773. 8. (1 Sh. 6 d.) The necessitarian; or, the question concerning liberty and necessity stated. 1783. 8. (2 Sh. 6 d.) Published: free thoughts on the subjects of a farther reformation of the church of England, with remarks of the editor by the author of a — expedient for terminating the present debates about subscription. 1771. 8. (2 Sh. 6 d.) (several single sermons.)

—— [John] *Surgeon at Sedbergh in Yorkshire.* Account of a singular fact in the practice of inoculation of the small-pox. (Med. Transact. Vol. 3. p. 385. London M. J. Vol. 7. P. 1.)

—— [Thomas] *M. D.* born.... died at Hackney, near London d. 29 Apr. 1782.

DAY, [Thomas] born 1748. died d. 28 Sept. 1789.

—— [Thomas] *Surgeon.* On the different ways of removing confined and infectious air —. 1784. 8. (1 Sh. 6 d.) übers. Altenb. 1788. 8.

DEACON, [....] *Jun.* Poems. 1790. 4. (4 Sh.)

—— [H....] On the venereal disease, gleets —. 1789. 8. (3 Sh. 6 d.)

DEANE, [Samuel] *F. A. A.* Account of yellow and red pigment, found at Norton, with the process

for

for preparing the yellow for ufe. (Mem. of B. A. Vol. I. p. 378.)

DEANE, [Silas] *Ambaſſadour of the XIII united provinces at Paris.* born at Groton, Connecticut 1736. died d. 23 Sept. 1789.

DEARBORN, [Benjamin] Defcription of a pump-engine, or, an apparatus to be added to a common pump. (Mem. of B. A. Vol. I. p. 520.) Defcription of a fire-engine of a new conſtruction. (Ibid. p. 523.)

DEASE, [William] *Surgeon to the united hoſpitals of St. Nicholas and St. Catharine, Dublin.* Obfervations on wounds of the head —. 1776. 8. (2 Sh. 6 d.) Introduction to the theory and practice of Surgery. Vol. I. 1780. 8. (3 Sh.) Obfervations in midwifery particularly on the different methods of affiſting women in tedious and difficult labours —. 1783. 8. (3 Sh.) überf. von C. F. Michaelis. Zittau u. Leipz. 1788. 8. Obfervations on venereal warts. (Med. Com. of Ed. Vol. 4. p. 335.) Obfervations on the extirpation of a cancerous ulcer in the lower lip. (Ibid. Vol. 5. p. 299.) Obfervations on the different methods of treating the venereal difeaſe. 1781. 8. überf. von C. F. Michaelis. Zittau 1790. 8. Account of the fatal effects produced by attempting to remove a ganglion by feton. (London M. J. Vol. 5. p. 172. überf. Samml. f. A. Th. 10. S. 157.

DEBRAW, [John] *Apothecary to Addenbrook's hoſpital at Cambridge.* Difcovery on the fex of bees, explaining the manner in which their fpecies is propagated —. (Phil. Transact. 1777. p. 15.)

DELAP, [John] *D. D.* Hecuba, a Tragedy. 1762. 8. *The royal fuppliants: a Tragedy. 1781. 8. (1 Sh. 6 d.) The captives, a Tragedy. 1786. 8. (1 Sh. 6 d.) Elegy on the death of the Duke of Rutland. 1788. 4. (1 Sh.)

DELAVAL, [Edward Huffey] *F. R. S. of London and of Gottingen.* Several electrical experiments. (Phil. Transact. 1761. p. 83.) Several experiments in electricity. (Ibid. 1762. p. 353.) Account of the effects of lightning on St. Bride's church, fleet-ſtreet June 18. 1764. (Ibid. 1764. p. 227.) Experiments and obfervations on the agreement between the fpecific gravities of the feveral metals and their colours

lours when united to glaſs, as well as thoſe of their other proportions. (Ibid. 1765. p. 10.) Experimental inquiry into the cauſe of the changes of colours in opake and coloured bodies. 1777. 4. (5 Sh.) Inquiry into the cauſe of the permanent colour of opake bodies. (Mem. of M. Vol. 2. p. 131.) überſ. (von Meyneke) 1788. 8.

DELL, [John] * Poetical effuſions of the heart. 1783. 8.

DEMPSTER, [George] Esq. Diſcourſe, containing a ſummary of the proceedings of the directors of the ſociety for extending the fiſheries of Great-Britain. 1789.

DENHAM, [James Stewart] Sir; Baronet, of Coltneſſ and Weſtſhield. born .... died d. 25 Dec. 1780.

DENMANN, [Thomas] M. D. *Phyſician - man - midwife to the Middleſex Hoſpital and Teacher of Midwifery in London.* On the puerperal fever and on puerperal convulſions. 1768. 8. (1 Sh. 6 d.) Ed. 3. 1785. 8. überſ. Altenb. 1777. 8. On the conſtruction and method of uſing vapor baths. 1769. 8. (1 Sh.) Obſervations to prove that in caſes where the upper extremities preſent, at the time of birth, the delivery may be effected by the ſpontaneous evolution of the child. (London M. J. Vol. 5. p. 64. p. 301.) On uterine haemorrhages depending on pregnancy and parturition. 1786. 8. (2 Sh.) On natural labours. 1786. 8. (2 Sh.) On preternatural labours. 1786. 8. (2 Sh.) Obſervations on the uſe of the globe peſſary. (London M. J. Vol. 7. P. 1.) überſ. Journ. f. Geburtsh. St. 1. Aphoriſms on the application and uſe of the forceps on preternatural labours and on labours attended with hemorrhage. 1786. 8. (2 Sh.) überſ. Journal f. Geburtsh. St. 2. Collection of engravings, tending to illuſtrate the generation and parturition of animals, with two plates of a ruptured and inverted uterus. 1786. fol. (13 Sh.) Introduction to the practice of midwifery. P. 1. 1787. 8. (6 Sh.) On difficult labours. P. 1. 1787. 8.

DENNE, [Samuel] F. A. S. Obſervations on Rocheſter Caſtle. (Arch. Vol. 6. p. 381.) Memoir on Hokeday. (Ibid. Vol. 7. p. 244.) Doubts and conjectures concerning the reaſon commonly aſſigned for inſerting or omitting the words eccleſia and
pres-

presbyter in Domesday Book. (Ibid. Vol. 8. p. 218.) Obfervations on the perfons called Waldenfes who where formerly tenants of the manor of Darenth in the county of Kent. (Ibid. Vol. 9. p. 292.) On the time when *William of Newburgh* wrote his hiftory. (Ibid. p. 310.)

DENNETT, [....] Examination of *Harris's* refearches on the licitnefs of the flave trade. 1788. 8. (2 Sh.)

DENT, [John] The candidate; a farce. 1782. 8. (1 Sh.) Too civil by half; a farce. 1783. 8. (1 Sh) The receipt tax; a farce. 1783. The lawyers panic; or Weftminfter Hall in an Uproar; a Prelude. 1785. 8. (1 Sh.) The force of love; in a feries of letters. Vol. 1. 2. 1785. 8. (5 Sh.)

DERBY, [John] *A. M: Chaplain of Lord Bifhop of Rochefter and Rector of Soushfleet and Longfield.* born .... died d 6 Oct. 1778.

DEVERELL, [Mary] *Mrs. Gloucefterfhire.* Sermons, on friendfhip, on gratitude to god, on mercy, on pride, on finful anger, on the advantages of early piety, on the unfearchablenefs of god's ways and the benefits of afflictive providence. 1774. 8. (5 Sh.) Mifcellanies in profe and verfe —. Vol. 1. 2. 1782. 12. (7 Sh) Theodora and Didymus or the exemplification of pure love and vital religion; an heroic poem 1785. 8. (5 Sh.)

DEVIS, [Ellen] *The accidence or firft rudiments of englifh grammar. 1774 8. (1 Sh. 6 d.) Ed. 3. 1778. 8. (1 Sh; 6 d.) Mifcellaneous leffons. 1784. 12. (2 Sh. 6 d.)

DEWELL, [T....] *M. D. Malmesbury, Wilts.* The philofophy of phyfic or phlogiftic fyftem —. 1784. 8. (1 Sh. 6 d.) Ed. 2 1785. 8. (3 fh. 6 d.)

DEXTER, [Samuel] *Esq.* Letter on the retreat of houfe-fwallows in Winter. (Mem. of B. A. Vol. I. p. 494.)

DIBDEN, [Charles] The Shepherd's artifice; a dramatic paftoral. 1765 8. (1 Sh.) Damon and Phillida, altered from Cibber. 1768. 8. * The wedding ring, a comic opera. 1773. 8. (1 Sh.) The deferter. 1773. 8. * The waterman or the firft of Auguft, an Opera. 1774. 8. (1 Sh.) * The two miferes; a mufical farce. 1775 8. (1 Sh.) The cobler; or, a wife of ten thoufand, a Ballad Opera. 1774.

1774. 8. The Metamorphofis, a comic Opera. 1775. 8. The Seraglio. 1776. 8. The Quaker, a comic Opera. 1776. 8. Poor Vulcan, a Burletta. 1778. 8. The gipfies, a comic Opera. 1778. 8. Rofe and Collin, a comic Opera. 1778. 8. The wives revenged, a comic Opera. 1778. 8. Annette and Lubin, a comic Opera. 1778. 8. The chelfea penfioner, a comic Opera. 1779. 8. The Mirror; or Harlequin every where. 1779. 8. The fhepherdeff of the alps, a comic Opera. 1780. 8. The islanders, a comic Opera. 1780. 8. Jupiter and Alcmena. 1781. 8. The marriage act. 1781. 8. Liberty Hall, or the teft of good fellow fhip. 1785. 8. Harveft home, a comic Opera. 1786. 8. (1 fh.)

DICK, [John] *Gardener.* The new gardiner's dictionary, or the whole art of gardening. 1769. fol. überf. von *J. E. Zeiher.* Th. 1. 2. Leipz. 1774. 8.

—— [William] *Surgeon of Artillery, Bengal Eftablifhment.* Obfervations on dropfies prevailing among the troops in the Eaft-Indies. (*Duncan's* M. C. Vol. 10. p. 207.)

DICKINSON, [....] Speech in the affembly of Pennfylvania —. 1764. 8. (6 d.) Reply to a piece, called the fpeech of *Jofeph Galloway.* 1765. 8. New effay on the conftitutional power of Great-Britain over the colonies in America —. 1774. 8. (2 fh.)

—— [Caleb] *M. D.* Inquiry into the nature and caufes of fever —. 1785. 8. (3 fh.) überf. von *J. Chr. Fahner.* Göttingen. 1787. 8.

DICKSON, [Adam] *A. M:* *Minifter at Whittingham.* born... died d. 25 March. 1776.

—— [James] *Fellow of the Linnaean fociety.* Plantae cryptogamicae. Fafcic. 1. 2. 1785. 1790. 4. (8 fh.) Collection of dried plants named on the authority of the Linnaean herbarium and other original collections. Fafc. 1. 1789. fol. (12 fh. 6 d.) Fafc. 2. 1790. fol. (12 fh.)

—— [Michael] *M. D:* *Phyfician at Taunton, Somerfetfhire.* born.... died d. 28 Dec. 1778.

—— [Stephen] *M. D:* *Profeffor of Phyfic in the city of Dublin.* F. R. *J. A.* Obfervations on pamphigus. (Tr. of I. A. 1787. p. 47. London M. J. Vol. IX. P. 3. überf. Samml. f. A. Th 13. S. 133.)

—— [Thomas] *M. D: F. R. S: Phyfician to the London Hofpital.* born.... died d. 1 June 1784.

DICK-

DICKSON, [William] *Formerly private secretary to the late Governor of Barbadoes Ed. Hay.* Letters on slavery. 1789. 8. (3 Sh. 6 d.)
DILLON, [John Talbot] *Couns of the Roman empire.* born in Ireland. Travels through Spain 1780. 4. (1 L. 1 sh.) übers. (durch *J. Andr. Engelbrecht*) Th. 1. 2. Leipz. 1782. 8. °Letters from an english traveller in Spain in 1778. 8. 1781. (6 sh.) Survey of the sacred roman empire. 1782. 8. (4 sh.) Translation of *Mengs's* Sketches of the art of painting. 1782. 8. (2 sh.) History of the reign of Peter the cruel, King of Castile and Leon. Vol. 1. 2. 1788. 8. (10 sh.) Historical and critical memoirs of the general Revolution in France in the Y. 1789. 1789. 4. (1 L. 1 sh.)
— [P...] *Surgeon of the* 105 *Regt. of foot.* Case of a fistula in Ano, cured by means of a caustic. (London M. J. Vol. 5. p. 392.) Case of an extrauterine foetus. (Ibid. P. 4.)
DIMSDALE, [Thomas] *M. D: F. R. S. Body Physician and actuel Counsellor of state to her imperial Majesty of all the Russies.* born.... died 1784.
DINE, [William] *Clerk of the parish of Chiddingly in Sussex.* Poems on several occasions —. 1771. 8. (1 sh.)
DINGLEY, [Somerville] Appendix to the XIV edition of *Burn's* justice. 1785. 8. (3 sh.) The parish officer's companion; or a new library of parish law. 1786. 8. (2 Sh. 6 d.)
DISNEY, [John] *D. D: F. A. S.* Four sermons on Christmas day. 1771. 8. °Thoughts on the great circumspection necessary in licensing public alehouses. 1776. 8. Reasons for resigning the Rectory of Panton and Vicarage of Swinderby — and quitting the church of England. 1783. 8. Memoir of the life and writing of *Arthur Ashley Sykes.* 1785. 8. (5 Sh.) °Dialogue between a common unitarian christian and an Athanasian. 1784. 8. Ed. 2. 1785. ' Published, the works, theological, medical, political and miscellanious of *John Jebb* M. D. 1787. 8. Vol. 1-3. (1 L. 1 Sh.) Published, *Sam. Disney's* (late Vicar of Halstead, Essex) Discourses on various subjects, with a preface. 1788. 8. (6 Sh.) (several single sermons.)
DISON,

DISON, [John] born.... died 1776.
DIXON, [George] *Captain.* Voyage round the world; but more particularly to the North-Weft-Coaft of America, by *Portlock* and *Dixon.* 1789. 4. (1 L. 1 Sh.) überf. von *J. R. Forfter.* 1790. 4. Voyage round the world. 1789. 8. (Ein Auszug) überf. Berlin. 1789. 8.
—— [Jofeph] *M. D. Phyfician in Whitehaven.* Hiftory of a cafe of Angina polypofa. (*Duncan's* M. C. Vol. 9. p. 254.) überf. Samml. f. A. Th. XI. S. 403. Account of appearances on the diffeftion of a child dying of hydrocephalus. (Ibid. Vol. 10. p. 312. überf. Samml. f. A. Th. XI. S. 685.)
DOBBS, [Francis] *Esq. Barrifter at law.* born in Ireland. The patriot king; or, irifh chief; a Tragedy. 1774. 8. (1 Sh. 6 d.) Letter to Lord North, on his propofitions in favour of Ireland. 1778. 8. (6 d.) Thoughts on the prefent mode of taxation in Great-Britain —. 1783. 8. (1 Sh.) Letter to Lord North and Mr. Fox. 1784. 8. Univerfalhiftory —. Vol. I. 1787. 12. (3 Sh.)
DOBSON, [Mary] *Mrs.* (Wife to *Matthew Dobfon's).* Translation of the life of Petrarch. Vol. 1. 2. 1775. 8. (12 Sh.) Ed. 2. Vol. 1. 2. 1776. 8. (12 Sh.) * Dialogue on friendfhip and fociety. 1776. 8. (2 Sh. 6 d.) * Translation of *St. Paley's* litterary hiftory of Troubadours. 1779. 8. (6 Sh.) * Translation of *St. Paley's* memoirs of ancient Chivalry. 1784. 8. (5 Sh.)
—— [Matthew] *M. D. Phyfician as Liverpool. F. R. S.* born.... died at Bath d. 25 July 1784.
—— [Robert] *M. D. Phyfician at Kirkham.* Diff. de Amenorrhoea. Edinb. 1771. 8. A cafe of a very obftinate ophthalmia, fucceffiully treated by an emetic and the confequent ufe of the Peruvian bark. (Med. Com. of Ed. Vol. 3. p. 411.)
DODD, [A... Charles] The contraft or ftriftures on felect parts of Dr. *Price's* additional obfervations on civil liberty —. 1777. 8. (1 Sh.)
—— [James Solas] *Surgeon and Manmidwife.* Natural hiftory of the herring. 1752. 8. (3 Sh.) Phyfical account of the cafe of *Elizab. Canning.* 1753. 8. (1 Sh.) * A fatyrical lefture on hearts. 1767. 8. (1 Sh.) All the prefcriptions contained in the new practi-

practice of Phyfic of *Thom. Marryat* — translated. 1774. 8. (2 fh. 6 d.) The antient and modern hiftory of Gibraltar — translated from the Spanifh: 1781. 8. (2 fh. 6 d.)

DODD, [William] *Doctor of Laws, Prebendary of Brecon and Chaplain in Ordinary to his Majefty.* born at Bourne, Lincolnfhire d. 29 March 1729. executed at Tyburn d. 27 June 1777.

DODDRIDGE, [....] *Mrs.* born :... died at Tewkesbury, Gloucefterfhire d. 20 Apr. 1790.

DOGERTY, [Thomas] Crown circuit affiftant; being a collection of precedents of indictments, informations, convictions by juftices, inquifitions, pleas —. 1787. 8. (9 fh.)

DOLLOND, [Peter] *Optician.* Account of an improvement in his new telefcopes. (Phil. Transact. 1765. p. 54.) Additions and alterations made to *Hadley's* quadrant, to render it more ferviceable at fea. (Ibid. 1772. p. 95.) Account of an apparatus applied to the equatorial inftrument for correcting the errors arifing from the refraction in altitude. (Ibid. 1779. p. 332.) Some accounts of the difcovery made by the late Mr. *John Dollond.* F. R. S. — 1789. 4. (1 fh.)

DONALDSON, [J....] at Edinburgh. Elements of beauty. 1780. 12. (2 fh.) überf. N. Bibl. der fchönen Wiff. Th. 27. S. 5-38. Ed. 2. with an analyfis of the human mind. 1787. 8. (3 fh.) Poems. 1786. 4. (2 fh. 6 d.)

—— [John] Mifcellaneous propofals for increafing our national wealth, 12 Millions a Year, and alfo for augmenting the revenue without a new tax —. 1790. 8. (1 fh. 6 d.)

—— [William] *late Secretary to the government of Jamaica.* Agriculture confidered as a moral and political duty. — 1777. 8. (3 fh. 6 d.)

DONAVAN, [John] *Surgeon.* Remarks upon the treatment and cure of venereal and fcorbutic diforders —. 1788. 8. (1 fh. 6 d.)

DONE, [William Stafford] *D. D. Prebendary of Lincoln and Arch-Deacon of Bedford.* born:... died d. 1 June 1783.

DONN, [Benjamin] *Mafter of the Academy at Kingfton near Taunton.* Mathematical effays on vulgar and decimal arithmetic —. 1758. 8. (6 ſh.) The accountant and geometrician; containing the doctrine of circulating decimals, logarithms, book-keeping and plane geometry —. 1766. 8. (6 ſh) Epitome of natural and experimental philoſophy including geography, with the uſe of the globe. 1770. 8. (2 ſh. 9 d.) The britiſh mariner's aſſiſtant; containing 40 tables adapted to the ſeveral purpoſes of trigonometry and navigation —. 1774. 8. (6 ſh.) The uſe of the Geoorganon and improved analemma or ſubſtitutes for the terreſtrial and celeſtial globe. 1788. 8. (1 ſh)

DORNFORD, [Joſiah] *of Lincoln's Inn: LL. D. of the Univerſity of Gottingen.* Translation of *Putter's* hiſtorical developement of the preſent political conſtitution of the germanic empire &c. with notes. Vol. 1-3. 1790. 8. (1 L. 1 ſh.)

—— [Joſiah] Two memorials to the committee appointed by the court of common-council —. 1784. 8. (1 ſh.) Addreſs to the livery and citizens of London on the proceedings of the court of common council-reſpecting Mr. Alderman *Clarke* and Mr. *Dornford.* 1785. 8. (6 d.) Seven letters - pointing out the cauſes of the depravity of the lower orders of the people, the corrupt ſtate of our goals. 1785. 8. (1 ſh.)

DOSSIE, [Robert] *Chymiſt.* born:... died d. 20 Febr. 1777.

DOUGALL, [William] *Surgeon at Keith.* Hiſtory of a caſe of Ileus, in which a conſiderable portion of the inteſtine was voided by ſtool. (*Duncan's* M. C. Vol. 9. p. 278.)

DOUGLAS, [....] Edwin, the baniſhed prince. 1784. 8.

—— [Andrew] *M. D: at London.* Diſſ. De variolae inſitione. Edinb. 1775 8. Account of the efficacy of Hemlock in ſchirrous caſe and ulcers. (Med. Obſ. Vol. 5. p. 113.) Obſervations on an extraordinary caſe of ruptured uterus. 1785. 8. (1 ſh. 6 d.) überſ. Journal für Geburtshelfer. St. 2. Obſervations on that ſpecies of haemorrhage which is occaſioned by an attachment of the placenta to the cervix uteri. (M. C. Vol. 1. p. 107.) Obſervations

vations on the rupture of the gravid uterus. 1789. 8. (3 ſh.)

DOUGLAS, [Archibald] *M. D. of London.* Caſe of a ſingular cough. (Med. Obſ. Vol. 6. p. 163.)

—— [Charles] *F. R. S. Captain of his Majeſty's ſhip the Emerald.* Experiments and obſervations upon a blue ſubſtance, found in the Peat Moſſ in Scotland. (Phil. Transaƈt. 1768. p. 181.) Account of the reſult of ſome attempts made to aſcertain the temperature of the ſea in great depths near the coaſts of Lapland and Norway. (Ibid. 1770. p. 39.)

—— [Francis] General deſcription of the eaſt coaſt of Scotland from Edinburgh to Cullen —. 1782. 8. (2 ſh. 6 d.)

—— [George] *Teacher of Mathematics in the Academy, at Ayr.* The elements of Euclid —. 1776. 8. (6 Sh.)

—— [James] *F. A. S.* °Travelling anecdotes through various parts of Europe. Vol. 1. 2. 1782. (12 ſh.) Ed. 2. (with the Author's name) (6 ſh.) On the antiquity of the earth. 1785. 4, (10 ſh. 6 d.) Nenia Britannica; or, an account of ſome 1000 ſepulchres of the ancient inhabitants of Britain 1786. fol. Numb. 1-5. (1 L. 5 ſh.) Letter to *Melvil's* obſervations on the Sword. (Arch. Vol. 7. p. 376.)

—— [John] *D. D: F. R. S: Biſhop of Carliſle.* Milton vindicated from the charge of Plagiariſm brought againſt him, by Mr. *Lauder.* 1750. (1 ſh. 6 d.) °The Criterion, or, miracles examined —. 1753. 8. (5 ſh.) °The Deteƈtion of *Archib. Bower.* 1757. 8. (2 ſh.)

—— [Robert] The variation of the compaſſ; containing 1719 obſervations to, in, and from the Eaſt-Indies, Guinea, Weſt-Indies and Mediterranean, with the latitudes and longitudes at the time of obſervation —. (Phil. Transaƈt. 1776. p. 18.)

—— [Robert] *Miniſter of Galaſhiels* Obſervations on the nature of oaths, and the danger of multiplying them. 1783. 8. (2 ſh.)

—— [....] *Lieutenant of the North Lincolnſhire Militia.* °*Guibert's* general eſſay on taƈtics translated. Vol. 1. 2. 1781. 8. (12 ſh.)

—— [Sylveſter] *of Lincoln's Inn.* Account of the Tokay and other wines of Hungary. (Phil. Transaƈt. 1773.

1773. p. 292.) Hiſtory of the cafes of controverted elections which were tried and determined during the firſt ſeſſion of the XIV parliament of Great-Britain —. Vol. 1 - 4. 1777. 8. (1 L.) Reports of cafes — determined in the Court of King's bench in the 19, 20, 21 Years of — George III. 1783. fol. (1 L. 16 ſh.)

DOW, [Alexander] *Lieutenant Colonel in the Eaſt - India company's Service.* born in Scotland... died in Eaſt - India 1779.

DOWNES, [Henry] *Miniſter at Sheffield.* Sermons on various ſubjects. Vol. 1. 2. 1784. 8. (10 ſh.)

DOWNING, [George] *Actor.* born.... died 1780.

DOWNMANN, [Hugh] *M. D. Phyſician at Exeter.* The land of the mules, a poem. 1767. 4. (2 ſh. 6 d.) Infancy, a poem. Book 1. 2. 3. 1775. 4. (4 ſh.) 1776. 8. (2 ſh.) 1788. 8. (2 ſh. 6 d.) *Lucius Junius Brutus*: or the expulſion of the Tarquins, an hiſtorical play. 1779. 8. (3 ſh.) The death ſong of *Ragnar Lodbroch*, King of Denmark translated from the latin of *Wormius.* 1781. 4. (1 ſh.) Editha, a Comedy. 1783. 8. (1 ſh. 6 d.)

DRAKE, [William] *A. M: F. A. S: Rector at Iſlaworth, Middleſex.* On the origin of the word romance. (Arch. Vol. 4. p. 142.) On two roman ſtations in Eſſex. (Ibid. Vol. 5. p. 137.) On the origin of the engliſh language. (Ibid. p. 306. p. 379.) Account of ſome diſcoveries in the church of Brotherton in Yorkſhire. (Ibid. Vol. 9. p. 253.) On the derivation of the engliſh language. (Ibid. p. 332.)

DRAPER, [William] *Sir. Knight, Baron, Lieutenant-General.* born.... died d. 8 Jan. 1787.

DRAY, [Thomas] *Surgeon.* Reflections on *Cadogan's* diſſertation on the gout and all chronic diſeaſes. 1772. 8. (6 d.)

DREW, [William] Translation of *Fontanieu's* art of making coloured cryſtals to imitate precious ſtones. 1788. 8. (2 ſh.)

DREWE, [Edward] *Major.* Military ſketches. 1784. 8. (2 ſh. 6 d.)

DRINK-

DRINKWATER, [John] *Captain of the late 72 regiment, or, royal Manchester Voluntairs.* History of the late siege of Gibraltar —. 4. 1786. (1 L. 7 sh)

DRUMMOND, [T...] *Surgeon at Bombay.* Account of the successful employment of Laudanum in the confluent small-pox. (*Duncan's* M. C. Dec. 2. Vol. 4. p. 300.)

DRURY, [Obrien] *Captain: of the royal Navy.* Observations on the magnetic fluid. (Tr. of I. A. 1788.)

—— [R....] Illustrations of natural history. Vol. 1-3. 1770-1782. 4. (7 L. 18 sh.) übers. durch *G. W. Fr. Panzer.* Nürnb. 1785. 4.

DRYDEN, [John] *Jun.* born.... died 17..

—— [John] *Surgeon in Jamaica.* Account of a rupture of the oesophagus from the action of vomiting. (*Duncan's* M. C. Dec. II. Vol. 3. p. 308.)

DRYSDALE, [W...] *Teacher of languages.* Popery dissected: or, a speech against the popish toleration bill —. 1779. 8. (1 sh.)

DUBOIS, [Dorothea] *Mrs.* (Daughter to the Earl *Anglesea.*) born.... died 1774.

DUCAREL, [Andrew Coltee] *LL. D: F. R. S: F. A. S: Commissary of the city and Diocese of Canterbury.* born at Greenwich 1714. died d. 29 May 1785.

DUCHE, [Jacob] *Preacher at Bow church in Cheapside.* Discourses on various subjects. Vol. 1. 2. 1779. 8. (10 sh. 6 d.) *Caspipina's* letters: containing observations on a variety of subjects literary, moral and religious — with the life and character of *Will. Penn.* Vol. 1. 2. 1777. 8. (5 sh.) (several single sermons.)

DUDLEY, [Henry Bate] *Clerk, Justice of the peace for the county of Essex.* Henry and Emma. 1774. 8. Rival candidates, a comic Opera. 1775. 8. (1 sh.) The blackamoor wash'd white, a comic Opera. 1776. 8. Flitch of Bacon, a comic Opera. 1779. 8. (1 sh.) The dramatic puffers. 1782. 8. The magic picture, a play. 1783. (1 sh. 6 d.) Remarks on *Gilbert's* last bill for the relief of the poor. 1788. 8. (1 sh.)

DUFF, [William] *A. M.* *Essay on original genius and its various modes of exertion in philosophy and the fine arts, particularly in poetry. 1767. 8. (5 Sh.) Critical obfervations on the writings of the moft celebrated original geniufes in poetry, a fequel to the effay on original genius. 1770. 8. (5 Sh.)

DUGUD, [Patrik] *Phyfician at Durham.* Hiftory of a convulfive diforder treated by the ufe of the flowers of zinc. (Med. Com. of Ed. Vol. 5. p. 84.)

DUIGENAN, [Patrick] *LL. D. Profeffor of common law in Trinity college, Dublin.* Theophilus Addreff to the nobility and gentry of Ireland. 17..

DULANCEY, [Oliver]. *Lieutenant Colonel.* Confiderations on the propriety of impofing taxes in the britifh colonies. 1765. 8. (1 Sh. 6 d.) Ed. 2. (with the author's name) 17..

DUN, [....] Sermons. Vol. 1. 2. 1790. 8. (10 Sh.)

DUNBAR, [James] *L. L. D. Profeffor of Philofophy, King's College, Aberdeen.* De primordiis civitatum oratio, in qua agitur de bello civili inter M. Britanniam et Colonias nunc flagranti. 1779. 4. (1 Sh. 6 d.) On the hiftory of mankind —. 1780. 8. (5 Sh.) Ed. 2. 1782. 8. (6 Sh.) überf. Leipz. 1781. 8.

DUNCAN, [....] Moral hints to the rifing generation, an epiftle of *Horace* —. 1783. 8. (1 Sh.)

—— [Andrew] *M. D. Phyfician to his Royal Highneff the Prince of Wales and Profeffor of the Univerfity of Edinburgh. F. R. S: F. A. S.* Diff. De alvi purgantium natura et vfu. Edinb. 1770. 8. Elements of Therapeutics. 1770. 8. (4 Sh.) Obfervations on the operation and ufe of Mercury in the venereal difeafe. 1772. 8. (3 Sh.) überf. Frankf. u. Leipz. 1773. 8. Medical cafes. 1778. 8. (5 Sh.) überf. Leipz. 1779. 8. Oratio de laudibus *Guil. Harvei.* 1778. 8. Account of the life and writings of *Alex. Monro* 1780. 8. (1 Sh.) Medical commentaries for the Year 1780. (6 Sh.) 1781. 1782. (6 Sh.) 1783. 1784. (6 Sh.) 1785. (6 Sh.) 1786. (6 Sh.) 1787. (6 Sh.) 1788. (6 Sh.) 1789. (6 Sh.) Heads of lectures on the theory and practice of Medecine. 17.. Ed. 2. 1781. 8. (3 Sh.) Ed. 4. 1788. 8. Letter to *Rob. Jones* — on the cafe of Mr. *J. B. Ifaacfon.* 1782. 8. (1 Sh.) *Will. Lewis's* translation of *Hoffmann's* fyftem of the practice of medicine revifed and completed. Vol. 1. 2. 1783. 8. (12 Sh.) Account of the late Dr. *John Parfons.* 1786. 8. (1 Sh.)

(1 Sh.) Account of good effects obtained from the ule of the vitriolic acid in the cure of obſtinate ſingultus. *(Duncan's* M. C. Dec. 2. Vol. 4. p. 371.)

DUNCAN, *[John] D. D. Rector of Southwarmborough, Hants.* Eſſay on happineſſ. 1762. 4. (2 Sh. 6 d.) Ed. 2. (with the author's name) 1773. 8. (5 Sh.) (Several ſingle ſermons.)

DUNCOMBE, [John] *M. A. Rector of St. Andrew's and St. Mary Bredman's and one of the VI preachers in Chriſt church*, Canterbury. born 1730. died d. 19 Jan. 1786.

DUNDAS, [David] *Colonel.* ' Principles of Military movements, chiefly applied to infantry —. 1788. 4. (1 L. 1 Sh.)

—— [David] *Surgeon at Richmond, in Surry.* On hydrophobia. (London M. J. Vol. VIII. P. 2.)

DUNDONALD, [....] Earl of. The preſent ſtate of the manufacture of ſalt explained: — 1785. 8. (2 Sh.) überſ. Leipz. 1787. 8. On the qualities and uſes of Coal tar and Coal Varniſh —. 1785. 8. (1 Sh]

DUNN, [Samuel] *Teacher of the mathematical and philoſophical ſciences, London.* Lecture on the aſtronomy and philoſophy of comets. 1759. 8. Some obſervations of the planet Venus, on the diſk of the Sun, June 6. 1761. with a preceding account of the method taken for verifying the time of that phaenomenon and certain reaſons for an atmoſphere about Venus. (Philoſ. Transact. 1762. p. 184.) Attempt to aſſign the cauſe why the Sun and Moon appear to the nacked eye larger when they are near the horizon : with an account of ſeveral natural phaenomena relative to this ſubject. (Ibid. 1762. p. 462.) Reaſons for a lunar atmoſphere. (Ibid. 1762. p. 578.) Account of the eclipſe of the Sun, Oct. 16. 1762. (Ibid. 1762. p. 644.) Account of an appulſe of the Moon to the planet Jupiter, obſerved at Chelſea. (Ibid. 1763. p. 31.) Remarks on the cenſure of Mercator's chart, in a poſthumous work of Mr. Weſt of Exeter. (Ibid. 1763. p. 66.) Account of a remarkable meteor, Oct. 6. 1763. (Ibid. 1763. p. 351.) Obſervations on the eclipſe of the Sun, April 1. 1764 at

Brompton Park. (Philof. Transact. 1764. p. 114.) Improvements of the doctrine of the fphere, aftronomy, geography, navigation. 1765. 4. (2 fh. 6 d.) Determination of the exacts moments of time, when the planet Venus was at external and internal contact with the Sun's limb in the tranlits of June 6th 1761. and 3 June 1769. (Phil. Transact. 1770. p. 65.) A new and general jntroduction to practical aftronomy. 1775. 8. (12 fh.) The navigator's guide to the oriental or indian feas. 1776. 8. (15 fh.) A new epitome of practical navigation or guide to the indian feas. 1778. 8. (9 fh.)

DUNSTER, [C....] A. M. The frogs, a Comedy translated from the greek of *Ariftophanes*. 1785. 4. (3 fh. 6 d.)

DUPRE', -[Edward] M. A. Fellow of Pembroke College. Sermons on various fubjects. 1782. 8. (6 fh.) (Several fingle fermons.)

—— [John] M. A. Fellow of Exeter College. Oxford. Sermons on various fubjects. Vol. 1. 2. 1787. 8. (12 fh.)

DURELL, [David] D. D. Principal of Hertford College, Oxford, Prebendary of Canterbury and Vice-Chancellor of Oxford. born.... died d. 16 Oct. 1775.

DURNFORD, [Charles] Barrifter at law. — and Edw. Hyde Eaft's reports of cafes argued and determined in the court of Kinch's bench from Michaelmas term 26 Georg III. to Michaelmas term 28 Georg III. Vol. 1. 2. 1788. (4 L. 9 fh.)

DWIGHT, [Timothy] The conqueft of Canaan, a poem. 1788. 12. (3 fh. 6 d.)

DYMOND, [Joſeph] ſee *Will. Wales*.

EASON, [Alexander] M. D. Phyfician in Dublin. A cafe of an imperforate hymen. (Med. Com. of Ed. Vol. 2. p. 187.) Account of the effects of lightning, in difcuffing a tumour of the breaft. (Ibid. Vol. 4. p. 82.) Account of the effects of electricity in removing a fixed contraction of the fingers. (Ibid. Vol. 5. p. 83.) Hiftory of a cafe of hydrocephalus fuccefsfully treated by the ufe of mercury. (*Duncan's* M. C. Vol. 8. p. 325.) On cryftallifation. (Mem. of M. Vol. 1. p. 29.) On the

On the ufe of acids in bleaching of linen. (Mem. of M. Vol. 1. p. 240.) On the afcent of vapour. (Ibid. Vol. 1. p. 395.)

EAST, [Edward Hyde] *Barrifter at law.* See *Charles Durnford.*

EDEN, [William] *LL. D. Member of Parliament.* ¤Principles of penal laws. 1771. 8. (5 fh.) Four letters to the Earl of Carlisle. 1779. 8. (2 fh. 6 d) Ed. 3. with a 5 letter. 1780. 8. (4 fh.) Letter to the Earl of Carlisle on the fubject of the late arrangement. 1786. 8. (1 fh.) Letter on the political arrangement. 1786. 8. (1 fh.) View of the treaty of commerce with France, figned at Verfailles 20 Sept. 1786. 1787. 8. (2 fh.)

EDGEWORTH, [Richard Lovell] *Esq. F. R. S: F. J. A.* Account of difcoveries in the turf bogs of Ireland. (Arch. Vol. 7. p. 111.) Experiments upon the refiftance of the air. (Phil. Transact. 1783. p. 136.) Account of the meteor of the 18 Aug. 1783. (Ibid. 1784. p. 118.) Account of fome experiments on wheel carriages. (Tr. of I. A. 1783.)

EDIE, [Georg] On englifh fhooting —. 1772. 8. (1 fh.)

EDMONSON, [Jofeph] *F. A. S.* born .... died d. 17 Febr. 1786.

EDMONSTONE, [William] *Surgeon.* On the prevention of an evil highly injurious to health. 1784. 8. (2 fh.) The reviewers corrected; or falfe criticifm analyfed —. 1785. 8. (6 d.)

EDWARDS, [....] *Mifs.* Otho and Rutha, a dramatic tale. 1781. 8.

—— [Bryan] Thoughts on the late proceedings of government refpecting the trade of the Weft-India Islands with the united ftates of North - America. 1784. 8. (1 fh.) Speech delivered at a free conference between the council and affembly of Jamaica held d. 25 Nov. 1789. — concerning the flave trade. 1790. 8. (2 fh.)

—— [Georg] *F. R. S: F. A. S.* born at Stratford, Effex d. 3 Apr. 1694. died d. 23 July. 1773.

—— [Georg] *Esq. M. D.* The aggrandiffement and national perfection of Great - Britain —. Vol. 1. 2. 1787. 4. (1 L. 5 fh.) The royal and conftitutional regeneration of Great - Britain —. Vol. 1. 2. 1790. 4. (15 fh.)

(15 fh.) The practical means of effectually exonerating the public burthens; of paying the national debts, and of raising the fupplies of war without new. taxes —. 1790. 4. (7 fh. 6 d.)

EDWARDS, [John] *B. A.* Aftronomical problems. (N. A. 1781.) Additions to the logarithmic folar tables annexed to the nautical Almanac of 1771. (N. A. 1781.) Directions for making the beft compofition for the metals of reflecting telefcopes; and the method of cafting, grinding, polifhing and giving them the true parabolic figure. (N. A. 1787.) Account of feveral compofition of metals and femi-metals, on which trials were made to find out the moft proper mixture for the fpecula of reflecting telefcopes. (N. A. 1787.) Account of caufe and cure of the tremors particularly affecting reflecting telefcopes more than refracting ones. (N. A. 1787.)

—— [John] *F. S. A.* On the plant called goofe-graff. 1784. 8. (1 fh.)

—— [John] *Major of Light Dragoons in the volunteer Army of Ireland.* The patriot foldier, a poem. 1784. 4. (2 fh)

—— [Jonathan] *A. M: Prefident of the College of New-Jerfey, New-England.* born.... died 17..

—— [Richard] *Clerk, Vicar of Mamble in the county of Worcefter and Curate of Pont-y-pool.* Letter to John Hanbury Esq. 1772 4. (1 fh.) Letter to Shute Barrington, Lordbifhop of Landaff. 1773. 4. (1 fh.)

—— [Thomas] *D. D.* A new englifh translation of the pfalms from the original hebrew — with notes —. 1755. 8. (6 fh.) The doctrine of irrefiftible grace proved to have no foundation in the writings of the new teftament. 1759. 8. (5 fh.) Prolegomena in libros V. T. poeticos; five Differtatio, in qua *Franc. Harii* — de antiqua hebraeorum hypothefin ratione et veritate niti, oftenditur —. 1762. 8. (3 fh. 6 d.) Epiftola ad *Rob. Lowth* in qua nonnulla, quae ad nuperae fuae de facra hebraeorum poefi praelectionum editionis calcem habet, expenduntur. 1765. 8. (1 fh.) Two differtations; on the abfurdity and injuftice of religious bigotry and perfecution — and on the principal qualifications and canons, neceffary for the right interpretation of of the New Teftament. 1767. 8. (1 fh. 6 d.) Duae differtationes: in quarum priore probatur, variantes lectiones et menda — non labefactare ejus auctoritatem in rebus, quae ad fidem et mores pertinent: in pofteriore vero, praedeftinationem Paulinam ad gentilium vocationem totam fpectare. 1768. 8. (2 fh.) Selecta quaedam *Theocriti* idyllia — cum notis. 1779. 8 (5 fh.) (Several fingle fermons.)

EELES, [Henry] On the caufe of thunder. (Phil. Transact. 1757. p. 524.) On the caufe of the afcent of vapour and exhalation and thofe of winds; and of the general phaenomena of the weather and barometer. (Ibid. 1759. p. 124.) Philofophical effays — containing a difcovery of the caufe of thunder. 1773. 8. (4 fh.)

EGAN, [Robert] The general exchanger: comprehending the principal direct and crofs-exchanges of Europe —. 1781. 4. (14 fh.)

EATON, [Samuel] *D. D.* born... died 17..

EGELSHAM, [Wells] *Printer.* born.... died d. 4 Apr. 1786.

EGERTON, [....] Theatrical remembrancer, containing a complete lift of all the dramatic performances in the englifh language —. 1788. 8. (3 fh. 6 d.)

—— [Charles] New hiftory of England in verfe —. 1780. 12. (3 fh.)

EKINS, [John] *M. A: Rector of Quainton, Bucks.* The loves of Medea and Jafon, a poem, translated from the greek of *Apollonius Rhodius's* Argonautics. 1770. 4. (3 fh. 6 d.)

ELIBANK, [....] *Lord.* *Confiderations on the prefent ftate of the peerage of Scotland — by a peer of Scotland. 1771. 8.

ELLERAY, [....] On transplanting Potatoe tops. *(Hunter's* G. E. Vol. 5. p. 241.)

ELLIOT, [John] *M. D.* Obfervations on the affinities of fubftances in fpirit of wine. (Phil. Transact. 1786. p. 155.) Experiments and obfervations on light and colours; and the analogy between heat and motion. 1787. 8. (3 fh.)

—— [John] *Apothecary at London.* born.... died in Newgate 1788.

ELLIOT,

ELLIOT, [R....] *A. B. formerly of Bennet College, Cambridge.* Dipping not baptizing: or, the author's opinion of the ſubjeƈt, mode and importance of water-baptiſm, according to ſcriptures. 1787. 8. (2 Sh. 6 d.)
—— [Robert] *Clergyman and Methodiſt.* born.... died d. 28 Dec. 1788.
—— [Thomas] *Miniſter of the Goſpel at Cavers.* Improvement of the method of correƈting the obſerved diſtance of the Moon from the Sun or a fixed ſtar. (T. of E. S. Vol. I. p. 191.)
—— [Thomas] *Fourcroy's* elementary leƈtures on chemiſtry and natural hiſtory — translated, with additions. Vol. 1. 2. 1785. 8. (12 Sh.)
ELLIS, [G....] * Memoir of a map of the countries comprehended between the black ſea and the Caspian, with account of the Caucaſian nations and vocabularies of their languages. 1788. 4. (9 Sh.)
—— [John] *F. R. S: Agent for the Province of Weſtflorida and for the Iſland of Dominica* born.... died d. 5 Oƈt 1776.
—— [Thomas] *Gardner at Lincoln.* Gardener's pocket Calendar. 1776. 12. (3 Sh.)
—— [William] *A. M. Maſter of the Grammarſchool at Alford in Lincolnſhire.* *Ariſtotle* on Government, translated. 1778. 4. (13 Sh.) Colleƈtion of Engliſh exerciſes; translated from *Cicero* —. 1782. 8. (2 Sh. 6 d.)
—— [William] *Aſſiſtant-Surgeon to both veſſels.* Narrative of a voyage performed by Capt. *Cook* and *Clerke* — during the Years 1776-1780. in ſearch of a North-Weſt paſſage between the continents of Aſia and America. Vol. I. 2. 1782. 8. (12 Sh.) überſ. Frankf. 1783. 8.
—— [William] *Apothecary in London.* On the cure of the venereal gonorrhoea. 1771. 8. (2 Sh. 6 d.)
ELPHINSTONE, [James] Analyſis of the french and engliſh language. Vol. I. 2. 1755. 8. (5 Sh.) Education, a poem. 1762. 8. (3 Sh.) *Apology for the monthly review. 1762. 8. (2 Sh.) Colleƈtion of poems from the beſt authors. 1763. 8. (3 Sh. 6 d.) The principles of the engliſh language digeſted; or engliſh grammar reduced to analogy. 1764. 8. Vol. 1. 2. (8 Sh.) The principles

ciples of the english language digested for the use
of schools. 1765. 8. (3 Sh.) Verses, english,
french, and latin. 1767. fol. (1 Sh.) Animadver-
sions upon elements of Criticism. 1771. 8. (2 Sh.
6 d.) A finishing plan of education. 1776. (6 d.)
Translation of *Martial's* epigramm with a comment.
1782. 4. (1 L. 1 Sh.) *Martialis* epigrammata.
1783. 8. (5 Sh.) *The hypercritic. 1783. 8.
(1 Sh.) Propriety ascertained in her picture, or
english speech and spelling reduced mutual gui-
des. Vol. 1. 2. 1787. 4.

ELSE, [Joseph] *Surgeon to St. Thomas's Hospital.*
born.... died d. 10 March 1780.

ELSTOB, [....] *Trip to Kilkenny, from Durham
by way of Whitehaven and Dublin in the Year
1776. 8. 1778. (2 Sh.)

ELVING, [Alexander] *Teacher of Mathematics in Edinburgh.* Synopsis of practical mathematics —. 1772.
12. (4 Sh)

EMERSON, [William] born d. 14 May. 1701. died
at Hurworth near Darlington d. 20 May 1782.

EMLYN, [Henry] of *Windsor.* Proposition for a
new order in architecture, with rules for drawing
the several parts. 1782. fol. (1 L. 1 Sh.)

EMMERICH. [A....] *Lieutenant Colonel.* The culture of forests with an appendix, in which the state of the royal forests is considered and a system
proposed for their improvement. 1789. 8. (2 Sh.
6 d.) The partisan in war; or the use of a corps
of light troops to an army. 1789. 8. (3 Sh.)

ENFIELD, [William] *LL. D. Lecturer on the belles
lettres in the dissenting Academy at Warrington,
Lancashire.* Sermons for the use of families. Vol.
1. 2. 1768. 1771. 8. (3 Sh.) übers. (von *J. C. F.
Schulz*) Halle 1774. Prayers for the use of families. 1770. 8. (3 Sh.) Ed. 2. 1777. 8. (4 Sh.)
Übers. von *F. E. Wilmsen.* Halle 1773. 8. *The
preacher's directory; or a series of subjects proper
for public discourses. 1771. 4. (6 Sh.) *The
english preacher: or sermons on the principal subjects of religion and morality, selected and abridged from various authors. Vol. 1-9. 1773. 8.
(1 L. 11 Sh. 6 d.) übers. Bremen. 8. Th. 1. 17..
Biographical sermons: or, a series of discourses on
the

the principal characters in scripture. 1777. 8. (3 Sh.) überf. Leipz. 1777. Effay towards the hiftory of Leverpool, drawn from papers left by the late M. *George Perry* and from other materials fince collected. 1774. fol. (12 Sh.) Obfervations on litterary property. 1774. 4. (2 Sh.) The fpeaker, or miscellaneous pieces felected from the beft englifh writers with an effay on elocution. 1775. 8. (6 Sh.) Exercifes in elocution. 1780. 8. (the *fecond* Part of the fpeaker) (3 Sh. 6 d.) Inftitutes of natural philofophy, theoretical and experimental. 1785. 4. (12 Sh.) (Several fingle fermons.)

ENGLEFIELD, [Henry] *Sir. Baronet. F. R. S: F. A. S.* Account of the appearance of the foil at opening a Well at Hanby in Lincolnfhire. (Phil. Transact. 1781. p. 345.) Obfervations on reading Abbey. (Arch. Vol. 6. p. 61.) Obfervations on the antient buildings at York. (Ibid. Vol. 6. p. 104.) Additions to Mr. *King's* account of Lincoln caftle. (Ibid. Vol. 6. p. 376.) Obfervation on the variation of light in the ftar Algol. (Phil. Transact. 1784. p. 1. & p. 5.) Tables of the apparent places of the comet of 1661. whofe return is expected in 1789. with a new method of ufing the reticule rhomboid. 1788. 4. (2 Sh. 6 d.) Letter to the author of the review of the cafe of the proteftant diffenters — with an abftract of, and fome general obfervations upon the laws now in force againft the englifh Protefting catholic diffenter. 1790. 8. (1 Sh. 6 d.)

ENGLISH, [Robert] *formerly Chaplain by the navy George.* Naval review, a poem. 1773. 4. (1 Sh.) Ed. 2. 1774. 4. (1 Sh. 6 d) Elegy on the death of Sir *Charles Saunders.* 1777. 4. (1 Sh.)

ENTICK, [John] *M A. Rector at Stapney.* born 1713. died d. 22 May 1773.

ERSKINE, [Andrew] Town eclogues — 1773. 4. (1 Sh. 6 d.)

—— [Charles] *Surgeon.* The inftitutions of medicinal pathology of *H. D. Gaubius* translated. 1778. 8. (4 Sh.)

—— [David] *Earl of Buchan in Scotland.* Speech of the Earl of Buchan. 1780. 4. (2 Sh. 6 d.)

—— [John] *D. D. Minifter of Edinburgh.* Theological Differtations: containing 1) the nature of the Sinai cove-

covenant. 2) The character and privileges of the apoftolic churches with an examination of Dr. *Taylor's* key to the epiftles. 3) The nature of faving faith. 4) the law of nature fufficiently promulgated to the heathens. 5) Attempt to promote the frequent difpenfing the Lord's fupper. 1766. 12. (3 Sh.) Shall i go to war with my American brethern? 1769. 8. (1 Sh.) Ed. 2. 1776. 8. Confiderations on the fpirit of popery. 1779. 8. °The equity and wisdom of adminiftration. 1776. 8. °Reflections on the rife, progreff and probable confequences of the contentions with the colonies. by a freeholder. 1776.

ERSKINE, [Robert] *Engineer.* The facts and accufations fet forth in a late pamphlet the conduct and treatment of *John Crookfhanks* proved to be falfe and groundleff. 1759. 8. (6 d.) Differtation on rivers and tides —. 1770. 8. (6 d.) Ed. 2. 1780. 8. (1 Sh.)

ESSEX, [James] of Cambridge: *F. A. S.* Remarks on the antiquity and the different modes of brick and ftone buildings in England. (Arch. Vol. 4. p. 73.) Some obfervations on Lincoln cathedral. (Ibid. p. 149.) On the origin and antiquity of round churches; and of the round church at Cambridge in particular. (Ibid Vol. 6. p. 163.) Defcription and plan of the ancient timber bridge at Rocheſter. (Ibid. Vol. 7. p. 305.) On Croyland abbey and bridge. (Biblioth. Topogr. Brit. Numb. 22. p. 525.)

ESTE, [Charles] *a Clergyman.* My own life. 1-87. 8. (1 Sh. 6 d.) (Principal Director of the newspaper, the World.)

—— [Charles] *Member of the company of Apothecaries in London.* Tracts on medical fubjects. 1776. 4. (1 Sh. 6 d.)

ESTWICK, [Samuel] *L. L. D.* Letter to Dr. *Tucker,* in anfwer to his humble addreff —. 1776. 8. (1 Sh. 6 d.) °Confiderations on the Negroe caufe. by a Weft- Indian. 1772. 8. (1 Sh.) Ed. 3. (with the author's name). 1788. 8. (2 Sh.)

EVANS, [Caleb] *M. A. Anabaptift Clergyman in Briftol.* Two fermons on the deity of the fon and holy fpirit. 1765. 8. Reply to the letter to him on his two fermons. 1765. 8. Letter to *John Wesley,*
occa-

occafioned by his calm addreff to the American colonies. 1775. 8. Reply to *Fletcher's* vindication of *Wesley's* calm addreff to our American colonies. 1775. 8. Political fophiftry detected; or — remarks on — *Fletcher's* — American patriotifm. 1776. 8. (3 d.) Publifhed: Mifcellaneous pieces in verfe and profe by *Theodofia* (Mrs. *Anne Steel's*) Vol. 1-3. 1781. 8. (3 Sh.) Chrift crucified, or the fcripture doctrine of the atonement — illuftrated in 13 Difcourfes. 1789. 8. (2 Sh.)

EVANS, [Evan] born.... died d. 4 Sept. 1788.

—— [John] *M. D. Phyfician in Liverpool.* Hiftory of a cafe of retroverted uterus. (Med. Com. of Ed. Vol. 6. p. 215.) Hiftory of an obftinate affection of the bowels, cured by the injection of a decoction of tobacco. (Ibid. p. 332.) Hiftory of a cafe of hydrocephalus, terminating fucceffully. (*Duncan's* M. C. Vol. 10. p. 299.) überf. Samml. f. A. Th. XI. S. 676. Hiftory of an uncommon fwelling of the lower extremities in a pregnant woman, terminating favourably immediately after an abortion. (Ibid. p. 302.) Cafe of Ganglion of the tendons, opened and fuccefffully treated. (London M. J. Vol. VIII. P. 2.)

—— [Thomas] *Solicitor in Chancery and one of the Attorneys of the court of King's bench in England.* Refutation of *Linguet's* memoirs of the baftile —. 1783. 8. (1 Sh. 6 d.)

EVANSON, [Edward] *M. A. Clergyman.* Three Difcourfes. 1) upon the man after God's own heart. 2) the faith of Abraham. 2) The feal of the foundation of God. 1773. 8. (1 Sh. 6 d.) Letter to the bifhop of Lichtfield (*Hurd*) on the prophecies of the New Teftament —. 1777. 8. (2 Sh.)

EWEN, [James] *Ovid's* Heroid; or epiftles from the heroines of Antiquity translated into englifh verfe. 1787. 8. (6 Sh.)

EWER, [J....] *M. D. Phyfician in Trinidad.* Account of the medicinal properties of a bark — from South-America. (London M. J. Vol. X. P. 2.) überf. Samml, f. A. Th. 13. S. 321.

EWING, [Alexander] *Teacher of Mathematics in Edinburgh.* Synopfis of practical mathematics. 1771. 8. 4 Sh.) Inftitutes of Arithmetic. 1773. 12. (2 Sh.)

EWING,

EWING, [John] *D. Provoſt of the Univerſity of Pennſylvania.* Calculation of the Tranſit of Venus over the Sun as it is to happen June 3. 1769. for the city of Philadelphia. (Tr. of A. S. Vol. I. p. 5.) Account of the obſervations on the tranſit of Venus over the Sun on the 3. of June 1769. and of the tranſit of Mercury Nov. 9. both as obſerved in the ſtate-houſe ſquare, Philadelphia. (Ibid. p. 42.) Improvement in the conſtruction of *Godfrey's* (commonly called *Hadley's*) Quadrant. (Ibid. App. p. 21.)

EYRE, [Joſeph] Obſervations on the prophecies relating to the reſtoration of the jews —. 1771. 8. (2 ſh. 6 d.)

FADEN, [William] *Geographer to his Majeſty.* Geographical exerciſes —. 1778. fol. (15 ſh.)

FAIRMAN, [William] *Teacher of Mathematics.* A new method for obtaining the longitude at ſea. 1783. 4. (1 ſh.) On geography, the uſes of the globes and aſtronomy —. 1788. 8. (4 ſh.)

FALCK, [N. ... D. ...] *M. D. at London.* The ready obſervator for determining the latitude. 1771. 4. (3 ſh.) Diſſertation on the diving veſſel projected by Mr. *Day*, and ſunk in Plymouth ſound —. 1775. 4. (2 ſh. 6 d.) Deſcription of an improved ſteam engine. 1776. 8. (2 ſh.) On the venereal diſeaſe. 1772. 8. (7 ſh. 6 d.) überſ. (von *J. W. Möller)* Hamburg. 1775. 8. The ſeaman's medical inſtructor —. 1774. 8. (4 ſh. 6 d.) On the medical qualities of mercury. 1776. 12. (3 ſh. 6 d.) überſ. Leipz. 1777. 8. Publiſhed: *Rich. Wilkes's* hiſtorical eſſay on the dropſy. 1777. 8. (7 ſh.) Guardian of health. Vol. I. 1778. 12. (3 ſh.)

FALCONAR, [Harriet] (born 1774.) and
—— [Maria] (born 1772.) Poems. 1788. 12. (3 ſh. 6 d.) Poems on Slavery. 1788. 8. (1 Sh. 6 d.)

FALCONBRIDGE, [Alexander] *late Surgeon in the African trade.* Account of the ſlave trade on the coaſt of Africa. 1788. 8. (9 d.) überſ. von *M. C. Sprengel.* Leipzig. 1789. 8.

FALCONER; [Magnus] *Surgeon and Prof. of Anatomy.* ſee *Will. Hewſon.* Synopſis of a courſe of lectures on anatomy and ſurgery. 1778. 8. (6 ſh.)

FALCONER, [Thomas] *Esq. of the city of Chester.*
Sketch of the materials for a new hiſtory of Cheſhire —. 1772. 4. (2 ſh. 6 d.)
—— [William] *M. D: F. R. S: Phyſician to the Bath Hoſpital.* ° The Shipwreck, a poem, by a ſailor. 1762. 4. (5 ſh.) Ed. 2. 1764. 8. (2 Sh. 6 d.) Diſſ. De nephritide vera. Edinb. 1766. The univerſal dictionary of the marine. 1769. 4. (1 L. 1 ſh) On the Bath waters. 1770. 8. (3 ſh.) Ed. 2. Vol. 1. 2. 1774. 8. (10 ſh.) Obſervations on Dr. *Cadogan's* Diſſertation on the gout and all chronic diſeaſes. Ed. 2. 1772. 8. (1 ſh. 6 d) überſ. (von *C. G. Selle*) Berlin. 1773. 8. Obſervations and experiments on the poiſon of copper. 1774. 8. (2 ſh.) On the water commonly uſed at Bath. 1775. 8. (3 ſh.) überſ. von *C. F. Sam. Hahnemann.* Leipz. 1777. 8. Experiments and obſervations. P. 1-3. 1777. 8. (2 ſh.) Obſervations on ſome of the articles of diet and regimen uſually recommended to valetudinarians. 1778. 8. (1 ſh.) Remarks on the influence of climate, ſituation, nature of country, population, nature of food and way of life. 1781. 4. (18 ſh.) überſ. (von *E. B. G. Hebenſtreit*) Leipz. 1782. 8. Account of the epidemic catharrhal fever, called the influenza. 1782. 8. (1 Sh.) *Matth. Dobſon* on fixed air with an appendix on the uſe of the ſolution of fixed alkaline ſalts — in the ſtone and gravel. 1785. 8. (4 Sh.) Remarks on the knowledge of the ancients. (Mem. of M. Vol. 1. p. 261.) On the influence of the ſcenery of a country on the manners of its inhabitants. (Ibid. p. 271.) Thoughts on the ſtyle and taſte of gardening among the ancients. (Ibid. p. 297.) Remarks on the knowledge of the ancients reſpecting glaſs. (Ibid. Vol. 2. p. 95.) On the influence of the paſſions upon the diſorders of the body. 1788. 8. (3 Sh.) überſ. von *C. F. Michaelis,* 1789. 8. On the efficacy of the application of cold water to the extremities in a caſe of obſtinate conſtipation of the bowels. (Mem. of M. S. of L. Vol. 2.) Remarks on the palſy. (Ibid.) On the preſervation of the health of perſons employed in agriculture, and on the cure of the diſeaſe incident to that way of life. 1789. 8. (1 Sh. 6 d.) Practical Diſſertation on the

medi-

medicinal effects of the Bath-waters. 1790. 8. (4 Sh.)

FALKENER, [....] *Surgeon at Southwell, in Nottinghamshire.* A case of the hydrophobia. (Med. Transact. Vol. 2. p. 222.)

FALKNER, [Thomas] Description of Patagonia and the adjoining parts of South-America —. 1774. 4. (7 Sh. 6 d.) übers. (von *S. H. Ewald*) Gotha. 1775. 8. übers. in *Hirschfeld's* Geschichte der Menschheit, Bändgen 3.

FALL, [Robert] Observations on the report of the committee of the house of Commons appointed to inquire into the state of the british fishery. 1786. 8. (2 Sh.)

FARLEY, [Edward] *Esq.* Imprisonment for debt unconstitutional and oppressive; proved from the fundamental principles of the constitution and the rights of nature. 1789. 8. (3 Sh.)

FARMER, [A... W...] "Free thoughts on the proceedings of the continental congress', held at Philadelphia Sept. 5. 1774. by a Farmer. 1775. 8. (1 Sh.) The congress canvassed; or, an examination into the conduct of the delegates at their grand convention held in Philadelphia Sept. 1. 1774 —. 1775. 8. (1 Sh.) View of the controversy between Great-Britain and her colonies —. 1775. 8. (1 Sh. 6 d.)

—— [Hugh] *Pastor of Protestant Dissenters at Walthamston near London.* born 1714. died d. 26 Febr. 1787.

—— [Richard] *D. D. Principal Librarian to the University of Cambridge.* On the learning of Shakespeare. 1766. 8. (1 Sh.)

FARQUHARSON, [William] *of Edinburgh. M. D.* Case of a scirrhous oesophagus. (Mem. of M. S. of L. Vol. 2.) Account of a singular case in midwifery. (*Duncan's* M. C. Dec. II. Vol. 3. p. 344.)

FARR, [Samuel] *M. D. F. R. S.* Diss. De Animo ut causa morborum. Lugd. Bat. 1765. 4. Extract of a meteorological journal for the Year 1767. kept at Plymouth. (Phil. Transact. 1768. p. 136.) — for the Year 1768. (Ibid. 1769. p. 81.) On the medical virtues of acids. 1769. 8. (2 Sh.) Philosophical enquiry into the nature, origin and extent of of animal motion. 1771. 8. (6 Sh.) Aphorismi de Marasmo, ex fummis medicis collecti. 1772. 4. (1 Sh. 6 d.) Extract of a meteorological journal for the Y. 1774. kept at Briftol. (Phil. Transact. 1775. p 194) — for the Y. 1775. (Ibid. 1776. p. 367.) — for the Y. 1776. (Ibid. 1777. p. 353.) — for the Y. 1777. (Ibid. 1778. p. 567.) — for the Y. 1778. (Ibid. 1779. p. 551.) On blood letting in confumptions. 1775. 8. (1 Sh.) überf. Samml. f. A, Th. 3. St. 1. S. 124.) Obfervations on the character and conduct of a phyfician. 17.. Translation of *Hippocrates's* hiftory of epidemics. 1780. 4. (1 L. 1 Sh.) On the ufe of cantharides in dropfical complaints. (Mem of M. S. of L. Vol. 2.) *Elements of medical jurisprudence. 1788. 8. (2 Sh. 6 d.)

FARRELL, [John] *A. M.* Translation of *Francis d'Ivernois's* view of the conftitution and revolutions of Geneva in XVIII Century. 1784. 8. (5 Sh.)

FARRER, [....] *Mrs.* (Wife of Capt. *Farrer.*) The appeal of an injured wife againft a cruel husband. 1788. 8. (2 Sh.)

—— [J....] *Mafter of the grammar-fchool at Witton le Wear in Durham.* M. *Corderii* colloquiorum centuria felecta —. 1785. 12. (1 Sh. 3 d.)

—— [John] *of Queen's College, Oxford.* The reign of death, a poem. 1780. 8. (1 Sh.) Selection of hebrew poems, translated. 1780. 4. (3 Sh. 6 d.) America, a poem. 1780. 4. (2 Sh.)

—— [W....] *M. D.* *Obfervations on fpecific medicines —. 1767. 8. (2 Sh. 6 d.) Account of the rickets in children and remarks on its analogy to the king's evil. 1773. 12. (1 Sh.)

FARROE, [....] *M. D.* The royal golden inftructor for Youth throughout the britifh dominions — being an abridgment of the royal univerfal britifh grammar and vocabulary. 1776. 12. (1 Sh. 6 d.)

FAULKNER, [B...] *of Little Chelfea.* Obfervations on the general and improper treatment of infanity with a plan for the more fpeedy and effectual recovery of infane perfons. 1789. 8. (1 Sh.)

—— [George] *Esq and Alderman.* Epiftle to *Gorges Edm. Howard*, with notes. Ed. VI. 1772. 8. (1 Sh.)

FAW-

FAWCETT, [Benjamin] *M. A.* Candid reflections on the doctrine of the Trinity. 1777. 8. Ed. 2. 1778. with appendix. 1780. 8. (2 Sh.) Observations on religious melancholy. 1780. 8. (1 Sh.) überf. von *J. F. Lehzen.* Leipz. 1785. 8. (Several single sermons.)

FAWCETT, [John] *Master of a Boarding school at Brearley-Hall near Halifax.* Critical expolition of the 9 chapter of the epistle to the Romans —. 1752. 8. (1 Sh.) The sick Man's employ or views of death and eternity realized. 1775. 12. (6 d.) Advice to Youth; or, the advantages of early piety —. 1778. 12. (1 Sh. 6 d.) Ed. III. 1786. 12. (1 Sh. 6 d.) Hymns —. 1782. 8. (2 Sh.) Death of Eumenio; a Poem. 1780. 8. (6 d.) The reign of death. a Poem. 1780. 8. (1 Sh.) Essay on anger. 1787. 12. (1 Sh. 6 d.)

FAWKES, [Francis] *M. A: Vicar of Hayes, Kent.* born in *Yorkshire.* died d. 26 Aug. 1777.

FAYERMAN, [Richard] *M. A.* Contemplation, a poetical essay, on the works of creation. 1776. 4. (2 Sh.)

FEARNE, [Charles] *Barrister of law; of the Inner temple, Conveyancer.* Impartial answer to the doctrine delivered in a letter, which appeard in the public advertiser on the 10th of Dec. 1769. under the signature of Junius. 1770. 8. (1 Sh.) ° Lexigraphical chart of landed property in England. 17.. Essay on the learning of contingent remainders and executory devises. 1772. 8. (1 Sh. 6 d.) Copies of opinions ascribed to eminent counsel on the will which was the subject of the case of Perrin v. Blake before the court —. 1781. 8. (1 Sh.)

FEARON, [Henry] *Surgeon to the Surry Dispensary.* On cancers. 1784. 8. (1 Sh. 6 d.) Ed. 2. 1786. 8. (2 Sh. 6 d.) Ed. 3. 1790. 8. (3 Sh. 6 d.) überf. Duisburg. 1790. 8. Account of a tumour, supposed to have been a diseased kidney. (M. C. Vol. I. p. 416.) Observations on cancers. (Mem. of M. S. of L. Vol. 2.) An improved method of amputating a cancerous breast. (London M. J. Vol. 4. p. 406.)

FELL, [Elizabeth] *of Newcastle.* Fables, odes and miscellaneous poems. 1771. 8. (3 Sh.) Poem on the

the times. 1774. 4. (1 fh.) Poems. 1777. 4. (4 fh.)

FELL, [John] a *Diſſenting Clergyman*. Genuine proteſtantiſm; or the unalienable rights of conſcience defended. 1773. 8. (1 fh. 6d.) A fourth letter to Mr. *Pickard* on genuine proteſtantiſm; 1775. 8. (1 fh.) Daemoniacs. Inquiry into the heathen and the ſcripture doctrine of Daemons, in which the hypotheſis of Mr. *Farmer* and others are conſidered. 1779. 8. (5 fh.) The idolatry of Greece and Rome diſtinguiſhed from that of other heathen nations. 1785. 8. (2 fh. 6d.)

FELLOWS, [John] *Grace triumphant, a ſacred poem — by Philantropos. 1770. 8. (2 fh.) Elegy on the death of *John Gill*, D.D. 1771. 8. (6d.) Hymn's on believers baptiſm. 1773. 12. (1 fh.) Elegiac poem on the death of *Aug. Montagu Toplady*. 1778. 8. (6d.) The Hiſtory of the holy bible in verſe —. Vol. 1-4. 1778. 12. (8 fh.) The proteſtant alarm; or, popiſh cruelty fully diſplayed —. 1780. 12. (3 fh.)

FENN, [John] *M.A: F.A.S.* Original letters, written during the reigns of Henry VI. Edward IV and Richard III. by various perſons of rank or conſequence. Vol. 1-4. 1787. 1789. 4. (4 L. 4 fh.)

FENNEL, [James] Statement of facts, occaſional of, and relative to the late diſturbances at the theatre royal, Edinburgh. 1788. 8. (1 fh.)

FENTON, [....] The Earl of Warwick, a Tragedy. 1767. 8. Poems. 1774. 4. (6 fh.)

FERGUSON, [Adam] *LL.D. Emeritus Profeſſor of Philoſophy in the Univerſity of Edinburgh*. Hiſtory of civil ſociety. 1766. 4. (15 fh.) überſ. (von C. F. *Jünger*) Leipz. 1768. 8. Inſtitutes of moral philoſophy. 1769. 8. (3 fh.) nachgedr. Mentz and Francfort. 1786. 8. überſ. von *Garve*. 1772. Hiſtory of the progreſſ and termination of the roman republic. Vol. 1-3. 1783. 4. (2 L. 12 fh. 6d.) überſ. von *C.D. Beck*. Th. 1-3. Leipz. 1784. 8.

—— [Andrew] *Gardener at Brentford*. The Gardener's univerſal guide. 1787. 8. (5 fh.)

—— [James] *F.R.S: Lecturer in Natural Philoſophy and Aſtronomy*. born at Keit in Bampſſhire 1710. died d. 16 Nov. 1776.

FERGU-

FERGUSON, [John] *A. M. Captain in the service of the East-India Company.* Dictionary of the hindostan language — with a grammar. 1773. 4. (2 L. 2 sh.)
—— [Robert] Poems. 1774. 12. (2 sh. 6 d.)
FERNYHOUGH, [William] *A. B.* Trentham park, a poem. 1789. 4. (1 sh.)
FERON, [J....] *late Surgeon-Major of the english squadron under M. de Ternay's command in North-America and of the Marine hospitals at Boston and in Rhode-Island.* Experiments on the waters of Boston. (Mem. of B. A. Vol. 1. p. 556.)
FERRAR, [J....] *Citizen of Limerick.* History of Limerick, ecclesiastical, civil and military from the earliest records to the Y. 1786. 1787. 8. (6 sh.)
FERRIS, [Samuel] *M. D. Extraordin. Member of the Roy. Soc. at Edinburgh.* Diff. De sanguinis per corpus vivum circulantis putredine. Edinb. 1784. Dissertation on Milk. 1785. 8. (3 Sh.) übers. von C. F. *Michaelis.* Leipz. 1787. 8.
FIELDING, [Charles John] The brothers, an eclogue. 1781. 4. (1 sh.)
FIGGES, [James] *Excise officer.* Excise Officer's vade mecum or ready assistant. 1783. 8. (2 sh. 6 d.)
FILSON, [John] The discovery, settlement and present state of Kentuke and an essay towards the topography and natural history of that important country. 1784. 8. (10 sh.) übers. Leipz. 1790. 8.
FINCH, [Thomas] Precedents in Chancery; being a collection of cases in Chancery from 1689 to 1722. Ed. II. 1786. 8. (10 sh. 6 d.)
FINDLAY, [Robert] *D. D. Professor of Divinity in the University of Glasgow.* Vindication of the sacred books and of *Josephus* — from various misrepresentations and cavils of *Voltaire.* 1770. 8. (5 sh. 6 d.)
FINGLASS, [Esther] *Miss.* The recluse, or history of Lady Gertrude Lesby. Vol. 1. 2. 1788. 8. (5 sh.)
FISHER, [Joseph] *of Drax, in Yorkshire. M. D.* Remarks upon the remarker on *Lindsey's* scripture confutation —. 1775. 8. (1 sh. 6 d.) Review of Dr. *Priestley's* doctrine of philosophical necessity —. 1779. 8. (1 sh. 6 d.) The practice of medicine made easy —. 1785. 8. (2 sh. 6 d.)

FISHER, [Joſhua] *F. A. S.* Caſe of a remarkable large tumour found in the cavity of the abdomen. (Mem. of B. A. Vol. 1. p. 537. Lond. M. J. Vol. 7. P. 3.)

FISKE, [Jonathan] *Bookſeller.* The caſe of *J. Fiſke* — tried and — acquitted at the ſeſſions in the Old Bailey — upon the infamous proſecution of *Patrik Roche Farrill.* 1781. 8. (1 Sh.) The life and transactions of *Margaret Nicholſon* —. 1785. 8. (1 Sh. 6 d.)

FITZGERALD, [George Robert] *Esq.* born.... executed for the murder of M'Donnel in Ireland 17..

—— [Gerald] *Fellow of Trinity-College, Dublin.* The academic ſportsman; or, a Winter's day; a poem. 1773. 4. (1 Sh.)

—— [Keane] *F. R. S.* Experiments on applying the Rever. D. *Hale's* method of diſtilling ſalt water to the ſteam engine. (Phil. Transact. 1760 p. 53. p. 370.) Attempt to improve the manner of working the ventilators by the help of the fire engine. (Ibid. 1760. p. 727.) Deſcription of a metalline thermometer. (Ibid. 1761. p. 823.) Experiments on checking the too luxuriant growth of fruit trees, tending to diſpoſe them to produce fruit. (Ibid. 1762. p. 71.) Deſcription of a new thermometer and barometer. (Ibid. 1762. p. 146.) Method of leſſening the quantity of friction in engines. (Ibid. 1763. p. 139.) Account of ſome improvements made on a new wheel barometer, invented by him. (Ibid. 1770. p. 74.) *Eſſay on the Eaſt-India trade, and its importance to this Kingdom —. 1770. 8. (1 Sh.) Letter to the directors of the Eaſt-India Company. 1777. 8. (1 Sh.) *Conſiderations on the important benefits to be derived from the Eaſt-India Company's building and navigating their own ſhips. 1778. 8. (1 Sh.) Experiments with Chineſe hemp ſeed. (Phil. Transact. 1782. p. 44.)

—— [Samuel] *Phyſician at Mullingar.* Hiſtories of two caſes: The discharge of a large calcareous concretion and the extraction of the bones of a foetus by the rectum. *(Duncan's* M. C. Vol. 8. p. 329.)

—— [William] *of Gray's Inn.* Ode to the memory of Capt. *James Cook.* 1780. 4. (1 Sh.)

FITZ-

FITZPATRICK, [J...] *of Dublin.* Account of extraordinary effects from the application of cold water after delivery. (*Duncan's* M. C. Vol. 9. p. 227.) History of a case of catalepsis successfully treated. (Ibid. Vol. 10. p. 242.)

FLAGG, [Henry Collins] *of South-Carolina.* Observations on the Numb.-Fish or torporific eel. (Tr. of A. S. Vol. 2. p. 170.)

FLEET, [Edward] Junior; B. A. *of Oriel College, Oxford.* Examination of *Maclaine's* answer to *Soame Jenyns* on his view of the internal evidence of the christian religion —. 1777. 8. (2 Sh.) Address and reply relative to his examination of *Maclaine's* answer to *Soame Jenyns* —. 1777. 8. (6 d.)

FLEMING, [Caleb] D. D. *Pastor of a Protestant dissenting church.* born 1698. died d. 21 July 1779.

—— [Thomas] *Minister of the Gospel at Kenmore.* Account of a remarkable agitation of the waters. of *Loch Tay.* (Tr. of E. S. Vol. 1. p. 200.)

FLETCHER, [Charles] M. D. Maritime state considered as to the health of seamen —. 1786. 8. (5 Sh.) The Cock-pit, a poem. 1787. 4. (2 Sh.)

—— [John] *Vicar of Madeley, Salop and Chaplain by the Earl of Buchan.* born.... died d. 14 Aug. 1785.

FLOOD, [Henry] Speech on the commercial treaty with France. 1787. 8. (1 Sh.)

FLOWER, [Henry] (born in America.) Observations on the gout and rhevmatism —. 1766. 8. (6 d.) Proofs of curing the gout, and other disorders —. Ed. 2. 1771. 8. (6 d.)

—— [Robert] The radix: a new way of making logarithms. 1771. 4. (3 Sh.)

FOGERTY, [....] Mrs. Memoirs of Col. *Digby* and Miss *Stanley.* Vol. 1. 2. 1773. 12. (5 Sh.) The fatal connexion. Vol. 1. 2. 1773. 12.

FOOT, [James] Penseroso; or, the pensive philosopher in his solitudes. a poem. 1771. 8. (4 Sh.)

—— [Jesse] *Surgeon at London.* On the diseases of the urethra. 1774. 8. (1 Sh. 6 d.) Ed. 2. 1781. Ed. 3. 1785. 8. überf. Altenb. 1777. 8. Observations on the new opinions of *J. Hunter* in his treatise on the venereal disease. P. 1-3. 1787. 8. (5 Sh. 6 d.) Ed. 2. 1787. 8. (8 Sh. 6 d.) On the bite of a mad doge —. 1788. 8. (2 Sh.) A new discovered

vered fact, of a relative nature, in the venereal poifon. 1790. 8. (1 Sh. 6 d.)

FOOTE, [Samuel] *Actor.* born at *Truro, Cornwall.* 1717. died d. 20 Oct. 1777.

FORBES, [Daniel] *Surgeon at Dornock.* Hiftory of a cafe of Ileus., in which great benefit was derived from the application of a blifter. (*Duncan's* M. C. Vol. 9. p. 266.)

—— [Eli] Account of the effects of lightning on a large rock in Gloucefter. (Mem. of B. A. Vol. I. p. 253.)

—— [Francis] The extenfive practice of the new husbandry —. 1778. 8. (5 Sh.) The improvement of wafte lands, viz, wet, moory land, land near rivers and running waters, peat land —. 1778. 8. (3 Sh. 6 d.)

FORD, [Edward] *Surgeon of the Weftminfter General Difpenfary.* An extraneous body cut out from the joint of the knee. (Med. Obf. Vol. 5. p. 329. überf. Samml. f. A. St. 5. S. 96.) A cafe of proptofis. (M. C. Vol. 1. p. 95.) Account of a method of curing the hydrophthalmis by means of a feton. (Ibid. p. 409.) Account of a hairy excrefcence in the facies of a new-born infant. (Ibid p. 444.) A cafe of hydrophthalmia fucceffully treated. (London M. J. Vol. 1. p. 346.) Account of a remarkable operation on a broken arm. (Ibid. Vol. 2. p. 46.) Cafe of a fatal ulceration of the bladder, occafioned by a caries of the os pubis. (Ibid. Vol. 3. p. 80. überf. Samml. f. A. Th. 8. S. 45.) Cafe of ftrangulated hernia. (Ibid. Vol. 6. p. 118.) Two cafes of fracture of the fcull. (Ibid. Vol. 8. P. 4.) Cafe of the fpontaneous cure of anevrifm, with remarks. (Ibid. Vol. 9. P. 2.) Remarks on hydrocephalus internus. (Ibid. Vol. 11. P. 1. überf. Samml. f. A. Th. 13. S. 369.)

FORD, [William] born 1736. died d. 26 Jan. 1783.

FORDE, [Brownlow] The miraculous cure, or the citizen outwitted, a farce. 1771. 8.

FORDYCE, [George] *M. D. F. R. S.* Differt. De Catarrho. Edinb. 1758 (fee *Smellie's* Thefaur.: Diff. Edin. Vol. 2. p. 501.) Elements of the practice of phyfic P. 1. 2. 1768. 8. (4 Sh. 6. d.) Ed. 2. 1771. 8. Ed. 3. 1784. überf. Kopenh. 1769. 8.
Ele-

Elements of Agriculture and vegetation. 1771. 8.
(2 Sh. 6. d.) überf. *Fr. Schwediauer.* Wien. 1778.
8. New Inquiry into the caufes symptoms and
cure of putrid and inflammable fevers. 1773. 8.
Of the light produced by inflammation. (Phil.
Transact. 1776. p. 504.) Examination of various
ores in the muſeum of Dr. *Will. Hunter.* (Ibid.
1779. p. 527.) A new method of effaying copper
ore. (Ibid. 1780. p. 30.) Account of fome experiments on the loſs of weight in bodies on being melted,
or heated. (Ibid. 1785. p. 361.) Account of an experiment on heat. (Ibid. 1787. p. 310.) The Croo-
nian lecture on muſcular motion. (Ibid. 1788. p. 23.)

FORDYCE, [James] D. D. *Minifter at Brechin.* (Brother to Sir *Will. Fordyce.*) The temple of Virtue; a
dream. 1756. 8. (1 Sh. 6. d.) ° Letters on the
eloquence of the pulpit. 1764. 8. (1 Sh. 6. d.)
Letters between Theodofius and Conftantia. 17..
° Sermons to young women. Vol. 1. 2. 1765. 8.
(6 Sh.) überf. Th. 1. 2. Leipzig. 1767. 8. The
character and conduct of the female fex. 1776.
8. (1 Sh. 6. d.) überf. Leipzig. 1776. 8. Addreff
to young men. Vol. 1. 2. 1777. 8. (7 Sh.) überf.
Th. 1. 2. Leipz. 1778. 8. Addreffes to the deity
1785. 8 (2 Sh. 6. d.) Ed. 2. 1787. (3 Sh.) Poems.
1787. 8. (3 Sh.)

—— [William] *Sir, Baronet. M. D. Phyfician at London.* Review of the venereal difeafe and its remedies. 1768. 8. (2 Sh.) Ed. 2. 1777. 8. Ed. 5. 1785.
8. überf. Altenburg. 1769. 8. Inquiry into the
caufes, fymptoms and cure, of putrid and inflammatory fevers —. 1773. 8. (3 Sh.) überf.: mit einem Anhang von dem Hectifchen Fieber und der
— Bräune. Leipz. 1774. 8. Fragmenta chirur-
gica et medica. 1784. 8. (3 Sh.) Attempt to discover the virtues of the farfaparilla root in the
venereal difeafe. (Med. Obf. Vol. 1. p. 149.) On
the virtues of the muriatic acid or fpirit of Sea - falt
in the cure of putrid difeafes. 1789. 8. (1 Sh.)

FOREST, [Theophilus] born: .... died d. 5 Nov.
1784.

FORREST, [Thomas] *Captain.* Voyage to new Guinea and the Moluccas, from Balambangan — during the Years 1774. 1775. 1776. with a vocabulary

ry of the Magindano tongue. 1779. 4. (1 L. 1 f
Sh. 6. d.) überf. im Auszug. Hamb. 1782. 8. *Ebe-
ling's* neue Sammlung von Reifebefchreib. Th. 3.
S. 1.   On the monfoons in India. 1783. 8. (2 Sh.)

FORSTER, [Nathaniel] *D. D. Rector of all faints, Colchefter and Tolleskunt knight's, Effex; Chaplain to
the Counteff Dowager of Northington.* born: ....
died d. 12 Apr. 1790.

FOSTER, [Anne Emelinda] *Mrs.* (maid-name *Mafter-
mann*) born 1747. died at Margate d. 24 March
1789.

—— [Edward] *M. D: Teacher of Midwifery in Dublin.*
born: .... died 17 . .

—— [John] born at Windfor 1731. died 1773.

—— [William] *Farrier.* The Gentleman's experienced
farrier; containing the methods of diet, exercife,
bleeding, purging — of horfes —. 1787. 8. (6 Sh.)

FOTHERGILL, [Anthony] *M. D: F. R. S. Northampton.* Diff. De febre remittente. Edinb. 1763.
8. Two cafes of an incontinency of urine cured
by a blifter to the region of the os facrum. (Med.
Obf. Vol. 3. p. ...) The cafe of a man affected
with a difficulty in paffing urine, occafioned by
a difcharge of wind from the urethra. (Med. Com.
of Ed. Vol. 2. p. 194.) Obfervations made during the laft froft at Northampton. (Phil. Transact.
1776. p. 587.) Account of the cure of the St.
Vitus's dance by electricity. (Ibid. 1779. p. 1.)
Account of an improved method of treating the
puerperal fever. (London M. J. Vol. 3. p. 411.)
On the nature and qualities of the Cheltenham water. 1785. 8. (1 Sh. 6. d.) Ed. 2. 1788. 8. (2 Sh.)
Obfervations on longevity. (Mem. of M. Vol. 1.
p. 355.) A fatal cafe of morbid enlargement of
the proftate gland, with a fingular appearance in
the bladder. (Mem. of M. S. of L. Vol. 1. p. 202.)
On the efficacy of the hyoscyamus or Henbane in
certain cafes of infanity. (Ibid. p. 310.) On the
efficacy of the gummi rubrum Aftringens Gambi-
enfe. (Ibid. Vol. 2.)

—— [John] *M. D: F. R. S: F. A. S.* (Quacker) born
d. 8 March. 1712. in Wensley Dale, Yorkfhire.
died d. 26. Dec. 1780.

FOWKE

FOWKE, [Francis] *Esq.* On the vina or indian lyre. (Afiat. Ref. Vol. 1. p. 295.)

FOWLER, [. . . . . .] General account of the calamities occafioned by the late tremendous hurricanes and earthquakes in the Weft-India islands —. 1781. 8. (1 Sh. 6. d.)

—— [John] *Surgeon at Ayton, Berwickſhire.* Some hints relative to the recovery of perfons drowned and apparently dead —. 1784. 8.

—— [Thomas] *M. D. Phyſician to the General Infirmary of the County of Hertford.* Diff. De methodo medendi variolas auxilio Mercurii. 1777. Hiſtory of two cafes from the poifonous effects of the feeds of the thorn apple. (Med Com. of Ed. Vol. 5. p. 161.) A remarkable cafe of the morbid effects of lightning, fuccefsfully treated. (Ibid. Vol. 6. p. 194.) Hiſtory of a cafe of rhevmatifm, cured by the volatile elixir of guajacum. (*Duncan's* M. C. 1780. p. 94. überf. Samml. f. A. Th. 6. S. 99.) Obfervations on the effects of different anthelmintics applied to earth-worms —. *Duncan's* M. C. Vol. 8. p 336.) Medical reports of the effect of tobacco principally — in the cure of dropfies and dyfuries with obfervations on the ufe of clyſters of tobacco in the treatment of colic. 1785. 8. (2 fh.) überf. Samml. f. A. Th. XI. S. 335.) Medical reports of the effect of arfenic in the cure of agues, remitting fevers and periodic head-aches. 1786. 8. (3 fh.) (London M. J. Vol, 7. P. 2.)

FOWNES, [Jofeph] *Diſſenting Miniſter at Shrewsbury.* born 1714. died d. 14 Nov. 1789.

FOX, [Charles James] *Member of Parliament* (born 1749.) Epiſtle from him, partridge fhooting, to J Townshend cruifing. 1779. 4. (1 fh.) Invocation to poetry, a poem. 17. . Lines addresfed to Mrs. *Crewe* of Chefhire. 17. . Speech to the Electors of Weftminſter. 1782. 8. (1 fh.) Speech on the Eaft-India Bill. 1783. 8. (1 fh.) *Fox* and *Pitt's* fpeeches in the houfe of commons. 1784. 8. (2 fh. 6. d.) Speech on the Irifh refolutions 1785. 8. (2 fh.) Speech on the 4th Irifh propofition. 1785. 8. (1 fh.) Reply to Mr. *Pitt* upon
re-

reporting the 4th propofition of the Irifh Syftem. 1785. 8. (6. d.)

FOX, [Edward] *Apothecary by the Princeff Amalia.* Formulae medicamentorum felectae. 1778. 8. (7 lh.)

—— [Henry] French and Englifh Dictionary —. 1769. 8. (4. fh.) View of univerfal modern hiftory of Chev. *Mehegan.* Vol. 1-3. 1779. (18 fh.)

—— [Jofeph] The parifh Clerk's vademecum being a collection of finging pfalms —. 1752. (6 d.) The Parifh Clerk's pocket companion —. 1778. 8. (2 Sh.)

FRANCIS, [Anne] *Miff.* Poetical translation of the fong of Solomon, from the briginal hebrew. 1781. 4. (7 Sh. 6. d.) The obfequies of Demetrius Poliorcetes. a Poem. 1785. 4. (1 Sh. 6. d.) Charlotte to Werter, a poetical epiftle. 1787. 4. (1 Sh. 6. d.) Mifcellaneous poems. 1790. 8. (3 Sh.)

—— [Benjamin] The conflagration: a poem. Ed. 2. 1786. 8. (1 Sh.)

—— [Philip] *Rector of Barrow in Suffolk.* born: .... died at *Barh*: d. 5 March. 1773.

—— [Philip] *Member of Parliament.* Original minutes — on the fettlement and collection of the Bengal revenues —. 1782. Speech in the houfe of Commons. 1784. 8. (1 Sh. 6. d.) Two fpeeches in the houfe of Commons on the Eaft-India Bill. 1784. 8. (1 Sh. 6. d.) Speech in the houfe of Commons. 1786. 8. (2 Sh.) Anfwer to the charges exhibited againft him Gen. *Clavering* and Colonel *Manfon* by Sir *Elijah Impey* — on his defence of the Nunducomar charge. 1788. 8. (1 Sh.)

FRANKLIN, [Benjamin] *LL. D.* born at *Bofton, North-America*, d. 17 Jan. 1706. died d. 17 Apr. 1790. (D' *Alembert* bewillkommte ihn bey feiner Aufnahme in die Franzöfifche Akademie mit diefen Worten: Eripuit fulmen coelo, mox fceptra tyrannis.)

—— [J.....] Account of a luminous arch. (Phil. Transact. 1790. p. 46.)

—— [Thomas] *D. D.* Chaplain in Ordinary to his Majefty, and Rector of Brafted, Kent. born: ..... died d. 15 March 1784.

FRANK-

FRANKLIN, [William] *Ensign on the Company's Bengal Establishment.* Observations made on a tour from Bengal to Persia in the Years 1786. 87. with a short account of the remains of the celebrated palace of Persepolis and other interesting events. London. 1790. 8. (6 Sh.) überſ. von *Joh. Reinh. Forster.* Berlin. 1790. 8.

FRANKLYN, [G......] Observations, occasioned by the attempts made in England to effectuate the abolition of the slavetrade —. 1780. 8. (2 Sh. 6. d.) Answer to *Clarkson's* essay on the slavery and commerce of the human species. 1789. 8. (5 Sh.)

FRANKS, [John] Observations on animal life and apparent death, from accidental suspension of the functions of the lungs, with remarks on the *Brunonian* system of Medicine. 1790. 8. (3 Sh.)

FRASER, [A......] Certain arrangements in civil policy necessary for the farther improvement of husbandry, mines, fisheries and manufactures in this kingdom —. 1785. 8. (1 Sh.)

—— [John] History of the agrestis Cornu copiae; or the new American grass; and a new botanical description of the plant —. 1789. fol. (2 Sh. 6. d.)

FREE, [B..: D...] *M. A.* Tyrocinium in hospitiis curiae: or, exercises for the first Year in the inns of court, preparatory to the study of the law. Vol. I. 2. 1784. 8. (6 Sh. 6 d.)

FRENCH, [G...] Fifteen minutes instructions on the venereal disease. 1776. 12. (1 Sh.)

—— [William] *Surgeon.* A case of hydrops ovarii and ascites. (Mem. of M. S. of L. Vol. I. p. 234.)

FREND, [W....] *M. A. of Jesus College, Cambridge.* Address to the member of the church of England and to protestant trinitarians in general, exhorting them to turn from the worship of three persons, to the worship of the one true god. 1788. 8. (2. d.) Thoughts on subscription to religious tests —. 1788. with Appendix. 1789. 8. (2 Sh.)

FRESTON, [A...] *A. M. Curate of Farley, Hants.* Elegy. 1787. 4. (6 d.) Poems on several subjects. 1787. 8. (2 Sh. 6 d.)

FREWEN, [Thomas] *M. D. of Lewes in Sussex.* Account of the condition of the town of Hastings after it had been visited by the small-pox. (Phil. Trans-

Transact. 1747. p. 108.) Letter in anſwer to Dr. *Watts.* 1756. 8. (6 d.) On the cure of the ſmall-pox by antidote. 1759. 8. (1 Sh.) Caſe of a patient, who voided a large ſtone through the perinaeum from the urethra. (Ibid. 1762. p. 258.) Caſe of a young man ſtupified by the ſmoke of ſea coal. (Ibid. 1762. p. 254.) Phyſiologia. 1780. 8. (6 Sh.)

FREWIN, [Richard] — — and *Will. Sims*; the rates of merchandiſe. 1782. 8. (7 Sh.)

FRY, [William] *Teacher of languages and mathematical ſciences.* A new vocabulary of the moſt difficult words in the engliſh language. 1785. 12. (2 Sh. 6 d.)

FRYER, [Edward] *M. D.* Ode to health: inſcribed to his Royal Highneſſ, Prince Auguſtus. Gottingen. 1788. 8. Ode to the genius of patriotiſm. Gottingen. 1789. 4.

FULLARTON, [William] *Member of Parliament. F. R. S. of London and Edinburgh; late Commander of the ſouthern army on the Coaſt of Coromandel.* View of the engliſh intereſts in India and an account of the military operations in the ſouthern parts of the Peninſula during the campaigns of 1782-1784 —. 1787. 8. (5 Sh.) Ed. 2. 1788. 8. (5 Sh.)

FULLER, [....] *Miſſ.* Alan Fitz-Osborne, an hiſtorical tale. Vol. I. 2. 1787. 12. (5 Sh.) ·°The ſon of Ethelwolf: an hiſtorical tale by the author of Alan Fitz-Osborne. Vol. I. 2. 1789. 8. (6 Sh.)

FULLER, [John] *Surgeon at Ayton, Berwickſhire.* New hints relative to the recovery of perſons drowned and apparently dead. 1784. 8. (1 Sh.)

—— [Stephen] *Agent for Jamaica.* The act of aſſembly of the iſland of Jamaica, for the better order and government of ſlaves - commonly called the conſolidated act —. 1788. 4. (2 Sh.) The new act of aſſembly of the iſland of Jamaica — being the preſent code noir of that iſland —. 1789. 4. (1 Sh.) Two reports from the committee of the houſe of aſſembly of Jamaica — on the ſubject of the ſlave trade and the treatment of the Negroes. 1789. 4. (1 Sh.) The code of laws for the government of the Negro-ſlaves in the Island of Jamaica. 1789. 4. (1 Sh.)

FULLMER. [Samuel] *Gardener.* Young gardener's beft companion —. 1781. 12. (2 Sh. 6 d.)

FURNEAUX, [Philipp] *D. D* born at *Tottneff, Devonfhire.* 1726. died d. 23 Nov. 1783.

FYFE, [Andrew] *Affiftant to Dr. Monro, Prof. of Anamy at Edinburgh.* °Syftem of Anatomy and phyfiology. Vol. 1. 2. 1786. 8. (15 Sh.) Ed. 2. (with the Author's name) Vol. 1-3. 1787. 8. (18 Sh.)

FYNNEY, [Fielding Belt] *Surgeon at Leek in Staffordfhire.* The hiftory of a cafe of imperforate hymen (Med. Com. of Ed. Vol. 3. p. 194.) Account of the extirpation of a polypous excrefcence from the os uteri. (Ibid. Vol. 4. p. 228.) A uncommon cafe in midwifery, accompanied with a luxation of the maxilla inferior, occafioned by convulfions. (*Duncan's* M. C. Vol. 9. p. 380.) Cafe of *Ann Davenport.* (Phil. Tr. 1777. p. 458.)

GABRIEL, [R. . . . . B. . . . .] *D. D. late fellow of Worcefter College, Oxford.* Facts relating to Dr. *White's* Bompton lectures. 1789. 8. (1 fh. 6. d.)

GADESBY, [R. . . .] Introduction to geography. 1776. (2 fh. 6. d.)

GAHAGAN, [Mathias] *Phyfician in Grenada.* Hiftory of a curious cafe of the tranflation of inflammation from the lungs to the brain ending fatally in hydrocephalus. (*Duncan's* M. C. Vol. 3. Dec. 2. p. 353.) Hiftory of two cafes, in which, after fuppuration at the Perinaeum, the urine was difcharged at preternatural openings. (Ibid. Dec. 2. Vol. 4. p. 271.) Hiftory of a cafe, in which fingular tumours from indurated and enlarged glands produced a fatal termination. (Ibid. p. 281.)

GALE, [......] °Effay on the nature and principles of public credit. Eff. 1. 2. 3. 4. 1784-1787. 8. (11 fh.)

—— [Benjamin] *F. A. A: F. S. Philad. and F. R. S.* Obfervations on the culture of Smyrna wheat. (Mem. of B. A. Vol. I. p. 381.) Hiftorical memoirs, relating to the practice of inoculation for the fmall pox in the britifh American provinces, particularly in New England. (Phil. Transact. 1766. p. 193.) Account of the fuccefsfull application of falt to wounds

wounds made by the bite of rattle fnakes. (Ibid. p. 244.)

GALE, [Roger] On the horologia of the antients. (Arch. Vol. 6. p. 133.)

GALLIARD, [Bradfhaw] Odes. 1774. 4. (2 fh. 6 d.)

GALLOWAY, [Jofeph] *Member of the American Congress.* Speech — in anfwer to the fpeech of *John Dickinfon.* 1764. 8. (2 fh.) * Candid examination of the mutual claims of Great Britain and the colonies —. 1775. 8. (1 fh.) überf. Hamburg. 1780. 8. The examination of *Jof. Galloway.* 1779. 8. (2 fh.)

GAMBOLD, [John] *A. M. Bifhop of Herrnhutian church at Nevils Court, Fetter Lane.* born: .... died d. 13 Sept. 1771.

GANDER, [Gregory] Poetical tales. 1779. 4. (1 fh.)

GANNETT, [Caleb] *A. M: F. A. A.* Obfervations of a folar eclipfe made at the Univerfity in Cambridge Oct. 27. 1780 (Mem. of B. A. Vol. I. p. 146.) Hiftorical regifter of the aurora borealis from Auguft 8. 1781. to Aug. 19. 1783. (Ibid. p 327.)

GARDEN, [Alexander] *M. D: F. R. S.* Account of the gymnotus electricus, or electrical eel. (Phil. Transact. 1775. p. 102.)

—— [James] * The hiftory of Henry III. King of France. 1783. 8. (6 fh.)

GARDINER, [John] *M. D. Prefident of the Royal College of Phyficians and F. R. S. of Edinburgh.* Diff. De Vino. 17.. A particular method of giving the folution of corrofive fublimate mercury in fmale dofes. (Eff. and Obferv. Edinb. Vol. 3. p. 380.) Obfervations on the animal oeconomy and on the caufes and cure of difeafes. 1784. überf. von *E. B. G. Hebenftreit.* Leipz. 1786. 8.

—— [Richard] *Captain of Marines on board his Majefty's fhips Rippon.* born : .... died ....

GARDNER, [Edward] Liberty, a poem. 1776. (2 fh.)

—— [John] *Surgeon at Betley, Staffordfhire.* Hiftory of a cafe in which there occurred a very uncommon prefentation of a child, to whofe neck there was attached a tumour nearly about the fize of the child's head. (Med. Com. of Ed. Vol. 5. p. 306.)

GARLICK, [William] *Surgeon at Marlborough.* Cafe of an enlargement of the fpleen; with an account of of some remarkable appearances obferved on opening the body of a gentleman whofe death was occafioned by a perforation in his bladder. (London M. J. Vol. 5. p. 186.)

GARNET, [John] *Lord-Bifhop of Clogher.* born..... died d. 1 March. 1782.

—— [Thomas] *M. D.* Experiments and obfervations on the horley-green fpaw near Halifax, with an account of two other mineral waters in Yorkfhire. 1789. 8. (2 fh.) Account of a fuppuration of the liver —. (*Duncan's* M. C. Dec. 2. Vol. 3. p. 303.)

GARRICK, [David] *Actor.* born at Hereford. d. 20 Febr. 1716. died d. 20 Jan. 1779.

GARTSHORE, [Maxwell] *M. D: F. R. S: F. A. S. Phyfician to the britifh Lying in Hofpital, St. Martins-Lane, Weftminfter.* Diff. De papaveris ufu — in parturientibus ac puerperis. Edinb. 1764. 8. Cafe of a fatal ileus. (Med. Obf. Vol. 4. p. ...) Two cafes of the retroverted uterus. (Ibid. Vol. 5. p. 381.) A cafe of difficult deglutition, occafioned by an ulcer in the oefophagus, with an account of the appearances on diffection. (M. C. Vol. I. p. 242.) A remarkable cafe of numerous births, with obfervations. (Phil. Transact 1787. p. 344. London M. J. Vol. X. P. I.) Obfervations on extra-uterine cafes and on ruptures of the uterus. (London M. J. Vol. VIII. P. 4.)

GAST, [John] *Deacon at Glandelagh.* The Rudiments of Grecian hiftory —. 1754. 8. (6 fh.) The hiftory of Greece —. 1782. 4. (1 L. 1 fh.)

GEACH, [Francis] *F. R. S. Surgeon at Plymouth.* Cafe of a man who had fix ftones taken out of the gall bladder. (Phil. Transact. 1763. p. 231.) Cafe of a man wounded in the left-eye with a fmall fword. (Ibid. 1763. p. 234.) Medical and chirurgical obfervations on inflammations of the eyes, on the venereal difeafe, on ulcers and gunfhotwounds. 1766. 8. (1 fh.) überf. Zittau und Görliz. 1768. 8. Obfervations on Dr. *Baker's* effay on the endemial colic of Devonfhire. 1768. 8. (1 fh.) Reply to Dr. *Saunders's* pamphlet, relative to the difpute concerning the Devonfhire cyder, 1769. 8. (1 fh.)

Obfervations on the prefent epidemic dyfentery. 1781. 8. (1 fh.) überf. Samml. f. A. Th. 7. S. 544.
GEDDES, [Alexander] D. D. *a Roman catholic Clergyman.* Select fatires of *Horace*, translated into englifh verfe. 1779. 4. (5 fh.) Profpectus of a new translation of the holy bible — compared with the ancient verfions, with various readings, explanatory notes and critical obfervations. 1786. 4. (7 fh. 6 d.) Queries, doubts and difficulties relative to a vernacular verfion of the holy fcriptures; being an appendix to a profpectus. 1787. 4. (3 fh. 6 d.) Letter to *Prieftley*, in which he attempt to prove that the divinity of Jefus Chrift was a primitive tenet of chriftianity. 1787. 8. (1 fh.) Letter to the Lord Bifhop of London. 1787. 4. (5 fh.) Propofals for printing by fubfcription a new translation of the holy bible. 1788. 4. (1 Sh; 6 d.) General anfwer to the queries, counfils and criticisms, that have been communicated to him fince the publication of his propofals for printing a new translation of the bible. London 1790. 4.
GENT, [Thomas] *Printer.* born: .... died 1778.
GENTLEMAN, [Francis] *Actor.* born in Ireland d. 23 Oct. 1728. died d. 21 Dec. 1784.
GERARD, [Alexander] D. D. *Prof. of Divinity, King's College, Aberdeen.* Plan of education in Marefhal's College. 1755. überf. (von *Gottl. Schlegel*) Riga. 1770. 8. (4 Sh.) überf. nebft *Voltaire's* und *Alembert's* Abhandl. über den Gefchmack: Breslau und Leipz. 1766. 8. Differtations on fubjects relating to the genius and the evidences of chriftianity. 1765. 8. (6 Sh.) On the Genius. 1784. 8. überf. von C. *Garve.* Leipzig. 1776. 8. Sermons. Vol. I. 2. 1782. 8. (10 Sh.)
GERARD, [James] *M. D. Phyfician in Liverpool.* The Hiftory of a fpeedy recovery after the operation of the trepan. (*Duncan's* M. C. Vol. 9. p. 272.) The hiftory of a cafe of ileus, terminating fatally with an account of the appearances on difflection. (Ibid. Vol. 10. p. 293.)
GIBBES, [P....] *Mrs.* Louifa Stroud. 17. The niece, or the hiftory, of Mifs Sukey Thornbey, a novel Vol. 1-3. 1787. 8. (9 Sh.)

GIBBON, [Edward] Eſſai ſur l'etnde de la litterature. 1760. 8. (2 Sh. 6 d.) translated into engliſh 1763. 8. (2 ſh.) Hiſtory of the decline and fall of the roman empire Vol. 1-6. 1775-1788. 4. (6 L. 6 Sh.) nachgedruckt Baſil. 1787. 8. Vol. 1-13. überſ. von *F. A. W. Weck* und *Schreiter*. Th. 1-4. Leipz. 1789. 8. überſ. von *C. W. v. R.* Th. 1-7. Magdeb. 1789. 8. überſ. u. abgekürzt (von *G. K. F. Seidel*) Berlin. 1790. 8. Hiſtoriſche Ueberſicht des römiſchen Rechts oder des 44ſten Cap. überſ. von *Hugo*. Göttingen 1789. 8. Das Leben des Attila, Königs der Hunnen. Lüneb. 1787. 8. Die Bekehrung des Kaiſers Conſtantins des Groſſen — überſ. (von *A. H. W. v. Walterſtern*) Altona 1784. 8. Vindication of ſome paſſages in the XV. XVI. Chapters of the hiſtory of the decline. 1770. 8. (2 Sh. 6 d.)

GIBBONS, [Thomas] *D D. Paſtor of Proteſtant Diſſenters in London.* born 1721. died d. 22 Febr. 1785.

—— [William] *Iron Manufacturer at Briſtol.* Reply to Sir *Lucius O'Brien* — on the preſent ſtate of the iron trade between England and Ireland. 1785. 8. (1 Sh. 6 d.)

GIBBS, [.....] *Mathematician and Muſician.* born: ... died at *Rhotherhite* d. ... Dec. 1779.

GIBSON, [John] *M. D.* On continual, intermitting, eruptive and inflammatory fevers. 1769. 8. (6 Sh.) The principles, elements, or primary particles of bodies —. 1772. 8. (2 Sh. 6 d.)

—— [John] *Surgeon and Man-midwife in Harwich.* Hints and admonitions - on the practice of midwifery. 1772. 12. (1 ſh.)

—— [Joſeph] *Merchant at Glaſgow.* Hiſtory of Glaſgow. 1777. 8. (5 ſh.)

—— [William] M. A. Conſcience; a poetical eſſay. 1772. 4. (1 ſh.) Religion; a poetical eſſay. 1775. 4. (2 ſh.) Jeruſalem deſtroyed: a poem. 1781. 4. (2 ſh.)

GIDDIES, [Alexander] Select ſatires of Horace. 1779. (5 ſh.)

GIFFORD, [Andrew] *D. D. F. A. S. Aſſiſtant to Joſeph Planta, Under-Librarian to the Britiſh Muſeum.* born d. 17 Aug. 1701. died d. 19 June 1784.

GIFFORD, [J. . . . .] ⁰ Reflections on the unity of God —. by *J. G.* 1782. 8. (1 fh.) Ed. 2. 1784. 8. (1 fh.) Ed. 4. 1786. 8. (3 fh.) ᶜ Letter to *John* Lord Archbifhop of Canterbury. 1785. 8. (1 fh.)

—— [Richard] *B. A. Rector of North Okendon, Effex.* Outlines of an anfwer to Dr. *Priefley's* difquifitions relating to matter and fpirit. 1781. 8. (2 fh. 6 d.)

GILBANK, [William] *A. M: Rector of St. Ethelburga, London, Chaplain to the Duke of Gloucefter.* The fcripture hiftory of Abraham. 1773. 8. (4 fh.) The day of Pentecoft, or man reftored. a poem. 1789. 8. (5 fh.)

GILBERT, [Thomas] *Esq. Commander of the Charlotte.* Voyage from new South Wales to Canton in the Year 1788. with views of the islands difcovered. 1789. 4. (8 fh.)

—— [Thomas] *Member of Parliament and Chairman of the committee of fupply and ways and means in the houfe of Commons.* Plan for the better relief and employment of the poor —. with a fupplement. 1781. 8. (2 fh. 6 d.) Obfervations on the bills for amending and rendering more effectual the laws relative to houfes of correction for the better relief — of the poor. 1782. 8. (6 d.) Confiderations on the bills for the better relief and employment of the poor. 1787. 8. (1 fh.) Heads of a bill for the better relief and employment of the poor and for the improvement of the police of this country —. 1787. 8. (1 fh.)

—— [W. . . . .] ᶜ Opinion on the power of courts martial to punifh for contempts; occafioned by the cafe of Major *John Browne* of the 76 Regiment. 1788 8. (1 fh. 6 d.)

GILDING, [Elizabeth] The breathings of genius, being a collection of poems. 1776. 8. (2 fh. 6 d.)

GILES, [William] On marriage. 12. 1771. (1 fh. 6 d.) Collection of poems on divine and moral fubjects. 1775. 8. (3 fh.)

GILL, [Jeremiah] Thoughts on a reform in the britifh reprefentation on government — and the affairs of Ireland —. 1785. 8. (6 d.)

—— [John] *D. D.* born: . . . . died d. 14 Oct. 1777.

GILL,

GILL, [Thomas] *Surgeon, Prescot, Lancashire.* Two cases of ulcer in the cheek, with which the salivary
duct communicated, cured. (*Duncan's* M. C. Dec.
2. Vol. 2. p. 322.)
GILLESPIE, [Leonard] *Surgeon of the Navy and
late Assistant Surgeon to his Majesty's Naval Hospital at St. Lucia.* Observations on the putrid ulcer.
(London M. J. Vol. 6. p. 373. übers. Samml.
F. A. Th. 12. S. 156.)
GILLIES, [John] *LL. D: F. R. S: F. A. S.* The
Orations of *Lysias* and *Isocrates*, translated from
the greek. 1778 4. (18 sh.) Die Einleitung hat
J. C. Macher überfezt unter dem Titel: Betrach-
tungen über die Gefchichte, Sitten und den Cha-
rakter der Griechen vom Schluss des Peloponnesi-
fchen Kriegs an bis zur Schlacht bey Chäronea.
Gött. und Bremen. 1781. 8. History of ancient
Greece, its colonies and conquests from the earliest
accounts till the division of the Macedonian empire
in the East. Vol. I. 2. 1786. 4. (2 L. 2 Sh.) übers.
Leipz. Th. I. 2. 1786. 8. View of the reign of
Frederik II. of Prussia with a parallel between that
Prince and Philipp II. of Macedon 1789. 8. (6 sh.)
—— [John] *D. D. Minister in Glasgow.* (born in Scot-
land.) Milton's paradise lost, illustrated with texts
of scripture 8. 1788. 3 Sh. 6 d.) Memoirs of the
life of *George Whitefield* M. A. Chaplain to the
Countess of Huntingdon. 1772. 8. (4 Sh.)
GILLINGWATER, [Edmund] *Overseer of the poor
at Harleston, Norfolk.* On parish work-houses.
1786. 8. (1 Sh.)
GILLUM, [W. .....] Miscellaneous poems — with
a farce called, what will the world say? 1787. 8.
(3 Sh.)
GILPIN, [J. .....] *Vicar of Wrockardine, Salop.*
J. Fletcher's essay upon the peace of 1783. translated from the french. 1785. 4. (2 Sh. 6 d.)
—— [John] Observations on the annual passage of her-
rings (Tr. of A. S. Vol. 2. p. 236.)
—— [Thomas] Account of a horizontal wind — mill.
(Tr. of A. S. Vol. I. p. 339.)
—— [William] *M. A. Vicar of Boldre in Newforest*, near
Lymington. The life of *Bernard Gilpin*. 1751. 8.
(5 Sh.) The life of *Hugh Latimer.* 1754. 8.
(2 sh)

(2 Sh.) The lives of *John Wicliff* and of the moſt eminent of his diſciple Lord *Cobham*, *John Huß*, *Jerome* of Prague and *Zisca* 1764. 8. (5 Sh.) überſ. von C. F. *Durrenhofer* Frankf. und Leipz. 1769. 8. Lectures on the catechiſm of the church of England. Vol. 1. 2. 1779. 8. (6 Sh.) Obſervations on the river Wye and ſeveral parts of ſouth Wales. 1782. 8. (12 Sh.) Ed. 2. 1789. 8. (17 Sh.) The life of *Thom. Cranmer*, Archbiſhop of Canterbury. 1784. 8. (3 Sh. 6 d.) Obſervations relative to pictureſque beauty made in the Year 1772. on ſeveral parts of England, particularly the mountains and lakes of Cumberland and Weſtmoreland. 1787. 8. Ed. 2. Vol. 1. 2. 1788. 8. (1 L. 11 Sh. 6 d.) Two ſermons. 1788. 8. (1 Sh. 6 d.) Obſervations relative to pictureſque beauty made in the Year 1776. on ſeveral parts of Great Britain particularly the highlands of Scotland. Vol. 1. 2. 1789. 8. (1 L. 16 Sh.) Expoſition of the new teſtament; intended as an introduction to the ſtudy of the ſcriptures, by pointing out the leading ſenſe and connexion of the ſacred writers. 1790. 4.

GILSON, [David] *M. A. Curate of St. Saviour's, Southwark*. Sermons on practical ſubjects. 1788. 8. (6 Sh.)

GIRDLESTONE, [Thomas] *M. D.* Eſſays on the hepatitis and spasmodic affections in India —. 1788. 8. (2 Sh.)

GIRTON, [Daniel] The complete pigeon — fancier or a new treatiſe on domeſtic pigeons —. 1779. 8. (1 Sh. 6 d.)

GISBORNE, [Thomas] *M. A.* The principles of moral philoſophy inveſtigated and applied to the conſtitution of civil ſociety —. 1789. 8. (3 Sh. 6 d.)

GLADWIN, [Francis] *Esq.* * The Ayin Akbary, or the inſtitutes of the emperor Akbar: translated from the original Perſian. 1777. 4. (5 Sh.) Ayeen Akbery, or the inſtitutes of the emperor Akber. translated from the original Perſian: Vol. 1 - 3 1783 - 1786. 4. Hiſtory of Hindoſtan, during the reigns of Jehangir, Shah Jehan and Aurungzebe. Vol. 1. 1788. 4. The memoirs of Khojeh Abdulkurreem, a Caſhmerian of diſtinction, who

who accompanied Nadir Shah on his return from Hindoſtan to Perſia — translated from the Perſian. Calcutta. 1788. 8. (5 Sh.) Narrative of the transactions in Bengal during the Soobahdaries of Azeem us Shan — Jaffer Khan —. translated from the Perſian. 1788. Calcutta. 8. (5 Sh.) Pundnameh, a compendium of Ethics, translated from the Perſian. Calcutta. 1788. 8. (—)

GLASS, [Thomas] M. D: of Exeter. *born: ..... died 17..

GLASSE, [George Henry] M. A. Rector of Hanwell, Middleſex. On the affinity of certain words in the language of the Sandwich and Friendly Isles in the pacific Ocean with the hebrew. (Arch. Vol. 8. p. 81.) (Several ſingle ſermons.)

—— [George Henry] A. B. Aedis Chriſti Alumnus. Translation of Maſon's Caractacus into greek. 1781. 8. (5 ſh.) Joh. Miltoni Samſon Agoniſtes, graeco carmine redditus cum verſione latina. 1788. 8. (5 ſh.)

—— [Samuel] D. D: F. R. S: Chaplain in Ordinary to his Majeſty. Advice from a Lady of Quality to her children, translated from the french. Vol. 1. 2. 1779. 8. (5 ſh.) (Several ſingle ſermons.)

GLENIE, [James] A. M. Lieutenant in the royal regiment of Artillery. Hiſtory of gunnery —. 1776. 8. (4 ſh. 6 d.) On the diviſion of right lines, ſurfaces and ſolids. (Phil. Transact. 1776. p. 73.) The general mathematical laws which regulate and extend proportion univerſally —. (Ibid. 1777. p. 450).

GLOSTER, [Archibald] of Antigua. Remarkable caſe of a tetanos and locked jaw cured by amazing quantities of opium. (Tr. of A. S. Vol. 1. p. 315.)

GLOVER, [Richard] Merchant. born 1711. died d. 25 Nov. 1785.

GOADBY, [Robert] Printer and Bookſeller at Sherborne, Dorſetſhire. born 1721. died 1778.

GODBOLD, [N. ......] On conſumptions, and their cure. 1786. 8. (1 ſh.)

GODDARD, [Peter Stephen] D. D. Maſter of Clare-Hall. born: .... died d. 8 Nov. 1781.

GODMAN, [Thomas] Surgeon to the Charterhouſe at London. born: .... died d. 30 Aug. 1784.

GODSCHALL, [William Man] *Esq. of Weſton Houſe in Surry, one of his Majeſty's juſtices of the Peace for that County.* General plan of parochial and provincial police. 1787. 8. (2 ſh.)
GODWIN, [William] *Diſſenting Clergyman.* Sketches of hiſtory: in VI ſermons. 8. 1784. (2 ſh. 6 d.)
GOLDSMITH, [Oliver] born at *Fernes in Ireland* d. 29 Nov. 1731. died d. 4 Apr. 1774.
GOLDSON, [William] *Member of the corporation of Surgeons.* An extraordinary caſe of lacerated vagina, at the full period of geſtation. 1787. 8. (1 ſh. 6 d.)
GOLLEDGE, [John] Free thoughts on the death threatened againſt Adam, in caſe of diſobedience. 1789. 12. (6 d.)
GOMERSALL, [ ] *Mrs. of Leeds.* *Eleonora, in a ſeries of letters. Vol. 1. 2. 1789. 8. (6 ſh.) The citizen. Vol. 1. 2. 1790. 8. (6 ſh.)
GOOCH, [Benjamin] *Surgeon at Shottisham in Norfolk.* Caſes and remarks in Surgery. 1758. 8. (4 ſh.) Ed. 2. Vol. 1. 2. 1769. On wounds and other chirurgical ſubjects - with an account of the riſe and progreſs of ſurgery and anatomy. 1768. 8. Vol. 1. 2. (14 ſh.) (Der zweyte Theil enthält: the caſes and remarks in Surgery.) Medical and chirurgical obſervations, as an appendix. 1773. 8. (5 ſh. 6 d.) Account of the cuticular glove. (Phil. Transact. 1769. p. 281. überſ Samml. F. A. Th. 1. St. 2. S. 1.) Remarks and conſiderations relative to the performance of amputation above the knee by the ſingle circular inciſion. (Phil. Transact. 1775. p. 273.) Remarks concerning anevryſms in the thigh. (Ibid. p. 378.)
—— [.....] *Mrs.* (Wife of *Will. Gooch*, Esq.) An appeal to the public, on the conduct of Mrs. Gooch, written by herſelf. 1788. 4. (2 ſh. 6 d.)
GOODENOUGH, [.....] born: .... died d. 27 Dec. 1781.
GOODHALL, [James] Florazene, or the fatal conqueſt 1754. 8. King Richard 2. altered and imitated from *Shakſpeare.* 1772. 8.
GOODRIDGE, [John] *Formerly Commander of one of his Majeſty's packet - boats ſtationed at Falmouth.* The phoenix; — or that the comet — is real phoe-
nix

nix of the ancients. 1781. 8. (3 ſh.) Series of obſervations on and a diſcovery of the period of the variation of the light in the bright ſtar called Algol. (Phil. Transact. 1783. P. 2.) On the period of the changes of light in the ſtar Algol. (Ibid. 1784. p. 287.) A ſeries of obſervations on and a diſcovery of the period of the variation of the ſtar marked δ by *Bayer* near the head of Cepheus. (Ibid. 1786. p. 48.)

GOODWIN, [T. . . . .] The loyal ſhepherd: or, the ruſtic heroine, a dramatic paſtoral poem —. 1779. 8. (1 ſh.)

— [W. . . . .] *Surgeon at Earl Soham in Suffolk*. Caſe of fragility of the bones. (London M. J. Vol. VI. p. 288.) Caſe of an encyſted tumour of the Eyelid which was found to contain hair. (Ibid. Vol. VI. p. 292.) Account of a caſe of mollities oſſium (Ibid Vol. VIII. P. I.)

GOODWYN, [Edmund] *M. D.* Diſſ. de morte ſubmerſorum. Edinb. 1786. The connexion of life with reſpiration; or, an experimental inquiry into the effects of ſubmerſion, ſtrangulation, and ſeveral kinds of noxious airs, on living animals: —. 1788. 8. (3 ſh.) überſezt von *C. F. Michaelis*. 1790. 8.

GORDON, [Duncan] *M. D.* Letter to *John Hunter*. 1786. 4. (1 ſh. 6 d.)

— [George] *Lord*. Letter to the Attorney General of England in which the motives of his Lordſhip's public conduct, from the beginning of 1780 to the preſent time, are vindicated. 1787. 8. (1 Sh. 6 d.)

— [Georg Alexander] *M. D.* Complete engliſh phyſician. 1779. 8. (2 Sh.)

— [Robert] *Surgeon to the* 54th *Regiment*. A remarkable caſe of deafneſſ cured by ſalivation. (Med. Com. of Ed. Vol. 3. p. 80.)

— [Thomas] *Esq.* Principles of naval architecture —. 1784. 8. (5 Sh.)

— [William] *D. D.* Hiſtory of the riſe, progreſſ and eſtabliſhment of the independence of the united ſtates of America; including an account of the late war; and of the XIII colonies from their origin to that period. Vol. 1-4. 1788. 8. (1 L. 4 Sh.)

GORDON, [William] *Master of the Mercantile Academy, Edinburgh* Institutes of Arithmetic, elementary and practical: the mensuration of surfaces and solids and the use of logarithms in all the parts of Arithmetic: to which are added tables of annuities, lives —. 1789. 8. (5 sh.)

GORSUCH, [William] *Minister of Holy-Cross in Salop.* Extract from the register of the parish of Holy-Cross in Salop, from 1760-1770. (Philol. Transact. 1771. p. 57.) Extract of the Register of the parish of Holy-Cross, Salop, from 1770-1780. (Ibid. 1782. p. 53.)

GOSLING, [—] *Mrs.* Moral essays and reflections. 1789 8. (3 Sh.)

GOSTLING. [William] *M. A. Vicar of Stone in the Isle of Oxney.* born 1705. died d. 9 March 1777.

GOUGH, [J. ....] *A. B. Rector of Kirk Ireton, Derbyshire.* ⁰ Discourse concerning the resurrection of bodies by Philalethes. 1789. 8. Ed. 2. (with the Author's name.) 1790. 8.

—— [Richard] *Esq. F. A. and R. S.* ⁰ Anecdotes of British Topography. 1768. 4. (1 L. 1 Sh.) Ed. 2. Vol. 1. 2. 1780. 4. (2 L. 12 Sh. 6 d.) ⁰Comparative view of the ancient monuments of India. 1785. 4. (5 Sh.) ⁰ Bibliotheca Topographica Britannica. Numb. I - XIII. 1781. 4. ⁰ Sepulchral monuments in Great Britain —. 1786. fol. (6 L. 6 Sh.) Observations on the round tower at Brechin, in Scotland. (Arch. Vol. 2. p. 83.) Conjectures on an antient tomb in Salisbury cathedral. (Ibid. p. 188.) On the deae matres. (Ibid. Vol. 3. p. 105.) Observations on some roman altars found 1771 near Graham's Dyke. (Ibid. p. 118.) Observations on the invention of cards and their introduction into England. (Ibid. Vol. 8. p. 152.) Observations in vindication of the authenticity of the Parian chronicle. (Ibid. Vol. 9. p. 157.) Observations on certain stamps or seals used antiently by the oculists. (Ibid. p. 227.) *W. Camden's* Britannia: or chorographical description of the flourishing kingdoms of England, Scotland and Ireland, translated and enlarged. Vol. 1-3. 1789. fol. (10 L.)

GOUR.

GOURLAY, [William] *M. D. Phyfician in the Island of Madeira and Member of the Med. Soc. of Edinb.* A cafe of encyfted farcocele. (*Duncan's* M. C. Vol. 9. p. 336.)

GOWER, [Foote] *M. D: F. A. S:* born: .... died d. 27 May. 1780.

GRAEME, [James] born at *Carnwath, Lanarkſhire* 1749. died 1771.

GRAHAM, [......] *Phyfician in Stirling.* On the external application of deadly nightſhade. (Med. Com. of Ed. Vol. 1. p. 419.) Account of violent pains from a particular ſpecies of worm under the ſkin. (*Duncan's* M. C. Dec. 2. Vol. 2. p. 366.)

—— [Catherine Macaulay] *Mrs.* (Maden Name' *Sawbridge;* Her firſt Husband was *Kenneth Macaulay.* DD. and Clergyman in Scotland: Her ſecond *Graham.*) Hiſtory of England from the acceſſion of James I. to the Revolution. Vol. 1 - 8. 1763 1782. 4. (6 L.) *Looſe remarks on *Hobbes's* rudiments of government and ſociety. 1767. 8. (1 ſh.) Ed. 2. 1769. 4. (1 ſh. 6 d.) Obſervations on *Edm. Burke's* thoughts on the cauſe of the preſent diſcontents. 1770. 8. (1 ſh.) A modeſt plea for the property of Copy - Right. 1773. 8. (1 ſh. 6 d.) Addreſs to the people of England, Scotland and Ireland on the preſent important criſis of affairs. 1774. 8. (6 d.) Hiſtory of England, from the revolution to the preſent time. Vol. 1. 1778. 4. (15 ſh.) On the immutability of moral truth. 1783. 8. (5 ſh.) Letters on education: with obſervations on religious and metaphyſical ſubjects. 1790. 8.

—— [Robert] *Esq. Prefident of the Delegates from the Burgeſſes.* Letter to *Will. Pitt* — on the reform of the internal government of the royal boroughs of Scotland. 1788. 8. (1 ſh. 6 d.)

—— [William] *Rector of Stapleton.* The eclogues of *Virgil,* translated into engliſh verſe. 1780. 8.

GRANGER, [Edmond] *Rector of Sowden and Vicar of Honiton Clift, Somerſetſhire.* born: .... died d. Sept. 1777.

—— [James] *Vicar of Shiplake, Oxfordſhire.* born: ... died d. 5 Apr. 1776.

GRANT,

GRANT, [......] *Minifter of the Gospel at Newcaftle.* Sermons, doctrinal and practical, on feveral fubjects. 1786. 12. (2 fh. 6 d.)
—— [Alexander] *Surgeon of his Majefty's Military Hospitals during the late war in North-America.* Obfervations on the ufe of opium in removing fymptoms fuppofed to be owing to morbid irritability. (London M. J. Vol. VI. p. 1. p. 131. überf. Samml. f. A. Th. XI. S. 68.)
—— [D....] *M. A. Vicar of Hutton-Rudby, Yorkfhire.* Two Differtations on popifh perfecution and breach of faith —. 1771. 8. (2 fh. 6 d.)
—— [George] *Surgeon.* Cafe of an abfceff in the lower part of the belly which communicated with the inteftine —. (London M. J. Vol. XI. P. 2.)
—— [James] *Advocate at the Scotifh Bar.* Origin of fociety, language, property, government, jurisdiction, contracts and marriage —. 1785. 4. (7 Sh. 6 d.)
—— [P.....] *Surgeon at Stonehaven.* Account of fingular effects from the external application of a ftrong infufion of tobacco employed for the cure of Plora. *(Duncan's* M. C. Dec. 2. Vol. I. p. 327. überf. Samml. f. A. Th. 13. S. 37.)
—— [William] *M. D. Phyfician to the Mifericordia Hospital in London.* born: .... died d. 30 Nov. 1786.
GRATTAN, [Henry] Speech on tithes. 1788. 8. (1 Sh. 6 d.)
GRAVES, [Richard] *Rector of Claverton and Vicar of Kilmerfden in the county of Somerfet.* (born at Mickleton in the County of *Gloucefter* d. 4 May 1715.) ° The fpiritual Quixote; or, the fummer's ramble of Mr. Geoffry Wildgoofe, a comic romance. Vol. 1-3. 1773. 8. (7 Sh. 6 d.) ° The love of order; a poetical effay. 1773. 4. (1 Sh. 6 d.) Peter of Pomfret. 17.. The diftreffed Anchoret. 17.. Poems. Vol. 1. 2. 17.. Columella. 1778. *Euphrofine, or amufements on the road of life. Vol. 1. 2. 1780. (6 Sh.) Echo and Narciffus. 1780. 8. ° Recollection of fome particulars in the life of the late *Will. Shenftone.* 1788. 8. (3 Sh.)
GRAY, [Alexander] *M. D. Surgeon to the 3*d *Reg. of Seapoys in the fervice of the Eaft-India Company in Bengal.* Hiftory of a cafe of rabies canina attended with fingular circumftances, and terminating

ting fatally, after a falivation had been induced by mercury. (*Duncan's* M. C. Dec. 2. Vol. 2. p. 304.)

GRAY, [Andrew] *D. D. Minifter of Abernethy.* Delineation of the parables of our bleffed faviour. 1777. überf. (von *Joh. Fried. Roos*). Hannover 1783. 8. (6 Sh.)

—— [Edward] *M. D: F. R. S.* Account of the epidemic catarrh of the Year 1782. (M. C. Vol. 1. p. 1.)

—— [Edward Whitaker] *M. D: F. R. S.* Obfervations on the manner in which glaff is charged with the electric fluid and difcharged. (Phil. Transact. 1788. p. 121.) überf. *Gren* J D P. Th. 1. S. 83. Obfervations on the claff of animals called, by *Linnacus* Amphibia; particularly on the means of diftinguifhing thofe ferpents which are venomous from thofe which are not fo. (Ibid. 1789. p. 21.)

—— [John] Translations of fome odes and epiftles of *Horace.* 1778. 8. (1 Sh 6 d)

—— [Robert] Key to the old teftament and apocrypha: in which is given an account of their feveral books, their contents and authors and of the times in which they were refpectively written. 1790. 8.

—— [Thomas] *Profeffor of modern hiftory at Cambridge.* born at *Cornhill* d. 26 Dec. 1716. died d. 30 July 1772.

GREATHEAD, [Bertie] The regent, a Tragedy. 1788. 8. (1 Sh. 6 d.) überf. unter dem Titel: der Statthalter. Berlin 1790. 8. Mannheim 1790. 8.

GREEN, [Charles] *Formerly Affiftant at the royal Obfervatory at Greenwich and* Lieut. *James Cook*, of his *Majefty's fhip the Endeavour.* born: ... died at fea in the paffage home from *Batavia* 17..

—— [John] *D. D. Bifhop of Lincoln.* born in *Yorkfhire* 1706. died d. 25 Apr. 1779.

—— [John] *M. D. Phyfician at Greenwich.* born: .... died d. 2 Jan. 1778.

—— [J.... L.....] *Surgeon at Peckham in Surry.* Defcription of a curious lufus naturae. (London M. J. Vol. 4. p. 403.)

—— [Thomas] *Esq.* Account of an ancient urn found in the parifh of Kilranelagh, in the county of Wicklow. (Tr. of J. A. 1787. p. 161.)

GREEN,

GREEN, [Rupert] The secret plot. a tragedy. 1777. 8.
—— [Valentine] F. A. S. Mezzotinto Engraver to his Majesty and to the Elector Palatine. Survey of the city of Worcester. 1764. 8. (5 Sh.) Review of the polite arts in France — under Louis the XIVth compared with their present state in England 1783. 4. (3 Sh.)
—— [William] M. D. born: . . . . died d. 30 Aug. 1788.
—— [William] M. A. Rector of Hardingham, Norfolk. The song of Deborah, reduced to metre; with a new translation and commentary —. 1753. 4. New translation of the prayer of Habakuk the prayer of Moses and the 139 psalm, with a commentary —. 1755. 4. (1 Sh. 6 d.) New translation of the psalms — with notes critical and explanatory — with a dissertation on the last prophetic words of Noah. 1763. 8. (3 Sh. 6 d.) Moral and religious essays upon various important subjects. by W. Green and John Penn. 1766. 12. Vol. 1. 2. (6 Sh.) New translation of Isaiah VII, 13. to the end of LIII. — with notes. 1776. 4. (1 Sh.) Poetical parts of the old testament — translated — with notes. 1781. 4. (6 Sh.) übers. (von J. F. Roos.) Giessen. 1783. 8.
GREENAWAY, [. . . . .] *A new translation of some parts of Ecclesiastes. P. 1-3. 1787. 8. (5 Sh. 4 d.)
GREENE, [Edward Burnaby] born: . . . . died d. 12 March. 1788.
—— [Thomas] of Ware, Herfordshire. born : . . . . . died 17..
GREENFIELD, [William] M. A: F. R. S. Edin. Minister at St. Andrew's church and Professor of Rhetoric in the University of Edinburgh. On the use of negative quantities in the solution of problems by algebraic equations. (Tr. of E. S. Vol. 1. p. 131.)
GREENLEAF, [Joseph] Account of an experiment for raising indian corn in poor land. (Mem. of B. A. Vol. 1. p. 383.)
GREENVILLE, [George] see Earl of Temple.
GREENWOOD, [J. . . .] Rhapsody on the Worcester election. 1776. 4. (1 Sh.)
—— [William] Fellow of St. John's College, Cambridge and Rector of Bignor, Sussex. A Poem written du-

during a shooting excursion on the moors. 1786:
4. (2 Sh.)

GREGORY, [G.....] *Curate of St. Nicholas's church in Liverpool. F. A. S.* · Essays historical and moral. 1785. 8. (5 Sh.) Ed. 2. 1788. 8. (6 Sh.) Sermons, with thoughts on the composition and delivery of a sermon. 1787. 8. (6 Sh) Translation of *Lowth's* lectures on the sacred poetry of the hebrews —. Vol. 1. 2. 1787. 8. (12 Sh) The life of *Thom. Chatterton* with criticisms on his genius and writings and a view of the controversy concerning *Rowley's* poems. 1789. 8. (5 sh.) °History of the christian church from the earliest periods to the present time. Vol. 1. 2. 1790. 8. (8 sh.)

—— [James] *M. D. Professor of Medicine in the University of Edinburgh.* (Son to *John Gregory*). Diss. 'De morbis coeli mutatione medendis. Edinb. 1774. 8. Conspectus Medicinae Theoreticae. Ed. 2. Vol. 1. 2. 1782. 8. (12 Sh.) Ed. 3. Vol. 1. 2. 1788. 8. (12 Sh.) überl. Leipzig. Th. 1. 2. 1784. 8. Theory of the moods of verbs (Tr. of E. S Vol. 2. p. 193.)

—— [John] *M. D: F. R. S. Professor of Medicine in the University of Edinburgh.* born at *Aberdeen* 1725. died d. 10 Febr. 1773.

GRENVILLE, [W..... W.....] *Speaker of the house of Commons.* Speech 1789. 8. (1 sh. 6 d.)

GREY, [Richard] *Prebendary at Paul's church, London.* born 1693. died 1771.

GRIEVE, [John] *M. D: F. R. S. Edin. late Physician to the Russian army at Nigene Nowgorod, now Physician in London.* The history of a case of inveterate dropsy, successfully treated with observations on the advantages from combining cathartics and diuretics. (*Duncan's* M. C. Vol. 9. p. 286) Account of the method of making a wine, called by the Tartars, Koumiss; with observations on its use in medicine. (T. of E. S. Vol. 1.'p. 178.) (London M. J. Vol. X. P. 2.)

—— [William] *Surgeon in Grenada.* On the use of the bark of the Angeline tree, as an anthelmintic. (*Duncan's* M. C. Vol. 9. p. 365.)

GRIFFIES, [Thomas] The journey to Brighton; an heroi-comic poem. 1788. 4. (2 sh. 6 d.)

GRIFFIN, [Gregory] *of the College of Eton.* The microcofm, a periodical work. 1787. 8. (7 fh.)
—— [Robert] Intereft tables on an improved plan—. 1775. 8. (6 fh.)
GRIFFITH, [Amyas] *Esq. late Surveyor of Belfaſt and formerly Inſpector general of the province of Munſter.* Oblervations on the Biſhop of Cloyne's pamphlet: in which the doctrine of tithes is illuſtrated and the argument for the infecurity of the proteſtant religion demonſtrated to be groundleſſ and viſionary. 1787. 8. (1 fh. 6 d.)
—— [Guyon] *D. D. Rector of St. Mary Hill.* born: .... died d. 1 Jan. 1784.
—— [Moſes] *M. D. at Colcheſter.* Practical obſervations on the cure of hectic and slow fevers and the pulmonary conſumption, with a method of treating feveral kinds of internal haemorrhages. 1775. 8. (2 Sh.) überf. Samml. f. A. Th. 6. S. 579.
GRIFFITHS, [Frances] *Mrs.* *Letters between Henry and Frances Vol. 1 - 6. 1756 - 1770. (17 Sh.)' * Memoirs of Ninon de l'Enclos, tranſlated. Vol. 1.2. 1761. (6 fh.) The platonic wife, a Comedy. 1765. 8. Amana. 1765. 4. The double miſtake, a Comedy 1766. 8. * Two novels, in letters. Vol. 1 - 4. 1768. (10 fh.) *The fchool for rakes, a Comedy. 1768. 8. (1 fh. 6 d.) *Tranſlation of Mad. de *Caylus's* Memoirs, anecdotes and characters of the court of Lewis XIV. Vol. 1. 2. 1770. 8. The fhipwreck and adventures of Monſ. *Pierre Viaud,* tranſlated from the French. 1771. 8. (4 Th.) Hiſtory of Lady *Barton,* in letters. Vol. 1. 2. 3. 1771. (7 fh. 6 d.) A wife in the right, a Comedy. 1772. 8. (5 fh.) The ſtory of Lady *Juliana Hartley,* a Novel, in letters. Vol. 1. 2. 1775. (6 Sh.) The Morality of *Shakeſpeare's* drama illuſtrated. 1775. 8. (7 Sh. 6 d.) Letter from. Monſ. *Desenfans* to Mrs. *Monrague* tranſlated 1777. 8. (1 fh. 6. d.) The times 1779. 8 Eſſays addreſſed to young married women. 1782. 8. (2 Sh. 6 d.) nachgedr. Berlin. 1787. 8.
GRIGG, [John] *Practitioner in Midwifery.* Advice to the female fex in general, particularly thoſe in a ſtate of pregnancy and lying — in woman. 1789. 8. (3 Sh. 6 d.) überf. Leipzig. 1791. 8.

CRIMSTON, [John] *Surgeon at Ripon.* Cafe of a fractured fcull unfuccefsfully treated. (London M. J. Vol. X. P. 3.)

GROOMBRIDGE, [William] Sonnets. 1789. 8. (1 Sh.)

GROSE, [......] Rules for drawing caricaturas, with an effay on comic painting. 1788. 8. (2 fh.)

—— [Francis] *F. R. S: F. A. S: Captain in the Effex militia.* The antiquities of England and Wales. Vol. 1-4. 1773. 4. (9 L. 1 Sh.) Ed. 2. Vol. 1-3. 1784. 8. (4 L. 9 Sh.) Collection of plans of the antiquities of England and Wales. 1775. 4. (10 Sh. 6. d.) Defcription of an ancient fortification near Chriftchurch Hampfhire. (Arch. Vol. 5. p. 237.) On ancient armours and weapons. 1786. 4. (2 L. 2 Sh.) - Provincial gloffary with a collection of local proverbs and popular fuperftitions. 1787. 8. (5 Sh.) Ed. 2. 1790. 8. (5 Sh.) Obfervations on antient fpurs. (Arch. Vol. 8. p. 111.) Military antiquities refpecting a hiftory of the english army from the conqueft to the prefent time. Vol. 1. 2. 1788. 4. (4 L. 4 Sh.) The Antiquities of Scotland. Numb. 1-18. fol. 1790. (3 L. 4 Sh.)

—— [John] *F. A. S.* Ethics, rational and theological with remarks on the general principles of Deifm. 1782. 8. (6 Sh.)

GROVE, [W.....] The faithful fhepherd, a Paftoral: tranflated from *Guarini.* 1782. 8.

GULLET, [Chriftopher] On the effects of elder in preferving growing plants from infects and flies. (Philof. Transact. 1772. p. 348.)

GURDON, [Philipp] *M. A. Fellow of Magdalen College, Oxford.* Sketch of the diftinguishing graces of the chriftian character —. 1778. 8. (2 Sh. 6 d.)

GUTCH, [John] *M. A. Chaplain of all Soul's College.* * Archbifhop *Sancroft's* Collectanea curiofa: or, mifcellaneous tracts, relating to the hiftory and antiquities of England and Ireland, the univerfities of Oxford and Cambridge and a variety of other fubjects. Vol. 1. 2. 1781. 8. *Ant. Wood's* Hiftory and antiquities of the colleges and halls in the Univerfity of Oxford — with a continuation to the prefent time —. 1786. 4. (1 L. 6 fh.)

GUTHRIE, [Matthew] *M. D. Phyſician at St. Petersburgh. F. R. S.* Obſervations on the plague, quarantaines —. (*Duncan's* M. C. Vol. 8. p. 345.) Nouvelles experiences pour ſervir a determiner le vrai point de congelation du mercure et la difference que lè degré de pureté de ce metal pourroit y apporter. à St. Petersburgh. 1785. 8. überſ. in Auszug in *Tralles* phyſikal. Taſchenbuch für das J. 1786. On the antiſeptic regimen of the natives of Ruſſia. (Phil. Transact. 1778. p. 622.) Account of the manner in which the ruſſians treat perſons affected by the fumes of burning Charcoal, and other effluvia of the ſame nature. (Ibid. 1779. p. 325.) On the effects of a cold climate on the land ſcurvy. (*Duncan's* M. C. Dec. 2. Vol. 2. p. 328. überſ. Samml. f. A. Th 13. S. 48.) On the climate of Ruſſia (Tr. of E. S. Vol. 2. p 213.)

GUY, [Melmoth] *Surgeon.* Select number of ſcirrhous and cancerous caſes. 1777. 8. (1 ſh.)

GWYNN, [John] London and Weſtminſter improved and illuſtrated by plans: 1771. 4. (9 ſh.)

HADLEY, [George] *Esq. Formerly Captain on the Bengal Eſtabliſhment.* Short grammar and vocabulary of the Moors language. 1771. 8. (1 ſh. 6 d.) Grammatical remarks on the Indoſtan language commonly called Moors. —. 1772. 8. (2 ſh. 6 d.) Ed. 3. 1784. 8. (4 ſh) Grammatical remarks on the perſian language —. 1776. 4. (7 ſh. 6 d.)

HAFFENDEN, [Richard] *Eſq.* Account of the effects of lightning on a houſe which was furniſhed with a pointed conductor at Tenterden, in Kent. (Phil. Transact. 1775. p. 336.)

HAIGH, [James] *Silk and Muslin Dyer, Leeds.* The dyer's aſſiſtant in the art of dying wool and woollen goods. —. 1778. 12. (5 ſh. 6 d.) A Hint to the dyers and Clothmakers —. 1780. 8. (6 d.)

HAIGTON, [J.....] *Surgeon, London.* The hiſtory of two caſes of the fractured Olecranon, with ſome remarks. (*Duncan's* M C. Vol. 9. p. 382.) Attempt to aſcertain the powers concerned in the act of vomiting —. (Mem. of M. S. of L. Vol. 2.) Caſe of hydrophobia. (London M. J. Vol. 6. p. 361.)

HAIR,

HAIR, [Lancelot] *Surgeon at Southminfter in Effex.* Remarks on Mr. *Lucas's* practical obfervations on amputation. (Lond. M. J. Vol. 7. P. 4.)

HALE, [.....] *Lieutenant-General.* Speech. 1785. 8. (1 fh.)

— [John] *Surgeon to the New Finsbury Dispenfary.* Cafe of a fracture of the fternum. (London M. J. Vol. VIII. P. 4.)

HALES, [Charles] Salivation not neceffary for the cure of the venereal difeafe in any degree whatever and all gleets curable. London 1764. 8. Letter, thoughts and obfervations in the cure of the venereal difeafe —. 1770. 8. (1 fh.)

— [William] D. D. *Rector at Killefandra.* Sonorum doctrina rationalis et experimentalis —. 1778. 4. (6 fh.) De Motibus planetarum —. 1786. 8. (1 fh. 6 d.) Analyfis aequationum —, 1786. 4. (10 fh.) Obfervations on the political influence of the doctrine of the *Pope's* fupremacy 1787. 8. (2 fh.) Survey of the modern ftate of the church of Rome, with additional obfervations on the doctrine of the Pope's fupremacy. 1789 8. (3 fh. 6 d.)

HALHED, [Nathaniel Braffey] *Officer of the Eaft-India Company at Hoogly in Bengal.* * A Code of gentoo laws; or ordinations of the pundits, from a perfian translation, made from the original, written in the Shancrit language. 1776. 4. Ed. 2. 1777. 8. (7 fh. 6 d.) Überf. von R. E. Rafpe. Hamb. 1778. 8. Grammar of the Bengal language. printed at Hoogly in Bengal. 1778. 4. (1 L. 1 fh.) Narrative of the events which have happened in Bombay and Bengal relative to the Maharatta empire fince July 1777. 1779. 8.

HALIDAY, [W.....] On the Siberian or Haliday Barley. (*Hunter's* G. E. Vol. 2. p. 87.)

HALL, [.....] *Captain.* * Hiftory of the civil war in America. Vol. 1. 1780. 8. (5 fh.)

— [.....] *Mrs.* * Moral tales — by lady * * 1783. 4. (2 fh. 6. d)

— [C....] *M D.* The family medical inftructor-with an appendix on canine madneff. 1785. 8. (2 fh. 6 d.)

— [Charles] *Surgeon to the 14th Regiment of Infantry.* Account of a new fpecies of palfy. (Med. Com. of Ed. Vol. 6. p. 71.)

HALL, [John] *of Broadstreet, Surgeon and Teacher of Anatomy in London.* Cafe of an anevrifm in the aorta and in the left carotid artery, which burft into the trochea. (Med. Obf. Vol. 6. p. 23.) Obfervations on the contents of medullary cells, droply. (London M. J. Vol. VII. P. 2.) überf. Samm. f. A. Th. 12. S. 17.)

—— [Ifaac] *Phyfician at Petersburgh in Virginia.* An uncommon tumour on the thigh fucceffully extirpated. (Med. Com. in Ed. Vol. 1. p. 89.)

—— [Richard] *Surgeon to the Manchefter infirmary.* Account of the fucceffful extirpation of a remarkable fchirrus of the fcrotum. (Lond. M. J. Vol. VIII. P. 1.)

—— [Samuel] *A. M. Chaplain to the Manchefter military affociation.* Sermon before the military affociation —. 1783. 4. (1 fh.) Attempt to fhew, that a tafte for the beauties of nature and the fine arts, has no influence favourable to morals. (Mem. of M. Vol. 1. p. 223.)

HALLIFAX, [Samuel] *D. D. Bifhop and Archdeacon at St. Afaph.* born 1730. died in Weftminfter. d. 5 March 1790.

HALYBURTON, [William] *D. D.* Georgics, in a feries of letters to a friend. 1782. 8. (6 fh.)

HAMILTON, [Alexander] *M. D. F. R. S. Profeffor of Midwifery at Edinburgh.* Elements of the practice of midwifery. 1776. 8. (5 fh.) Treatife of midwifery. 1781. 8. (6 fh.) überf. von *J. P. Ebeling.* Leipz. 1782. 8. Outlines of the theory and practice of midwifery. 1783. 8. (5 fh.) *Will. Smellie's* anatomical tables with explanations and an abridgment of the practice of midwifery. 1787. fol. (2 L. 5 fh.)

—— [Auguftus] *M. A.* Account of the tranfit of Mercury over the fun of Nov. 12. 1782., obferved at Cook's Town in Ireland. (Phil. Transact. 1783. P. 2.)

—— [Charles] Esq. *Officer in the Service of the Eaft-India Company, on the Bengal eftablifhment.* Hiftorical relation of the origin, progreff and final diffolution, of the government of the Rohilla Afgans, in the northern provinces of Hindoftan, compiled from a perfian Msct. —. 1787. 8. (5 fh.) Defcription

ption of the Mahwah (or Maduca) tree. (Afiat. Ref. Vol. 1. p. 300.)

HAMILTON, [Charles] *The patriot. a Tragedy. 1784. 8. (1 fh. 6 d.)

—— [Hugh] *D. D. F. R. S. Dean of Armagh.* De fectionibus conicis. 1758. 4. (10 fh. 6 d.) The properties of the mechanic powers demonftrated, with fome obfervations on the methods that have been commonly ufed for that purpofe. (Phil. Transact. 1763. p. 103.) On the nature of evaporation and feueral phaenomena of air, water and boiling liquors. (Ibid. 1765. p. 146.) Geometrical treatife of the conic fections — translated from the latin. 1773. 4. (12 fh.) *Four introductory lectures in natural philofophy. 1773. 8. (2 fh.) Attempt to prove the exiftence and abfolute perfection of the fupreme unoriginated being. 1785. 8. (3 fh. 6 d.)

—— [James Archibald] *D. D. Member of Roy. Irifh Acad.* Account of Parhelia feen at Cookftown Sept. 24. 1783. (Tr. of J. A. 1787. p. 23.)

—— [James Edward] 1 and 2 letter to the people of England, upon the prefent crifis. 1790. 8. (1 Sh.) Attempt to explain the termes Democracy, Ariftocracy, Oligarchy, Monarchy and Despotifm. 1790. 8. (6 d.)

—— [R. . . . .] *LL. D. Profeffor of Philofophy at Aberdeen.* Syftem of Arithmetic and book keeping. with a fupplement containing anfwers to the arithmetical queftions. 1788. 8. (2 Sh. 6 d.)

—— [Robert] *D. D. Profeffor of Divinity in the Univerfity of Edinburgh.* born: . . . . died d. 2 Apr. 1787.

—— [Robert] *LL. D. Mafter of the academy at Perth.* Introduction to Merchandize. Vol. 1. 2. 1777. 8. (9 Sh.)

—— [Robert] *M. D. Phyfician at Ipswich.* The duties of a regimental furgeon confidered; with obfervations on his general qualifications. Vol. 1. 2. 1788. (10 Sh.) überf. von Hunczovsky. Wien 1790. 8.

—— [Robert] *M. D: F. R. S. and Phyfician at Lynn-Regis, Norfolk.* Account of a fuppreffion of urine cured by a puncture made in the bladder through the anus. (Phil. Transact. 1776. p. 578.) Thoughts on eftablifhing a fund for fick foldiers and their wives.

wives. 1783. 8. (1 Sh.) Defcription of the influenza.
1782. 8. (1 fh.) überf. Samml. f A. Th. 8. S. 52.)
Account of a fucceffiull method of treating inflammatory difeafes, by mercury and opium. *(Duncan's* M.
C. Vol 9. p. 191. überf. Samml. f. A Th. XI. S. 265.)
Cafe of angina pectoris, from which it would appear
that the complaint is fometimes hereditary. (Ibid.
Vol. 9. p. 307) A cafe of a difeafed tefticle fucceffiully treated. (London M. J. Vol. 4. p. 172.)
Several inftances of the good effects of opium in
mortifications. (London M. J. Vol. 5. p. 75. p.
190.) Remarks on the means of obviating the
fatal effects of the bite of a mad dog, or other ra-
bid animal. 1785. 8. (5 Sh.) überf. von *C. F. Michaelis.* Leipz. 1787. 8. A cafe of hydrophobia.
(London M. J. Vol. 7. P. 1.) Cafe of worms
difcharged through an opening in the navel. (London M. J. Vol. 7. P. 4.) Hiftory of a cafe in
which an epiftaxis occurred vicarious to the men-
ftrual difcharge. *(Duncan's* M. C. Dec. 2. Vol. 1.
p. 337.) Hiftory of a remarkable cafe of noftal-
gia affecting a native of Wales and occurring in
Britain. *(Duncan's* M. C. Dec. 2. Vol. 1. p. 343.)
Remarks on the influenza in fpring 1782. (Mem.
of M. S. of S. Vol. 2.) The duties of a regimental furgeon confidered; with obfervations on
his general qualifications. Vol. 1. 2. 1788. 8. (10
Sh. 6 d.) Account of a diftemper by the common people in England vulgary called the mumps.
(London M. J. Vol. XI. P. 2. Tr. of E. S. Vol. 2. p. 59.)

HAMILTON, [Thomas] *Student of Medicine at Edinburgh.* On the benefit of cyder in the cure of
dropsy and on the induction of artificial emphyfema.
(Duncan's M. C. Dec. 2. Vol. 2. p. 370.) überf.
Samml. f. A. Th. 13. S. 76.

—— [William] *A. M. F. T. C. D. M. R. J. A.* Letters concerning the northern coaft of Antrim, in Ireland —.
1786. 8. (4 fh.) überf. (von *Kühn*) Leipz. 1787. 8.
Account of experiments made to determine the temperature of the earth's furface in the kingdom of
Ireland in the Y. 1788. (Tr. of J. A. 1788. p. 143.

—— [William] *Sir. Britannic Majefty's Envoy to the Court of
Naples. Knight Baron. F. R. S.* Account of the
late

late eruption of Mount Vesuvius Nov. 17. 1764. (Phil. Transact. 1767. p. 192.) Account of the eruption of mount Vesuvius in 1767. (Ibid. 1768. p. 1.) Some farther particulars of mount Vesuvius and other Volcanos in that neighbourhood. (Ibid. 1769. p. 18.) Account of a Journey to mount Etna. (Ibid. 1770. p. 1.) Remarks upon the nature of the soil of Naples and its neighbourhood. (Ibid. 1771. p. 1. p. 48.) Observations on mount Vesuvius, mount Etna and other Vulcanos. 1772. 8. (3 sh. 6. d.) Schola Italica picturae — The Italian school of painting. fol. 1773. (4 L. 14 sh.) Account of the effects of a thunder storm on the 15th of March 1773 upon the house of Lord *Fylney* at Naples. (Phil. Transact. 1773. p. 324.) Campi Phlegraei; or observations on the Volcanos of the two Sicilies. Vol. 1. 2. 1776. Supplem. 1779. fol. (15 L. 4 sh.) On the discoveries at Pompeji. (Arch. Vol. 4. p. 160.) überf. von *C. G. Murr.* Nürnb. 1780. 4. Account of certain traces of Volcanos on the banks of the Rhine. (Phil. Transact. 1778. p. 1. überf. Samml. zur P. u. Ng. Th. 2. S. 453.) Account of an eruption of mount Vesuvius in Aug. 1779. (Ibid. 1780. p. 42.) Account of some scoria from iron works, which resemble the vitrified filaments. (Ibid. 1782. p. 50.) Account of the earthquakes which happened in Italy from Febr. to May 1783. (Ibid. 1783. p. 169.) überf. von *L. Wittenberg.* Altona 1783. 8. Some particulars of the present state of mount Vesuvius; with the account of a Journey into the province of Abruzzo and a voyage to the island of Ponza. (Ibid 1786. p. 365. überf. Dresden 1787. 4.

HAMPE, [John Henry] *M. D:* at *London.* born 1697. died 1777.

HAMPSON, [John] A blow at the root of pretended Calvinism, or real Antinomianism. 1788. 8. (1 sh.)
—— [George] *M. A.* Candid remarks upon *Taylor's* discourse entitled, the scripture doctrine of atonement examined. 1752. 8. (1 sh 6 d.). Answer to *Priestley's* objections to the doctrine of the atonement by the death of Christ in the history of the corruptions of Christianity. 1785. 8. (2 sh.)

HAMPTON, [James] *Rector of Moor-Monkton and Folkton.* born: .... died d. 15 July 1778,
HANBURY, [W.....] *A. M. Rector of Church-Langton, Leicestershire.* Essay on planting —. 1758. 8. (1 sh.) History of the rise and progress of the charitable foundations at Church-Langton —. 1767. 8. (6 sh.) Complete body of planting and gardening. Vol. 1. 2. 1771. fol. (4 L. 4 sh.)
HANCOCK, [Blith] *Teacher of the Mathematics.* The doctrine of eclipses, both solar and lunar —. 1783. 8. (3 sh.) The astronomy of comets. 1786. 8. (2 sh. 6 d.)
HANDASYD, [Talbot Blayney] Account of antiquities near Bagshot. (Arch. Vol. 7. p. 199.)
HANDS, [Elizabeth] *Mrs.* (Wife of a Blacksmith.) The death of Ammon, a poem. 1790.
HANGER, [George] *Major to the Cavalry of the British Legion.* Address to the army on *Tarleton's* history of the campaigns of 1780 et 1781. 1789. 8. 4 sh.)
HANKIN, [Edward] *A. M.* Panegyric on Great Britain —. 1786. 8. (1 sh.) Reflections on the infamy of smuggling —. 1790. 8. (1 sh.)
HANLEY, [P....] *M. D.* Account of an extraordinary steatomatous tumour in the abdomen of a woman. (Phil. Transact. 1770. p. 131.) überf. Samml. f. A Th. 2. S. 139.)
HANSARD, [Hugh Iosiah] Letters and thoughts which may promote christian knowledge and justice. 1784. 8.
HANWAY, [Jonas] *Commissioner of the victualling office.* born at *Portsmouth, Hampshire* d. 12 Aug. 1712. died at *London* d. 5 Sept. 1786.
HARDHAM, [John] born: .... died d. .. Sept. 1772.
HARDWICK, [Thomas] *F. A. S.* Observations on the remains of the amphitheatre of Flavius Vespasian at Rome as it was in the Year 1777. (Arch. Vol. 7. p. 369.)
HARDWICKE, [....] *Earl of*, born d. 20 Dec. 1720. died d. 16 May. 1790.
HARDY, [Francis] *Esq. M. R. J. A.* Thoughts on some particular passages in the Agamemnon of *Aeschylus*. (Tr. of J. A. 1788. p. 55.)

HARDY, [James] *M. D. of Barnſtaple, Devonſhire.* Examination of what has been advanced on the colic of Poitou and Devonſhire —. 1778. 8. (3 Sh. 6 d.) Anſwer to Dr. *Riollay's* letter on the origin of the gout. 1780. 8. (1 Sh.)

—— [.....] *Admiral.* Chronological liſt of the captains of the royal navy from 1673 to 1783. 1788. (7 Sh. 6 d.)

—— [Samuel] *Rector of little Blackenham in Suffolk.* The Theory of the moon —. 1752. 8. (1 Sh.) Account of the nature and ends of the holy euchariſt —. 8. 1763. (1 Sh.) Translation of *Scheffer's* treatiſe on the emendation of dioptrical teleſcopes —. 1769. 8. (1 Sh. 6 d.) The principal prophecies of the old and new teſtament - compared and explained. 1770. 8. (6 ſh.) Vindication of the church of England, in requiring ſubſcription to her 39 articles of religion. 1773. 8. (1 Sh.) Translation of St. Paul's epiſtle to the hebrews. 1783. 8. (1 Sh. 6 d.)

HARGRAVE, [Francis] *Esq. Barriſter at law.* On the caſe of *James Somerſett,* a Negro, lately determined by the court, of King's Bench : wherein it is attempted to demonſtrate the preſent unlawfulneſſ of domeſtic ſlavery in England, to which is prefixed, a ſtate of the caſe. 1772. 8. (2 Sh.) Argument in defence of literary property. 1774. 8. (1 ſh. 6 d.) Collection of ſtate trials and proceedings for high treaſon and other crimes and miſdemeanours. Vol. I-XI. fol. 1781. (11 Guin.) Collection of tracts relative to the law of England, from Manuſcript. 1787. 4. Vol. I. (1 L. 7 ſb.) *Edw. Coke's* commentary upon Littleton. Ed. XIII. with additions and notes by *Fr. Hargrave* and *Charles Butler* —. 1788. fol. (3 L. 3 Sh.)

HARGROVE, [E......] Hiſtory of the caſtle, town and foreſt of *Knaresborough* with *Harrogate* and its medicinal waters —. 1782. 8. (1 Sh. 6 d.) Ed. 4. 1789. 8.

HARINGTON, [John Herbert] Deſcription of a Cave with an inſcription near Gyá, (Aſiat. Reſ. Vol. 1. p. 276.)

—— [Henry] *A. B. of Queen's College, Oxford.* Nugae antiquae; being a miſcellaneous collection of

origi-

original papers in profe and verfe: written in the reigns of Henry VIII. Edward VI. Mary, Elizabeth, James I. felected from authentic remains of *John Harrington* —. 1769. 8. (3 Sh.) Ed. 2. 1775. Vol. 1. 2. (3 Sh.)

HARLEY, [George Davies] *of the Theatre-Royal, Norwich.* Monody on the death of Mr. *John Henderfon* late of Covent-Garden Theatre. 1787. 4. (2 fh.)

HARMER, [Thomas] *Diffenting Minifter at Waresfield, Suffolk.* born: .... died d. 27 Nov. 1788.

HARPER, [Andrew] The oeconomy of health; or, a medical effay: containing new and familiar inftructions for the attainment of health, happinefs and longevity —. 1789. 8. (2 Sh.) On the real caufe and cure of infanity —. 1789. 8. (2 Sh.)

HARPLEY, [T......] *T. Harpley* and *W. Sancroft* poems on various fubjects, moral, fentimental, fatyrical and entertaining 1785. 8 (3 Sh.)

HARRINGTON, [.....] *Mrs.* "New and elegant amufements for the ladies of Great Britain. by a Lady. 1772. 8. (2 Sh. 6 d.)

—— [Robert] *M. D.* Enquiry into the firft and general principles of animal and vegetable life. —. 1781. 8. (5 Sh.) Thoughts on the properties and formations of the different kinds of air —. 1785. 8. (5 Sh.) Letter to *Prieftley, Cavendifh, Lavoifier* and *Kirwan* endeavouring to prove, that their newly adopted opinions of inflammable and dephlogiftical airs forming water; and the acids being compounded of the different kinds of air, are fallacious. 1788. 8. (3 fh.)

—— [Thomas] Science improved; or, the true theory of the univerfe —. 1774. 4. ('7 Sh. 6 d.)

HARRIS, [James] *F R. S. Truftee of the Britifh Mufeum.* born at *Clofe, Salisbury*: 1708. died d. 21 Dec. 1780.

—— [Jofeph] *Secretary.* born 1751. died d. 31 Aug. 1789.

—— [Mofes] The Aurelian; or hiftory of Englifh infects. 17.. The englifh Lepidoptera: or, the Aurelian's pocket companion —. 1775. 8. (2 Sh.)

—— [R ....] Scriptural refearches on the licitnefs of the flave trade. —. 1788. 8. (1 Sh. 6 d.)

HAR-

HARRIS, [Richard] *M. D. Physician at Clonmel.* Collectanea hibernica medica. Nro. I. 1783. 8. (2 Sh. 6 d)
—— [William] *D. D. Dissenting Clergyman at Honiton, Devonshire.* born: ..... died d ... Febr. 1770.
—— [William] *Prebendary of Landaff and Curate of Cairell.* Observations on the Julia strata and on the roman stations, forts, and camps in the counties of Monmouth, Breeknock, Caermarthen and Glamorgan. (Arch. Vol. 2. p. 1.)

HARRISON, [.....] *Lieutenant.* The travellers, a comedy. 1788. 8. (1 Sh. 6 d.)
—— [......] Memoires of Charles Frederic, King of Prussia by *Sam. Johnson,* LL. D. with notes and a continuation, with translations of select poems written by the King of Prussia. 1786. (6 Sh.)
—— [Edward] *Member of the royal medical society at Edinburgh.* Letter to Dr. (*Will.*) *Stevenson,* occasioned by a postscript published in the IId Edition of his medical cases —. 1782. 8. (1 Sh.)
—— [Gustavus] Agriculture delineated: or, the farmer's complete guide; — —. 1775. 8. (5 Sh.)
—— [John] *Surgeon, of Mountstreet, Berkeleysquare.* The remarkable effects of fixed air in mortifications of the extremities, with a history of some worm cases. 1785. 8. (1 Sh.) On the cure of the dry belly - ach. —. 1786. 8. (1 Sh.) A case of the stone in the urinary bladder, successfully treated; by giving water impregnated with fixed air, by means of salt of tartar and weak spirit of vitriol. (Mem. of M. S. of L. Vol. 1 p. 225.) History of some remarkable cures in worm cases by a mild and efficacious medicine —. 1786 8.
—— [John] *Mechanician.* born at *Fulby* in the parish of *Wragby* 1693. died d. 24 March 1776.
—— [Richard] *M. A. Minister of Brompton Chapel and Lecturer of St. Peter's, Cornhill.* Institutes of English grammar. 1780. 8. (Several single sermons)
—— [R. ...] *Musical Professor.* Sacred harmony; or, a collection of psalm tunes, ancient and modern —. 8. 1784. (5 Sh.)

HARROD, [W....] The antiquities of Stamford and St. Martin. Vol. I. 2. 1786. 8. (7 Sh.)

HARSTON, [Hall] The counteſſ of Salisbury. a Tragedy. 1767. (1 ſh. 6 d.) Youth, a poem. 1773. 4. (2 Sh.)

HART, [Cheney] M. D. In the Commiſſion of the peace, for the County of Salop and ſenior Phyſician of the Infirmary at Shrewsbury. born 1726. died d. 21 June 1784.

HARTE, [Walter] M. A. born: .... died at Bath. 1773.

HARTLEY, [David] Esq. Member of Parliament in Yorkſhire. Speech on the ſtate of the nation and the preſent civil war in America. 1776. 4. (1 Sh.) Letters on the American War —. 1778. 4. (3 Sh.) Two letters — to the committee of the county of York. 1780. 8. (6 d.) Addreſſ to the committee of the county of York. 1781. 8. (1 Sh.) Conſiderations on the propoſed renewal of the bank Charter. 1781. 8. (1 Sh.) Addreſſ to the — Mayor and Corporation — of the Trinity houſe and to the — burgeſſes of the town of Kingſton upon Hull. 1784. 8. (1 Sh.)

—— [James] born ..... died 1780.

—— [Thomas] M. A. Rector of Winwick, Northamptonſhire. born: .... died d. 10 Dec. 1784.

—— [Winchcombe Henry] Member of Parliament. Addreſſ to the public on the loan. 1781. 8. (6 d.)

HARTSON, [Hall] born in Ireland .... died d. .... March. 1773.

HARVEST, [George] M. A. Fellow of Magdalen College. Collection of ſermons — on various ſubjects. 1763. 8. (4 Sh.) Reaſonebleneſſ and neceſſity of ſubſcription. 1772. 8. (2 Sh 6 d.)

HARVEY, [Stanhope] Esq. On ſoot uſed upon graſſ grounds. (Hunter's G. E. Vol. 5. p. 267.)

HARWOOD, [Buſick] F. R. S. Profeſſor of Anatomy in the Univerſity of Cambridge. Synopſis of a courſe of lectures on anatomy and phyſiology. 1787. 8. (2 Sh. 6 d.)

—— [Edward] D. D. Letter to Caleb Evans occaſioned by his curious confeſſion of faith. 1767. 8. (1 Sh.) New introduction to the ſtudy and knowledge of the new teſtament. Vol. 1. 2. 1767. 1771. (11 Sh.) überſ. von J. Cph. Fr. Schulz. Th. 1-3. Halle 1770. Liberal translation of the New Teſtament. Vol.

Vol. 1. 2. 1768. (12 Sh.) The melancholy doctrine of predestination expoled and the delightful truth of universal redemption reprefented. 1768. 8 (1 Sh. 6 d.) Five Differtations: 1) on the Athanafian doctrine: 2) on the Socinian sheme. 3) On the perfon of Christ. 4) On the rife, progreff, perfection and end of Christ's kingdom. 5) On the caufes which probably conspired to produce our Saviour's agony. 1772. 8. (4 Sh.) überf (von Krüger) Berlin 1774. 8. überf. Leipzig 1774 8. The life and character of Jefus Christ. 1773. 8. (4 Sh. 6 d.) On temperance and intemperance. 1774. 8. (2 Sh. 6 d.) überf Leipzig 1776. 8. Abaucit Mifcellanies on historical theological and critical fubject — translated from the french. 1774. 8. (6 Sh.) Catulli, Tibulli, Propertii Opera 1774. 8. (3 Sh.) New Teftament — with notes. Vol. 1. 2. 1776. 8. (7 Sh.) (La Roche,) Memoirs of Miff Sophie Sternheim translated. Vol. 1. 2. 1776. (6 Sh.) Sermons on the parable of the sower. 1777. 8. (3 Sh. 6 d.) Biographia claffica: The lives and characters of the greek and roman claffics 1777. Vol. 1. 2. (6 Sh.) View of the various editions of the greek and roman claffics. 1775. 8. (3 Sh.) überf. von F. K. Alter. Wien 1778. 8. On the focinian sheme. Ed. 2. 1784. 8. (1 Sh. 6 d.) überf. von J. C. F. Schulz. Leipz. 1773. 8. The cafe of Harwood; an obftinate palfy-relieved by electricity. 1784. 8. (1 Sh.) Letter to the Rev. S. Badcock, the Monthly reviewer, in which his uncharitablenefs, ignorance and abufe of Dr. Prieftley are exposed. 1784. 8. (1 Sh.)

(Several fingle fermons.)

HARWOOD, [Thomas] *of Univerfiry College, Oxford.* De death of Dion, a Tragedy. 1787. 8. (1 Sh. 6 d.) Annotations upon genefis; —. 1789. 8. (5 Sh.)

HASSEL, [J. . . . .] Tour of the Isle of Wight. Vol. 1. 2. 1790. 8. (1 L. 11 fh. 6 d.)

HASTED, [Edward] *F. R. S: F. A. S.* Letter to Dr. *Ducarel*, concerning Chesnut trees. (Phil. Transact. 1771. p. 160.) Hiftory and topographical furvey of the county of Kent. Vol. 1-3. 1778-1790. fol. (5 L. 5 Sh.)

HASTIN-

HASTINGS, [Thomas] The tears of Britannia; a poem on the death of William Earl of Chatham. 1778. 4. (1 Sh.)
—— [Warren] *late Governor General of Bengal.* Narrative of the late transaction at Benares. 1782. 8. (2 Sh. 6 d.) Narrative of the insurrection, which happened in the Zemeedary at Benares. Calcutta 1782. 4. (10 Sh. 6 d.) Letter to the court of directors of East India Company 1783. 8. (1 Sh. 6 d.) Letter - with remarks and authentic documents. 1786. 8. (1 Sh.) The defence at the bar of the houfe of commons. P. 1. 2. 1786. 8. (5 Sh.) Review of the state of Bengal. 1786. 8. (3 Sh.) auch unter dem Titel: Memoirs relative to the state of India. 1786. 8. (4 Sh.) The prefent state of the East Indies. 1786. 8. (2 Sh.) Letter to the court of Directors relative to their censure on his conduct at Benares - with a letter - on the subject of money privateley received. 1786. 8. (1 Sh. 6 d.) Answer to the articles exhibited by the knigths, citizens and burgeffes in parliament affembled — in maintenance of their impeachment against him for high crimes - fupposed to have been by him committed. 1788. 8. (4 Sh.)

HATSELL, [John] *Esq. Clerk to the houfe of commons.* Collection of cafes of privilege of parliament from the earlieft records, to the Year 1628. 4. (6 Sh.) Vol. 1. 1778. Precedents of proceedings in the houfe of commons, under feparate titles; with observations. Vol. 1-3. 1781. 4. (16 Sh.)

HATTON, [Thomas] *Watchmaker.* Introduction to the mechanical part of Clock and watch work —. 1773. 8. (6 Sh. 6 d.) Effay on Goldcoin. 1773. 8. (2 Sh.)

HAVARD, [Neaft] *Town Clerk of the Borough of Tewkesbury.* born: .... died d. Jan. 1787.
—— [William] *Actor.* born: .... died. d. 20 Febr. 1778.

HAWEIS, [Thomas] *LL. B. Rector of Aldwinkle and Chaplain to the Earl of Peterborough.* Evangelical principles and practice —. 1763. 8. (5 Sh.) Improvement of the church catechism —. 1776. 12. (2 Sh.) Scriptural refutation of the arguments
for

for polygamy. —. 1781. 8. (1 Sh. 6 d.) Hints respecting the poor. 1788. 8. (1 Sh.)
(Several single sermons.)
HAWES, [William] *Apothecary*. *M. D.* Account of the late Dr. Goldsmith's illness, so far as relates to the exhibition of Dr. *James's* powders —. 1774. 4. (1 sh) Examination of *John Wesley's* primitive physic. 1776. 8. (1 sh. 6 d.) Address against to hasty interments. 1777. 8. Address on the recovery of suspended animation —. 1782. 8. (2 sh.) *Editor of Reports of the humane society, instituted in the year 1774. for the recovery of persons apparently drowned, for the years 1781 and 1782. 8. Address on the important subject of preserving the lives of its inhabitants. 1782. Observations on the general bills of mortality. 1783. 8. (3 sh.)
HAWKE, [....] *Mrs.* ° Julia de Gramont, a Novel. Vol. 1. 2. 1788. 12. (7 sh.)
HAWKESBURY, *Lord.* see *Charles Jenkinson*.
HAWKESWORTH, [John] LL. D. *of Bromley in Kent.* born 1719. died d. 17 Nov. 1773.
HAWKINS, [A. ...] Translation of *Mignot's* history of the Turkish or Ottoman empire from 1300-1740. Vol. 1-4. 1788. 8. (1 L. 4sh.)
—— [George] *Esq.* The Royal letter Writer. 17.. On female education. 1781. 8. (1 sh 6 d)
—— [John Sidney] *Sir, Knight.* One *of his Majesty's justices of the peace of Midlesex and Chairman of the Court of quarter session.* born: 1718. died d. 21 May. 1789.
—— [John] Address to *Priestley*; containing an apology for those who conscientiously subscribe to the articles of the church of England; and in particular, to the doctrines of the trinity —. 1788. 8. (1 sh. 6 d)
—— [Thomas] *M. A. of Magdalen-College, Oxford.* The origin of the english drama. Vol. 1-3. 1773. 8. (9 sh.)
—— [William] *M A.* Discourses on scripture mysteries. 1787. 8. (5 sh.) Poems, chiefly pastoral. 1787. 8. (1 sh.)
HAWTHORN, [John] *Light Dragoon in the Inniskilling regiment.* Poems. 1779. 4. (3 sh.)
HAY, [Charles] *Captain.* Description of a roman hypocaust

' cauſt discovered near Brecknock. (Arch. Vol. 7. p. 205. Vol. 8. p. 441.)

HAYES, [....] Natural hiſtory of british birds. 1775. fol. (5 L. 15 ſh. 6 d.)

—— [Samuel] *M. A. Fellow of Trinity college. Uſher of Weſtminſter ſchool.* Duelling, a poem. 1775. 4. (1 ſh.) Prayer, a poem. 1777. 4. (1 ſh) Prophecy, a poem. 1777. 4. (1 ſh.) The nativity of our ſaviour, a poem. 1778. 4. (1 ſh.) The Aſcenſion, a poetical eſſay. 1781. 4. (1 ſh.) Hope, a poem. 1783. 4. (1 ſh. 6 d.) Creation, a poem. 1784. 4. (1 ſh.) The exodus, a poem. 1785. 4. (2 ſh.) Publiſhed *Sam. Johnſon's* ſermon for the funeral of his wife. 1788. 8. (1 Sh) Publiſhed *John Taylor's* L. L. D. ſermons on different ſubjects. Vol. 1. 2. 1789. (10 Sh.) Verſes on his Majeſty's recovery. 1789. 4. (1 Sh. 6 d.) Thanksgiving ſermon. 1789. 4. (1 Sh.).

HAYES, [Thomas] *Surgeon at London.* *Addreſſ to the public on the dangerous conſequences of neglecting common coughs and colds. 1784. 8. (1 Sh. 6 d.) Ed. 2. with the Author's name) 1785. Ed. 3. 1786. 8. (2 Sh. 6 d.) überſ. von *C. F. Michaelis.* Leipz. 1787. 8. Remarks on the nature and treatment of intermittents, as they occurred at *Hampſtead* in the ſpring of 1781. (London M. J. Vol. 2. p 267. überſ. Sammml. f. A. Th. 7. S. 493.

—— [Thomas] *Surgeon at Hampſtead.* born:... died 17...

HAYGARTH, [John] *M. D: F. R. S.* A caſe of angina pectoiis, with an attempt to inveſtigate the cauſe of the diſeaſe by diſſection and a hint ſuggeſted concerning the method of cure. (Med. Transact Vol. 3. p. 37.) Apparent effects of mercury in caſes that were ſuppoſed hydrocephalus. (Med. Obſ. Vol. 6. p. 58.) Experiments on the cerumen or earwax in order to discover the beſt method of diſſolving it when cauſing deafneſſ. (Ibid. p. 198.) Bill of Mortality for Cheſter for the Y. 1772. (Phil. Transact. 1774. p. 67.) Bill of Mortality for Cheſter for the Y. 1773. (Ibid. 1775 p. 85.) Bill of Mortality for Cheſter for the Y. 1774. (Ibid. 1778. p. 131.) Obſervations on the population and diſeaſes of Cheſter in the Year 1774. (Ibid.

(Ibid. 1778. p. 131.) Account of a newly invented machine for impregnating water or other fluids with fixed air. (Mem. of M. Vol. I. p. 41.) Inquiry how to prevent the small pox. 1784. 8. (3 Sh.) überf. von *J. F. L. Cappel*. Berlin. 1786. 8.

HAYLEY, [William] at *Eartham*. ⁰ Poetical epistle to an eminent painter. (Mr. *Romney*) 1778. 4. ⁰Elegy on the ancient greek medal. 1779. 4. (1 Sh. 6 d.) ⁰Epistle to a friend on the death of *John Thornton*. 1780. 4. (1 Sh.) Essay on history, in 3 Epistles to *Edw. Gibbon*. 1780. 4. (7 Sh. 6 d.) ⁰Ode inscribed to *John Howard*. 1780. 4. (1 Sh. 6 d.) The triumphs of temper; a poem. 1781. 4. (6 Sh.) Essay on epic poetry. 1782. 4. (10 Sh. 6 d.) Plays. 1784. 4. (12 Sh.) Poems and plays. Vol. 1-6. 1785. 8. (1 L. 1 Sh) * Philosophical historical and moral essay on old maids; by a friend to the sisterhood. Vol. 1-3. 1785. 8. (10 Sh. 6 d) überf. Leipz. Th. 1-3. 1786. 8. Occasional stanzas. 1788. 4. (2 Sh.)

HAYSHAM, [John] M. D. Account of the jail fever, as it appeared at *Carlisle* in the Year 1781. 1782.

HAYTER, [Thomas] A. M. Fellow of King's College, Cambridge. Preacher at his Majesty's Chapel in Whitehall. Remarks on *Hume's* dialogues concerning natural religion. 1780. 8. (1 Sh. 6 d.) Two sermons. 1788. 8. (1 Sh.)

HAYWOOD, [...] *Mrs.* A new present for a servant maid: containing rules for her moral conduct —. 1771. 12. (2 Sh.)

HEADLEY, [Henry] A. B. at *Norwich*. born 1765. died d. 15 Nov. 1788.

HEALDE, [Thomas] M. D: F. R. S. Lumleyan Lecturer at the college of physicians and senior physician of the London Hospital. On the use of oleum asphalti in ulcers of the intestines, lungs and other viscers. 1769. 8. (1 Sh.) The new pharmacopoea of the royal college of physicians of London, translated into english with notes —. 1788. 8. (5 Sh.)

HEARD, [William] Valentine day; a musical drama. 1775. 8. The Snuffbox; or a trip to bath, a comedy. 1775. 8. (1 Sh.) A sentimental journey to Bath,

Bath, Briſtol and their environs; a poem, with miscellaneous pieces. 1778. 4. (5 Sh.)

HEARNE, [Gilbert] *of Hertford. Antiquarian.* born: .... died d. 17 Sept. 1771.

HEASEL, [Anthony] The ſervant's book of knowledge, containing tables of wages —. 1773. 8. (1 Sh. 6 d.)

HEATHCOTE, [Ralph] *D. D. Clergyman.* Sketch of Lord *Bolingbroke's* philoſophy. 1754. 8. (1 Sh. 6 d.) The uſe of reaſon aſſerted in matters of religion or natural religion the foundation of revealed. Ed. 2. 1755. 8. (1 Sh. 6 d.) Reply to Dr. *Paſſen* Sermon on St. *Peter's* chriſtian apology. 1756. 8. (2 Sh.) A diſcourſe upon the being of God: againſt Atheiſts in two ſermons. 1763. 4. (1 Sh.) * Letter to the Lord Major — from an old ſervant. 1762. 8. (1 Sh. 6 d.) Sylva or the wood. 17.. The Irenarch: or juſtice of peace's manual. 2) miſcellaneous reflections upon the laws, 'policy, manners. 3) Aſſize ſermon. 1781. 8. (3 Sh.)

(Several ſingle ſermons.)

HEBERDEN, [William] *M. D: F. R. S: F. A. S.* Antithyriaca, eſſay on Mithridaticum and Theriaca. 1755. 8. Remarks on the pumpwater of London and on the methods of procuring the pureſt water. (Med. Transact. Vol. 1. p. 1.) Obſervations on the Ascarides. (Ibid. p. 60.) On the effect of common ſalt in an extraordinary caſe of worms. (Ibid. p. .) Of the night-blindneſs or Nyctalopia. (Ibid. p. 60.) On the chicken-pox. (Ibid. p. 427.) The epidemical cold, in June and July 1767. (Ibid. p. 437.) On the hectic fever. (Ibid. Vol. 2. p. 1.) Remarks on the pulſe. (Ibid. p. 18) Account of a disorder of the breaſt. (Ibid. p. 59.) Account of the diseaſes of the liver. (Ibid. p. 123.) Account of the nettle rash. (Ibid. p. 173.) Account of the noxious effects of ſome fungi. (Ibid. p. 216.) Account of the angina pectoris. (Ibid. Vol. 2. p... Vol. 3. p...) Of the measles. (Ibid. Vol. 3. p. 389.) The method of preparing Ginseng root in China. (Ibid. Vol. 3. p...) A table of the mean heat of every month for ten Years in London from 1763 to 1772. incluſively. (Phil. Transact. 1788. p. 66.)

HECK-

HECKFORD, [William] *Esq.* Characters, or historical anecdotes of all the kings and queens of England. 1789. 8. (3 Sh.)

HEDLEY, [William] System of practical arithmetic and three forms of book-keeping —. 1779. 8. (2 Sh. 6 d.)

HEELY, [Joseph] *Esq.* Letters on the beauties of Hagley, Envil and the Leasowes, with observations on the modern taste in gardening. Vol. I. 2. 1777. 12. (5 Sh.) Überf. Leipz. 1779. 8.

HELLINS, [John] *Curate of Constantine, in Cornwall.* Theorems for computing logarithms. (Phil. Transact. 1780. p. 388.) A new method of finding the equal roots of an equation by division. (Ibid. 1782. p. 417.) Mathematical essays on several subjects —. 1788. 4. (7 Sh. 6 d.)

HELME, [Elizabeth] *Mrs.* Louisa, or the cottage on the moor. Vol. 1. 2. 1787. 8. (6 Sh.) Clara and Emmelina, or the maternal benediction. Vol. 1. 2. 1788. 8. (6 Sh.) *Vaillant's* travels from the Cape of good Hope into the interior parts of Africa — translated from the french. Vol. 1. 2. 1790. 8. (12. sh)

HELSHAM, [Henry] *Surgeon at Stoke in Norfolk.* Account of different medical cases. (*Duncan's* M. C. Dec. 2. Vol. III. p. 278.)

HEMMING, [John] *M. D: Physician to the Offulston dispensary.* History and chemical analysis of the mineral water lately discovered in the city of Gloucester —. 1789. 8. (1 Sh.)

HENDERSON, [Andrew] *M. A.* Arsinoe: or, the incestuous marriage, a tragedy. 1752. 8. (1 Sh.) *Voltaire's* history of Frederik, King of Sweden, translated. 1752. 8. (1 Sh. 6 d.) Memoirs of Dr. *Archib. Cameron* —. 1753. 8. (1 Sh.) Memoirs of the Field-Mareshal *Leopold* Count *Daun* — translated from a french Manuscript —. 1757. 8. (1 Sh. 6 d.) Memoirs of the life and actions of *James Keith* Field-Mareshal in the Prussian armies —. 1759. 8. (1 Sh.) Considerations whether the act of parliament establishing a militia through England ought to extend to Scotland in time of war? 1760. 8. (1 Sh.) The life of *William* the Conqueror, Duke of Normandy and King of England. 1764. 8. (2 Sh. 6 d.) The life of *William Augustus*

ſtus Duke of Cumberland —. 1766. 8. (5 Sh.)
Letter to the Lord Biſhop of Cheſter on his ſermon before theLords. 1774. 8. Letter 1. 2. to *Sam. Johnſon* on
his journey to the Weſtern Isles. 1775. 8. (1 ſh. 6 d.)

HENDERSON, [John] *B. A.* born at *Bellegarance in
Ireland* d. 27 March 1757. died d. 2 Nov. 1788.

HENDERSON, [Stewart] *Surgeon of his Majeſty's
ſhip Aſtrea, at Jamaica.* Account of the ſucceſſfull
treatment of an ulcer of the leg, with remarks on
ulcers of the legs in general, in warm climates.
(*Duncan's* M. C. Dec. 2. Vol. 3. p. 292.)

HENDERSON, [William] *M. D. Member of the R.
Med. Soc. of Edinb.* Obſervations concerning thoſe
things which are probable or in ſome meaſure ascertained relative to the hiſtory and cure of the plague.
1789. 8. (1 ſh. 6 d.)

HENDY, [James] *M. D. Phyſician general to the militia and one of the phyſicians to the general dispen-
ſary at Barbadoes.* On glandular ſecretion —.
1775. 8. (2 ſh.) On the glandular diseaſe of Barbadoes. 1784. 8. (2 ſh. 6 d.) überſ. von *A. F. A. Diel.*
Frankf. 1788. 8. Vindication of the opinions and
facts, contained in a treatiſe of the glandular diſeaſe
of Barbadoes. 1789. 8. (3 ſh.)

HENLEY, [Samuel] *F. S. A: Rector of Rendlesham,
Suffolk.* Obſervations on the ſubject of the IV
eclogue, the allegory in the third georgic and the
primary deſign of the aeneid of *Virgil*, with remarks on ſome coins of the jews. 1788. 8. (2 ſh.
6 d.)

—— [Samuel] *Curate of Northall in Middlesex.* Diſſertation on the controverted paſſages in St. Peter
and St. Jude concerning the angels that ſinned and
who kept not their firſt eſtate. 1778. 8. (2 ſh.)

—— [William] *F. R. S.* Account of the death of a
perſon destroyed by lightning in the chapel in Tot-
tenham-Court-road and its effects on the building.
(Philoſ. Transact. 1772. p. 131.) Experiment concerning the different efficacy of pointed and blun-
ted rods, in ſecuring buildings againſt the ſtroke
of lightning. (Ibid. 1774. p. 133.) Account of
ſome new experiments in electricity —. (Ibid. 1774.
p. 389.) Remarks on Mr. *Haffenden's* account of
the effects of lightning on a houſe furniſhed with a
poin-

pointed conductor at Tenterden in Kent. *(* Ibid. 1774. p. 336.*)* Experiments and obfervations on a new apparatus, called, a machine for exhibiting perpetual electricity. (Ibid. 1776. p. 513.) Experiments and obfervations in electricity. (Ibid. 1777. p. 85) Obfervations and experiments tending to confirm Dr. *Ingenhousz's* theory of the electrophorus; and to fhew the impermeability of glafs to electric fluid. (Phil. Transact. 1778. p. 1049.) überf. Samml. zur P. u. N. G. Th. 2. S. 536.

HENRY, [Robert] *D. D. Minifter of Edinburgh.* F. A. S. *Edinb.* Hiftory of Great - Britain trom the firft invafion of it by the Romans under Julius Cefar. Vol. 1 - 5. London. 1771 - 1785. 4. (5 L. 5 fh.) Letter to the Authors of the Critical Review. (Crit. Review. Vol. 46. p. 320.)
 (Several fingle fermons.)
—— [Thomas] *Apothecary at Manchefter* F. R. S. Account of an improved method of preparing magnefia alba. (Med. Transact. Vol. 2. p. 226.) Experiments and obfervations on the preparation, calcination and medicinal uses of magnefia alba. 1773. 8. (2 fh. 6 d.) Account of the medicinal virtues of magnefia alba — 1773. 8. Letter to Dr. *Glafs*, containing a reply to his examination of the ftrictures on Dr. *Glafs's* magnefia. 1774. 8. (6 d.) Experiments on the comparative powers of foft and hard water in diffolving refinous fubftances. *(Percival's* Effays. Ed. 3. Vol. 1.) Letter on the folution of lead in water impregnated with nitrous air. *(Prieftley's* Exper. and Obs. on air. Vol. 1. p. 323.) *Lavoifier* effays phyfical and chemical translated. 1776. 8. (7 fh.) Account of the earthquake which was felt at Manchefter and other places, on the 14th day of Sept. 1777. (Phil. Transact. 1778. p. 221.) On the effects of fixed air in preserving fruit and its influence on vegetation, milk —. *(Prieftley's* Exp. and Obs. on air. Vol. 3. p. 369.) On the action of lime and marl as manures; and the making of artificial marl for the purposes of Agriculture *(Hunter's* G. E. Vol. 5. p. 65.) Account of a method of preserving water at fea from putrefaction. 1781. 8. (2 fh.) *Lavoifier's* effays on effects produced by various pro-

processes on atmospheric air. 1783. 8. (2 sh. 6 d.) Memoirs of *Alb. Haller.* 1783. 8. (2 sh. 6 d.) Instances of the medicinal effects of magnetism. (London M. J. Vol. 3. p. 303.) On the advantage of litterature and philosophy in general and especially on the consistency of literary and philosophical with comercial pursuits. (Mem. of. M. Vol 1. p. 7.) On the preservation of sea water from putrefaction by means of quicklime. (Mem. of M Vol. 1. p. 41.) On the natural history and origin of magnesian earth, particularly as connected with those of seasalt and of nitre, with observations on some of the chemical properties of that earth, which have been hitherto, either unknown or undetermined. (Ibid. p. 448.) Experiments and observations on ferments and fermentation. 1785. 8. (Ibid, Vol. 2. p. 257.) übers. Samml. zur P. u. Ng. Th. 3. S. 643. Observations on the influence of fixed air on vegetation and on the probable cause of the difference in the results of various experiments, made on that subject. (Ibid p. 341.) A case of a head-ach attended with uncommon symptoms. (Mem. of M. S. of L. Vol. 1. p. 294.)

HENRY, [William] *of Lancaster.* Description of a self-moving or sentinel register (Tr. of A. S. Vol. 1. p. 286.)

HERBERT, [William] *of Cheshunt, Herts. Jos. Ames's* typographical antiquities: or account of the origin and progress of printing in Great-Britain and Ireland — considerably augmented. Vol. 1-3. 1785-1790. 4. (1 L. 1 Sh.)

HERIOT, [George] *Descriptive poem, written in the West-Indies. 1781. 4. (2 sh.)

HERON, [Robert] see *Pinkerton.*

HERRIES, [John] *M. A.* The elements of speech. 1773. 8. (4 sh) Sermon on the frequent and enormous crime of suicide. 1774. 4. (1 sh.)

HERRING, [Thomas] *Archbishop of Canterbury.* born : .... died 1774.

HERVEY, [Chr. ...] *Esq.* Letters from Portugal, Spain, Italy and Germany in the years 1759-1761. Vol. 1-3. 1785. 8. (18 sh.)

—— [G.... A....] see *Payne.*

HEWGILL, [Edwin] *Ensign and Adjutant in the Cold-stream*

stream Regiment of foot guards. J. G. Tielke's field Engineer; or, inſtructions upon every branch of field fortification translated —. Vol. 1. 2. 1789. 8. (1 L. 8 Sh.)

HEWLETT, [John] *A. M. of Magdalene College, Cambridge, Lecturer of the united pariſhes of St. Vedaſt, Foſterlane and St. Michael le Querne.* Sermons on different ſubjects. 1786. 8. (6 ſh.) Introduction to reading and ſpelling, written on a new plan —. 1786. 8. (1 ſh.) Vindication of the authenticity of the parian chronicle in answer to a diſſertation on that ſubject. 1789. 8. (4 ſh.) Answer to ſome critical ſtrictures, relative to the controversy on the authenticity of the parian chronicle in a letter to *J. Robertſon* —. 1789. 8. (1 ſh. 6 d.)

HEWSON, [William] *F. R. S. and Teacher of Anatomy*: born at *Hexham* in *Northumberland*. d. 14 May. 1739. died d. 1 May 1774.

HEY, [Richard] *L. L. D. Fellow of Magdalen College Cambridge and Barriſter at Law of the middle temple.* Diſſertation on the pernicious effects of gaming. 1783. 8. (1 ſh. 6 d.) Diſſertation on duelling. 1784. 8. (1 ſh. 6 d.) Observations on the nature of civil liberty and the principles of government. 1776. 8. (1 ſh.)

—— [William] *F. R. S. Surgeon-General to the Infirmary at Leeds.* Account of an extrauterine foetus. (Med. Obs. Vol. 3. p. ...) Account of a rupture of the bladder from a ſuppreſſion of urine in a pregnant woman. (Ibid. Vol. 4. p. 58.) Experiments on fixed air and an account of its utility as a medicine in putrid fevers. (Phil. Transact. 1772. p. ...) On the effects of fixed air, applied by way of clyſter. (*Prieſtley's* Experim. on air: Vol. I. p. 292.) überſ. Samml. f. A. Th. 3. S. 272. Account of the effects of electricity in the amauroſis. (Med. Obs. Vol. 5. p. 1.) Experiments to prove that there is no oil of vitriol in water impregnated with fixed air. (*Prieſtley's* experiments on air. Vol. 1. p. 288.) On the acidity of fixed air: (Ibid. Vol. 3. p. 383.) Observations on the blood. 1779. 8. (1 ſh.) Account of ſome luminous arches. (Phil. Transact. 1790. p. 32.).

HEYDON, [C.....] *Jun.* The new aftrology 1786.
12. (2 fh. 6 d.)
HEYLYN, [Peter] *D. D. Prebendary of Weftminfter.*
A help to englifh hiftory —. 1774. 8. (8 fh.)
HEYSHAM, [John] *M. D. Phyfician at Carlisle in Cumberland.* Diff. De rabie canina. Edinh. 1777.
8. Account of the jail fever, or typhus carcerum —. 1782. 8. (1 fh) Account of a painful affection of the antrum maxillare, from which three insects were discharged. (M. C. Vol. 1. p. 430.) A remarkable case of epilepsy and dysphagia fpasmodica cured by the use of cuprum ammoniacum. *(Duncan's* M. C. 1780. p 428. and p. 438.)
HICKS, [George] *M. D Phyfician to the Weftminfter Hospital.* Diff. De Enteritide. Edinh. 1768. 8. A cafe of peripnevmony, attended with emphysema. (M. C. Vol. 1. p. 173.)
HIFFERNAN, [Paul] born in *Ireland:* .... died d 12 Jun. 1777.
HIGGINS, [Bryant] *M. D.* Actual fire and detonation produced by the contact of tinfoil, with the falt composed of copper and the nitrous acid. (Phil. Transact 1773. p. 137) Philosophical effay concerning light. Vol. 1. 1776. 8. (6 fh.) On the use of an amalgam of zinc, for the purpose of electrical excitation. (Phil. Transact. 1778. p. 861.) Experiments and observations made with the view of improving the art of compofing and applying calcareous cements and of preparing quicklime —. 1780. 8. (5 fh.) Experiments and obfervations relating to acetous acid, fixable air, dense inflammable air, oils and fuel —. 1786. 8. (6 fh.)
—— [William] *of Pembr. Coll. Oxford.* Comparative view of the phlogiftic and antiphlogistic theories — with an analyfis of the human calculus and observations on its origin —. 1789. 8. (7 fh.)
HIGHMORE, [Anthony] *Jun. Attorney at law.* Doctrine of bail in civil and criminal cases. 1783. 8. (4 fh.) Review of the hiftory of Mortmain —. 1787. 8. (4 fh.)
—— [John] Journal of travels made through the principal cities of Europe, — translated from the French of *M. L. Dutens* —. Ed. 2. 1782. 8. (3 fh. 6 d.)

HIGH-

HIGHMORE, [Joseph] *Painter and Professor by the Academy of Painting, Sculpture, at London.* born in the Parish of St. *James, Garlickhithe*, London. d. 13 Jun. 1692. died d. 3 March. 1780.

HILL, [Brian] *A. M. Chaplain to the Earl of Leven.* Henry and Acasto: a moral tale. 1785. 8. (1 sh.) (Several single sermons.)

—— [James] *Surgeon at Dumfries in Scotland* Account of the discharge of feces mixed with the urine from the urethra of a woman. (Med. Com. of Ed. Vol. 2. p. 192.) Account of singular appearances from affections of the liver in two cases. (Ibid. p. 303.) The history of an anomalous tumour on the eyebrow of a child of 15 months old. (Ibid. Vol. 3. p. 313.) Cases in Surgery, particularly of cancers and disorders of the head from external violence with observations. 1775. 8. (4 sh. 6 d.) History of a large prolapsus uteri. (Med. Com. of Ed. Vol. 4. p. 88.)

HILL [John] *Sir. Knight of the Polar-Star. Botanist to the royal garden at Kew.* born: 1717. died d. 21 Nov. 1775.

—— [John] *M. A: F. R. S. Edin. and Professor of Humanity in the University of Edinburgh.* Essay upon the principles of historical composition, with an application of those principles to the writings of *Tacitus*. (Tr. of E. S. Vol. 1. p. 76. et pag. 181.) übers. von *J. G. Buhle*: Philos. u. Histor. Abhandl. der Wissensch. zu Edinburgh Th. 1 S. 123.

—— [Richard] *Baronet and Member of Parliament.* (a Methodist.) *Pietas Oxoniensis: or, an account of the expulsion of VI students from St. Edmon-Hall —. 1768. 8. (1 sh.) *Goliath slain being a reply to Dr. *Nowell's* Answer to pietas Oxoniensis —. 1769. 8. (2 sh. 6 d.) *Review of all the doctrines taught by — *John Wesley* containing an answer to a book: a second check to Antinomianism. 1771. 8. (1 sh. 6 d.) *Five letters to the Rev. *M. F—r.* relative to his vindication of the minutes of — *John Wesley* — by a friend. 1771. 8. (6 d.) *Some remarks on a pamphlet, entitled, a third check to Antinomianism by the author of pietas Oxoniensis. 1771. 8. (3 d.) Logica Weslejensis —. 1773. 8. (1 sh.) The finishing stroke;

ke; containing fome ftrictures on *Fletcher's* logica Genevenfis. 1773. 8. (1 fh.) A prefent for your neighbour; or, the right knowlege of god and of ourfelves. 1773. 8. (4 d.) Three letters — to — *J. Fletcher* — fetting forth reafons for declining any further controversy relative to *Wesley's* principles. 1774. 8. (6 d.) ° A groff impofition upon the public detected, or, Archbishop *Cranmer* vindicated from the charge of Pelagianism — by the author of pietas Oxonienfis — 1775. 8. (6 d.) Pietas Redingenfis, or, a vindication of — *John Hallward's* fermon. 1776. 8. (6 d.) The gofpell fhop, a Comedy. 1778. 8. (2 Sh) The bleffings of polygamy difplayed in an — addreff to *Martin Madan*, occafioned by his work' Thelyphthora. 1781. 8. (3 fh.) The tables turned a letter to the author of a pamphlet observations on the election of members for the borough of Ludlow. 1781. 8. (6 d.) *The skyrocket: or thoughts during the cafter receff of Parliament, on feveral very important fubjects and on feveral recent events. 1781. 8. (1 fh.) A fhort catechism, containing the fundamental principles of Chriftianity. 1788. (6 d.)

HILL, [Robert] *Esq. of Cambridge.* Poems on feveral occafions —. 1775. 8. (5 fh.)

—— [Rowland] *M. A.* Impofture detected and the dead vindicated —. 1777. 8. (6 d.) Answer to *J. Wesley's* remarks upon the defence of the character of Whitefield and others. 1778. 8. (6 d.)

—— [Thom. F. . . . .] *Antient Erfe poems —. 1784. 8. (—)

HILDITCH, [Ann] *Miff.* Rofa de Montmorien. Vol. 1. 2. 1787. 12. (5 fh.)

HINDE, [Robert] *of the fix Clerks Office.* The modern practice of the high court of Chancery —. 1785. 8. (9 Sh.)

—— [. . . . . .] *Captain of the Royal Regiment of light Dragoons.* born: .... died d. 29 Sept. 1786.

HINGESTON, [James] *M. A. Vicar of Raydon in Suffolk.* Discourses upon the divine covenants: or, an enquiry into the origin and progreff of religion, natural and revealed. Part. 1. 1771. 8. (5 fh.)

HIRD, [William] *M. D. at Leeds in Yorkshire.* (a Quaker) born 1724. died d. 23 Aug. 1782.

HITCH-

HITCHCOCK, [—] The macoroni. a Comedy. 1773. 8. The coquet; or, the miſtakes of the heart. a Comedy. 1777. 8.

HITCHIN, [Edward] *B. D. Diſſenting Miniſter.* born 1726. died d. 11 Jan. 1774.

HOADLEY, [John] *LL. D. Chancellor of the Dioceſe of Wincheſter.* born d. 8 Oct. 1711. died d. 16 March. 1776.

HOBHOUSE, [Thomas] Elegy to the memory of *Sam. Johnſon.* 1784. 4. (6 d.) ✣Kingsweſton hill, a poem. 1784. 4. (1 Sh. 6 d.) Ed. 2. (with the Author's name.) 1787. 4. (1 ſh. 6 d.)

HOBSON, [John] *Miniſter of a congregation of proteſtant diſſenters at Kingswood Worceſterſhire.* Diſcourſe on prayer. 1787. 8. (6 d.) Remarks upon *George Croft's* ſermon, the teſts laws defended. 1790. 8. (1 Sh.)

HODGE, [....] *Farmer.* The hampſtead conteſt; —. 1776. 4. (6 d.)

HODGES, [William] *R. A.* Select views in Aqua tinta of Antiquities in India, drawn on the ſpot in the Years 1780-1783. Vol. 1. 2. Numb. 1-12. fol. (12 L. 12 ſh.) überſ. von Riem. Heft. 1. Berlin. 1789. fol.

HODGSON, [....] Miscellaneous poems. 1788. 4. (1 ſh. 6 d.)

—— [Henry] *Curate of Market Rasen, Lincolnſhire.* Letters to Mrs. *Kindersley.* 1778. 8. (6 d.) The duty of universal benevolence enforced; in 3 ſermons. 1778. 8. (1 ſh.) Effuſions of the heart and fancy; in verse and prose. 1779. 8. (3 ſh. 6 d.)

—— [Bernard] *L. L. D. Principal of Hertford College Oxford.* Salomon's ſong translated from the hebrew. Oxford. 1786. 4. (5 Sh.) The proverbs of Salomon, translated. 1788. 4. (7 ſh. 6 d.)

——. [Henry] *Letter — on the right of fishing in public ſtreams. 1787. 8. (1 Sh.)

—— [Thomas] Cursory observations on *Phil. Stern's* medical advice to the conſumptive and aſtmatic people of England —. 1784. 8. (1 Sh.)

HODSON, [J.....] *M. D.* Jesus Chriſt the true god —. 1787. 12. Vol. 1. 2. (5 Sh) The Young's chriſtian's introduction to the knowledge of his god and ſaviour Jeſus Chriſt. 1788. 12. (6 d.)
The

The worship of Jesus Chrift, as the true god of heaven and earth vindicated. 1789. 8. (6 d.)

HODSON, [William] M A. *Fellow of Trinity college.* The dedication of the temple of Solomon: a poetical effay. 1770. 4. (1 Sh.) "Arfaces, a tragedy. 1775. 8. (1 Sh. 6 d.) "Zoraida, a Tragedy, with obfervations on Tragedy. 1780. 8. (1 fh. 6 d.) The adventures of a night, a farce. 1783. 8.

HOGG, [John] Thanksgiving fermon. 1759. (6 d.) *Nathan.* Lardner's hiftory of the heretics of the two firft centuries after Chrift, with additions. 1780. 4. (18 fh.)

HOLCROFT, [Thomas] *Actor at Drury-Lane Theater.* (born in the county of *Lancafter.*) Elegies: on the death of *Sam. Foote*: on age. 1777. 4. (1 fh.) The Crifis; or, love and fear, a Comedy. 1778. Duplicity, a Comedy. 1780. 8. (1 fh. 6 d.) Alwyn; a novel. Vol. 1. 2. 1780. Human happinefs; or, the fceptic, a poem. 1783. 4. (3 fh.) The family picture, or domeftic dialogues on amiable and interefting fubjects. Vol. 1. 2. 1783. 8. (6 fh.) The noble peafant; a comic opera. 1784. 8. (1 fh 6 d) The follies of a day, a Comedy. 1784. 8. (*Foucher d'Obfonville's*) Philofophical effays on the manners of various foreign animals, with obfervations on the laws and cuftoms of feveral eaftern nations translated from the french. 1784. 8. (5 fh.) *Beaumarchais* follies of a day or the marriage of Figaro, a Comedy, translated. 1785. 8. (1 fh. 6 d.) Mad. *Genlis's* — Tales of the caftle — translated. Vol. 1-5. 1785. 8. (15 fh.) The choleric fathers, a comic Opera. 1785. 8. (1 fh. 6 d.) An amorous tale of the chaste loves of Peter the long and of his — Dame *Blanche Bazu.* 1786. 8. (3 fh. 6 d.) Mad. *Genlis's* facred dramas translated. 1786. 8. (5 Sh.) Caroline of Lichtfield translated from the french. Vol. 1-3. 1786. 8. (9 Sh.) Seduction, a Comedy. 1787. 8. (1 Sh. 6 d.) The life of *Frederik Baron Trenck*, translated from the german. Vol. 1-3. 1788. 8. (12 Sh.) *Lavater's* effays on phyfiognomy — translated. Vol. 1-3. 1789. 8. (5 L. 5 Sh.) *Frederik's II.* Hiftory of my own time — translated. Vol. 1. 2. 1789. 8. (7 Sh.)

HOLDEN, [John]   Eſſay towards a rational ſyſtem of Muſic. 1770. 4. (7 Sh. 6 d.)
HOLDER, [....] at *Barbadoes*.   Syſtem of french accidence and ſyntax —. 1782. 12. (3 Sh. 6 d.) Ed. 2. 1790. 8. (3 Sh. 6 d.)   Eſſay on the ſubject of Negroe Slavery, with a particular reference to the Island of *Barbadoes*. 1788. 8. (1 Sh.)
HOLE, [Richard] *LL. B.*   *Homer's* hymn to Ceres, translated into english verſe. 1781. 8. (2 Sh.)   Arthur; or the northern enchantment, a poetical romance. 1789. 8. (4 Sh.)
HOLLAND, [Samuel] *Esq. Surveyor General of Lands for the Northern diſtrict of America.*   Some Eclipſes of Jupiter's ſatellites, obſerved near Quebec. (Phil. Transact. 1774. p. 171.)   Aſtronomical obſervations, for aſcertaining the longitude of ſeveral places in North-America. (Ibid. p. 182.)
HOLLIDAY, [F....]   Introduction to practical gunnery; or, the art of engineering —. 12 1757. (3 Sh.)   Introduction to fluxions —. 1777. 8. (6 ſh.)
HOLLINGBERY, [Thomas] *D. D. Archdeacon of Chicheſter and Chaplain in Ordinary to his Majeſty, F. R. S: F. A. S.   Alex. Cunningham's* hiſtory of Great-Britain from the revolution in 1688 to the acceſſion of George I. with *Will. Thomſon's* account of the author and his writings. Vol. 1. 2. 1787. 4., (1 L. 16 ſh.) überſ. Breslau. Th 1. 2. 1789. 4.
HOLLINGSWORTH, [Henry] *of Elk-Ridge.*   The method of deſtroying wild garlic. (Tr. of A. S. Vol. 1. p. 241.)
—— [S....]   *Account of the preſent ſtate of Nova Scotia. 1786. 8. (3 ſh.)   On the manners, governments and ſpirit of Africa — with obſervations on the preſent application to Parliament for aboliſhing Negroe ſlavery —. 1788. 4. (2 ſh. 6 d.) überſ. Halle. 1790. 8.
HOLLIS, [Thomas] *F. R. S: F. A S.*   born in London d. 14 Apr. 1720. died d. 1 Jan. 1774.
HOLLOWAY, [John]   Letter to Dr. *Price* containing a few ſtrictures upon his ſermon ,,The love of our country. 1790. 8. (6 d.)
—— [Robert] *Gent of Gray's Inn   Attorney at law.*
*Letter to the citizens of London on a very intereſting

esting subject. 1771. 8. (1 sh.) Letter to *John Wilkes* on the extortion and expression of sheriffs officers —. 1771. 8. (1 Sh.) Letter to Sir *John Fielding*. 1772. 8. (1 Sh. 6 d.) Letter to the jury who convicted Mr. *Shelly* the Silverfmith —. 1781. 8. (1 Sh.) The rat-trap --. 1773. 8. (2 Sh. 6 d.)

HOLMANN, [Charles'] *Surgeon at Milverton, in Somersetshire*. History of a cafe in which symptoms of pulmonary consumption were suddenly relieved by the expectoration of a piece of carious bone. (London M. J. Vol. VII. Part 2.)

HOLMES, [Edward] *M. A. Mafter of Scorton fchool. Newcaftle*. Comment on the Apoftle's creed, for the use of unlearned chriftians. 1788. 12. (6 d.) Attempt to prove the materiality of the foul, by reafon and fcripture —. 1789. 8. (2 sh.)

—— [Robert] *D. D. Profeffor of Poetry in the Univerfity of Oxford*. Alfred, an ode, with fix fonnets. 1778. 4. (1 sh. 6d.) Eight fermons at *Bampton's* lecture. 1782. 8. (5 sh.) Four tracts. 1) on the principle of religion, 2) on the principle of redemption 3) on the angelical meffage to the virgin Mary. 4) On the refurrection of the body, with a discourse on humility. 1788. 8. (5 sh.) The *firft* annual account of the collation of the MSS. of the LXX verfion. 1789. 8. The *fecond* annual account —. 1790. 8.

HOLROYD, [John] fee Lord *Sheffield*.

HOLT, [J. . . .] Characters of the kings and Queens of England. Vol. 1-3. 1786-1788. 8. (8 sh. 6 d.)

HOLWELL, [John Zephaniah] *F. R. S.* (Formerly Servant of the Eaft India Company.) Narrative of the deplorable deaths of the english gentlemen and others, who where fuffocated in the blackhole, in Fort William at Calcutta in the kingdom of Bengal in the night fucceeding the 20 day of June 1756. 8. 1757. (1 sh.) Addrefs to the proprietors of Eaft India ftock. 1763. 4. (2 sh.) India tracts— containing 1) addrefs to the proprietors of Eaft India ftock. 2) Refutation of a letter from certain gentleman of the Council at Bengal. 3) important facts regarding the Eaft India company's affairs in Bengal from the Y. 1752 to 1760. 4) Narrative of the deplorable deaths of the english gentlemen

men —. 5) defence of Mr. *Vanfittart's* conduct. 1763. 4. (6 fh.) Interefting hiftorical events relative to the provinces of Bengal and the empire of Indoftan. P. 1-3. 1764-1771. 8. (9 Sh. 6 d.) überf. mit Anmerk. von *J. F. Kleuker.* Leipz. 1778. 8. Account of the manner of inoculating the fmallpox in the Eaft-Indies. 1767. 8. (1 fh.) Account of a new fpecies of oak. (Phil Transact. 1772. p. 128.) New experiment for the prevention of crimes. 1786. 8. (1 fh.) Differtations on the origin, nature and purfuits of intelligent beings and on divine providence, religion and religious worship —. 1787. 8. (2 fh. 6 d.)

HOLWELL, [William] *B. D: F. A. S*: *Chaplain in Ordinary to the King.* The beauties of *Homer*, felected from the Iliad. 1775. 8. (4 fh.) Extracts from Mr. Pope's translation corresponding with the beauties of *Homer* —. 1776. 8. (4 fh.)

HOLYOKE, [Edward Auguftus] *M. D: F. A. A: F. M. S.* A Bill of mortality for the town of Salem for the Years 1782 and 1783. (Mem. of B. A. Vol. 1. p. 546.)

HOME, [Everard] *F. R. S: Surgeon.* Defcription of a new marine animal.. (Phil. Transact.. 1785. p 333.) Account of Mr. *Hunter's* method of performing the operation for the popliteal anevrism. (London M. J. Vol. 7. P. 4. Vol. 8. P. 2.) Differtation on the properties of pus. 1788. 4. (überf. Samml. f. A. Th. 12. S. 653.)

—— [Francis] *M. D. Profeffor of Medicine and of Materia medica in the Univerfity at Edinburgh.* Diff. De febre remittente. Edinb. 1750. 4. On the contents and virtues of Dunfe fpaw — 1751. 8. (3 fh. 6 d.) Experiments on bleaching. 1756. 8. (4 fh.) überf. Leipz. 1777. 8. Principia medicinae. 1758. 8. (5 fh.) Ed. 2. 1762. überf. Frankf. u. Leipz. 1772. überf. von *J. F. Ehrmann.* Nürnb. 1778. 8. The principles of agriculture and vegetation. 1758. 8. (3 fh.) Ed. 3. 1776. überf. von *J. Cph. Wöllner.* Berlin. 1779. 8. Medical facts and experiments. 1759. 8. (4 fh.) überf. durch *G. H. Koenigsdörfer.* 1768. 8. Inquiry into the nature caufe and cure of the croup. 1765. 8. (1 fh.) Cli-

N nical

nical experiments hiftories and diffections. 1780. 8.
(6 fh.) überf. Leipz. 1781. 8.

HOME, [Henry] fee Lord Kaims.

—— [John] Clergyman. (born in Scotland.) °Douglas,
a Tragedy. 1757. 8. (1 fh. 6 d.) °Agis, a Tragedy. 1758. 8. (1 fh. 6 d.) °The fiege of Aquileja; a Tragedy. 1760. 8. (1 fh. 6 d.) °The fatal discovery, a Tragedy, 1769. 8. (1 fh. 6 d.)
°Alonzo, a Tragedy. 1773. 8. (1 fh. 6 d.). °Alfred, a Tragedy. 1778. 8.

—— [Robert] Surgeon to the Savoy. The efficacy
and innocency of folvents —. 1783. 8. (1 fh. 6 d.)
überf. Samml. f. W. A. St. 8. S. 61.

HOMER, [Philip Bracebridge] A. M. Magdalen-College,
Oxford. Anthologia; or, a collection of flowers.
In blank verfe. 1789. 4. (1 fh.)

HOOD, [Robert] D. D. Minifter of the Chapel in Hanover Square, Newcaftle. Sermon on the nature
of Chrift's Kingdom. 1780. 8. (6 d.) XIV. Termons on various fabjects. 1782. 8. (5 fh.)

HOOK, [James] Houts of love. 17.. The wreath:
a collection of Arietts for the voice and Harpsichord.
1788. (5 Sh.)

HOOLE, [...] Critical effays on fome of the poems
of feveral english poets by *John Scott*, Esq. with
an account of his life and writings. 1785. 8. (5 fh.
3 d.)

—— [Charles] Clergyman; (Son to *John Hoole*) °Modern manners; in a feries of familiar epiftles. 1781.
8. (2 fh. 6 d.) °Aurelia, or the conteft: a poem,
1783. 4. (2 fh. 6 d.)

—— [John] Auditor to the Eaft-India Company. Translation of *Taffo's* Jerufalem delivered. Vol. 1. 2. 1762.
8. (12 fh.) Translation of *Metaftafio's* works.
Vol. 1. 2. 1767. 8. (6 fh.) Translation of *Metaftafio's* Artaxerxes, the Olympiad, Hypsipile, Titus,
Demetrius, Demophon. Vol. 1. 2. 1767. 8. Cyrus;
a Tragedy. 1768. 8. (1 fh. 6 d.) Timanthes: a
Tragedy. 1770. 8. (1 fh. 6 d.) Translation of
Ariofto's Orlando furiofo. Vol. 1-5. 1773-1783.
8. (1 L. 11 fh. 6 d.) Cleonice; princeff of Bithynia: a Tragedy. 1775. 8. (1 fh. 6 d.)

—— [Samuel] A. M. Sermons, 1786. 8. (5 Sh.) Edward:

ward, or the curate; a poem. 1787. 4. (3 sh.)
Poems. Vol. 1. 2. 1790. 8. (6 sh.)

HOOPER, [John] *Surgeon*, *Fellow of Medical Society*. History of a case of cicuta. (Mem. of M. S. of L. Vol. 2.)

—— [Joseph] *Surgeon*. F. M. S. Cases of hydrocephalus internus. (Mem. of M. S. of L. Vol 1. p 165.) A case of Angina pectoris. (Ibid. p. 238.) The case of a retroverted uterus (Med. Obs. Vol. 5. p. 104.) A second case of a retroverted uterus (Ibid. p. 378.) Case of the uterus lacerated by the force of the labour pains. (Mem. of M. S. of L. Vol. 2.)

HOOPER, [William] *M. D.* Baron *Bielfeld's* letters translated. Vol. 1 - 4. 1768. 8. (11 sh.) Baron *Bielfeld's* elements of universal erudition translated. Vol. 1 - 3. 1770. 8. (18 sh.) Memoirs of the Year 2500 translated. Vol. 1. 2. 1772. 8. (5 sh.) Rational recreations, in which the principles of members and natural philosophy are clearly and copiously elucidated —. Vol. 1 - 4. 1774. 8 (1 L. 1 Sh.) *Geßner's* new idyls translated. 1775. fol. (16 Sh.) *Helvetius* on man, his intellectual faculties and his education, translated. Vol. 1. 2. 1777. 8. (12 Sh.)

HOPE, [John] *M. D: Professor of Medicine and of Botany at Edinburgh.* F. R S. born at Edinburgh d. 10 May 1725. died d. 10 Nov. 1786.

—— [John] born :... died at *Newcastle upon Tyne* d. ... Jun. 1785.

—— [John] *Esq.* Letters on certain proceedings in Parliament, during the sessions of the Years 1769 and 1770. 8. 1772. (1 Sh. 6 d.) Thoughts in prose and verse. 1780. 8. (6 Sh.) Letters on credit. 1784. 8. (1 Sh. 6 d.)

HOPKINS, [William] *B. A: Vicar of Bolney and Master of the Grammar-school of Cuckfield, Sussex.* Exodus; a translation with notes. 1784. 4. (7 Sh.)

HOPKINSON, [Francis] *Esq. Judge of the Admiralty in Pennsylvania.* Description of a machine for measuring a ship's way thro' the sea. (Tr. of A. S. Vol. 2. p. 159.) Account of a worm in a horse's eye. (Ibid. p. 183.) An improved method of quilling a harpsichord. (Ibid. p. 185.)

HOPSON, [Charles] *M. D. Physician in London.* Diss.

De Tribus in uno. Lugd. Bat. 1767. 4. *J. G. Zimmermann* on the dysentery translated. 1771. 8.
(4 Sh.) Effay on fire. 1781. 8. (2 Sh. 6 d.) °Tranſ-
lation of *J. G. Zimmermann's* treatiſe on experience
in Phyſic. Vol. 1. 2. 1782. 8. (12 Sh.) *Wiegleb's*
general ſyſtem of Chemiſtry, translated from the
german. 1789. 4. (1 L. 7 Sh.)
HOPSON, [Edward] *Esq. of Norwich.* °Rational
conduct of the human mind, moral and religious —.
1777. 12. (3 Sh.)
HORBERRY, [Matthew] *D. D. Rector of Standlake,
Oxfordshire and Canon Reſidentary of Lichifield.*
born:... died 17..
HORDE, [Thomas] *Jun. Esq.* *Leander and Hero,
a Tragedy, 1769. 8. °Zelida, a Tragedy. 1772. 8.
Damon and Phebe, an Opera. 1774. 8. Dramatic
love. 17.. Disappointed Villany. 17.. The
Empiric. 17.. As the world goes. 17.. Para-
diſe of fools. 17.. Pretended puritain. 17.. It
was right at the laſt. 17.. The whimſical ſere-
nade. 17.. The female pedant. 17.. Intrigue
in a Cloister; a farce. 1786. 8. (1 ſh.)
HORN, [Henry] Eſſays concerning iron and ſteel —.
1773. 12. (2 Sh. 6 d.)
—— [John] The description and uſe of the new invented patent univerſal ſowing machine for broad-
caſting, or drilling every kind of grain, pulſe and
ſeed. 1786. 8. (1 ſh. 6 d.)
HORNE, [George] *D. D. Dean of Canterbury and Preſident of Magdalen · College, Oxford.* State of the
caſe between *Js. Newton* and *Hutchinson.* 1752 8.
(1 Sh. 6 d.) View of Mr. *Kennicott's* method of
correcting the hebrew text —. 1759. (6 d.) Commentary on the pſalms. Vol. 1. 2. 1776. 4. (1 L.
1 Sh.) Discourſes on ſeveral ſubjects and occaſions. Vol. 1. 2. 1779. 8. (12 Sh.) °Letter to
Adam Smith — on the life, death and philoſophy
of *Dav. Hume*, by one of the people called chris-
tians. 1777. 8. (1 ſh.) °Letters on infidelity by
the author of a letter to Dr. *Ad. Smith.* 1784. 8.
(3 Sh.) (Several ſingle ſermons.)
—— [John] ſee *Tooke.*
HORNSBY, [Thomas] *M. A: Profeſſor of Aſtronomy
in the Univerſity of Oxford. F. R. S. of London and
of*

of Gottingen. On the parallax of the Sun. (Phil. Transact. 1763. p. 467.) Observations on the solar eclipse April 1, 1764. at Oxford. (Ibid. 1764. p. 145.) Account of the improvements to be made by observations of the transit of Venus in 1769. (Ibid. 1765. p. 326.) Observations on the transit of Venus and eclipse of the Sun, June 3. 1769. (Ibid. 1769. p. 172.) The quantity of the Sun's parallax, as deduced from the observations of the transit of Venus, on June 3. 1769. (Ibid. 1771. p. 574.) Inquiry into the quantity and direction of the proper motion of Arcturus; with some remarks on the diminution of the obliquity of the ecliptic. (Ibid. 1773. p. 93.

HORSLEY, [Samuel] *D. D. F. R. S. Lord Bishop of St Davids.* Computation of the distance of the sun from the earth. (Phil. Transact. 1767. p. 179.) Attempt to determine the height of the sun's atmosphere from the height of the solar spots above the sun's surface. (Ibid. p. 398.) On the computation of the sun's distance from the earth, by the theory of gravity. (Ibid. 1769. p. 153.) Observations on the transit of Venus and eclipse of the Sun June 3. 1769. (Ibid. 1769. p. 183.) Difficulties in the *Newtonian* theory of light. (Ibid. 1770. p. 417.) Supplement. (Ibid. 1771. p. 547.) *Apollonii Pergaei* Inclinationum libri 2. 1770. (9 sh.) The sieve of *Eratosthenes*, being an account of his method of finding all the prime numbers. (Phil. Transact. 1772. p. 327.) *De Luc's* rules, for the measurement of heights by the barometer, compared with theory reduced to english measures of length and adapted to *Fahrenheit's* scale of the thermometer; with tables and precepts for expediting the practical application of them. (Ibid. 1774. p. 214.) Remarks on the observations of *(Phipp's)* voyage towards the Northpole, for determining the acceleration of the pendulum, in latitude 79° 50'. 1774. 4. (1 sh.) An abridged state of the weather at London in the Year 1774. (Phil. Transact. 1775. p. 167.) De polygonis area vel perimetro maximis et minimis, inscriptis circulo, vel circulum circumscribentibus. (Ibid. p. 301.) An abridged state of the weather at London in the Y. 1775.

1775. (Ibid. p. 354.) *Js. Newtoni* Opera, cum commentario. Vol. 1. P. 1. 2. Vol. 2-5. (8 L. 11 sh.)
*Letters from the Archdeacon of St. Alban's, in reply to Dr. *Priestley* —. 1784. 8. (3 sh.)
(Several single sermons.)

HORSLEY, [William] born 1701. died d. 22 Febr. 1776.

HOSSACK, [Colin] *M. D: Physician to his late R. H. Frederik, Prince of Wales.* born 1706. died d. 11 Dec. 1782.

HOTHAM, [Richard] Reflections on East-India shipping. 1773. 8. (1 Sh.) On the East-India shipping for the Year 1773. 1774. 4. (2 Sh.) Appendix. 1775. 4. (6 d.)

HOUGH, [John] *of the Inner-Temple.* The pastor —. 1777. 4. (1 Sh.) Second thought is best, an Opera. 1778. 8. (1 Sh.)

HOULSTON, [Thomas] *M. D: Physician to the Liverpool Infirmary.* Diss. De inflammatione. Lugd. Bat. 1767. 4. A new method of treating the smallpox, translated from the latin of *J. F. Closs*. 1767. 8. Il presente metodo d'innestare il vajuolo del *D. T. Dimsdale.* Napoli. 1768. Lettres sur les ravages de la petite verole et les inoculations faites a Montpellier. (Journal de Medec. 1771. Fevr. et Avril.) Lettre sur les purgatifs drastiques resineux. (Journ. de Medec. 1771. Oct. Journal Encyclopedique. 1771. Vol. V.) On the Liverpool Spa-Water. 1773. 8. (1 Sh.) Observations on mineral poisons. (Med. Com. of Ed. Vol. 6. p. 325.) Observations on canine madness. (*Duncan's* M. C. Vol. 8. p. 304.) Case of a boy poisoned by the root of hemlock-dropwort. (London M. J. Vol. 2. p. 40.) On poisons and use of mercury in the cure of obstinate dysenteries. 1784. 8. (1 Sh.) Ed. 2. 1787. 8. (1 Sh. 6 d.) übers. Altenb. 1786. 8. übers. Samml. f. A. Th. 10. S. 373. A remarkable instance of a patient's recovery after taking a very large dose of corrosive sublimate. (London M. J. Vol. 6. p. 271.) Experiments on the duration of the infectious power of variolous matter. (Ibid. Vol. VII. P. 1.) Remarks on the hydrophobia and on the efficacy of the Ormskirk medicine for the bite of a mad dog. (*Duncan's* M. C.

C. Dec. 2. Vol. 1. p. 330. überf. Samml. f. A. Th. 13. S. 39.)

HOULSTON, [William] *Surgeon*. Cafe of injury of the brain, occafioned without any blow or external violence upon the head. (London M. J. Vol. 5. p. 292.) *J. O. Inflamond's* furgical tracts — with notes. 1790. 4. (1 L. 1 Sh.)

HOUNSFIELD, [George] *Surgeon at Sheffield in Yorkshire*. On the good effects of electricity in four cafes of a diseafed tefticle. (Lond. M. J. Vol. VII. P. 3.)

HOWARD, [Frederic] Earl of *Carlisle*. Poems: 1) Upon the death of Mr. *Gray*. 2) For the monument of a favourite fpaniel. 3) Another infcription for the fame. 4) Translation from *Dante*, Canto 33. 1773. 4. (1 fh.) The father's revenge; a Tragedy. 1783.

—— [George Edmond] *Esq. Attorney in Dublin*. Cafes on the laws againft the further growth of popery in Ireland. 1775. 8. (6 fh.) Almeyda; or the rival kings: a Tragedy. 1770. 8. (1 fh. 6 d.) The fiege of Tamor; a Tragedy. Ed. III. 1773. 8. (1 fh. 6 d.) Miscellaneous works, in verse and prose. Vol. 1. 2. 3. 1782. 8. The female gamefter, a Tragedy. 1778. 12.

—— [John] *F. R. S. Sheriff of the county of Bedford*, born at *Lower Clapton*. 1725., died d. 20 Jan. 1790.

—— [John] *Surgeon*. On the medical properties of mercury. 1782. 8. (2 fh.) On the method of curing the hydrocele by means of a feton. 1783. 8. (1 fh. 6 d.) On the natural hiftory and cure of the venereal disease. Vol. 1. 2. 1787. 8. (10 fh.) überf. von C. F. *Michaelis*. Th. 1. 2. 1790. 8.

—— [Sarah] Thoughts on female education —. 1783. 12. (1 fh.)

HOWE, [William] *Sir*. Narrative of his conduct during his late command of the King's troops in North-America with fome observations on the letters to a nobleman. 1780. 4. (3 fh.)

HOWEL, [James] Defcription of the people and country of Scotland — a fatire. 1788. 12. (6 d.)

—— [Thomas] *M. D.* Journal of the paffage from India — through Mesopotamia, Armenia, and Natolia

tolia or Afia minor —. 1789. 8. (5 fh.) überf. in *Sprengel's* und *Forster's* N. Beitr. zur Völker und Länderk. Th. 3. S. 1.

HOWLET, [John] *A. B. Vicar of Great Dunmow, Effex.* Examination of Dr. Price's effay on the population of England and Wales and the doctrine of an increased population in this kingdom, with remarks on Dr. Price's argument of a decreased population — 1781. 8. (2 fh. 6 d.) * Political enquiry into the consequences of inclofing wafte lands and the causes of the present high price of butchers meat. 1785. 8. (2 fh. 6 d.) Enquiry into the influence which enclosures have had on the population of this kingdom. 1786. 8. (1 fh.) On the population of Ireland. 1786. 8. (1 fh. Enclosures a cause of improved agriculture, of plenty and cheapnefs of provifions, of population, and of both private and national wealth, being an examination of two pamphlets — 1787. 8. (2 fh.) The insufficiency of the causes to which the increase of our poor and of the poor's rates have been commonly ascribed with enquiry on the mortality of countryhouses of induftry —. 1788. 8. (2 fh. 6 d.) (Several fingle fermons.)

HOYLAND, [.....] Odes. 1785. 4. (1 fh.)

HUBBARD, [Leverett] *M. D. of Newhaven in Connecticut.* Hiftory of a gangrene of the scrotum. (Mem. of M. S. of L. Vol. 1. p. 462.)

HUDDART, [.....] *Captain.* Sketch of the ftraits of Gaspar, a paffage between the islands of Banks and Billiton, with remarks for failing through the ftraits. 1788. 8. (5 fh.)

—— [Joseph] Account of persons who could not diftinguish colours. (Phil. Transact. 1777. p. 260.)

HUDDESFORD, [William] *B. D. Keeper of the Ashmolean Museum at Oxford.* born: .... died d. 11 Oct. 1772.

HUDSON, [R.....] The Land valuer's affiftant. 1781. (3 fh. 6 d.)

—— [Thomas] Miscellaneous poems. 1788. 4. (1 fh.)

—— [William] *F. R. S. Horti Chelseani: Praefectus et Praelector botanicus.* Catalogue of the 50 plants from Chelsea garden presented to the royal fociety
by

by the — company of Apothecaries for the Year. 1767. (Philos. Transact. 1770. p. 541.) Flora Anglica. 1762. 8. Ed. 2. Vol. I. 2. 1778. 8. (10 fh. 6 d)

HUGHES, [.....] *Mrs.* Poems. 1784. 8. (3 fh.) Moral dramas intended for private representation. 1790. 8. (3 fh.)
—— [Benjamin] *Curate of Wisbich St. Peter's in the Isle of Ely.* An Epiſtle to Junius. 1774. 4. (2 fh. 6 d.) Simon Magus, a poem. 1775. 4. (2 fh.)
—— [Charles] *Profeſſor of Horsemanship.* — The complete Horseman; or, the art of riding made easy. 1772. 8. (1 fh.)
—— [Samuel] *M. A.* Creation, a poem. 1785. 4. (1 fh.)
—— [T....] *Surgeon at Stroud water, in Gloucestershire.* Case of cancer of the breaſt, with remarks. (London M. J. Vol. X. P. 1.)
—— [Thomas] *M. A.* The ascenſion: a poetical eſſay. 1780. 4. (1 fh.)
—— [W.....] *M. A.* Sermon on abolition of slavery in the british Weſt Indies. 1788. 4. (1 Sh.) Answer to Mr. *Harris's* ſcriptural researches on the licitneſſ of the slave trade. 1788. 8. (1 Sh.) Ed. 2. 1788. 8. (1 Sh.)

HULKE, [William] *of Deal in Kent.* Account of a remarkable ſpasmodic affection. (London M. J. Vol. 5. p. 389.)

HULL, [Thomas] *Actor at Covent-Garden theatre' and Deputy-manager there.* Pharnaces, an Opera. 1765. 8. (1 Sh.) The ſpanish lady, a muſical entertainment. 1765. 8. The perplexities, a Comedy. 1767. 8. The fairy favour. 1767. 8. The royal merchant; an Opera. 1767. 8. (1 fh. 6 d.) *Preſton's* genuine lettes from a gentleman to a young lady his pupil — revised and published with notes by *Thom. Hull.* Vol. I. 2. 1772. (6 fh.) The prodigal ſon, an Oratorio 1773. 4. (1 fh.) Henry the ſecond, or, the fall of Rosamond: a Tragedy. 1774. 8. (1 fh. 6 d.) Richard Plantagenet, a legendary tale. 1774. 4. (2 Sh.) Select letters between late Ducheſſ of Somerset and others on the manners of the republic of Venise and ſome poetical pieces. Vol. I. 2. 1778. 8. (12 fh.) Alteration of *James Thomson's* Edward and Eleonora, a Tragedy. 1775. 8. (1 ſh.)

HULME, [Nathan:] *M. D. Phyſician in Ordinary to the city of London lying in Hospital.* Diſſ. De ſcorbuto. Edinb. 1765. 8. De Natura, causa, curationeque ſcorbuti. 1768. 8. (3 ſh.) On the puerperal fever —. 1772. 8. (3 Sh.) überſ. Leipzig. 1772. 8. Oratio de re medica cognoscenda et promovenda —. 1777. 4. (1 Sh. 6 d.) A —remedy for the relief of the ſtone and gravel, the ſcurvy. — 1778. 4. (2 Sh.) überſ. Leipz. 1778. 8. überſ. von *J. Lippert.* Wien. 1781. 8.

HUME, [A.....] *M D. Every woman her own phyſician* —. 1776. 12. (2 Sh.)

—— [David] born at *Edinburgh* d. 26 Apr. 1711. died d. 25. Aug. 1776.

—— [David] *Esq. Advocate, F. R. S. Edin. and Profeſſor of Scots Law in the Univerſity of Edinburgh.* Account of Sir *Thom. Miller* of Glenlee, Bart. Lord Preſident of the Court of Seſſion and F. R. S. Edin. (Tr. of E. S Vol. 2. App. p. 63.)

HUMPAGE, [Benjamin] *Surgeon.* On the rupture called hydrocele: explaining the anatomy of the parts affected; with objections to the inciſion, ſeton —. 1788. 8. (1 Sh.)

HUMPHRIES, [David] *Esq. Colonel in the ſervice of the United States.* Poem to the united ſtates of America. 1785. 4. (2 Sh.) Poem on the happineſſ of America. 1786. 4. (2 Sh.)

HUNT, [John] *Surgeon.* On the circulation of the blood and the effects of bleeding 1787. 8. (2 Sh.)

HUNTER, [Alexander] *M D: F. R. S: Phyſician at York.* Diſſ. De Cantharidibus. Edinb. 1751. 4. °Georgical eſſays. Vol. 1 – 5. 1770 - 1777. (11 Sh.) On drill - ſowing (G. E. Vol. 3. p. 109.) On Top-Dreſſings (Ibid. p. 167.) On the preparation of carrots for the use of ſeamen on long voyages. (Ibid. Vol. 5. p. 1.) On nutritive lime. (Ibid. p. 182.) On carrots for the use of the diſtiller. (Ibid. p. 263.) *John Evelyn* ſilva: or discourse of foreſt trees and the propagation of timber, with notes. 1776. 4. (2 L. 12 Sh. 6 d.) Ed. 2. Vol. 1. 2. 1786. 4. (2 L. 15 Sh.) *J. Evelyn* terra, a philosophical discourse of earth — with notes — 1778. 8.

8. (3 Sh.) Ed. 2. 1787. 4. (5 Sh.) On the Buxton waters. 1776. 8.

HUNTER, [David] D. D. *Minifter at St. Andrew's in Scotland.* Observations on the hiftory of Jesus Chrift —. Vol. 1. 2. 1770. 8. (7 Sh.)

—— [Henry] D. D. Sacred Biography or the hiftory of the Patriarchs from Abraham to Isaac. Vol. 1-4. 1784-1788. (1 L. 4 Sh.)

(Several fingle fermons.)

—— [John] M. D: F. R. S: *and Phyfician to the Army.* (Brother of *Will. Hunter.*) Natural hiftory of the human teeth, explaining their ftructure, use, formation, growth and diseases. 1771. 4. Supplement. 1778. 4. (1 L. 1 Sh.) überf. Th. 1. 2. Leipz. 1780. Diff. De Hominum varietatibus et harum caufis. Edinb. 1775. 8. On the digeftion of the ftomach after death. (Phil. Transact. 1772. p. 447.) Anatomical observations on the torpedo. (Ibid. 1773. p. 481.) Account of certain receptacles of air in birds, which communicate with the lungs, and are lodged both among the fleshy parts and in the hollow bones of those animals. (Ibid. 1774. p. 205.) Observations on the Gillaroo trout, called in Ireland the Gizzard trout. (Ibid. p. 310.) Account of the Gymnotus electricus. (Ibid. 1775. p. 395.) Experiments on animals and vegetables, with respect to the power of producing heat. (Ibid, p. 446. überf. Samml. z. P. und Ng. Th. f. S. 420.) Proposals for the recovery of people apparently drowned. (Ibid. 1776. p. 412. überf. Samml. f. A. Th. 4. S. 144.) Of the heat — of animals and vegetables. (Ibid. 1778. p. 7.) Account of the free martin. (Ibid. 1779. p. 279.) Account of a woman who had the fmallpox during pregnancy and who feemed to have communicated the fame disease to the foetus. (Ibid. 1780. p. 128.) Account of an extraordinary pheasant. (Ibid. p. 527.) Account of the organ of hearing in fish. (Ibid. 1782. p. 379.) Account of the fucceffiull treatment of a fuppofed hydrocephalus internus. (Med. Obs. Vol. 6. p. 52.) Some experiments made upon rum, in order to ascertain the cause of the colic, frequent among the foldiers in the Island of Jamaica in the Years, 1781. and 1782. (Med. Transact.

Transact. Vol. 3. p. 227.) Account of a cafe of an uncommon disease in the omentum; and of a double kidney on one fide of the body with none on the other. (Ibid p. 250.) Observations on the disease commonly called the jail or hospital fever. (Ibid. p. 345.) Experiment to determine the effect of extirpating one ovarium upon the member of young produced. (Phil. Transact. 1787. p. 233. London M. J. Vol. IX. P. I.) Observations tending to fhew that the wolf, jackal and dog are all of the fame fpecies. (Phil. Transact. 1787. p. 253. 1789. p. 160.) Observations on the ftructure and oeconomy of Whales. (Ibid. p. 371.) On the veneral disease. 1786. 4. (1 L, 1 Sh) Überf. Leipzig. 1787. 8. Observations on certain parts of the animal oeconomy. 1787. 4. (16 Sh.) Observations on the case of mollities offium with remarks on that disease. (London M. J. Vol. VIII. P. I.) Some observations on the heat of wells and fprings in the Island of Jamaica and on the temperature of the earth below the furface in different climates. (Phil. Transact. 1788. p. 53. Überf. *Gren* J. d. P. Th. 1. S. 111.) Observations on the diseases of the army in Jamaica and on the beft means of preserving the health of Europeans, in that climate. 1788. 8. (5 Sh.)

HUNTER, [John] *M. A: F. R S. Edin. and Profeſſor of Humanity in the Univerſity of St. Andrews.* Grammatical eſſay on the nature, import, and effect of certain conjunctions; particularly the greek Δε. (Transact. of E. S. Vol. 1. p. 113.)

—— [Thomas] *M. A. Vicar of Weaverham, Cheshire.* born : .... died d. .. Jul. 1777.

—— [William] *Phuſician extraordinary to the Queen and Profeſſor of Anatomy in the Royal Academy,* born at *Kilbridge* in the county of *Lanerk* d. 23 May 1718. died d. 15 March. 1783.

—— [William] *M A. Rector of St. Anne, Lincoln.* Letter to Dr. *Prieſtley* in answer to his letter — on the fubject of the repeal of the teft act. 1787. 8. (1 Sh.) (Several fingle fermons.)

—— [W......] *A. M. Surgeon.* Concise account of the kingdom of Pegu; its climate, produce, trade-

go,

government and inhabitans —. 1785. 8. (5 Sh.)
überf. *Ebelin'gs* Neue Samml. von Keifebef.hreib.
Th. 9. S. 397 —. Account of fome artificial caverns near Bombay, (Arch. Vol. 7. p. 286.)

HUNTINGDON, [William] Letter to Mr. *Caleb Evans* — containing a few remarks on a circular letter drawn up by him —. 1790. 8. (1 Sh. 6 d.)

HUNTINGFORD, [George James] *A. M. Fellow of new College, Oxford.* Introduction to the writing of greek —. Ed. III. P. I. 2. 1782. (4 fh. 6 d.) Metrica quaedam monoftrophica. 1783. 8. (3 fh.) Apology for the monoftrophics with a fecond collection of monoftrophics. 1784. 8. (4 fh. 6 d.)

—— [J. . . . .] *Secretary to the fociety for the Increase and Encouragement of good fervants.* The laws of mafters and fervants confidered — with an account of a fociety, formed for the encrease and encouragement of good fervants. 1790. 8. (2 fh. 6 d.)

HURD, [Richard] *D. D. Lord Bishop of Worcefter F. R. S. of Gottingen.* °*Horatii* Ars poetica, Epiftola ad Pisones: with an english commentary and notes. 1749. 8. (3 Sh.) The opinion of an eminent lawyer concerning the right of appeal from the Vice-Chancellor of Cambridge to the fenate, fupposed by a fhort, hiftorical account of the jurisdiction of the Univerfity: by a fellow of a College. 1751. 8. Ed. 3. 17... Letter tho the author of a further inquiry. 1752. 8. The delicacy of friendship. 1755. 8. Remarks on *Dav. Hume's* effay on the natural hiftory of religion. 1757. 8. Letter to Mr. *Mafon* on the marks of imitation. 1757. 8. Dialogues moral and political with letters on Chivalry and romances. 1758. 8. (5 Sh.) Ed. 2. 1762. Ed. 3. Vol. 1-3. with two dialogues on the use and abuse of foreign travel. 1764. (9 Sh.) überf. von *L. H. Hölty.* Th. 1. 2. Leipz. 1775. 8. *Letters on chivalry and romance. 1761. 8. (2 Sh.) Introduction to the ftudy of the prophecies concerning the chriftian church — in XII fermons. 1772. 8. (5 Sh.) überf. Leipzig. 1778. 8. Edition of the felect works of *Abrah. Cowley*, with notes. Vol. 1. 2. 1772. (6 Sh.) Sermons Vol. 1-3. 1781. 8. (15 Sh.) *Discord a fatire 4. 17..
°*Jerem.*

° *Jerem. Taylor's* moral demonftration of the truth of the chriftian religion. 1776. 8.
(Several fingle fermons.)

HURDIS, [James] *M. A.* Critical Diſſertation upon the true meaning of the word החיצים, Genes. x. 21. 1790. 8. (1 Sh.)

HURLY, [James] *B. A. Mafter of the grammar – fchool and curate of St. James's in Taunton.* Ecliptical aftronomy reftored to its natural fimplicity —. 1771. 8. (3 Sh.)

HURN, [William] Heath hill, a poem. 1777. 4. (2 Sh. 6 d.) The bleſſings of peace and guilt of war, a lyric poem. 1784. 4. (2 Sh.)

HURRY, [Thomas] Tables of intereſt, from one pound to five hundred millions for one day —. 1786. 12. (3 Sh.)

HURTLEY, [Thomas] *of Malham.* Account of fome natural curiofities in the environs of Malham in Craven, Yorkshire. 1786. 8. (5 Sh.)

HUSSEY, [Garret] *M. D: Phyfician to the Merchants-Quay Hofpital, Dublin.* Inquiry into the caufe and cure of fevers. 1784. 8. (6 Sh.) überſ. Mayns. 1789. 8.

HUSTLER, [....] *Manufacturer.* °Obfervations on the bill - for preventing the exportation of Wool —. 1788. 8. (6 d.)

HUTCHINS, [John] *M. A: Rector of the holy Trinity in Warsham and of Swyre, Dorfetshire.* born 1698. died 1773.

—— [Richard] *Rector of Lincoln College, Oxford.* born at Eyden, Northamptonshire 1698. died 1781.

—— [Thomas] *Governor of Albany Fort, in Hudfons-Bay.* Experiments on the dipping needle, made by defire of the royal fociety. (Phil. Transact. 1775. p. 127.) Account of the fucceſs of fome attempts to freeze quickfilver, at Albany-Fort, in Hudfon's-Bay in the Y. 1775. with obfervations on the dipping needle. (Ibid. 1776. p. 174.) Topographical defcription of the river Ohio, Kenhawa, Sioto, Cherokee, Wabash, Illinois, Miffiffippi. 1778. 8. Experiments for afcertaining the point of mercurial congelation. (Phil Transact. 1783. P. 2.) Defcription of a remarkable rock and

and cascade, near the western side of the Youghiogeny river. (Tr. of A. S. Vol. 2. p. 50.)

HUTCHINSON, [....] *Lieut. Governor.* History of the colony of Massachusetts-Bay, from the first settlement thereof in 1628. Vol. 1. 2. 1775. 8. (12 Sh.)

—— [B....] *Vicar at Kimbolton in the county of Huntingdon.* Calendar of the weather for the Year 1781 —. 1782. 8. (1 Sh.) Observations on the dryness of the Year 1788. (Phil. Tr. 1789. p. 37.) überf. *Gren* J. d. P. Th. 2. S. 79.) Account of a luminous arch. (Phil. Transact. 1790. p. 45.)

—— [John Hely] *His Majesty's Principal Secretary of State for the Kingdom of Ireland, Provost of Trinity-College, Dublin and Privy Counsellor.* Commercial restraints of Ireland. 1779. Letter to constituents of the city of Cork in defence of Mr. Pitt's Irish propositions. 1785.

—— [William] F. A. S. The spirit of masonry —. 1776. 8. (3 Sh. 6 d.) Oration at the dedication of free mason's Hall in Sunderland in the county of Durham. 1778. 4. (1 Sh.) View of Northumberland. Vol. 1. 2. 1778. 4. (1 L. 10 Sh.) History and antiquities of the county palatine of Durham. Vol. 1. 2. 1787. 4. (1 L. 1 Sh.) Account of antiquities in Lancashire. (Arch. Vol. 9. p 211.)

—— [William] *Mariner and Dockmaster of Liverpool.* On practical seamanship —. 1777. 4. (12 Sh. 6 d.)

HUTCHISSON, [John] *M. D: of Dublin.* Case of chronic tetanus, cured — by the use of electricity. (Mem. of M. S. of L. Vol. 2. p. 138.)

HUTTON, [Charles] *LL. D. F. R. S. Lond. and Edin. Professor of Mathematiks in the Royal Military Academy at Woolwich.* On mensuration both in theory and practice. 1771. 4. (15 Sh.) Ed. 2. 1788. 8. (15 Sh.) The principles of bridges. 1772. 8. (2 Sh. 6 d.) The diarian miscellany, consisting of all the useful and entertaining parts, both mathematical and poetical, extracted from the Ladies diary — with many additional solutions and improvements. Vol. 1-5. 1775. 8. (1 L. 9 Sh.) A new and general method of finding simple and quickly-converging series; by which the proportion of the

the diameter of a circle to its circumference may easily be computed to a great number of places of figures. (Philof. Transact. 1776. p. 476.) Demonftration of two theorems mentioned in article XXV of the Philof. Transact. for the Year 1775. (Ibid. p. 600.) The force of fired gun-powder and the initial velocities of cannon balls, determined by experiments. (Ibid. 1778. p. 50) Account of the calculations made from the furvey and meafures taken at Schehallien, in order, to afcertain the mean denfity of the earth. (Ibid 1778. p. 689.) Of cubic equations and infinite feries. (Ibid. 1780. p. 387.) Calculations to determine at what point in the fide of a hill its attraction will be the greateft. (Ibid. 1780. P. 1.) Project of a new divifion of the Quadrant. (Ibid. 1784. p 21.) Tables of the products and powers of numbers. 1784. fol. (7 Sh. 6 d.) Mathematical tables: containing common, hyperbolic and logiftic logarithms. 1785. 8. (14 Sh.) Tables of interest from one pound to 500 millions for one day —. 1786. 8. (3 Sh.) Key to *Hutton's* Arithmetic —. 1786. 8. (3 Sh.) Tracts mathematical and philofophical. 1786. 4. (14 Sh.) The compendious meafurer. 1786. 8. (3 Sh.) Abftract of experiments made to determine the true refiftance of the air to the furfaces of bodies, of various figures, and moved through it with different degrees of velocity. (Tr. of I. A. Vol. 2. p. 29.)

—— [James] *M. D:* *at Edinburgh. F. R. S. Edin.* Confiderations on the nature, quality and diftinctions of coal and culm —. 1777. 8. (1 Sh.) The theory of rain. (Tr. of E. S. Vol. 1. p 41) Theory of the earth; or an inveftigation of the laws obfervable in the compofition, diffolution and reftoration of land upon the globe. (Ibid. p. 209.) Of certain natural appearances of the ground on the Hill of Arthur's feat. (Ibid. Vol. 2. p. 3.) Answer to the objections of M. *De Luc*, with regard to the Theory of rain. (Ibid. Vol. 2. p. 39.) On written language as a fign of fpeech. (Ibid. Vol. 2. p. 5.)

HUTTON, [W.....] *F. A. S. Edin.* Hiftory of Birmingham. 1782. 8. (7 Sh. 6 d.) Journey from Birming-

Birmingham to London. 1785. 12. (2 ſh. 6 d.)
The court of requeſts —. 1787. 8. (6 Sh.) The
battle of Bosworth-field between Richard III. and
Henry Earl of Richmond 1485 —. 1788. 8. (5 ſh.)
Diſſertation on juries: with a deſcription of the
hundred court as an appendix to the court of requeſts. 1789. 8. (1 ſh.)

JABET, [William] B. A. *Lecturer of St. Bartholomew's
Chapel in Birmingham.* born : .... died 17..

JACKMAN, [Isaac] *a Gentleman of Ireland.* The
Mileſian, a Ballad Opera. 1776. 8. All the world's
a ſtage, a farce. 1777. 8. The divorce, a farce.
1782. 8. Hero and Leander. 1787. 8. Almirina.
1787.

JACKSON, [Andrew] born 1695. died d. 25 July
1778.

—— [......] Thoughts on the causes of the delay of
the Weſtminſter ſcrutiny. 1784. 8. (1 ſh.)

—— [Humphrey] *Esq. F. R. S: of Patterſea* in *Surrey.*
On the invention of engraving and printing in chia-
ro oscuro — and the application of the making
paper-hangings of taſte, duration and elegance.
1754. 4. Account of the discovery of the manner
of making iſinglaſſ in Ruſſia; with a particular deſcription of its manufacture in England from the
produce of Britiſh fiſheries. (Phil. Transact. 1773.
p. 1.)

—— [John] of *Clement's — Lane.* Account of the diſcoveries in digging a ſewer in Lombard-ſtreet and
Birchinlane. 1786. (Arch. Vol. 8. p. 116. et
p. 127.)

—— [Lawrence] *B. D: Prebendary of Lincoln.* born : ...
died d. 26 Febr. 1772.

—— [Robert] *M. D. Phyſician at Stockton in the county
of Durham.* Observations on the connexion of the
new and full moon with the invaſion and relapſe
of fevers. (Lond. M. J. Vol. VIII. P. 1. überſ.
Samml. f. A. Th. 12. S. 83.) On the ſupposed
influence of the moon in fevers. (Lond. M. J.
Vol. VIII. P. 3. überſ. Samml. f. A. Th. 12.
S. 548.)

—— [Seguin, Henry] *M. D. Phyſician to the Weſtminſter
general dispensary in London.* Diſſ. De phyſiol:
et

et patholog: dentium cruptione. Edinb. 1778. 8.
On fympathy. P. 1. 2. —. 1781. 8. (4 fh.) Hiftory of a fingular affection of respiration with an
account of the appearances on diffection. (Med.
Com. of Ed. Vol. 6. p. 208.) The case of a
patient whose ftomach, on diffection, was found
to contain two piftol bullets. (Ibid Vol. 4. p....)

JACKSON, [Theodore] *A. M.* Addreff to the Queen, Prince of Wales and the public relative to his Majefty's unhappy fituation. 1788. 4. (1 fh.)

—— [William] *of Lichtfield Close.* The beauties of nature displayed —. 1769. 8. (5 fh.) Letter to the
monthly reviewers in reply to their critique on
his beauties of nature displayed. 1770. 8. (1 fh.)

—— [William] *B. D. Student of Chriftchurch and Preacher to the fociety of Lincoln's Inn.* The Conftitution of the feveral independent ftates of America.
1783. 8. (6 fh.) (Several fingle fermons.)

—— [William] *Organift and Composer of Exeter.* Lyci-
das. 1767. 8. The Metamorpholis, a comic Opera. 1783. * Thirty letters on various fubjects.
Vol. 1. 2. 1783. 8. (4 fh.) Ed. II. (with the Author's name.) Vol. 1. 2. 1784. (4 fh.)

—— [William] *Member of the corporation of Surgeons.*
Observations on the inefficacious use of irons in cafes of luxations and diftortion of the ancle joint
and children born with deformed and crooked feet.
1787. 8. (1 fh.)

JACOB, [Edward] *F. A. S.* born 1710. died d. 26
Oct. 1788.

—— [Edward] *Jun. Surgeon at Faversham, in Kent.*
Case of an extra - uterine foetus. (London M. J.
Vol. VIII. P. 2.).

—— [J.....] Observations on the ftructure and draught
of wheel carriages. 1773. 4. (6 fh.) Animadverfions on the use of broad wheels and the preservation of the public roads. 1773. 4. (1 fh. d d.)

JAGO, [Richard] *M. A: Vicar of Snitterfield, Warwickshire: Rector of Kimcote, Leiceftershire.* born: ....
died d. 8 Apr. 1781.

JAIK, [James] The life of *Servetus*, the Antitrinita-
rian. 1771. (4 fh.)

JA-

JAMES, [Charles] *Esq. Petrarch* to *Laura*, a poetical epiftle. 1787. 4. Poems. Vol. 1. 2. 1789. 8. (6 Sh.)
—— [Robert] *M. D.* born: .... died d. 23 March. 1776.
—— [Thomas] *Lieutenant - Colonel.* The hiftory of the Herculean ftraits, now called the ftraits of Gibraltar —. Vol. 1. 2. 1771. 4. (2 L. 2 fh.)
JAMESON, [Thomas] *Surgeon of his Maj-fly's Navy.* On diluents and enquiry of the human body —. 1789. 8. (2 fh. 6 d.) überf Leipz. 1790. 8.
JAMIESON, [J.....] *A. M: F. A. S. Scot.* The forrows of slavery, a poem. 1789. (2 Sh.)
JANES, [Thomas] *of Briftol.* The beauties of the poets, or, a collection of moral and facred poetry, from the moft eminent authors. 1778. 8 (3 fh.)
JARDINE [......] *Artillerie-Major.* Observations on the tranfit of Venus June 3. 1769. at Gibraltar. (Phil. Transact. 1769. p. 347.) Observations on the eclipse of the fun June 4. 1769. at Gibraltar. (Ibid.) Letters from Barbary, France, Spain, Portugal — by an Officer. Vol. 1. 2. 1788. 8. (12 fh.) überf. im Auszug. Leipz. 1790 8.
JAY, [James] *M. D.* Letter to the governors of the college of New York respecting the collection that was made in 1762 and 1763. for the colleges of Philadelphia and New York. 1771. 8. (1 fh.) Reflections and observations on the gout. 1772. 8. (2 fh.) Letter to the Univerfities of Oxford and Cambridge — in respect to the collection that was made for the colleges of New York and Philadelphia. 1773. 8 (6 d.)
IBBETSON, [.....] Thoughts on bonds of refignation. 1783. 8. (1 fh.)
—— [James] *D. D. Archdeacon of St. Alban's*, *Rector of Bushy.* born: .... died d. 9 Aug. 1781.
—— [James] *Esq. Barrifter at Law.* On the judicial cuftoms of the Saxon and Norman age. 1780. 4. (1 fh. 6 d.) Differtation on the national affemblies under the Saxon and Norman governments. 1781. 4. (2 fh.)
JEBB, [John] *M. D: F. R. S.* (formerly *Minifter at Homersfield*, *Suffolk.* born in London d. 16 Febr. 1736. died d. 2 March. 1786.

JEBB, [Samuel] *M. D. Phyſician at Stratford.* born: ...
died at Derby. 1772.
JEFFERSON, [......] Poems. Ed. 2. 1773. 8.
(2 ſh. 6 d.)
—— [Thomas] °Summary view of the rights of British
America. 1774. 8. (1 ſh. 6 d.) Notes on the
ſtate of Virginia; — with a map. 1788. 8. (7 ſh.)
JEFFRIES, [......] Narrative of the two aerial voyages of Dr. *Jeffries* with Monſ. *Blanchard:* ,with
meteorological observations and remarks —. 1785.
4. (7 ſh. 6 d.)
JENKINS, [Joseph] *A. M.* Calm reply to the firſt
part of de *Courcy's* rejoinder —. 1778. 8. (1 Sh.)
Discourses on ſelect paſſages of the ſcripture hiſtory,
Vol. 1. 2. 1779. 8. (6 Sh.) The inconſiſtency
of infant ſprinckling with chriſtian baptism — a
reply to *Matth. Henry's* treatise on baptism. 1784.
8. (1 Sh.) The beauty of a believer's baptism. —
1778. 12. (2 d.)
JENKINSON, [Charles] Lord *Hawkesbury.* (Son
of a Clergyman in Oxfordshire.) °Discourse on
the eſtablishment of a national and conſtitutional
force in England. 1756. 8. (1 Sh.) °Discourse
on the conduct of the government of Great-Britain
in respect to neutral nations, during the present
war. 1757. 4. (2 ſh. 6 d.) Collection of treaties
of peace, commerce and alliance between Great-
Britain and other powers from the Y. 1619 to
1734. 1781. (2 ſh. 6 d.) Collection of all the
treaties of peace, alliance and commerce, between
Great-Britain and other powers from the Y. 1648
to 1783. Vol. 1-3. 1785. 8. (18 Sh.)
—— [James] Generic and ſpecific description of British plants translated from the genera et ſpecies
plantarum of *Linnaeus.* 1775. 8. (5 ſh. 3 d.)
JENNENS, [Charles] born: .... died 1773.
JENNER, [Charles] *M. A. Rector of Claybrooke in the
County of Leiceſter.* born: .... died d. 11 May.
1774.
—— [Edward] Observations on the natural hiſtory of
the Cuckoo. (Phil. Transact. 1788. p. 219.)
JENNER, [J..... C.....] *Surgeon at Painſwick in
Glouceſtershire.* Cases of an excrescence in the
ure-

urethra of a female patient fuccefsfully treated.
(Lond. M. J. Vol. VII. P. 2.) Account of a general inoculation at Painswick. (Ibid. p. 109.
überf. Sämml. f. A. Th. 12. S. 52.) On the
efficacy of arfenic in intermittents. (Ibid. Vol. IX.
P. 1.)

JENNINGS, [Jos.] *of Fenchurchftreet.* born: ....
died d. 2 Jan. 1782.

JENYNS, [Soame] born in London 1705. died d. 18
Dec. 1787.

JEPHSON, [Robert] Esq. *Officer in the Irish Army.
Member of Parliament in Ireland.* * Braganza;
a Tragedy. 1775. 8. (1 fh. 6 d.) The law of
Lombardy; a Tragedy. 1779. 8. (1 fh. 6 d.)
The count of Narbonne; a Tragedy. 1781 8. (1fh.
6 d.) The hotel, or fervant with two mafters,
a farce. 1784. 12. The campaign or love and
war; an Opera. 1785. Julia or the italian lover,
a Tragedy. 1787. 8. (1 fh. 6 d.)

JERNINGHAM, [John] *A Roman Catholic and brother to Sir William Jerningham.* Poems on various fubjects —. 1766. 8. (2 fh.) Amabella:
a poem. 1767. 4. (1 fh.) The Deserter; a poem.
1769. 4. (1 fh.) The funeral of Arabert, Monk
of la Trappe: a poem. 1771. 4. (1 fh.) Faldoni
and Teresa. 1773. 4. (1 fh) The fwedish curate, a poem. 1773. 4. (1 fh.) Poems. 1774. 8.
(2 fh. 6 d.) The fall of Mexico, a poem. 1775.
4. (2 fh. 6 d.) Fugitive poetical pieces. 1778. 8.
(1 Sh. 6 d.) The ancient english wake; a poem.
1779. 4. (1 Sh. 6 d.) Honoria or the day of all
fouls, a poem, with other poetical pieces. 1782.
4. (1 fh. 6 d.) The rise and progrefs of fcandinavian poetry; a poem in two parts. 1784. 4.
(2 fh.) Poems. Vol. I. 2. 1786. 8. (5 fh.) Enthufiasm; a poem. 1789. 4. (2 fh.)

JESSE, [William] *Rector of Dowles and Chaplain to
the Earl of Glasgow.* Parochialia; or observations
on the discharge of parochial duties —. 1787. 8.
(2 Sh. 6 d.) Defence of the eftablished church:
or, letters — in which Dr. *Prieftley's* arguments
againft fubscription and the peculiar doctrines of
chriftianity, are examined. 1788. 12. (2 fh. 6 d.)

JESSE, [William] *Vicar of Hutton-Cranswick, Yorkshire.* Remonstrance to the proteſtant aſſociation containing observations on their conduct —. 1780. 8. (1 Sh.)
JESTON, [H. ....] *M. A. Maſter of the Royal Grammar School at Henley-upon-Thames.* The ſacred drama of Joseph ſold by his Brethren; and other poems. 1790. 8. (1 ſh. 6 d.)
ILLINGWORTH, [James] *D. D.* The ſigns of the times: or a ſyſtem of true politics —. 1781. 8. (1 Sh. 6d.). Sermon on the duty to God and the king. 8. (6 d.)
IMISON, [John] *Mechanician at London.* born: .... died d. 16 Aug. 1788.
IMPEY, [John] The new inſtructor clericalis —. 1782. 8. (8 Sh.) Office of Sheriff, ſhewing its hiſtory and antiquity —. 1786. 8. (9 Sh.)
INCHBALD, [Elizabeth] *Mrs. Actreſs at Covent-Garden Theatre.* (Her maiden name *Simpson.* born. 1756.) The mogul tale; a farce. 1784. J'll tell you what, a comedy. 1786. 8. (1 Sh. 6 d.) "Appearance is againſt him, a farce. 1786. (1 Sh.) "The widows vow, a farce. 1786. 8. (1 Sh.) Such things are, a play. 1787. 8. (1 Sh. 6 d.) Ed. 2. 1788. 8. (1 Sh. 6 d.) All on a ſummers day. 1788. Midnight hour, translated from the French of *Dumaniant.* 1787. The child of nature; a dramatic piece. 1788. 8. (1 Sh. 6 d.) The married man, a comedy. 1789. 8. (1 Sh. 6 d.)
INGLEFIELD, [Ann] *Mrs.* Iuſtification, containing the proceedings in the eccleſiaſtical court, before the right worſhipful *Peter Calvert.* LL. D. 1788. 8. (2 Sh.)
—— [John] *Captain in the Navy.* Narrative,. concerning the loſs of his majeſty's ſhip the Centaur —. 1783. 8. (1 Sh.)
INGRAM, [Dale] *Surgeon to the Chriſt's Hospital.* Eſſay on the gout. 1743. 8. Practical cases and observations in ſurgery, with remarks —. 1751. 8. (4 Sh.) Translation of *Verdier's* Anatomy of the human body —. 1753. 8 (6 Sh.) Account of the ſeveral plagues in the world ſince. 1346 —. 1755. 8. (2 Sh. 6 d.) *Verdier's* Anatomy of the human body, translated. 1756. 8. Origin and

nature

nature of magnefia alba and the properties of Ep-
fom waters —. 1768. 8. (1 Sh.) The blow or
inquiry into the causes of the late *Mr. Clarke's*
death —. 1769. 8. (.1 Sh.) Impartial enquiry
into the cause and death of the late *Will. Scawen.*
1777. 8. (3 Sh.)

INGRAM, [Robert] *Vicar of Wormingford and Boxted
in Eſſex.* Explanation of the prophecy of the feven
vials or the feven laſt plagues contained in the revelation of St. John. Chap. 6. 7. 1780. 8. (1 Sh.)
Further observations — on the prophecy of the 7
vials —. 1783. 8. (1 Sh.) Expofition of Isaiah's
vifion Chap. VI. 1784. 8. (6 d.) View of the
great events of the 7 plague, or period, when the
myſtery of God fhall be finiſhed. Apoc. X. 7.
1786. 8. (3 d.)

INNES, [George] *of Aberdeen.* Fourteen discourses on
practical fubjects. 1783. 12. (3 Sh.)

—— [James Dunbar] *A. M. Surgeon at London.* On
the venereal disease —. 1783. 8 (2 Sh)

—— [John] *Proſector at Edinburgh.* Description of the
human muscles —. 1776. 8. (3 Sh.) Eight anatomical tables of the human body —. 1776. 4.
(6 Sh. 6 d.)

JODREL, [Richard Paul] *Sir, Knight. F. R. S: F. A. S:
M. D: Phyſician to the Nabob of Arcot.* A widow
and no widow, a Comedy. 1780. 8. (1 Sh. 6 d.)
Illuſtrations of Euripides, on the Jon and the Bac-
chae. 1781. 8. (10 Sh.) The Knight and friars;
an hiſtoric tale. 1785. 4. (2 Sh.) The perfian
Heroine; a Tragedy. 1786. 4. (6 Sh.) 8. (3 Sh.)
*Seeing is believing, a Comedy. 1786. 8. (1 Sh.)
Select dramatic pieces —. 1787. 8. (6 Sh.)
Illuſtrations of Euripides, on the Alceſtis. 1790. 8.

JOEL, [Thomas] Introduction to English grammar.
1775. 12. (1 Sh.)

JOHNSON, [.....] *Mrs.* Retribution. 17.. The
gameſters. 17.. Califta a novel. Vol. 1. 2. 1789.
8. (5 Sh.)

—— [Alexander] *M. D.* Account of a Society at Amſterdam, inſtituted in the Y. 1767. for the recovery of drowned persons. 1773. 8. (2 Sh.) überſ.
nach der 12. Ausg. Hamburg. 1788. 8. Collection

of authentic cases, proving the practicability of recovering persons vifibly dead by drowning, fuffocations, ſtifling, ſwooning, convulſions and other accidents. 1773. 8. (2 Sh.)

JOHNSON, [Cuthbert] *M. D: of Sherborne, Dorset.* The hiſtory of a dropsy of the ovarium, terminating fatally, with an account of the appearances on diffection. *(Duncan's* M. C. 1780. p. 91.)

—— [Henry] Introduction to logography —. 1783. 8. (2 Sh.) (Das Buch ſelbſt iſt auf dieſe Art gedruckt.)

—— [J.....] A complete abridgment of the law reſpecting gaming and usury —. 1787. 8. (1 Sh. 6 d.)

—— [James] *Surgeon at Lancaſter.* Observations on the internal use of the vitriolum album in a case of epilepsy and in diarrhoea. (Med. Com. of Ed. Vol. 5. p. 311.) Case of hydatids discharged by coughing. (London M. J. Vol. VI. p. 293.) Case of pyuria ſucceſſfully treated. (Ibid. p. 295. Überſ. Samml. f. A. Th. XI. S. 213.) Case of a fractured ſcull ſucceſſfully treated. (Ibid. p. 354.) A Case of plumbſtones retained in the inteſtines. (Ibid. p. 355.)

—— [John] *M. A: Chaplain in Ordinary to his Majeſty.* An enigmatical queſtion, relating to things ſacred and divine. 1755. 8. (1 Sh.) Evangelical truths vindicated —. 1758. 8. (1 Sh.) Review of the Prebendary of *Litchfield's* ſermon and addreſſ to Quakers. 1762. 8. (9 d.) Divine truth, being a vindication of the three immutable attributes — of God — 1769. 8. (3 ſh) Addreſſ to *Sam. Fisher* of Norwich, concerning the errors charged upon him by the fictitious Quaker —. 1773. 8. (6 d.) The riches of gospel grace opened in XII Discourses — Vol. 1. 2. 1776. 8. (8 ſh.) A ſcriptural illuſtration of the book of the revelation. 1779. 8. (5 ſh.) Observations on the military eſtabliſhment and discipline of his majeſty the King of Pruſſia — translated from the French. 1780. 8. (2 Sh.)
(Several ſingle ſermons.)

—— [Robert Wallace] *M. D: Phyſician at Brentford.* Friendly cautions to the heads of families. 8. 17.. New ſyſtem of midwifery, in 4 parts founded on
practi-

practical observations, the whole illustrated with
copper plates. 1769. 4. (1 L. 1 sh.) Ed. 2. 1777.
4. (1 L. 1 sh.) überf. von *J. C. Loder.* Th. 1. 2.
Leipz. 1782. (Überf. Samml. f. WA. St. 2. S. 92.
u. S. 95.)

JOHNSON, [Samuel] *LL. D.* (Son of a Bookseller
at *Litchfield, Warwickshire.*) born at *Litchfield.*
1709. died d. 14 Dec. 1784.

— [William] *Sir. Baronet.* born: .... died at *Johnson-hall* in the province of *New-York in America.*
d. 11 July. 1774.

JOHNSTON, [Alexander] *Surgeon in the Royal Navy.*
History of two cases of amputation, in which compression of the artery was successfully made by the finger of an assistant, as there was no room for applying the Tourniquet. (*Duncan's* M. C. Dec. 2. Vol. 3. p. 366.)

JOHNSTONE, [.....] *(Lessing's)* Disbanded officer: or the baroness of Bruchsal; (translated.) 1786. 8. (1 sh. 6 d.)

— [Edward] *M. D. F. R. S. of Edinb: Physician to the general hospital at Birmingham.* Diss. De febre puerperali. Edinb. 1779. 8. Case of angina pectoris. (Mem: of M. S. of L. Vol. 1. p. 306.) History of a case of obstinate obstipatio, depending on a stricture of the rectum. (Med. Com. of Ed. Vol. 5. p. 302.) History of a case of puerperal fever; with remarks on the treatment of that affection in general. (*Duncan's* M. C. 1780. p. 98.) überf. Samml. f. A. Th. 6. S. 103.

— [James] *M. D. Physician at Kidderminster, Worcestershire.* born: .... died. d. 2 Aug. 1783.

— [James] *A. M. Rector of Maghera-Cross.* Anecdotes of Olave the black, king of Man and the hebridian princes of the Somerled family — —. 1780. 8. (2 sh.) Lodbrokar — quida; or, the deathsong of Lodbroc — with an English translation. 1783. 8. The Norwegian account of *Haco's* expedition against Scotland 1263 —. 1786. 8. (3 sh.) Antiquitates Celto-Normanniae, containing the chronicle of Man and the Isles —. Copenhagen. 1786. 4. (10 sh. 6 d.) Antiquitates Celto Scandicae, s. series rerum gestarum inter nationes Britannitannicarum infularum et gentes feptentrionales. 1786. 4. (10 fh. 6 d.)

JONES, [A......] The art of playing at Skittles; or the laws of nine pins. 1773. 12. (1 fh.)

—— [Daniel] *of Hindsdale*. Account of Weftriver mountain, and the appearance of there having been a Volcano in it. (Mem. of B. A. Vol. I. p. 312.)

—— [E......] *Teacher of the claffics and geography, at Bromley, Kent.* The Young geographer and aftronomer's beft companion. 1773. 12. (3 fh. 6 d.) *Cicero's* Brutus, or the hiftory of the famous orators — translated. 1776. 8. (6 fh.)

—— [Edward] *of Henblas, Llanddersel, Merionetshire.* Mufical and poetical relics of the welsh bards —. 1784. fol. (1 L. 1 fh.)

—— [G......] *An journeyman Woll-Comber.* Miscellaneous poetic attempts. 1786. 8. (3 fh.)

—— [Henry] born at *Drogheda* in *Ireland:* died d. .... Apr. 1770.

—— [J......] *Prefident.* Remarks on the english language. 1775. 4. (1 fh.)

—— [John] *at Indian River, Worcefter County, Maryland.* Account of a new fpecies of Grape Vines. (Tr. of A. S. Vol. I. p. 340.)

—— [John] *Schoolmafter in Kidderminfter.* Elegy on winter and other poems; with a memory of the late Lord *Lyttelton.* 1779. 4. (1 fh.)

—— [Philipp] *Tailor:* On crookednefs or diftortions of the fpine —. 1788. 8. (4 fh.)

—— [R......] *Lieutenant of Artillery.* On skating. 1772. 8. (2 fh. 6 d.)

—— [Robert] *M. D: F. A. S. at Edinb.* Inquiry into the ftate of Medicine, on the principles of inductive philosophy. 1782. 8. (5 fh. 3 d.) Inquiry into the nature, causes and termination of nervous fevers —. 1789. 8.

—— [Rowland] *of the Inner temple.* The origin of language and nations —. 1764. 8. (10 fh. 6 d.) Hieroglyfic or a grammatical introduction to an universal hieroglyfic language —. 1768. 8. (2 fh. 6 d.) The philosophy of words —. 1769. 8. (2 Sh.) The circles of Gomer; or an effay towards an inveftigation and introduction of the english as an universal language —. 1771. 8. (5 fh.)

The

The Jo triads; or the tenth Muse —. 1773. 8.
(2 fh. 6 d.)

JONES, [Thomas] *of Briftol.* born:.... died 17..
—— [Thomas] *Surgeon at Bingley, near Bradford,
Yorkshire, late Surgeon to the Leed's infirmary.*
A Cafe of a flap operation united by tne firft intention. (*Duncan's* M. C. Vol. 9. p. 326.).
—— [W......] On the art of Mufic —. 1785. fol.
(1 L. 1 Sh.)
—— [W......] *Clerk, Curate of Shinfield and Swallowfield.* Neceffity and advantages of education.
1786. 8. (2 Sh.)
—— [William] *Sir, Knight, one of the judges of
the supreme court of judicature at Calcutta in the
Eaft - Indies. Prefident of the Afiatik Society.
F. R. S.* (Formerly Barrifter at Law, fellow of Univerfity College, Oxford.) Hiftoire de Nader-Chah, connu sous le nom de Thahmas Kuli Kahn, Empereur de Perse. Vol. 1. 2. 1770. 4. (1 L. 4
fh.) überf. Greifswald 1773. 4. The Hiftory of
the life of Nader Schah, King of Perfia. 1773. 8.
(6 fh.) (Ein Auszug aus dem Franzöfifchen.)
*Diflertation fur la litterature orientale. 1771. 8.
(1 fh.) Grammar of the Perfian language. 1771.
4. (10 fh. 6 d.) Lettre a M. *Anquetil du Perron* dans laquelle eft compris l'examen de sa traduction des livres attribués a Zoroaftre. 1771. 8.
überf. *Hifsmann's* Magazin für die Philofophie Th.
3. S. 9. *Poems, confifting chiefly of translations from the Afiatic languages, with two eflays, on the poetry of the Eaftern nations and on the arts, commonly called imitative. 1772. 8. (4 fh.)
Ed. 2. 1777. 8. (6 fh.) Poetkos Afiaticae commentariorum libri VI. 1774. 8. (9 fh.) recudi curavit *J. G. Eichhorn.* Lipfiae 1777. 8. The fpeeches of *Isaeus*, in causes concerning the law of succeffion to property at Athens —. 1779. 4. (10 fh.
6 d.) *Inquiry into the legal mode of suppresfing riots. 1780. 8. (1 fh.) Eflay on the law of bailments. 1781. 8. (2 fh.) Speech to the affembled inhabitants of the counties of Middlesex and
Surrey —. 1782. 8. (6 d.) The Mahomedan
law of succeffion to the property of inteftates, in
arabic with a translation and notes 1782. 4. (5 fh.)
The

The Moallakat, or seven Arabian poems, which were suspended on the temple at Mecca; with a transtion and arguments. 1783. 4. (10 sh. 6 d.) On the orthography of Afiatik words in roman letters. (Afiat. Res. Vol. I. p. 1.) Discourse on the inflitution of a society for enquiring into the biflory, civil and natural, the antiquities, arts, sciences and litterature of Afia. 1784. 4. (1 sh. 6 d.) 1 Afiat. Res. Vol. I. p. 1.) On the Gods of Greece, Italy and India. (Ibid. p. 221.) A converfation with Abram an Abyffinian, concerning the city of Gwender and the Sources of the Nile. (Ibid. p. 383. überf. in *Sprengel's* und *Forster's* Länder - und Völker - Kunde. Th. 3. S. 189. überf. in *Eichhorn's* Bibliothek Th. 2. S. 1020.) Second Anniversary discourse on the Hindus. (Ibid. p. 405.) The third discourse on the Hindus. (Ibid. p. 415.) *Sacontala; or the fatal ring: an Indian drama by *Calidas* translated from the original Sanscrit and Pancrit. 1790. 4.

JONES, [William] *A. M: Rector of Paston in Norshamptonshire, Minifter of Nayland, Suffolk. F. R. S.* *A full answer to the effay on spirit —. 1753. 8. (2 sh. 6 d.) The catholic doctrine of a Trinity — proved from fcripture. 1757. 8. (2 sh.) Effay on the first principles of natural philofophy. 1762. 4. (9 sh.) Remarks on the principles and spirit of a work: the Confeffional 1770. 8. (2 Sh. 6 d.) Zoologia ethica, a disquifition concerning the mosaic diftinction of animals into clean and unclean. 1771. 8. (2 Sh.) Three Differtations on life and death. 1771. 8. (1 Sh. 6. d.) Hiftory of all the religious houfes in the counties of Devon and Cornwall, before the diffolution. 1779. 8. (2 Sh. 6 d.) Phyfiological disquifitions, or, discourses on the natural philofophy of the elements —. 1781. 4. (1 L. 1 Sh.) Courfe of lectures on the figurative language of the holy fcripture and the interpretation of it from the fcripture itself. 1787. 8. (6 Sh.) (Several fingle fermons.)

—— [William] *F. R. S.* born: .... died 17...
—— [William] *Surgeon in Birmingham.* Account of two cases of insanity, one of which was cured by
the

the use of the fox glove; also a cafe of hemoptyfis cured by the same remedy. *(Duncan's* M. C. Dec. II. Vol. I. p. 302. et 380. überf. Samml. f. A. Th. 13. S. 23.) Account of an expeditious cure of a fractured scull, with remarks on the case by *Rob. Mynors.* (London M. J. Vol. 5. p. 278.

JORTIN, [John] D. D. *Arch-Deacon of London, Rector of St. Dunstan in the East and Vicar of Kensington.* born in *London* d. 23 Oct. 1698. died d... Aug. 1770.

IRELAND, [John] The Emigrant. a poem. 1785. 4. (1 Sh.) Letters and poems by *John Henderson* with anecdotes of his life. 1786. 8. (4 Sh)

—— [Samuel] A picturesque tour through Holland, Brabant and part of France, made 1789. Vol. I. 2. 1790. 8. (2 L. 12 Sh. 6 d.)

IRONSIDE, [.....] *Lieutenant-Colonel.* Of the culture and uses of the son or sun — plant of Hindoftan with an account of the manner of manufacturing the Hindoftan paper. (Philos. Transact. 1774. p. 99.)

IRVING, [Ralph] *M. D.* Experiments on the red and quill peruvian bark with observations on its hiftory, made of operation and uses. 1785. 8. (3 Sh.) überf. Leipz. 1787. 8. Some remarks on the supposed effects of lime and magnefia in promoting the solubility of peruvian bark. (Lond. M. J. Vol. 7. P. 4.) *The Edinburgh new Dispensatory — by Gentlemen of the faculty at Edinburgh. 1786. 8.

—— [Thomas] *M. D. Physician at Lisburne.* Account of a singular fracture of the cranium; and of the haemorrhage, from amputation of penis, stopt by flight compreffion for a few minutes. *(Duncan's* M. C. 1790. Dec. 2. Vol. 5. p. 363.)

IRWIN, [Eyles] *In the service of the East-Indian-Company.* Bedukah, or the self devoted, an Indian pastoral. 1776. (2 Sh. 6 d.) A series of adventures in the course of a voyage up the red sea, on the coasts of Arabia and Egypt — in the Year 1777. in letters to a lady. 1780. 4. (15 Sh.) Ed. 3. Vol. 1. 2. 1787. 8. (12 Sh.) überf. (durch *Joh. Andr. Engelbrecht.*) Leipzig 1781. 8. ⁕ Eastern eclogues —. 1780. 4. (2 Sh. 6 d.) Occafional epi-

epiftles, written during a journey from London to Busrah in the Gulph of Perfia in the Years 1780 and 1781. —. 1783. 4. (3 Sh.) Ode to *Robert Brooke* — occafioned by the death of Hyder Ally. 1784. 4. (1 Sh. 6 d.)

JUBB, [George] *D. D. Profeffor of Hebrew in the Univerfity of Oxford.* born: .... died d. 13 Nov. 1787.

JUNIPER, [Julius] *Poet Laurent to the Royal College of Phyficiant.* The Brunoniad: an heroic poem, in VI Cantos, containing a folemn detail of certain commotions which have, of late, divided the kingdom of phyfic againft itself, a critical and truly Homerican catalogue of our prefent Luminaries of Medicine —. 1789. 4. (3 Sh. 6 d.)

JUSTAMOND, [John Obadiah] *Surgeon to the Weftminfter hofpital. F. R. S.* born: .... died d. 27 March. 1786.

IVERY, [John] *Teacher of Mufic at Norrhaw in Hertfordshire.* The Hertfordshire melody; or, pfalm-Singer's recreation —. 1773. 8. (2 Sh. 6 d.)

IVES, [Edward] *Surgeon in Eaft-India.* born: .... died d. 25 Sept. 1786.

—— [John] *F. R. S. and F. A. S. Suffolk Herold extraordinary.* born at Yarmouth 1751. died d. 9 June 1776.

KAIMS, [Lord] (HENRY HOME.) *Judge in the courts of Seffion and Jufticiary at Edinburgh.* born: .... died d. 27 Dec. 1782.

KEAN, [T....] A new and easy method of finding the longitude at fea. 1774. 8. (1 Sh. 6 d.)

KEARNEY, [Michael] *D. D. Profeffor of Hiftory at Dublin.* Lectures concerning hiftory. 1776. 4. (2 Sh. 6 d.)

KEARSLEY, [G.....] Annual Taxtables, including all the new ones of the Year 1785 —. 1785. 8. Table of trades for — the benefit of young men. 1786. 8. (1 Sh.)

KEATE, [George] *F. R. S: F. A, S.* Account of the ancient hiftory, present government and laws of the republic of Geneva. 1760. 8. (3 Sh.) The alps, a poem. 1763. 4. (1 Sh. 6 d.) The ruins of Netley Abbey, a poem. 1764. 4. (6 d.) *Poem to to the memory of Mrs. *Cibber*. 1766. 4. (6 d.) Ferney, an epiftle to Mr. *Voltaire*. 1767. 4. (1 Sh.) The monument in Arcadia, a poem. 1773. 4. (2 Sh). Sketches from nature, taken and coloured in a journey to Margate. Vol. 1. 2. 1779. 8. (5 Sh.) nachgedr. Dresden 1784. 8. Poems. Vol. 1. 2. 1781. 8. The mummy, an epiftle to *Angel. Kauffmann*. 1781. 4. (2 Sh.) Obfervations on the roman earthen ware found in the sea on the kentish coaft between whiftable and reculver on the borders of the isle of Thanet. (Arch. Vol. 6. p. 125.) A probationary ode for the Laureatship. 1787. 4. (2 Sh.) Diftreffed poet, poem. 1787. 4. (4 Sh.) Account of the Pelew-Islands — compofed from the journals and communications of Capt. *Henr. Wilfon* and fome of his officers — 1783. - 1788. 4. (1 L. 1 Sh.) nachgedr. Bafil. Vol. 1. 2. 1790. 8. überf. von *G. Forfter*. 1789. 8. The interefling and affecting hiftory of Prince Lee Boo, a native of the Pelew-Islands, brought to England — with a short account of thofe islands, and a sketch of the manners and cuftoms of the inhabitants. 1789. 12.

KEATE, [T. . . . .] *Surgeon extraordinary to her Majefty and Surgeon to the Prince of Wales and Duke of York*. Cases of the hydrocele with obfervations on a peculiar method of treating that diseafe. 1788. 8. (2 Sh.)

—— [William] *M. A. Prebendary of Wells and Rector of Lavefton, Somerset*. Examination of Dr. *Price's* and *Prieftley's* fermon, 1790. 8. (2 Sh.) The addrefs of *Will. Bull* — to *Will. Poole* —. 1790. 8. (1 Sh.) Quotation againft quotation, or curfosy obfervations on Dr. *Prieftley's* letters to the inhabitants of Birmingham —. 1790. 8. (1 Sh. 6 d.) (Several fingle sermons.)

KEEBLE, [John] *Organift of St. George's Church at London*. The Theory of harmonics: or an illuftration of the Grecian harmonica —. 1784. fol. (1 L. 1 Sh.)

O'KEEFE, [John] *Actor in the Irish Stage*. (born in Ireland) Tony lumpkin in town, a farce. 1780. 8. (1 Sh.)

KEELING, [Bartholom.] *M. A. Rector of Tiffield and Bradden, in Northamptonshire and Chaplain to the Earl*

Earl Temple. Three sermons on St. Paul's wish. 1766. 8. (2 Sh.) Three discourses on Moses's petition and Character. 1767. 8. (1 sh. 6 d.) Eight discourses of the behaviour of the malefactor's crucified with our bleſſed Lord. 1773. 8. (3 Sh.)

KEIR, [Archibald] Thoughts on the affairs of Bengal. 1772. 8. (1 sh. 6 d.) Of the method of diſtilling as practised by the natives at Chatra in Ramgur, and in the other provinces, perhaps, with but little variation —. (Aſiat. Res. Vol. 1. p. 309.)

—— [James] *Esq. of Stourbridge.* F. R. S: F. A. S. Edinb. *Macquer's* Dictionary of chemiſtry translated. Vol. 1. 2. 1771. 4. (1 L. 8 Sh.) On the cryſtallization observed on glaſſ. (Phil. Transact. 1776. p. 530.) *Treatise on the various kinds of permanently elaſtic fluids or gases 1777. 8. Experiments on the congelation of the vitriolic acid. (Phil. Transact. 1787. p. 267.) Dictionary of Chemiſtry. Part. 1. 1789. 4. (10 sh.) Experiments and observations on the diſſolution of metals in acids, and their precipitations; with an account of a new compound acid menſtruum; useful in ſome technical operations of parting metals. (Phil. Transact. 1790. p. 359.)

—— [William] *M. D. Phyſician to St. Thomas's Hospital at London and Lecturer on Chemiſtry in London.* born at Perth in Scotland 1753. died d. 6 Jun. 1783.

KEITH, [Alexander] *Esq.* F. R. S: F. A. S. Edinb. Description of a mercurial level. (Tr. of E. S. Vol. 2. p. 14.)

—— [George Skene] *M. A. Miniſter of Keith - Hall, Aberdeenshire.* Sermons and discourses on ſeveral occaſions. 1785. 8. (5 Sh.)
(Several ſingle ſermons.)

—— [Thomas] *Teacher of the Mathematics.* Introduction to the ſcience of geography. 1787. 12. (1 sh. 6 d.) The complete practical arithmetician. 1788. 8. (3 sh.)

KELHAM, [Robert] *of Lincolns Inn.* Dictionary of the Norman or old French language —. 1779. 8. (6 sh.) Domesday book illuſtrated —. 1788. 8. (5 sh.)

KELLIE, [George] *Surgeon in Leith.* Account of the paracentelis being performed in the thorax, for the cure of an emphysema. (Med. Com. of Ed. Vol. 2. p. 427.)

KELLY, [Hugh] (O'-KELLY.) *Member of the Middle Temple at London.* born on the Banks of *Killarney Lake in Ireland.* 1739. died. d. 3 Febr. 1777.

KELSALL, [R.....] *Lieutenant.* Thoughts on the present manner of quartering the troops on the coaſt —. 1784. 8. (6 d.)

KELSO, [Hamilton] *M. D.* On elementary air. 1786. 8. (1 ſh.)

KEMBLE, [John] *Aƈtor.* (Brother to Mrs. *Siddons.* born at *Lancashire.*) The pilgrim a comedy of *Fletcher,* altered. 17.. The palaces of *Mersey.* 17.. Fugitive pieces. 1780. 8. (1 ſh. 6 d.) The maid of honour, a comedy, altered from *Maſſinger.* 1785. Projeƈts, a farce. 1786. Criticism on the performance of Hamlet. 1788. 8. (6 d.) The farm-house, a Comedy. 1789. 8. (1 ſh.) Love in many masks: altered from Mr. *Behn's* Rover. 1790. 8. (1 ſh. 6 d.) The tempeſt; or, the enchanted Island: written by *Shakespeare:* with additions from *Dryden.* 1790. 8. (1 ſh. 6 d.)

KEMEYS, [John Gardner] *Eſq. of Plantain garden river plantation in Jamaica and of Bartholey in the County of Monmouth.* Refleƈtions by the late additional duties on ſugars and on rum —. 1783. 8. (2 ſh. 6 d.)

KENNEDY, [James] Description of the piƈtures, ſtatues, buſtos, baſſo — relievos, and other curioſities at the Earl of *Pembroke's* House at *Wilton* —. 1758. 8. (2 ſh. 6 d.) Description of the antiquities and curioſities in Wiltonhouse illuſtrated with 25 engravings —. 1770. 4. (16 ſh.)

—— [John] *Reƈtor of Bradley in Derbyshire.* A new method of ſtating and explaining the ſcripture chronology —. 1752. 8. (5 ſh.) Examination of *Jackson's* chronological antiquities. 1753. 8. (1 ſh. 6 d.) The doƈtrine of a commensurability between the diurnal and annual motions —. 1753. 8. (6 d.) A complete ſyſtem of aſtronomical chronology, unſolding the ſcriptures —. 1763. 4. (1 L. 5 ſh.) Discuſſion of ſome important and uncertain

'certain points in chronology —. 1773. 8. (1 ſh.) Explanation and proof of the complete ſyſtem of aſtronomical chronology —. 1775. 8. (1 ſh. 6 d.)

KENNICOTT, [Benjamin]- D. D. *Canon of Chriſt-church, Keeper of the Radcliffe Library and Vicar of Culham, Oxfordshire.* born at *Totrneſſ, Devonshire.* 1718. died d. 18 Aug. 1783.

KENRICK, [.....] ⁕Lecture on the perpetual motion. P. 1. 2. 1770. 4. (5 ſh.)

—— [.....] *Millot's* elements of the hiſtory of England, from the invaſions of the romans to the reign of George II. translated: Vol. 1. 2. 1771. 8. (8 ſh.)

—— [William] *LL. D.* born: ..... died d. 9 June. 1779.

KENT, [Nathaniel] *of Fulham.* Hints to gentlemen of landed property. 1775. 8. (5 ſh.)

KENTISH, [Richard] *M. D: F. A. S. Edin.* Experiments and observations on a new ſpecies of bark —. 1785. 8. (2 ſh. 6 d.) überſ. Leipz. 1787. 8. Eſſay on ſea-bathing and the internal uſe of ſea water. 1786. 8. (1 ſh. 6 d.) Oration on the method of ſtudying natural hiſtory —. 1787. 8. (2 ſh.) Advice to gouty perſons. 1789. 8. (1 ſh. 6 d.) Hiſtory of a caſe of universal latent cancer. *(Duncan's* M. C. Dec. 2. Vol. 1. überſ. Samml. f. A. Th. 13. S. 18.)

KENTON, [James] Eſſay on death, a poem. 1777. 4. (2 ſh. 6 d.)

KER, [L. ....] *M. B.* Minor poems, or poetical pieces. 1787. 4. (1 Sh.)

KERR, [James] *Surgeon to the civil hospital at Bengal.* Account of the tree producing the terra japonica. (Med. Obs. Vol. 5. p. 148.) The culture of the white poppy and preparation of opium in the province of Bahar. (Ibid. p. 317.) Natural hiſtory of the inſect which produces the gum laua. (Phil. Transact. 1781. p. 374. überſ. Samml. zur P. u. Ng. Th. 3. S. 479.)

—— [James] *Captain.* ⁕Narrative of the rise and rapid advancement of the Mahratta ſtate; translated from the Perſian into Engliſh. 1782. 8. (2 Sh. 6 d.)

—— [Robert] *F. R. S: F. A. S. Edinb. Lavoiſier* elements of chemiſtry translated —. 1789. 8. (10 Sh.) *Bertholet's* eſſay on the new method of bleaching, by means of oxygenated muriatic acid; with an
ac-

account of the nature, preparation and properties of that acid and its application, translated. 1789. 8.
KEYES, [John] The practical bee-malter —. 1781. 8. (4 Sh)
KIDDELL, [John] Three Differtations on the infpiration of the holy fcriptures. 1779. 8. (2 Sh.) überf. von *J. S. Semler.* Halle. 1783. 8.
(Several fingle fermons.)
KILGOUR, [Thomas] *Surgeon in Jamaica.* The hiftory of a case, in which worms in the nose, productive of alarming fymptoms, were fuccefsfully removed by the use of tobacco. *(Duncan's* M. C. Vol. 8. p. 75.)
KIMBER, [E. ....] The peerage of England —. 1766. 8. (3 Sh.) The peerage of Scotland —. 1767. 18mo. (3 Sh.) The peerage of Ireland. 1768. 12. (3 Sh) E. *Kimber* and R. *Johnson,* The baronetage of England —. Vol. 1-3. 1771. 8. (1 L. 1 fh.)
KINDAN, [.....] On the conftruction of a mine augar. 1788. (2 Sh.)
KINDERSLY, [.....] *Mrs.* Letters from the island of Teneriffe, Brazil, the Cape of good hope and the-Eaft-Indies. 1777. 8. (3 Sh. 6 d.) überf. Leipzig 1777. 8.
KING, [Edward] *F. R. S: F. A. S. and late Prefident of the Society of Antiquaries.* On the English conftitution and government. 1766. 8. (2 Sh. 6 d.) Attempt to account for the universal deluge. (Phil. Transact. 1767. p. 44.) Attempt to account for the formation of fpars and chryftals. (Ibid. p. 58.) Account of a very remarkable aquatic insect. (Ibid. p. 72.) Observations on *J. Lloyd* account of Elden Hole in Derbyshire. (Ibid. 1771. p. 250.) Account of the effects of lightning at Steeple, Ashton and Holt in the county of wilts on the 20 June 1772. (Ibid. 1773. p. 231.) Observations on a fingular fparry incruftation found in Somertfhire. (Ibid. 1773. p. 241.) Remarks on the Abbey church of Bury St. Edmund's in Suffolk. (Arch. Vol. 3. p. 311.) Account of the great feal of Ranulph Earl of *Chefter,* and of two ancient inscriptions found in the ruins of St. Edmund Bury Abbey. (Ibid. Vol. 4. p. 119.) Observations on antient caftles, (Ibid. p. 364. Vol. 6. p. 231.)

P 2

Ob-

Observations on antient castle. 1777. 4. Account of an old piece of Ordnance. (Ibid. Vol. 5. p. 147.) Account of a petrefaction found on the coast of East-Lothian (Phil. Transact. 1779. p. 35.) *Proposals for establishing, at sea, a marine school, or seminary for seamen —. 1785. 8. (1 Sh.) *Morsels of criticism, tending to illustrate some few passages in the holy scripture upon philosophical principles and an enlarged view of things. 1788. 4. (1 L. 1 Sh.)

KING, [John] Thoughts on the difficulties and distresses in which the peace of 1783. has involved the people of England. 1783. 8. (1 Sh. 6 d.)

—— [John Glen] *D. D Rector of Wormley, Preacher at Spring Garden Chapel. F. R. S: F. A. S.* born at Norfolk. 1732. died d. 3 Nov. 1787.

—— [Richard] The frauds of London detected. 1779. 12. (1 Sh.)

—— [Samuel Croker] *Dublin.* Case of a feather or pen, XI inches in length, which was fortunately extracted from the oesophagus of a man, who had put it into his throat to excite vomiting, and had let it slip down. (Med. Obs. Vol. 5. p. 231.)

—— [Thomas] *Actor at Drury-Lane Theater.* (born in London 1730.) Love at first sight. 1763. 8. *Neck or nothing, a farce. 1765. 8. (1 Sh.) *A peep behind the curtain; or the new rehearsal, a comedy. 1766. 8. (1 Sh.) Wit's last stake, a comedy. 1769. 8. (1 Sh.)

KINGLAKE, [Robert] *Surgeon at Chipping-Norton, in Oxfordshire.* Account of a case, in which a part of the femoral artery was dilated in consequence of its being laid bare by a wound and which was successfully treated by obliterating the cavity of the artery, at that part, by compression. (London M. J. Vol. VIII. P. 4.) Account of a remarkable disease of the heart, lungs and one of the external mammae —. (Ibid. Vol. X. P. 4.)

KINGSFORD, [William] Appeal to the scriptures in general, on the universality of divine love to man and the universal extent of our saviour's death. 1788. 8. (5 Sh.) Vindication of the baptists from the criminality of a charge exhibited against them by Mr. *Wesley*. 1789. 8. (2 d.) Three letters to Mr. *Wesley*, containing remarks on on a piece lately published with his approbation: and three challenges to all the methodifts in the kingdom. 1789. 8. (1 Sh.)

KINNAIRD, [William] *Apothecary in Edinburgh.* Experiments and observations on the temperature of the atmosphere and on the viciffitudes to which it is fubjected from different causes. *(Duncan's* M. C. Vol. 9. p. 425.)

KINNERSLEY, [Ebenezer] New Experiments in electricity. (Phil. Transact. 1763. p. 84.) On fome electrical experiments made with Charcoal. (Ibid. 1773. p. 38.)

KIPPIS, [Andrew] *D. D: F. R. S: F. A. S.* Vindication of the proteftant diffenting minifters, with regard to their late application to parliament. 1772. 8. (1 fh. 6 d.) Ed. 2. 1773. 8. (2 fh.) überf. Brittifches theolog. Magazin. Th. 4. S. 529. u. S. 721. Biographia Brittannica. Vol. 1 - 4. 1778 - 1789. fol. (6 L. 7 fh. 6 d.) Six Discourses delivered by *John Pringle,* with the life of the author. 1783. 8. (6 fh.) *Confiderations on the provifional treaty with America and the preliminary articles of peace with France and Spain. 1783. 8. (2 fh. 6 d.) Observations on the late contefts in the royal society. 1784. 8. (2 fh. 6 d.) The life of Capt. *James Cook.* 1788. 4. (1 L. 1 fh.) nachgedr. Bafil. Vol. 1. 2. 1788. 8. überf. Th. 1. 2. Hamb. 1789. 8. The life of *Nath. Lardner,* prefixed to the firft volume of the works of *N. Lardner.* 1788. 8. *Jos. Fownes's* enquiry into the principles of toleration, with some account of the author. 1789. 8. (2 fh 6 d.)

KIRBY, [Thomas] Effay on criticism. in the course of which the theory of light and the gravity of the earth are confidered. 1758. 8. (6 d.) Analyfis of the electrical fire —. 1778. 8. (6 d.)

KIRK, [M. ....] *of Wilderspool, near Manchefter.* On the beft method of raifing early potatoes. *(Hunter's* G. E. Vol. 5. p. 185.)

KIRKE, [Robert] *Advocate.* Minutes and proceedings of a Court - Martial held on *John Crookshanks* — formerly Captain of his Majefty fhip the Lark. 1772. 8. (2 fh. 6 d.)

P 3

KIRK-

KIRKLAND, [Thomas] *M. D. Phyfician at Ashby de la Zouch, Leiceftershire.* On Gangrenes. 1754. 8. (1 fh 6 d.) überf. von *Huth.* Nürnberg 1761. 8. On the use of spunge after amputations. (Med. Obs Vol. 2. p. 278.) On the methods of suppreffing haemorrhages from divided arteries. 1763. 8. (1 fh.) On the cure of those diseases which are the causes of fevers. 1767. 8. (1 fh. 6 d.) Reply to *Maxwell's* answer to *Kirkland's* effay on fevers —. 1769. 8. (2 fh.) Observations upon *Pott's* general remarks on fractures. 1770. Appendix. 1771. 8. (2 fh. 6 d.) überf. Altenb. 1771. 8. On child-bed fevers — with two differtations on the brain and nerves. 1774. 8. (3 fh.) überf. von *J. C. F. Sherf.* Gotha 1778. 8. Animadverfions on Dr. B —'s treatise on the King-cough, with an effay on the hooping cough. 1774. 8. Thoughts on amputation with an effay° on the use of opium in mortifications. 1780. 8. (2 fh.) (° überf. Samml. f. A. Th. 5. S. 555.) Inquiry into the present ftate of medical surgery. Vol. 1. 2. 1783. 1786. 8. (12 fh. 6 d.) überf. Leipzig 1785. 8. On the use and abuse of mercury in the cure of the syphilis. (London M. J. Vol. VII. p. 1. überf. Samml. f. A. Th XI. S. 714.)

KIRKPATRIK, [H.....] Sermons on various subjects —. 1785. 8. (5 fh.)

—— [J.....] *M. D: at London.* born:.... died 1770.

—— [James] *Esq. Lieutenant Colonel in the Eaft-Indies Company service.* °Confiderations on the expediency of a corps of light troops to be employed on detached service in the Ealt-Indies. 1769. 8. (1 fh.) Ed. 2. with the Author's name 1781. 8. (1 fh.)

KIRSHAW, [Thomas] On the comparative merit of the ancients and moderns, with respect to the imitative arts. (Mem. of M. Vol. 1. p. 405.)

KIRWAN, [Richard] *F. R. S: F. I. A.* Experiments and observations on the specific gravities and attractive powers of various saline substances. (Phil. Transact. 1781. p. 6. 1782. p. 129. 1783. p. 15.) überf. von *Lor. Crell.* Berlin u. Stettin. 1783. 8. Remarks on *Cavendish's* experiments on air. (Ibid. 1784. p. 154. — 178.) Elements of Mineralogy. 1784. 8. (5 fh.) überf. von *L. Crell.*

L. Crell. 1785. 8. Remarks on specific gravities taken at different degrees of heat and an easy method of reducing them to a common standard. (Phil. Transact. 1785. p. 267.) Experiments on hepatic air. (Ibid. 1786. p. 118.) Essay on phlogiston and on the constitution of acids. 1787. 8. (3 sh. 6. d.) Estimate of the temperature of different latitudes. 1787. 8. (3 sh.) On the variations of the barometer. (Tr. of J. A. 1788. p. 43.) Observations on coral mines. (Ibid. p. 157.) *Lor. Crell.* sammlete diese Schriften zusammen und gab sie unter dem Titel heraus: Physisch chemische Schriften. Th. 1-3. Berlin 1788. 8.

KITCHEN, [Thomas] *Hydrographer to his Majesty.* born: .... died d. 19 July 1784.

KITE, [Charles] *Surgeon at Gravesend in Kent.* Account of a remarkable nervous affection. (London M. J. Vol. 3. p. 300.) A case of paralysis of the lower extremities successfully treated by an issue. (Ibid. p. 405.) Recommendation of electricity for the cure of the cataract. (Ibid. Vol. 7. P. 2. übers. Samml. f. A. Th. XII. S. 43.) Account of two cases of violent constipation of the bowels, the first treated by the internal and external application of coldwater; the second by a discharge of matter from the vagina. (Ibid. Vol. VIII. P. 2. übers. Samml. f. A. Th. 12. S. 551.) On the recovery of the apparently dead. 1788. 8. (5 sh.) Übers. von *C. F. Michaelis.* Leipzig 1790. 8.

KNIGHT, [D.... M....] Proposal for peace between Great Britain and North America —. 1779. 8. (6 d.)

—— [Francis] *Surgeon to the Coldstream Regim. of Foot-Guards.* Two cases of obstructed liver, followed by dropsy, succesfully treated by mercurial friction. (Med. Transact. Vol. 3. p. 368.) On the effect of a large dose of saccharum saturni. (London M. J. Vol. 4. p. 286.)

—— [J.....] The ears of Chesterfield and parson Goodmann; translated from the French of *Voltaire.* 1786. 12. (1 sh. 6 d.)

—— [Samuel] *A. M. of Trinity College, Cambridge.* *Elegies and sonnets. 1785. 4. (3 sh.) Ed. 2. with the Author's name. 1786. 4. (3 Sh.)

KNIPE, [Eliza] Six narrative poems. 1787. 4. (3 Sh. 6 d.)
—— [Reft] The new birth —. 1771. 8. (1 Sh. 6. d.)
KNOWLES, [Thomas] D. D. *Prebendary of Ely.* Answer to an eſſay on spirit —. 1753. 8. (1 Sh. 6 d.) Observations on the divine miſſion and adminiſtration of Moses. 1763. 8. (1 Sh. 6 d.) Letters between Lord *Hervey* and Dr. *Middleton* concerning the roman senate. 1778. 4. (12 Sh.) On the paſſion. 1780. 8. (3 Sh.) Primitive chriſtianity; or, teſtimony from the writers of the firſt four centuries, to prove that Jesus Chriſt was worshipped as God from the beginning of the chriſtian church. 1789. 8. (2 Sh. 6 d.) (Several ſingle sermons.)

KNOX, [Hugh] *D. D. Miniſter of the Gospel in St. Croix.* Discourses on the truth of revealed religion and other important ſubjects. Vol. 1. 2. 1768. (6 Sh.) Letter to *Green* pointing out some difficulties in the calviniſtic scheme of divinity —. 1772. 12. (1 Sh. 6 d.) The moral and religious miscellany. 1775. 8.
—— [John] born: .... died at *Dalkeith*, near *Edinburgh*. 1790.
—— [Viceſimus] at *Tunbridge, in Kent.* M. A. °Eſſays moral and litterary. 1777. 8. (4 Sh. 6 d.) with the Author's name. Ed. 2. Vol. 1. 2. 1778. 8. (7 Sh. 6 d.) Ed. 3. Vol. 1. 2. 1782. 8. (7 Sh. 6 d.) Ed. 4. Vol. 1. 2. 1784. 8. (8 Sh.) überſ. von *J. P. Bamberger.* Th. 1. 2. Berlin 1781. 8. Liberal education: or, a practical treatise on the methods of acquiring useful and polite learning. 1781. 8. (3 Sh. 6 d.) Ed. 7. Vol. 1. 2. 1785. 8. (6 Sh.) Ed. 10. Vol. 1. 2. 1790. 8. (12 Sh.) °*Juvenalis* in uſum ſcholarum. 1784. 8. (5 Sh.) °*Horatius* in uſum ſcholarum. 1784. 8. (6 Sh.) Letter to Lord *North*, Chancellor of the Univerſity of Oxford. 1789. 8. (6 d.)
—— [William] *late Under-Secretary of the late American Department.* °Observations upon the liturgy —. 1789. 8. (3 Sh.) *Extraofficial ſtate papers — for the preservation of the conſtitution and promoting the prosperity of the British empire. 1789. 8. (4 Sh.) °Conſiderations on the present ſtate of the nation —. 1790. 8. (1 Sh. 6. d.)

KNOX, [William] *M. D:* *of the Northern Regiment of Scots Fencibles.* Hiftory of a cafe in which cataracts in both eyes were removed by electricity. (*Duncan's M. C.* Vol. 9. p. 303.)

KUCKAHN, [T.... S.....] On the preservation of dead birds. (Philos. Transact. 1770. p. 302.)

KYLE, [Thomas] *Gardener to the Bar. Steuart of Moredun.* On forcing fruit trees. 1784. 8. (3 Sh.)

KYNASTON, [In....] *M. A.* born at *Chefter* d. 5 Dec. 1728. died at *Wigan* in *Lancashire* d... June 1783.

LABILLIERE, [Peter] *Major.* Letters to the majefty of the people and a declaration of those rights of the commonalty of Great Britain and Ireland without which they cannot be free. 1784. 8. (6. d.)

LACY, [John] *The Universal syftem: or mechanical cause of all the appearances and movements of the vifible heavens —. 1779. 8. (1 fh.)

LAMBE, [Robert] *Vicar of Norham upon Tweed.* Hiftory of the battle of Floddon in verse, written about the time of Queen Elizabeth —. 1774. 8. (4 fh.) Hiftory of Cheff —. 1774. 8. (2 Sh. 6 d.)

LAMBERT, [George] Sermons on various subjects. Vol. 1. 2. 1779. 1788. 8. (9 Sh.)

—— [James] *Landscape-Painter at Lewes.* Account of a very extraordinary effect of lightning on a bullock at *Swanborow* in the parish of *Iford* near *Lewes*, in *Suffex.* (Phil. Transact. 1776. p. 493.)

LAMONT, [David] *D. D. Chaplain to his Royal Highneff the Prince of Wales.* Sermons. Vol. I. 2. 1780-1787. (11 Sh.)

LAMPORT, [William] born:.... died at *Honiton*, *Devonshire* d. 5 March 1788.

LANCASTER, [Nathanael] *Rector of Stanford Rivers Effex.* born:.... died 1775.

LANDELLS, [James] *M. A.* Collection of prose and verse. 1782. 12. (2 Sh. 6. d.)

LANDEN, [John] *F. R. S.* born at *Peakirk* in *Northamptonshire* d. 23 Jan. 1719. died d. 15 Jan. 1790.

LANDMANN, [J....] *Profeffor of Fortification and Artillery to the Royal Military Academy at Woolwich.* (*Saldern's*) Elements of tactics and introduction to military evolution for the infantry; translated from the German —. 1787. 8. (7 Sh. 6 d.)

LANE, [John] *Secretary to the Commiffioners.* The report of the Commiffioners — appointed to examine, take and ftate, the public accounts of the kingdom. Vol. 1-3. 1785. 1787. 4. (3 L. 16 Sh.)
—— [Rachael] *Mrs. Midwife.* Addreff to pregnant ladies, and others, pointing out such women as are fit to be inftructed and particularly to be employed in the practice of midwifery. 1785. 8.
—— [Timothy] F. R. S. Account of two persons having a bronchocele, wherein the use of burnt sponge appeared to have a very conliderable effect. (Mem. of M. S. of L. Vol. 1. p. 217.)
LANGFORD; [Abraham] born 1711. died d. 18 Sept. 1774.
—— [William] D. D. born 1704. died d. 23 Apr. 1775.
LANGHORNE, [John] D. D. *Rector of Blagdon, Somersetshire.* born at *Kirby Stephen, Westmoreland*, 17.. died d. 1 Apr. 1779.
—— [William] *M. A: Rector of Hawkinge and Minifter of Folkftone in Kent.* Job, a poem. 1760. 4.· (2 Sh. 6 d.) Poetical paraphrase on part of the book of Isaiah. 1761. 4. (2 Sh. 6 d.) *Plutarch's* lives. Vol. 1-6. 1770. 8. (1 L. 11 Sh. 6 d.) Sermons. Vol. 1 2. 1773. 8. (7 Sh.)
LANPHIER, [Simon] *Phyfician, Waterford.* Hiftory of a case of rheumatism, cured by electricity. (*Duncan's* M. C. Vol. 8. p. 314.)
LATHAM, [John] Observations on the earth quake at Lifton Nov. 1. 1775. made at Zsusqueira. (Phil. Transact. 1759. p. 411.) Case of a man seized with a fever from the effects of meal-duft. (Ibid. 1770. p. 451.) Account of an extraordinary dropfical case. (Ibid. 1779. p. 54.) General fynopfis of birds. Vol. 1-3. and supplem. 1782-1787. 4. (8 L. 13 Sh.)
LATTER, [Mary] *Mrs. a Shopkeeper at Reading in Berkshire.* born: .... died d. 4 March 1777.
LAUDER, [William] *Profeffor of the Ecclefiaftical Hiftory and Mathematik at Dundee.* born: .... died 1771.
LAUGHTON, [George] *D. D. of Richmond in Surry.* The progreff and eftablishment of chriftianity in reply to *Gibbon's* XV Chapt. of the decline and fall of

of the roman empire. 1780. 4. (1 Sh. 6 d.) Hiſtory of ancient Egypt. 1774. 8. (5 Sh.)
(Several ſingle ſermons.)
LAVINGTON, [.....] *M. D: at Taviſtok in Devonſhire.* born: .... died d. 12 Oct. 1782.
—— [John] *Jun.* The caſe of deſertion and affliction conſidered in a courſe of sermons on the Pſ. 77, v. 1-10. 1789. 12. (3 Sh.)
LAURENTS, [Philippe] born 1737. died d. .. Nov. 1787.
LAW, [Edmund] *D. D. Lord Biſhop of Carliſle.* born in the pariſh of *Cartmel* in *Lancaſhire* 1702. died d. 14 Aug. 1787.
LAWRENCE, [Thomas] *M. D. Phyſician in London.* born d. 25 May 1711. died at *Canterbury* d. 6 June 1783.
LAWRIE, [John] *A. M.* Hiſtory of the wars in Scotland, from the battle of the Grampian hills in the Year 85 to the battle of Culloden in the Year 1746. 1785. 12. (3 Sh.)
LAWSON, [John] *B. D: Rector of Swanscombe in Kent.* born: .... died d. 13 Nov. 1779.
—— [Robert] *Surgeon at Leith.* Account of the diſſection of two ſingular caſes. (*Duncan's* M. C. Dec. II. Vol. 3. p. 299.)
LAYARD, [Charles Peter] *D. D: F. R. S: F. A. S:* Charity, a poetical eſſay. 1773. Poetical eſſay, on duelling. 1776. 4. (1 Sh.) (Several ſingle ſermons.)
—— [Daniel Peter] *M. D: F. R. S: of London and of Gottingen. F. A. S:* Caſe of a fracture of the os ilium, and its cure. (Phil. Transact. 1753. p. 537.) Account of a young lady, who had an extraordinary impoſtume formed in her ſtomach. (Ibid. 1756. p. 406.) Account of the earth quake March 8. 1749-50, at London. (Ibid. 1756. p. 621.) On the uſefulneſſ of inoculation of horned cattle to prevent the contagious diſtemper among them. (Ibid. 1760. p. 528.) Caſe of a diſeaſed eye. (Ibid. 1760. p. 747.) On the bite of a mad dog. 1763. 8. Ed. 2. 1766. Ed. 3. 1772. Account of the Somersham water in the county of Huntingdon. 1767. 8. and in Phil. Transact. 1766. p. 10.) Directions to prevent the contagion of the jail diſtemper. 1772. 8.

Phar-

Pharmacopoea in ufum gravidarum puerperarum et infantum recens natorum. 1772. 8. Ed. 2. 1776. On the nature, cause and cure of the diftemper among the horned cattle. 1757. 8. Ed. 2. 1770. and in Phil. Transact. 1780. p. 536.)

LEACH, [Edmund] *Surveyor.* Treatise of universal inland navigations and the use of all sorts of mines. 1790. 8. (5 Sh.)

—— [Thomas] *Esq: of the Middle Temple, Barrifter at Law.* Cases in Crown law, determined by the 12 judges, by the court of King's Bench — from the 4th Year of Geo. II. to the 29th Year of Geo. III. 1789. 8. (0 Sh. 6 d.)

LEAKE, [John] *M D: Phyfician to the Weftminfter Lying in Hospital.* On the Lisbon diet drink. 8. 17.. Observations on the child-bed fever, on uterine haemorrhagies and convulfions and other acute ficknefles in pregnancy. 1773. 8. (5 Sh.) überf. Leipzig 1775. 8. A Lecture introductory to the theory and practice of midwifery. 1773. 4. (2 Sh. 6 d.) aus diefer überfezt: von der Verhütung der erblichen Krankheiten: Samml. f. A. Th. 2. St. 2. S. 67. Medical inftructions towards the prevention and cure of chronic or slow diseases peculiar to women. 1777. 8. (6 Sh.) Syllabus: or generals heads of a course of lectures on the theory and practice of midwifery. 1787. 8. (1 Sh.)

—— [Stephan Martin] born: .... died 1773.

LEDWICH, [Edward] *LL. B: Vicar of Aghaboe, Queen's County Ireland. F. A. S. of London, Dublin and Edinburgh.* On the religion of the Druids. (Arch. Vol. 7. p. 303.) Observations on our antient churches. (Ibid. Vol. 8. p. 165.) °Antiquities of Ireland. Nro. 1. 1789.

LEE, [Arthur] *Esq. F. A. A.* Account of the effects of lightning on two houses in the city of Philadelphia. (Mem. of B. A. Vol. 1. p. 247.)

—— [Francis Bacon] Letter to *Sheridan.* 1757. 8. (6 d.) The debauches, a poem. 1771. 4. (2 Sh.) Translation of *Tiffot's* eflay on the disorders of people of fashion. 1771. 8. (3 Sh.)

—— [Harriet] *Miff: at Bath.* Errors of innocence; a novel. Vol. 1-5. 17.. New peerage; or our eyes may deceive us, a Comedy. 1787. 8. (1 Sh. 6 d.)

LEE,

LEE, [James] *Nurseryman at Hammersmith in Middlesex.* Introduction to botany — extracted from the work of *Linnaeus.* 1760. 8. Ed. III. 1776. 8. (7 Sh. 6 d.)

—— [John] *M. D: Phyſician at Bath:* F. R. S. Narrative of a ſingular gouty case, with observations. 1782. 8. (1 Sh.) überſ. Samml. f. A. Th. 8. S. 91.

—— [John] *Actor at Bath.* born: .... died. d. 19 Febr. 1781.

—— [Sophia] *Miſſ.* (Siſter of *Harriet Lee.*) The Chapter of accidents: a Comedy. 1780. 8. (1 Sh. 6 d.) überſ. von *Leonhardi:* neu bearbeitet von *Schroeder.* Berlin. 1782. 8. *The receſſ; or the tale of other times. Vol. 1-3. 1783. (13 Sh. 6 d.) überſ. unter dem Titel *Ruinen.* 17.. °The hermit's tale, a poem. 1787. 4. (2 Sh.)

—— [William] *Maſter of an Academy in lower Tooting, Surry.* Elegiac poem, sacred to the memory of a father. 1788. 8. (2 Sh.)

—— [William] *Sir. Baronet.* On the use of water impregnated with fixed air, in preserving flesh meat from putrefaction. (*Prieſtley's* Experiments of Natur. Philoſ. Vol. I. p. 461.)

LEECHMAN, [William] *D. D: Principal of the college of Glasgow.* born at *Dolphington, Lankershire.* 1706. died d. 3 Dec. 1785.

LEEDES, [John] *Surgeon, Hemingſton, Suffolkshire.* Account of a case of scorbutus occurring on shore, and terminating succeſſfully. (*Duncan's* M. C. Dec. 2. Vol. 3. p. 320.)

LEGGE, [Thomas] The law of outlawry and practice in civil actions. 1779. 8. (2 Sh. 6 d.)

LEIGH, [John] *M. D.* Experimental inquiry into the properties of opium and its effects on living subjects with observations on its history, preparations and uses. 1786. 8. (2 Sh. 6 d.)

LEIGHTON, [Francis] *of Shrewsbury.* Memoir concerning the roman baths discovered 1788. at Wroxeter, the ancient Uriconium or Viroconium. (Arch. Vol. 9. p. 323.)

LEITH, [Charles] *M. D: at Johnſtone near Montrose.* History of a very uncommon convulſive cough cured

red by the flowers of zinc. (Med. Com. of Ed. Vol. 6. p. 343.)

LELAND, [Thomas] *D. D.* born: .... died. 17..

LEMON, [George William] *Rector of Geyronthorpe and Vicar of Eaſt Walton, Norfolk.* Graecae grammaticae rudimenta —. 1774. 12. (2 ſh. 6 d.) Two tracts and additional observations on the greek accents by the late *Edw. Spelmann*, and the voyage of *Aeneas* from Troy to Italy —. 1775. 8. (2 ſh. 6 d.) English etymology; or a derivative dictionary of the english language —. 1783. 4. (1 L. 6 ſh.)

LEMPRIERE, [.....] *of Pembroke College, Oxford.* *Bibliotheca claſſica, or a claſſical dictionary; containing a full account of all the proper names mentioned in ancient authors, with tables of coins, weights and measures in use among the greeks and romans. 1788. 8. (8 ſh.)

LENOX, [Charlotta] *Mrs.* (Her maiden name *Ramsay*: born at *New York in North America.*) *The female Quixote: or, the adventures of Arabella. Vol. 1. 2. 1751. 8. (6 ſh.) *Shakespeare illuſtrated or the novels and hiſtories on which the plays of *Shakespeare* are founded —. 1752. 8. (6 Sh.) *The memoirs of the counteſſ of Berci, taken from the French. Vol. 1. 2. 1755. (6 Sh.) *Henrietta, a novel. Vol. 1. 2. 1757. (6 Sh.) *Philander, a dramatic paſtoral. 1757. 8. (1 Sh.) *Brumoy's* greek theater, translated. Vol. 1-3. 1759. 4. Sophia, a novel. Vol. 1. 2. 1761. (6 Sh.) Memoirs of *Sully* translated. 17.. The ſiſter, a comedy. 1769. 8. (1 Sh. 6 d.) *De la Valliere* meditations and penitential prayers translated. 1774. 8. (2 Sh. 6 d.) Old city manners; a comedy; altered from the original *Eaſtward Hoe*, written by *Ben Jonson* —. 1775. 8. (1 Sh.) Euphemia. Vol. 1-4. 1790. 8. (12 Sh.)

LEROUX, [J....] *Esq. Juſtice of peace for the counties of Herford and Middlesex.* Thoughts on the present ſtate of the prisons of this country. 1781. 8. (1 Sh.)

LESLIE, [Charles] *Surgeon at Cork.* Account of the operation for the aneurism being performed upon the

the femoral artery with fucceff. (Med. Com. of Ed. Vol. 2. p. 176.)

LESLIE, [John] *A. M. Profeſſor of Greek, King's College, Aberdeen.* born: .... died d. 30 Jun. 1790.

— [Matthew] *Esq.* On the Pangolin of Bahar. (Afiat. Ref. Vol. 1. p. 376.)

— [Patrick Dugud] *M. D: F. R. S: Phyſician at Durham.* born 1751. died at *Lisbonne.* d. 12 March. 1783.

LETCHWORTH, [Thomas] *Miniſter of the Goſpel among the Quakers.* born: .... died 17..

LETHIEULLIER, [Smart] Obſervations on fepulchral monuments. (Arch. Vol. 2. p. 291.)

LETTICE, [John] *B. D: Vicar of Peaſemarch, Suſſex.* The converſion of St. Paul, a poetical eſſay. 1765. 4. (1 Sh.) The antiquities of Herculanum, tranſlated from the Italian by *Thom. Martyn* and *John Lettice.* Vol. 1. 1773. 4. (3 L. 3 Sh.) Two fermons —. 1788. 4. (1 Sh. 6 d.)

LETTSOM, [John Coakley] *M. D: F. R. S: F. A. S. Phyſician extraordinary to the London Lying — in Hoſpital.* Obſervationes ad hiſtoriam theae pertinentes. Lugd. Bat. 1769. 4. The natural hiſtory of the tea-tree with obſervations on the medical qualities of tea and effects of tea-drinking. 1772. 4. (4 ſh.) überſ. Leipz. 1776. 8. The naturaliſts and travellers companion 1772. 8. Reflections on the general treatment and cure of fevers. 1772. 8. (2 ſh.) Medical memoirs of the general diſpenſary in London for part of the Years 1773. 1774. —. 1774. 8. (5 ſh,) überſ. Altenb. 1777. 8. Improvement of medicine in London, on the baſis of public good. 1775. 8. (1 ſh. 6 d.) Obſervations preparatory to the use of Dr. *Meyersbach's* medicines. 1776. 8. (1 ſh.) Letter — upon general inoculation 1778. 4. (6 d.) Hiſtory of the origin of medicine. 1778. 4. (5 ſh.) Obſervations on *Dimsdale's* remarks on the letter — upon general inoculation. 1779. 8. (1 ſh.) Anſwer to *Dimsdale's* review of *Lettsom's* obſervations on *Dimsdale's* remarks —. 1779. 8. Conſiderations on the propriety of a plan for inoculating the poor of London at their own habitations. 1779. 8. (6 d.) Obſervations on the plan for eſtabliſhing a dispensary

sary and medical society. 1779. 8. (1 fh.) On the danger of fragrant flowers in a close room (Monthly Review Vol. 62. p. 504.) "Letter to the King on the subject of a new proposed inftitution in the medical department: (a public Profefforfhip of Anatomy and Surgery) 1781. 4. (1 fh. 6 d.) Biographical account of Capt. *J. Carver.* 1781. 8. (2 fh.) Some account of the late *John Fothergill* M. D. 1783. 8. (3 fh.) Publifhed: *J. Fothergill's* Works. *Vol.* 1. 2. 1783. 8. (12 fh.) Ed. 2. 1784. 4. (1 L. 11 fh. 6 d.) Vindication of Dr. *Lettsom's* conduct relative to the late election at the Finsbury dispenfary —. 1786. 8. (6 d.) Hiftory and diffeation of an extraordinary intro susception. (Phil. Tranfact. 1786. p. 305.) Cases of palpitation of the heart. (Mem. of M. S. of L. Vol. 1. p. 77. überf. Samml. f A. Th. 12. S. 596.) Some remarks on the effects of lignum Quaffiae amarae. (Ibid. p. 128) Observations on fome cases of hydrocephalus internus (Ibid. p. 169.) On a disease, succeeding the transplanting of teeth. (Ibid. p. 330.) Case of a biliary calculus. (Ibid. p. 373.) Memoirs of *Jacques Barbeu Dubourg*, Profeffor Med. of Paris. (Ibid. p. 476.) *Commerell*, on the culture and use of the Mangel Wurzel, translated. 1787. 8. Hiftory of two cases of hydatides renales. (Mem. of M. S. of L. Vol. 2. p. 32.) Of the digitalis purpurea in hydropic diseases. (Ibid. p. 145.) Case of a diseased rectum. (Ibid. p. 308.) Hiftory of some of the effects of hard drinking. 1789. 4. (6 d.)

LEVESON, [G. . . . .] M. D. On the blood — 1776. 8. (2 fh. 6 d.) überf. Berlin 1782.. 8. On the epidemical fore throat, with the method of treatment. 1778. 8. (1 fh. 6 d.) Ed. 2. 17.. überf. nach der 2ten Aufl. Berlin 1783. 8.

LEVELYN, [William] Treatise on the Sabbath. 1783. 8. (2 fh. 6 d)

LEVI [David] *a Jew,* Account of the rites and ceremonies of the jews. — 1783. 8. (4 fh. 6 d.) Answer to Dr. *Prieftley's* letter to the jews. P. 1. 2. 1789. (5 fh.) Lingua facra: or, a grammar and dictionary of the Hebrew, Chaldee and Talmudic dialect. Vol. 1-3. 1789. 8. (2 l.. 16 fh. 6 d.) The
Pen-

Pentateuch — in Hebrew, with the Englifh translation and notes by *Lion Soesmans*, corrected and translated by *Dav. Levi*. Vol. 1-5. 1789. 8 (1 L 8 fh.)
LEVISON, [G . . .] *M. D: Phyfician to the Medical Asylum at London*. On the blood. 1776. 8. (1 fh.) Account of the epidemical sore throat. 1778. 8.
LEWIS [. . . .] *Mifs*. Poems, moral and interefting. 1788. 8. (4 fh.)
—— [John] Uniting and monopolizing farms — disadvantageous to the land - owners and highly prejudicial to the public — 1767. 8. (6 d.) Remarks on an inquiry into the connexion between the present price of provifions and the fize of farms — 1773. 8. (2 fh.)
—— [Hardwicke] *Esq*. Excurfion to Margate, in June 1786. — with anecdotes of well known characters. 1787. 8. (2 fh. 6 d.)
—— [L...] *Esq*. Lord Walford. Vol. I. 2. 1789. 8. (6 fh.)
—— [Meyer] *Operator for the teeth, at Oxford* On the formation, ftructure and use of the teeth. 1772. 8. (1 Sh.)
—— [P . . . .] *Actor*. Miscellaneous pieces in verse — 1775. 4. (2 Sh. 6 d.)
—— [P. . . .] *M. D*. Inquiry into the nature and properties of common water, with observations on its medicinal qualities. 1790. 8. (3 Sh. 6 d.)
—— [William] *M. D: F. R. S: Phyfician at Kingfton, Surry*. born: . . . . died d. 19. Jan. 1781.
LEY, [Charles] *Land-Surveyor*. The nobleman, gentleman, land-fteward and furveyor's complete guide — 1787. 8. (3 Sh. 6 d.)
LEYBOURN, [William] Defcription of an entertaining and useful inftrument called *Gunter's* quadrant. 1772. 8. (1 Sh.)
LIDDEL, [R. . . .] *Purser in the Royal Navy*. The seaman's new vade mecum; containing a practical effay on naval book-keeping — 1787. 8. (5 Sh.)
LIGHTFOOT, [John] *A. M: Rector of Gotham, Nottinghampfhire and Chaplain to the Duchefs Dowager of Portland; F. R. S*. born: . . . . died d. 20 Febr. 1788.
LIMBIRD, [James] *Surveyor to the corporation*. Account of the ftrata observed in finking for water at Bofton, Lincolnfhire. (Phil. Transact. 1787. p. 50)

LINCOLN, [Benjamin] *Esq. F. A. A.* Account of several ſtrata of earth and ſhells in the banks of York-river, in Virginia; of a ſubterraneous paſſage and the sudden descent of a very large current of water from a mountain, near Carlisle; of a remarkably large spring near Reading in Pennsylvania and of ſeveral remarkable springs in the ſtates of Pennsylvania and Virginia (Mem. of B. A. Vol. I. p. 372.) Letter on the ingrafting of fruittrees and the growth of vegetables: — (Ibid. p. 388.)

LIND, [James] *M. D: Phyſician at Windſor.* On the putrid and remitting ten fever, which raged at Bengal in the Y. 1762. translated from the latin. 1772. 8. (1 Sh.) überſ. von *J. N. Petzold.* Leipz. 1773. 8. On the efficacy of vitriolic aether in removing the gout in the ſtomach. (London M. J. Vol. VI. p. 53. überſ. Samml. f. A. Th. XI. S. 97.) Remarks on the supposed influence of the moon in fevers. (Ibid. Vol. VIII. P. 2. überſ. Samml. f. A. Th. 12. S. 546.) On the efficacy of mercury in the cure of inflammatory diseases and the dysentery. (Ibid. Vol. VIII. P. 1. überſ. Samml. f. A. Th. 12. S. 91.) A Case of taeniae hydatigenae or hydatids, succeſſfully treated by the use of mercury. (Ibid. Vol. X. P. 1.)

—— [John] *M. D: Phyſician to the Royal Hospital at Haslar.* A case, ſhewing the efficacy of flowers of zinc, in the epilepsy. (Lond. M. J. Vol. VII. P. 1.)

—— [John] *Barriſter at Law, F. R. S: F. A. S:* born: . . died d. 12 Jan. 1781.

LINDSAY, [John] *D. D. Rector of the parish of St. Catherine at Jamaica.* born: . . . died d. 3 Nov. 1788.

LINDSEY, [Theophilus] *M. A: Clergyman.* Apology on reſigning the vicarage of *Catterick*, *Yorkshire*. 1774. 8. (3 ſh.) Farewell addreſſ to the pariſhioners of *Catterick*. 1774. 8. (6 d.) * The book of common prayer reformed, upon the plane of Dr. *Sam. Clarke*. 1774. 8. (4 ſh.) Sequel to the apology on reſigning the vicarage of *Catterick*, *Yorkshire*. 1776. 8. (6 ſh.) Two Diſſertations 1) on the preface to St. John's Gospel. 2) on praying to Jesus Chriſt. 1779. 8. (2 ſh. 6 d.) The

The catechist: or, an inquiry into the doctrine of the scriptures concerning the only true god and object of religious worship. P. 1. 2. 1783. 8. (2 sh.) Historical view of the state of the unitarian doctrine and worship from the reformation to our own times —. 1783. 8. (6 sh.) Vindiciae *Priestleianae*: an address to the students of Oxford and Cambridge. 1788. 8. (6 sh. 6 d.) A second address to the students of Oxford and Cambridge, relating to Jesus Christ and the origin of the great errors concerning him. 1790. 8. (4 sh.) (Several single sermons.)

LIPSCOMB, [William] *A. M: Chaplain to the Earl of Dorlington.* Poems. 1784. 4. (3 sh. 6 d.)

LITTLE, [Daniel] *F. A. A.* Observations upon the art of making steel. (Mem. of B. A. Vol. 1. p. 525.)

LIVINGSTONE, [....] *One of the heads of the Congress at New-York.* born: ..... died d. 22 Febr. 1776.

LLOYD, [....] *Austrian Major General.* born: .... died. 1783.

—— [....] *Surgeon at Wrexham.* The case of a flatulent tumour on the head, opened and cured. (Med. Obs. Vol. 6. p. 192.)

—— [Evan] *A. M: Vicar of Lanfair, near Ruthim, Denbigshire.* born: .... died d. 6 Febr. 1776.

—— [George] *F. R. S.* born 1708. died d. ... Nov. 1783. at *Barowby* in the *West-riding of Yorkshire.*

—— [John] *F. R. S.* Account of *Eldenshole* in *Derbyshire* with some observations upon it by *Edw. King.* (Phil. Transact. 1771. p. 350.) Account of an earthquake at *Hafodunos* near *Denbigh.* (Ibid. 1781. p. 331.) Account of an earthquake.. (Ibid. 1783. p. 104.)

—— [John] *A. B.* Thesaurus ecclesiasticus — containing an account of the valuation of all the livings in England and Wales, their charge in the king's books, respective patrons —. 1788. 8. (7 sh. 6 d.)

LOBO, [Daniel] *Notary Public and Translator of the Modern Languages.* Nomenclature; or dictionary Engl. Fr. Span. und German —. 1776. 4. (12 sh.)

LOCH, [David] *Merchant and Inspector General of the Fisheries in Scotland.* born: .... died d. 21 Febr. 1780.

LOCHÉE, [Lewis] *Master of the Military Academy at*
little

little Chelsea. On military education. 1773. 8. (2 ſh.) Syſtem of military mathematics. Vol. I. 2. 1776. 8. (12 ſh.) On caſtrametation. 1778. 8. (4 ſh.) On encampments. 1779. (4 ſh.) Elements of fortification. 1780. 8. (6 ſh.) Elements of field fortification. 1783. 8. (4 ſh.)

LOCKMAN, [John] *Secretary on the British Herring Fishery.* born: .... died d. 2 Febr. 1771.

LOFT, [Capel] *JC.* The praises of poetry; a poem. 1775 8. (2 ſh.) Observations on *Wesley's* second calm addreſs and incidentally on other writings upon the american queſtion. 1777. 8. (1 ſh.) Observations on Mrs. *Macaulay's* hiſtory of England —. 1778. 4. (2 ſh. 6 d.) Principia cum juris univerſalis, tum praecipue anglicani. Vol. I. 2. 1779. 8. (6 ſh.) *An argument on the nature of party and faction. 1780. 8. (1 ſh.) Eudoſia; or a poem on the universe. 1781. 8. (2 ſh. 6 d.) *Translation of the firſt and ſecond Georgic of *Virgil.* 1784. 8. (2 ſh. 6 d.) *Eſſay on the law of libels —. 1785. 8. (2 ſh. 6 d.) Three letters on the queſtion of regency. 1789. 8. (1 ſh. 6 d.) Obſervations on the firſt part of Dr. *Knowle's* teſtimonies from the writers of the firſt four centuries. 1789. 8. (2 Sh. 6 d.) Hiſtory of the corporation and teſt acts. 1790. 8. (1 Sh.) Remarks on the letter of *Edm. Burke* concerning the revolution in France and on the proceedings in certain ſocieties in London, relative to that events. 1790. 8. (2 Sh.)

LOFTIE, [William] *Surgeon at Canterbury.* born 1700. died 1778.

LOFTUS, [Smyth] *M. A: Vicar of Coolock.* Reply to the reasonings of Mr. *Gibbon,* in his hiſtory of the decline and fall of the roman empire —. 1778. 8. (1 ſh.)

LOGAN, [......] at *Edinburgh.* Diſſertation on the government, manners and ſpirit of Aſia. 1787. 4. (1 Sh. 6 d.)

—— [John] *F. R. S: Miniſter of Leith.* born: .... died d. 28 Dec. 1788.

LONG, [Robert] *D. D: F. R. S: Maſter of Pembroke-Hall and Profeſſor of Aſtronomy and Geometry in the Univerſity of Cambridge.* born: .... died d. 16 Dec. 1770.

LONGFIELD, [John] *M. D: at Cork in Ireland.*

Lon-

Longitude of *Cork* deduced from aftronomical observations: (Phil. Transact. 1779. p. 163.)
LONGMATE, [B. ....] Supplement to the 5 Edit. of *Collins's* peerage of England —. 1784. 8. (7 Sh. 6 d.)
LONNERGAN, [Andrew] *Teacher of the Military Sciences.* The fencer's guide —. 1772. 8. (7 Sh.)
LONSDALE, [.....] °The fpanish rivals, a mufical farce. 1784. 8. (1 Sh.)
LORIMER, [J. ....] Letter, containing fome remarks on the climate, vegetable productions — of Weftflorida. (Tr. of A. S. Vol. I. p. 250.) Description of a new dipping-needle. (Phil. Transact. 1775. p. 79.)
LORT, [Michael] *D. D: F. R. S: Vice Prefident of A. S. Rector of S. Matthew Friday-ftreet of St. Michael Mile-end, near Colchefter, Prebendary of St. Pauls.* born: ..... died d. 5 Nov. 1790.
L'OSTE, [Charles] *A. M: Rector of Langton in Lincolnshire.* The truth of the chriftian religion, a poem —. 1776. 8. (5 Sh.)
LOTHIAN, [William] *D. D: Minifter of Canongate:* born at *Edinburgh* d. 5 Nov. 1740. died d. 17 Dec. 1783.
LOTT, [Yeoman] °Addrefs to the people of England: containing an enquiry into the cause of the great fcarcity of timber throughout the dominions belonging to his majefty —. 1766. 8. (1 fh. 6 d.) °Important hints towards an amendment of the royal dock-yards. by a man of Kent. 1767. 8. (1 Sh.) The case of the late agent of the royal hospital at Plymouth fuperceded in July 1774 —. 1776. 8. (1 fh. 6 d.) Proposals for the benefit of the naval fervice. 1776. 8. (1 fh. 6 d.)
.LOVE, [James] *Actor.* (His real name was *Dance.*) born: .... died 1774.
LOVEFUN, [A..... G. .....] A new cure for the fpleen: being a collection of advertisements humorous, curious, farcical, fatirical —. 1778. 8. (1 fh.)
LOVELASS, [Peter] *of the Inner temple.* The will, which the law makes: or, how it difpoles of a person's eftate, in case he dies without a will—. 17..
(the same book under the title:) On inteftacy and wills. 1786. 8. (3 fh. 6 d.) Ed. 3. (with the title:) The laws difposal of person's eftate who dies without

out a will or testament. 1786. 8. (3 sh. 6 d.) Explanation of the law concerning the bills of exchange, promissory notes and the evidence on a trial by jury relative thereto: with description of Banknotes and the privilege of attornies. 1789. 8. (3 Sh.)

LOW, [....]. Chiropodologia; or a scientific enquiry into the causes of corns, warts, onions and other painful or offensive cutaneous excrescences —. 1786. 8. (3 sh.)

LOWDELL, [Stephen] *Surgeon: F. M. S.* The case of a burn and another of stones in the kidnies. (Mem. of M. S. of L. Vol. I. p. 315.)

LOWE, [John] Jun. of *Manchester*. Liberty or death; by which is vindicated the obvious practicability of trading to the coast of Guinea for its natural productions —. 1790. 4. (1 sh)

LOWNDES, [Francis] *Medical Electrician.* Observations on medical electricity —. 1787. 8. (1 sh. 6 d.)

LOWTH, [Robert] *D. D. Lord-Bishop of London.* born 1711. died d. 3 Nov. 1787.

LUCAS, [Bernard] *of Chesterfield, Derbyshire.* The solution of the quadrature. 1788. 4. (1 sh. 6 d.)

—— [Henry] *A. M.* Love in disguise: an Opera. 1767. Tears of Alnwick; a pastoral elegy in memory of the late Duchess of Northumberland. 1777. 4. (1 sh.) Visit from the shades; or, Earl *Chatham's* Adieu to his friend Lord *Camden* —. 1778. 4. (2 sh. 6 d.) Poems to her Majesty. 1780. 4. (10 sh. 6 d.) The earl of Somerset: a Tragedy. 1780. 4. The cypress-wreath; or meed of honour, a poem to the memory of Lord *Rob. Manners.* 1782. 4. (1 sh.) Alnwick's condolence; a pastoral elegy — in memory of the late - Duke of Northumberland. 1786. 4 (1 sh.)

—— [James] *Surgeon to the Leed's Infirmary.* Account of a singular nervous case. (Med. Obs. Vol. 5. p. .) On the amputation of the ankle with a flap. (Ibid. p. 323.) On cataracts. (Ibid. p. 250.) Observations on amputation. (London M. J. Vol. 7. P. 3. Vol. 9. P 1.) Remarks on elastic bandages. (Ibid.) Remarks on febrile contagion. (Ibid. Vol. X. P. 3.) A case of retention of urine —. (Ibid. Vol. XI. P. 2.) Account of the singular effects of music on a patient. (Ibid.)

(Ibid.) Hints on the management of women in certain cases of pregnancy. (Mem. of M. S. of L. Vol. 2. p. 409.)

LUCAS, [Robert] *B. D. of Trinity College.* Translation of *Homer's* hymn to Ceres. 1781. 4. (3 sh.) Three sermons on the subject of sunday schools — with few hints on parochial clubs. 1787. 8. (2 sh.)
(Several single sermons.)

—— [William] *of the Middle temple.* The laws concerning horses: or every horsekeeper his own lawyer. 1786. 8. (1 sh. 6 d.)

LUCKOMBE, [Philipp] see *Thomas Pride.*

LUDERS, [Alexander] *Barrister at Law, of the Inner-Temple.* Reports of the proceedings in committees of the house of commons, on controverted elections —. Vol. 1. 2. 1785. 1789. (14 sh.)

LUDLAM, [William] *M. A: F. R. S: Rector of Cockfield and Vicar of Norton,* born: ..... died d. 16 March. 1788.

LUFFMANN, [John] Account of Antigua — written in the Years 1786-1788. 8. 1789. (1 Sh.) überf. von *J. H. Wiedmann.* Leipzig. 1790. 8.

LUKENS, [John] *Surveyor General of Pennsylvania.* Account of the transit of Venus over the sun's disc, as observed at Norriton June 3d 1769. (Tr. of A. S. Vol. 1. p. 8.) Observations on the transit of Venus June 3. 1769. in Philadelphia. (Phil. Transact. 1769. p. 289.)

LUND, [John] Ducks and peas, or the London rider, a farce. 1776. 8.

LUSIGNAN, [....] °History of the revolt of Ali Bey against the Ottoman porte, including an account of the form of government of Egypt with a description of grand Cairo and of several celebrated places in Egypt, Palestine and Syria. 1783. 8. (5 sh.) überf. Leipzig. 1784. 8. °Series of letters - containing a voyage and journey from England to Smyrna, from thence to Constantinople and to England —. Vol. 1. 2. 1788. 8. (12 Sh.) überf. *Ebeling's* Neue Samml. von Reisebeschr. Th. 10. S. 129.

LUSON, [Hewling] *of the Navy Office.* Inferior politics, of considerations on the wretchedness and profligacy of the poor, especially in London and its vicinity —. 1786. 8. (2 Sh. 6 d.)

LUT.

LUTTRELL, [Edward] *Surgeon at Tunbridge.* A case of a gangrene, after caſtration ſucceſsfully treated by giving alkalis and acids ſeparately. (Mem. of M. S. of L. Vol. 1. p. 60. überſ. Saml. f. A. Th. 12. S. 572.)
—— [Temple] Bill — for the more easy and effectual manning of the royal navy —. 1777. 8. (1 Sh.)
LYNN, [W.....] *Surgeon.* The ſingular case of a lady, who had the ſmallpox during pregnancy and who communicated the ſame disease to the foetus. 1786. 8. (6 d.)
LYON, [John] *Miniſter of the Gospel at Dover, Kent.* Experiments and observations in electricity. 1780. 4. (12 Sh.) Further proofs that glaſs is permeable by the electric effluvia —. 1781. 4. (3 Sh.) Description of a Roman bath, discovered at *Dover*. (Arch. Vol. 5. p. 325.) Account of a ſubſidence of the ground near Folkſtone on the coaſt of Kent. (Phil. Transact. 1786. p. 220.)
LYONS, [Israel] *Aſtronomer, with Capt. Phipps in his voyage to the Northpole.* born: ... died d. 1 May 1775.
LYSONS, [Daniel] *M. D: Phyſician at Bath and late Fellow of all Souls, College.* Description of the cepphus. (Phil. Transact. 1762. p. 135.) Case of the late Rev. *James Bradley.* (Ibid. 1762. p. 635.) Case of a girl who ſwallowed three pins and discharged them at the shoulder. (Ibid. 1769. p. 9.) On the effects of camphire and calomel in continual fevers —. 1771. 8. (1 Sh. 6 d.) Farther observations upon the effects of camphire and calomel in the dropsy; upon bath waters —. 1771. 8. (1 Sh.) überſ. Leipzig. 1774. 8. On Elmbark. (Med. Transact. Vol. 2. p. 203.) Practical eſſays upon intermitting fevers, dropſies, diseases of the liver, the epilepsy, the colic, dysenteric fluxes and the operation of calomel. 1772. 8. (3 Sh.) Ed. 2. 1783. 8. (5 Sh.)
—— [Samuel] *F. A. S.* Account of ſome roman antiquities discovered at Combend farm, near Cirenceſter, Gloucestershire. (Arch. Vol. 9. p. 319.)
LYTTELTON, [George] *Lord.* (Baron of Frankley in Worceſtershire.) *Privy-Counseller: F. R. S.* born d. 17 Jan. 1708. died d. 22 Aug. 1773.

www.ingramcontent.com/pod-product-compliance
Lightning Source LLC
Chambersburg PA
CBHW032148230426
43672CB00011B/2482